RACING GUIDE

2005

Statistics • Results

Previews • Training centre reports

Contributors: Amy Bennett, Adam Bull, Neil Clark, Chris Cook, Nick Deacon, Steffan Edwards, Tony Jakobson, Kel Mansfield, Steve Mellish, Peter Naughton, Mark Nelson, Dave Nevison, Ben Osborne, Nick Watts, Graham Wheldon, Richard Williams.

Grateful thanks also to Clemency and Romily Gillespie.

Designed and edited by Nick Watts and Adam Bull

Published in 2005 by Raceform,
Compton, Newbury, Berkshire RG20 6NL
Raceform Ltd is a wholly owned subsidiary of MGN Ltd

A catalogue record for this book is available from the British Library.

ISBN 1-904317-86-3

Printed by Cox & Wyman, Reading

racing & football outlook

Contents

Outlook

Editor's introduction

Let's just remind ourselves of some of last season's memorable moments, so we can start on the right foot when we begin our punting this season.

The first point, that cannot be emphasised enough, is the significant rise in the number of horses now based with Saeed bin Suroor at his Newmarket stables.

Godolphin had a rather quiet season in 2003, by their own high standards, and as a result Sheikh Mohammed decided that his Godolphin operation would accommodate a lot more of their own horses.

The decision couldn't have been more successful and last year (2004) was momentous. Their two-year-olds especially, helped re-establish the owner and trainer on the daily racing circuit and put them back at the top of the tree.

They were prepared to win small races, day in day out, and send their youngsters to tracks they had never ventured to previously.

Frankie Dettori was one of the main beneficiaries of this turnaround and he couldn't fail to win the title of Champion Jockey from Kieren Fallon, after a nine year wait.

The Italian has famously never won the Derby, but surely this will be his year, whether it be on Dubawi or whatever colt they decide to pin their hopes on.

Our Newmarket correspondent can help in this area and every week in the RFO, as he reports from the gallops at HQ.

Still in training at Newmarket is Ouija Board, the filly that took top honours last year, having performed admirably in four different countries.

It is hard to envisage any of her own sex dethroning the Champion filly. The colts had better watch their backs too when the King George and Arc come around, as Lord Derby's filly looks to be very special indeed.

Talking of superstars, the usually dominant Ballydoyle yard seem to have lost that magical ingredient needed to send out winners consistently at the highest level.

Jamie Spencer has certainly had enough, and has quit his job to ride more horses this side of the water.

It is noticeable that many of the horses that inhabit Aidan O'Brien's Tipperary stables are performing better in the latter part of the season. Namely Footstepsinthesand, Oratorio, Ad Valorem and Yehudi, who all look promising.

Our Irish reporter gives us his view, and tries to establish some reasons for this disparity. Have a read of Jerry M's column for some additional advice on which Irish nags to include in your list of horses to follow.

For big-race advice look no further than our trends data and analysis provided in the Big-handicap records section. Here you will find some fundamental rules to follow when you're considering a bet on a heritage handicap on a Saturday afternoon.

Perhaps one of the most informative pieces in this years Flat Annual is Graham Wheldon's track-by-track guide to draw biases and stalls positions.

It is surprising how much can be learnt, and it is a useful guide to refer to when races look tricky and indeed when they are not.

Most of us know about the extreme biases that occur at Beverley and Chester, but what about certain distances at Doncaster, Newmarket and York? You may well be surprised at the results.

Our breeding expert, Amy Bennett, kicks off a brand new section entitled Pedigrees for Punters.

And talking of experts, we still have Dave Nevison, Steve Mellish and Time Test delivering the goods. Enjoy!

Profiles for punters

Nerys Dutfield

NERYS DUTFIELD: together with one of her best, the Group-winning, flying grey Misty Eyed

FOR THOSE big yards lucky enough to enjoy the patronage of a wealthy Arab benefactor, two-year-old winners are just a numbers game.

For every couple of ordinary ones they get, they might get a potential star, and so the conveyor belt goes on.

However for the smaller yard, the skill involved in picking out a youngster for a relatively modest sum and pitching it in with, and winning against the big boys, is considerable.

Step forward Nerys Dutfield, who in recent seasons has repeatedly humbled bigger yards with her shrewd selection policy among the juvenile brigade.

Smittenby, a modestly-bred filly by the failed stallion Tenby started the ball rolling by winning the Listed Oh So Sharp Stakes at Newmarket in 1998, beating a better fancied Maktoum Al Maktoum-owned, Ed Dunlop-trained runner-up.

Then, a couple of years later, Lady Dominatrix (apparently named after Nerys!) came along, winning a Listed race at Ascot and a Group 3 at Newbury in the same season.

Convent Girl also did her bit, by winning four races and being placed in a Listed event, but surely the title of 'Queen of the Bargains' must go to the 3,200Irgns Misty Eyed.

She was modestly-bred, by the Jack Berry-trained sprinter Paris House out of a Lomond mare, and early on even her trainer had doubts: "She didn't look all that good when I bought her, but I thought I could go on with her."

What an understatement that turned out to be. Misty Eyed won the Molecomb Stakes as a two-year-old, as well as finishing runner up in both the Flying Childers, and the following season in the King's Stand at Royal Ascot.

Dutfield often targets the Royal meeting with her babies and they never seem to disgrace themselves. Spirit Of Chester and Celtic Spa both made the journey last season, with the former finishing second in the Albany Stakes to Jewel In The Sand at odds of 40-1.

The last couple of seasons probably haven't gone quite as well as she would have hoped for, and last season the horses were ravaged by health problems. Indeed, after Celtic Spa's victory at Nottingham last May, Dutfield was moved to comment: "The horses have been coughing and coughing. A lot of them have been working well at home, but they haven't been running well. It's most frustrating."

The boxes have all been steam-cleaned in the close season in an effort to rid the yard of 'the bug', and if early results are anything to go by then it's worked.

My Gacho won at Southwell on January 3 in the hands of the useful stable apprentice Amy Baker, while La Professoressa finished second over hurdles at Huntingdon at odds of 100-1 later in the month.

It's no suprise that Dutfield excels with two-year-olds. She has accumulated seven children of her own, including the youngest Declan, who is apparently nicknamed the 'Killarney Kid' due to his arrival nine months after the Listowel Festival. After that, managing horses must be a piece of cake - they can't answer back.

The stables themselves are based a stone's throw away from the coastal resort of Seaton in deepest Devon - a location that brings its own advantages in the summer: "The climate here in Devon helps with the juveniles. Our stables are so much warmer than other locations."

There are 40 boxes at Crabhayne Stables, together with a seven furlong All-Weather gallop which has a steep uphill section to finish with. Believe me, the horses will be fit after going up there a few times.

Stalls training is well catered for too - an important part of a two-year-old's education. Dutfield has two sets of stalls with one two-bay and one three-bay arrangement.

Juvenile contests can so often be won with a swift exit from the stalls, and it is a feature of Dutfield's training that it's hard to recall any of her horses misbehaving at the start and losing races in the stalls.

With illness hopefully behind the stable now, Dutfield can look forward to a better season this time around and, while there are no guarantees in this game, it's a fair bet that we'll see Nerys at Royal Ascot taking on, and possibly beating the big guns again.

CELTIC SPA (on the rails in fourth): running soundly behind Beaver Patrol at the Curragh

Dutfield's demons

Aoninch

5yo chestnut mare

Inchinor - Willowbank (Gay Fandango)

"She has won a couple on the Flat at Bath and Warwick in 2003. We gave her a taste of hurdles at Folkestone last November and she ran well for a long way. She will go summer jumping when the time comes, as she likes a bit of decent ground."

Celtic Spa

3yo grey filly

Celtic Swing - Allegorica (Alzao)

"She did well for us last season, considering a lot of our horses weren't right during the season. She won at Nottingham early on, and then ran a great race in the Windsor Castle at Royal Ascot to finish a close fifth behind Chateau Istana. We took her to Ireland for a valuable race at the Curragh in August over 6f and she picked up some valuable prizemoney coming fourth. She ran on the All-Weather over the winter, but it didn't seem to suit her. She likes a bit of cut in the gound."

My Gacho

3yo bay colt

Shinko Forest - Floralia (Auction Ring)

"This one has got a really nice temperament, and got the year off to a good start when winning at Southwell over 6f. Our apprentice Amy Baker set her off in front and she had just enough in reserve to hold on, from a horse [Cerebus] who has won since. He is a very generous type."

Royal Axminster

10yo bay gelding

Alzao - Number One Spot (Reference Point)

"A real favourite in the stable. He is approaching the veteran stage now, but doesn't let us down, and is a great horse through which Amy [Baker] can learn off. They won together at Chepstow last season, where he stuck it out in front to hang on. He will pop up during the season."

Spirit Of Chester

3yo bay filly

Lend A Hand - It Takes Two (Alzao)

"Is still a maiden, but was a star for us last season in an otherwise disappointing year. She didn't win, but she was second in the Albany at Royal Ascot behind Jewel In The Sand, and then came third behind Soar in the Lowther at York, which is pretty good form. She did suffer a hairline pelvis fracture afterwards, but she was having a holiday anyway so it didn't make much difference. Probably wants 7f, and should get further. She is exciting"

Withering Lady

3yo bay filly

Tagula - Princess Oberon (Fairy King)

"Was a good seventh in the Weatherbys Super Sprint at Newbury behind Siena Gold, and won at Beverley soon after that. Had a couple of runs on the All-Weather over the winter, so is having a bit of a break, but will be back on turf this summer, and is worth looking out for."

Wood Spirit

3yo bay filly

Woodborough - Windomen (Forest Wind)

"Had four runs for us last season, the best of which came at Beverley late in the season, when fourth on good to soft ground. Had a go on the All-Weather last November, but has had a nice break since and could do well with a bit of cut in the ground."

Woodsley House

3yo bay colt

Orpen - Flame And Shadow (Turtle Island)

"Didn't win last season, but put up some great efforts. Was second on his debut at Salisbury, and was runner-up twice more before finishing fifth in the Horris Hill at Newbury on his last start behind Cupid's Glory. The ground was very soft that day, but he seemed to cope with it well enough and should win his races this season over 1m"

Although they aren't named yet, there are a couple of two-year-olds who Nerys is keen on. One is a filly by **Bold Edge out of a mare named **Noor El Hoodah**, who happens to be a half-sister to the stable's Listed winner Smittenby. The other is a filly by **Bold Fact** out of a mare, named **Willow Dale**, a winner for David Elsworth. You've been warned!*

Profiles for punters

Mark Polglase

MARK POLGLASE

SOLOMON'S MINE

DRIVING INTO Southwell racecourse really does feel like you are on the road to nowhere.

Having left the petrol station - seemingly the last bastion of civilisation - an age ago, a road of romanesque straightness and longevity greets you with no apparent ending.

However, just as you start to doubt that there is anything of any significance down this remote track, the racecourse, and a measure of relief, home into view, as too does the sign that indicates Mark Polglase trains racehorses here.

Polglase moved here in 1998 from Newmarket . Once upon a time, Paul Blockley and Richard Marvin were next-door neighbours, but with the racecourse authorities unhappy at the burgeoning equine population taking shape, Blockley and Marvin both vacated, to leave the durable Polglase as the last man standing.

It's an eerily quiet place on non-racedays, which is probably a good thing, for horses and trainer alike. For, in his previous role in the Army as a Coldstream Guard, Polglase would have seen enough action to last a lifetime during stints in Iraq during the first Gulf War, and in Northern Ireland during the height of The Troubles.

On leaving the Army, Polglase went to work as assistant trainer to Robert Armstrong in Newmarket for three years, during which time the stable achieved a notorious success when Maroof made all to cause a 66-1 shock in the Queen Elizabeth II Stakes at Ascot.

Apprenticeship duly served, Polglase then set up himself, and achieved some eye-catching early successes through the likes of Dahlidya, Swift and King Priam, who was claimed out of the Martin Pipe stable for £7,000 and has since won a stack of races and been placed in two consecutive Lincolns.

What has really helped Polglase since the move to Southwell though has been the consistent patronage of big player Paul Dixon - he of Milk It Mick fame.

The two have formed a handy alliance and have been rewarded with a steady stream of winners. Solomon's Mine has done well for the combo, winning at the Doncaster Lincoln meeting in 2003, but undoubtedly the star of the show over the last few seasons has been the sprinter No Time.

He enjoyed a memorable spring in 2003, breaking the track record whilst winning a £29,000 handicap at Ascot, before following up in the Listed Field Marshal Stakes at Haydock, which remains Polglase's solitary Listed-class victory as a trainer.

No Time was at it again in the spring of 2004, notching a quick double at Lingfield on the All-Weather, and once again revealed his appealing trait of breaking track records, smashing the existing 5f time in the hands of Mr Dettori.

Allied to the support of owner Dixon is a small, close-knit team of dedicated staff including Polglase's extremely helpful wife Sandy.

And importantly too, in an industry which can break hearts and test patience to the absolute limit, team Polglase give the impression that they enjoy what they do, and don't mind having some fun along the way.

This attribute saw the ex-Coldstream Guardsman accompany staff in March 1999 to Nottingham nightclub Essence for a very belated Christmas bash.

Of the night, Polglase remembers that: "I found it a totally enlightening experience.

"I enjoyed pretending I was quite cool, but I was surprised at how little I could hear for the next day or so!"

Essence is unlikely to be a word that the Polglases forget either. Not because they had the time of their lives at the discotheque of the same name, but rather that their 'night' spawned the title of their entry into that year's Ten To Follow competition.

'Other people' win that don't they? Not in 1999 they didn't. The Essence team broke well, went further clear in July (scooping the paltry £10,000 monthly prize) before easing down close home to win with lengths to spare for a first prize of £130,000.

The handicapper inevitably raised them for that success and they've failed to win again since, but in that competition, a monthly dividend as well as an outright win would normally be considered the preserve of a madman's dreams.

Normality has long since returned to the yard after those heady days. The 100-winner mark was breached when Alizar romped home in a seller in December of 2003, and appropriately, the winner came at Southwell.

Quite understandably, a significant proportion of Polglase winners have come at his adopted home, but it would be entirely wrong to think that the horses can't operate anywhere else, although Polglase does admit that: "We do seem to do better on flat tracks such as Doncaster and York. I can't remember us having too many winners at undulating tracks such as Chepstow."

To counter the threat of familiarity breeding contempt, Polglase is installing a grass gallop at a satellite yard in nearby Retford.

In this way, the horses can become better accustomed to turf racing, while not forgetting their roots on the All-Weather, which looks set to become an unstoppable juggernaut during the coming years, with more and more AW tracks planned.

As it stands, the fact that the 'AW' is at its busiest during the winter months places Polglase in a handy position, albeit a personal one. It means that his quieter period is during the summer, which allows him time to nip down to Cornwall and indulge his other passion of surfing.

Polglase, wife Sandy and twins Fergus and Tara head down to the west country about three or four times a year for some much-needed battery-recharging, and to make the most of the waves. And although Polglase professes to be of only modest ability, it's odds-on that he feels more at home on a surfboard than he does on a nightclub dance floor.

Polglase's prospects

Alpaga Le Jomage

3yo bay gelding

Orpen – Miss Bagatelle (Mummy's Pet)

"Had some good form for Brian Meehan last season, including when fourth behind Siena Gold in the Weatherbys Super Sprint at Newbury.

"He had his first run for us at Southwell in December and we fancied him, but he disappointed and has now been gelded. He has plenty of ability and works well, so hopefully he should win us a few on turf this season."

Beauteous

6yo chestnut gelding

Tagula - Beauty Appeal (Shadeed)

"Took advantage of Banded racing last April - where he won four times within a week on all three All-Weather tracks.

"He has had a nice long break since then and is just coming back to full fitness. He will have a few runs on the All-Weather to get him ready before returning to turf.

"He's one to bear in mind."

Bold Blade

4yo bay gelding

Sure Blade - Golden Ciel (Septieme Ciel)

"Seems to be a much better horse on the All-Weather than on turf so that is probably where he will stay. He's at his best over staying trips, possibly around the 2m mark, although he has won over shorter. He has won at Wolverhampton and Southwell."

Hamburg Springer

3yo bay gelding

Charnwood Forest - Kyra Crown (Astronef)

"He has plenty of ability, but is difficult to catch right.

"We dropped him in trip to 6f at Southwell in January and he won well under a good ride from Chris Catlin.

"He ought to progress and could turn out to be a bit better than his current mark."

Miss Malone

3yo bay filly

Daggers Drawn - Queen Molly (Emarati)

"We picked her up from Richard Hannon's yard, where she had some great form from last season, including a second behind Cheveley Park winner Magical Romance at Kempton.

She will have a few runs on the All-Weather before starting her turf campaign and we'd hope to pick up a few races with her over 6f or 7f. She could be well handicapped at the moment."

ALPAGA LE JOMAGE (fourth from right, white face): finshing fourth behind Siena Gold

Nicholas Nickelby

5yo grey gelding

Fayruz - Alasib (Siberian Express)

"Versatile sort who goes equally as well on turf as the All-Weather. He won at Southwell last November at 28-1, but should really have got his head in front before then. He wouldn't want the ground too fast on turf."

No Time

5yo bay horse

Danetime - Muckross Park (Nomination)

"He has been a tremendous flagbearer for the stable, having won the Listed Field Marshal Stakes at Haydock in 2003, as well as a £29,000 handicap at Ascot, where he broke the track record. He also holds the course record at Lingfield for 5f - which he broke under Frankie Dettori last March. He's a real speed horse, and is better at 5f than 6f, so look out for him in all the big turf sprint handicaps."

Piccleyes

4yo bay gelding

Piccolo - Dark Eyed Lady (Exhibitioner)

"Another one we got out of the Richard Hannon stable and he could turn out to be well handicapped. He was third for us on New Year's Day under Eddie Ahern, and on that showing he should be capable of winning races on the All Weather over 6f."

Solomon's Mine

6yo bay gelding

Rahy - Shes A Sheba (Alysheba)

"He is being aimed at the 2m2f handicap at the Lincoln meeting, which he won in 2003. He ran at Wolverhampton in January behind Moayed on his first run back following a break, but the 1m trip was far too short. He will now be stepped back up in trip, and will have a few sighters before the Doncaster race. He likes to get his toe in."

Tally

5yo chestnut gelding

Tagula - Sally Chase (Sallust)

"A solid, decent handicapper who is gradually slipping down the weights to an attractive mark. He is capable of winning over 6f or 7f and goes on any ground. Might just need freshening up a bit, but will pop up again."

Mark currently has three two-year-olds who are worthy of note. **Ullah Pendragon is from the first crop of Aidan O'Brien's Group 1 winner **Beckett**, out of **Marathon Maid** (who won as a two-year-old). He is described as a precocious sort who has plenty of speed and will be out early. The other two have yet to be named, but one is a filly by **Montjeu** out of **Castara Beach** who will stay well and is related to winners, while the other is a filly by **Brave Act** (won Solario Stakes for Mark Prescott at two), out of **Faypool**, who has had five offspring, all of whom have won as two-year-olds.*

NO TIME (right): seen here scoring in record-breaking fashion at Ascot in March 2003

Profiles for punters

Geraldine Rees

THE TWO FACES OF GERALDINE REES: 1982, Cheers and all that; now a respected trainer

ALTHOUGH Geraldine Rees started training horses under her own name in 1998, the legacy left for her really dates back to June 19, 1992 and the Wokingham Handicap at Royal Ascot.

Geraldine's father, Captain Jim Wilson entered two horses in the race. Profilic managed 15th, but the mare Red Rosein defied odds of 33-1 (and a Mark Johnston-trained favourite in second) to win the race under Gary Carter.

By all accounts, Red Rosein could be difficult and highly strung, but she also displayed admirable tenacity and a killer instinct when the winning post was in sight.

These were all valuable qualities to pass down the genes in her new career as a broodmare, and on the retirement in 1998 of her father, Rees would have the pleasure of training Red Rosein's progeny.

They didn't disappoint. Out of seven foals produced by the Wokingham winner, five won. Young Rosein and Chief Response got the ball rolling, but the exploits of the third foal, Proud Boast, really were eyecatching, and served to put Rees on the map as a trainer.

She won the Listed Rous Stakes at Newmarket back in 2002, having already scooped the Gosforth Park Cup in the very same season.

Her final foal, Rosein, is currently in

training and looks like following the family tradition already.

Of course there were others that helped Rees in her new career, such as Miss Fit, Katie Komaite and Piccolo Cativo, who struck up a great rapport with Angela Hartley, the pair winning six races together.

Hartley, now retired from race-riding, still works at the yard and plays a vital role, while adding to the continuity are the aforementioned three horses - all now retired - and now producing the next wave of inmates at Rees's petite training establishment in rural Lancashire.

There are seven broodmares currently housed at Moor Farm, all of whom ran for the stable, and most of whom won - the future looks bright.

Rees's statistics might not look startling in terms of winners recorded, but it must be borne in mind that it is only a small stable. At present there are 15 horses in training, and the number has never departed much from that figure.

What is impressive however is that a high proportion of horses to pass through Rees's hands have won, have often been multiple winners, and have gone off at good prices.

Thus Miss Fit won her first three starts as a two-year-old, Baby Barry has won twice at Goodwood, and Beach Buoy defied a nine-month absence to win at 33-1. This proves that, given the material, Rees can get the winners.

She equates training racehorses to running a classroom: "Horses are like human beings. You get some industrious triers, some talented high-flyers, while others are good but don't want to work or are too insecure and not tough enough to stand racing.

"All you can do is get them as fit as you can, and make sure they are happy and relaxed, but they've got to want to win."

Rees has done particularly well with sharp two-year-olds, and admits she has absolutely no inclination to train staying chasers, which could be seen as a little surprising, given her history as the first lady rider to complete the Grand National when she rode Cheers into eighth place in 1982.

It's not something that she thinks about now, naturally enough considering it was 23 years ago, but it's still a momentous achievement, particularly back then, when the fences were 'real' fences.

The chance very nearly didn't arise at all. She was due to partner Gordon's Lad in the race but he went lame and the dream looked over.

They tried to buy Cheers, but were outbid by Charlie Mackenzie and all seemed lost. However the new owners decided to book Rees anyway for the ride and the dream was back on.

As ever with the National, the partnership needed their slice of fortune, and it could all have ended in tears going to Becher's second time round.

Two loose horses were causing mayhem to the backmarkers as Cheers approached the fence. Rees made a quick decision to head to the right, the loose horses went left and refused, taking out horses on the inner, and disaster was averted.

The rest of the fences were negotiated safely, and although Cheers got very tired after the last, the partnership remained intact and history was made.

Rees had no time to rest on her laurels, as she was riding in the very next race, but admits that while connections had a big party that night, she slipped quietly away from the course struggling to take it all in. She had another try the following year on Midday Welcome, but they fell at the first.

In the years following her Grand National exploits, Rees learnt her trade under the watchful eye of her father until the role reversal in 1998 that saw Rees take over.

She admits that she found the prospect a daunting one at first, especially in a small stable where: "You have to do a bit of everything in the yard because there aren't may staff to go round. I'm a hands-on trainer, so aside from tending to the horses, I've got to make the entries, drive the horsebox occasionally and be a jack of all trades."

When speaking of ambitions for the future, Rees modestly hopes that: "I just want to get the best out of all the horses in the yard. In terms of numbers, it's nice to reach double figures each season, but I just want to let the horses realise their potential."

With the broodmare angle helping things along, together with a small, close-knit team (comprising mainly of her father and Angela Hartley), it's easy to see Rees realising, if not exceeding her aims, and as the 'Cheers' episode proved, she isn't someone to be underestimated.

Rees's racers

Baby Barry

8yo bay gelding

Komaite - Malcesine (Auction Ring)

"We've had him since he was a foal, and although he's now eight years old, he still retains plenty of enthusiasm. He's had a good winter break, but there are no early plans for him, and he will be out later on.

"He's quite well handicapped, and has now won twice at Goodwood so we might take him down there again. We've had tremendous success with Baby Barry's dam Malcesine, and she's produced another good one for us here."

Benny The Bus

3yo bay gelding

Komaite - Amy Leigh (Imperial Frontier)

"A tremendous character, a real likely lad who took a while to get the hang of what was required.

"The penny appeared to have dropped on his fourth start for us though when he almost won at Catterick at odds of 33-1. He was lent on close home and wasn't beaten far, and we thought we may get the race in the stewards room, but we didn't.

"We tried him on the All-Weather in the winter, but it was the end of a long season and he didn't show his best. He will start off on the sand this season, and he's really improved since his two-year-old days so we should be able to pinch a race with him."

Calculaite

4yo bay gelding

Komaite - Miss Calculate (Mummy's Game)

"A real gentleman to deal with, who is a lot stronger this year. He won for us at Carlisle last season by 10l, although it was only a banded event. His full brothers Sandles and Playtime Blue have both won, and we'd hope to win a few more with him too, probably over a 1m trip."

Ellen Mooney

6yo chestnut mare

Efisio - Budby (Rock City)

"A lovely filly who loves soft ground, and who ran well at Wolverhampton in February.

"She is due to be covered by Lend A Hand at some stage too, but she will carry on afterwards. You can run mares up to 120 days into their pregnancy and it has been known to improve them sometimes."

BABY BARRY (right): winning for the first time at Goodwood in the hands of Richard Quinn

Lark In The Park

5yo chestnut mare

Grand Lodge - Jarrayan (Machiavellian)

"She is new to us this season, having been trained by Mark Brisbourne previously. She struggled last season, but as a result is now well-handicapped. Her last win came in August 2003 over 1m on firm ground at Bath."

Newcorp Lad

5yo bay gelding

Komaite - Gleam Of Gold (Crested Lark)

"Consistent type who gets on well with Tony Culhane - all of his three wins have come with Tony riding, and two of those came at Hamilton. His last win came at Newcastle last September where he won by 5l, so he has ability, and should win some more this season.

He is another horse by Komaite, who is a sire we've had a lot of success with. Unfortunately he's not here any more, but most of his progeny have done us proud - as this one has."

Owed

3yo bay gelding

Lujain - Nightingale (Night Shift)

"Had three runs for us last season, and ran really well on the last of those when fourth behind Tara's Treasure at Thirsk over 6f.

He has since been gelded, which has helped him a lot, and his best trip would probably besf, as he was staying on in the Thirsk race."

Rosein

3yo bay filly

Komaite - Red Rosein (Red Sunset)

"She is a lovely filly with a great temperament and a very sweet nature. She's out of my father's Wokingham winner Red Rosein, and shows plenty of ability herself.

"She won at Southwell on her debut under Joe Fanning last May and, really ran on well once she new what was required.

"We then stepped her up in grade and went for the Listed Hilary Needler at Beverley, but she didn't pick up as well as we expected.

"She finished seventh, and wasn't beaten that far, only beaten about 3l, but we found her to be coughing afterwards, so it probably wasn't her true form.

"She had one more outing at Ripon in August, finished sixth, again not beaten far, and then we put her away.

"She will probably start again in mid-April in handicaps, and we will take it from there, but she is good, and if she turns out anything like her mother, then we are in for a lot of fun."

In the juvenile division, Geraldine Rees has several names worth noting. The filly **Miss Tickle, is by **Komaite**, out of a mare called **Miss Fit**, who was a very sharp two-year-old for the stable, winning her first three starts. Miss Tickle has shown plenty of ability, and is "nicely forward". **Kildonan Castle**, is by **Forzando** out of the stable's winning mare (pictured below) **Katie Komaite**. He is well put together and "goes nicely."*

Profiles by Nick Watts

KATIE KOMAITE (right): dam of Kildonan Castle powering home in the mud at Pontefract

2005 Preview

Outlook

Ante-Post

by
Steffan Edwards

2,000 Guineas

The interesting thing about the 2,000 Guineas market is that, although it's headed by a perfectly sound favourite based on last season's juvenile form, if reports are to be believed the horse in question looks highly likely to miss the race.

Shamardal won the Vintage Stakes and Dewhurst in impressive style last year and was rightly crowned top two-year-old in the International Classifications as a result.

He'd be the one to beat if lining up at Newmarket, but since he left Mark Johnston's yard for Godolphin it seems that dreams of Kentucky Derby glory may well have been pinned to him.

By Giant's Causeway, who came so close to winning the Breeders' Cup Classic, out of a full-sister to Dubai World Cup winner Street Cry, it's easy to see why Godolphin are planning to enter him for the US Triple Crown races. They also have a more than able deputy for the 2,000 in the shape of **DUBAWI**.

The first offspring of Dubai Millennium to set foot on a racecourse, he made a winning debut at Goodwood before going on to pick up a Group 3 at Newmarket and the Group 1 National Stakes at The Curragh.

The fact that he achieved so much at two is remarkable as he's bred to do much better as a three-year-old. His dam won the Italian Oaks and he looks sure to get 1m4f in time, but it would be unwise to assume that he won't have the speed for the Guineas, as the highlight of his win in Ireland was his ability to quicken.

Clearly very well regarded, nothing would please Sheikh Mohammed more than to see a son of his favourite horse win a Classic, and Dubawi has a major chance of achieving that for him.

Maiden winner **Rob Roy**'s prominence

DUBAWI (left): Dubai Millennium's legacy starting to show with this 2,000 Guineas type

in the market is reminiscent of his trainer's Golan prior to that one's Guineas victory. He's clearly in the could-be-anything category as well, but it's worth noting that, while Golan's maiden win came over a subsequent Group 3 winner, Rob Roy could only finish 3l in front of something which has been beaten since in banded maidens.

ETLAALA was disputing favouritism for this race after his impressive victory in the Champagne Stakes. Repeatedly short of running room and forced to switch, he looked sure to go down as an unlucky loser, but he actually produced a terrific turn of foot to make up lost ground and win cleverly.

A son of Selkirk, there were grounds for believing that he would handle the soft conditions in the Dewhurst, but in the event he failed to act on it. That performance can be easily written off, and in the circumstances it's a surprise to see that his odds for the Guineas have doubled. Back on good ground or faster, Etlaala's turn of speed will make him a threat to all.

The Derby looks a more suitable target for **Motivator**, who might struggle for pace at Newmarket. In two starts to date, including when winning the Racing Post Trophy impressively, he's shown stamina to be his strong suit and a liking for soft ground. History shows that the ground at Newmarket is rarely testing on Guineas weekend.

Oratorio was kept busy last year, running seven times in all. He progressed throughout, though, rounding off with a win in a French Group 1 and the runner-up spot in the Dewhurst on unsuitably soft ground. A tough, admirable type, he looks sure to run his race in the Guineas and certainly has frame possibilities.

Grey Swallow hacked up in the Killavullan Stakes in 2003, and last year's winner **Footstepsinthesand** looks another promising type. Although he's only run on soft ground so far, Aidan O'Brien and Jamie Spencer both believe he'll be much happier on a fast surface, and the Guineas mile should suit him down to the ground.

O'Brien's Middle Park winner **Ad Valorem** is of less interest Guineas-wise, as both his pedigree and style of racing suggest sprinting will be his game.

Perfectperformance failed to run his race in the Dewhurst and is better judged on his win in the Royal Lodge, but even that form would put him short of the level required to win a Guineas.

One of Godolphin's most interesting three-year-olds for the forthcoming season is **Belenus**, who impressed when winning on his debut at Newmarket last summer. A good-looking son of Dubai Millennium, he'll get 1m2f in time but should have the speed for the Guineas, although the worry with him is whether the first Classic will come too soon.

Layman was only beaten narrowly by Oratorio in France, and is bred to come into

2,000 Guineas — Newmarket, 30th April 2005

	Bet365	*Chandler*	*Coral*	*Hills*	*Lads*	*PPower*	*SJames*	*SGraham*
Shamardal	4	7-2	**5**	4	**5**	4	4	3
Dubawi	6	7	6	7	6	6	7	**8**
Oratorio	**16**	14	14	14	14	14	14	14
Rob Roy	16	14	**20**	14	14	14	16	16
Ad Valorem	12	**16**	14	**16**	**16**	**16**	**16**	**16**
Footstepsinthesand	16	14	**20**	16	16	16	**20**	16
Etlaala	**16**	12	12	12	14	14	12	14
Motivator	14	**16**	**16**	**16**	14	**16**	12	**16**
Tiger Dance	**25**	**25**	**25**	**25**	**25**	**25**	**25**	**25**
Belenus	**25**	**25**	**25**	**25**	**25**	**25**	**25**	**25**
Echo Of Light	25		25	**40**	33	25	33	25
Layman	20	**25**	20	**25**	**25**	20	20	20
Home Affairs	**40**	-	33	**40**	33	33	28	33
Elliots World	**50**	25	40	33	40	-	33	33

each-way 1/4 odds, 1-2-3

Others on application, prices correct at time of going to press

his own as a three-year-old, but he's now with Godolphin, and they have a stronger candidate for the race.

Montgomery's Arch is a smart performer but he has to find improvement from somewhere to trouble the best of these, while Godolphin lesser lights **Windsor Knot** and **Librettist** are both promising types for the season ahead, but the Guineas might be flying a bit high. The same can be said for **Oude**, who's prone to taking a keen hold in his races, something which contributed to his defeats in both the Acomb and Champagne Stakes.

The Coventry Stakes winner **Iceman** ran well throughout last season but was found out at the top level. He'll have to find improvement from somewhere if he's going to turn the tables on the likes of Shamardal, Oratorio, Ad Valorem and Etlaala.

Cupid's Glory is a mudlover and probably isn't good enough anyway, but **Diktatorial** is more interesting.

Andrew Balding's already tasted Classic success with Casual Look in the Oaks two years ago, and Diktatorial looks a live outsider for this year's 2,000.

A gutsy winner of the Somerville Tattersalls Stakes on his final start at two, he needs to improve a good deal on that to play a part at Newmarket, but he's sure to have strengthened up over the winter and looks the type to do a lot better at three.

Unexposed, well-bred maiden winners who could develop into candidates if they progress fast enough include the Aidan O'Brien pair **Grand Central** and **Tiger Dance**. The former is a son of Coronation Stakes winner Rebecca Sharp and the latter a full-brother to Giant's Causeway.

Forward Move, owned by the Queen and trained by Richard Hannon is another potential joker in the pack. He looked good when winning at Newmarket last term.

1,000 Guineas

Last season's 1,000 Guineas winner Attraction was an untypical winner. She wasn't bred to get a mile and came to the race having been absent through injury since July.

She beat a bad field – the only one of her rivals to go on and win a European Group race later in the season was Red Bloom, who won a four-runner Group 3, and all in all I think we can dismiss last year's result as a blip. I expect this year's race to go to a filly who has taken a more conventional route to Newmarket.

As I mentioned last year, the key stats for the race are as follows. Firstly, each of the last 23 winners had Group-race form as a two-year-old. Secondly, sixteen of the last 23 winners finished first and/or started favourite for at least one of the following four races: Ascot's Fillies' Mile, Longchamp's Prix Marcel Boussac and Newmarket's Cheveley Park Stakes and Rockfel Stakes. Another three winners finished runner-up in one of these informative races.

This year's nine qualifiers are **Playful Act**, **Maids Causeway**, **Echelon**, **Divine Proportions**, **Titian Time**, **Magical Romance**, **Suez**, **Damson** and **Penkenna Princess**.

Divine Proportions is a worthy favourite, having beaten the colts in the Prix Morny over 6f and shown her stamina for a mile with a clear-cut win in the Marcel Boussac.

It's worth noting that her rider Christophe Lemaire, who partnered Denebola to victory in the previous year's Boussac, was quoted afterwards as saying that this filly is "much, much better than Denebola".

A half-sister to Whipper, who was fifth in the 2,000 last year, she could not have done any more at two and sets the standard. There is one big negative, however, which is that she has yet to be confirmed for the race.

At the time of writing, connections are planning to give her an entry for the French and English Guineas and choose nearer the time. Although her chance, were she to be confirmed for Newmarket, is obvious, 5-1 is a short enough price given the doubts. I'd rather back her on the day.

The filly she beat in France, **Titian Time**, is a sister to Queen Mary winner Shining Hour, but had no problem with the mile at Longchamp. She clearly has plenty of ability, but she did enjoy the run of the race that day, and her trainer, successful in the 1,000 Guineas with Lahan in 2000, has a stronger candidate in **Playful Act**.

Purely on breeding the May Hill and Fillies' Mile winner is an Oaks filly, but Kazzia and Imagine (Irish 1,000) are both recent examples of middle-distance-bred fillies succeeding over the mile trip. John Gosden's filly is not short of speed and, as a proven front-runner, could well make an impact. The likeliest scenario, though, is that she runs well without winning: in other words, a nice trial for Espom.

Maids Causeway finished behind Playful Act at Doncaster and Ascot and was found a weak Rockfel.

She beat **Penkenna Princess** by only a short-head on that occasion and, given that that filly had been beaten in a nursery two starts earlier, the form is nothing to get carried away about.

There's no reason why she should turn the tables on the Gosden filly and I expect her to play only a minor role at Newmarket.

The Fillies' Mile third **Dash To The Top** is another who looks more an Oaks filly.

Echelon, who was sent off favourite for the aforementioned Ascot Group 1 on the back of her impressive maiden victory at Newbury, found the step up to top company just a bit too much for her at that stage of her career.

The fact that she also enjoyed a far from clear run suggests she wasn't seen at her best at Ascot, and it wouldn't be a surprise to see this half-sister to Chic step up considerably on that bare form this season. Her dam won the Coronation Stakes and she has "miler" written all over her.

The Cheveley Park form doesn't look that strong, given that it was run on loose ground, won by a 40-1 shot, and the first five all finished in a heap. Nevertheless, the winner **Magical Romance**, who is clearly suited by some ease, promises to be well suited by the step up to a mile this season, and she cannot be dismissed lightly. In contrast, both **Suez** and **Soar** are likely to struggle to see out a stiff mile, and it wouldn't be a surprise to see them contesting the top sprint races later in the season.

Sent off at odds-on for the race, **DAMSON** was a big disappointment in third. She might not have been suited by the ground, though, and connections suggested it may have been one run too many at the end of a long season.

Whatever the reason, her previous form entitles her to serious consideration for the Guineas. An impressive winner of the Queen Mary at Royal Ascot, she later went on to beat Oratorio in the Group 1 Phoenix Stakes, form which was franked when that colt went on to win a Group 1 race himself in France and finish runner-up to Shamardal in the Dewhurst.

She'll get a mile no problem and, at 12-1, looks to have plenty going for her.

Shanghai Lily didn't get the chance to prove herself in Group company last season, as she was a late withdrawal from the

1,000 Guineas — Newmarket, 1st May 2005

	Bet365	*Bl Sq*	*Coral*	*Hills*	*Lads*	*PPower*	*SJames*	*Tote*
Divine Proportions	4	4	4	4	**5**	9-2	4	4
Damson	**12**	**12**	**12**	10	8	10	9	10
Playful Act	**12**	10	10	**12**	10	10	10	10
Echelon	14	-	16	16	14	16	12	**20**
Suez	12	14	**20**	12	14	12	14	14
Discuss	20	20	**25**	**25**	16	16	20	**25**
Magical Romance	20	**25**	**25**	16	**25**	20	16	**25**
Shanghai Lily	**20**	14	16	**20**	16	16	16	16
Cherokee	25	-	**33**	**33**	25	25	20	**33**
Dash To The Top	**33**	-	25	**33**	**33**	25	**33**	20
Fen Shui	**33**	-	**33**	**33**	25	**33**	**33**	**33**
Intriguing	**25**	**25**	**25**	**25**	**25**	**25**	**25**	**25**
Shohrah	**40**	-	**40**	25	25	**40**	25	33
Whazzat	33	**50**	25	20	33	25	25	33

each-way 1/4 odds, 1-2-3

Others on application, prices correct at time of going to press

Rockfel because of the testing ground, but her easy wins in two starts to date have shown her a smart filly in the making.

While she couldn't be rated too highly on a strict reading of the form, she looks the type who's sure to do better at three. There are no concerns on the stamina front as she's by a Guineas winner out of a nine-furlong winner, and her trainer, also responsible for Echelon, is in the enviable position of holding two strong cards for the race.

Aidan O'Brien's best chance appears to lie with **Cherokee**, who disappointed on soft ground in the Rockfel but had previously shown smart form on fast ground when beating two Pattern-placed performers in a Group 3 race on her debut.

Stablemate **Silk And Scarlet** is another who has to put behind her a disappointing effort on her final start, having earlier looked a classy performer in the making.

One of the more interesting outsiders is the Barry Hills-trained **WHAZZAT**. Hills has a poor strike-rate with his juvenile debutantes, but she beat two subsequent Group-race winners in stablemate Maids Causeway and Cours De La Reine on her debut in a Newbury maiden, showing plenty of guts to battle back after being headed.

As her trainer said: "she's not that big, but she has a bit of fire about her." Ten days later she turned up at Royal Ascot for the Chesham Stakes, the only filly in the field, and ran out an impressive winner from some solid performers.

Wilko, Hearthstead Wings and In Excelsis, who finished third, fourth and fifth respectively, all got closer to the top-class colt Dubawi on subsequent starts than they did to Whazzat!

For a filly with what is undoubtedly a middle-distance pedigree, she has a decent amount of speed and a fine turn of foot. She was due to step up into Group company after Ascot, but suffered a setback and was given the rest of the season off.

Obviously this isn't ideal, but her owner was quoted in the autumn as saying: "I think the break in racing has actually benefited her as it's given her a bit of time, and she should be a nice prospect for next year."

A filly who already has decent form in the book and could go right to the top, her price is big enough to take the chance that she reappears fit and well.

Of the others, **Clear Impression** starts the season a maiden and isn't sure to stay a mile, while **Birthstone** is interesting, although Godolphin have many possibles.

Oaks

Unfortunately, in contrast to previous years, the Oaks market isn't full of milers who can be easily dismissed.

The betting is headed by a worthy favourite in Playful Act. She's already shown high-class form at the top level, and her pedigree just screams middle distances.

By Sadler's Wells out of a Musidora winner, her brother Percussionist was a close fourth in last year's Derby, and her half-sister Echoes In Eternity won the Park Hill over an extended 1m6f. One couldn't hope for better breeding with the Oaks in mind.

There is only one minor concern, and that's the ground. Percussionist handled good ground well enough on Derby Day, but completely failed to give his running on fast ground in the Irish equivalent.

John Gosden himself stated that Playful Act wouldn't run in the Fillies' Mile if it was firm and, although she won the race on ground officially described as good to firm, there had been rain beforehand.

Indeed, her winning time was almost a second and a half slower than that recorded by Red Bloom the previous year. It's difficult to argue against her having a major chance, though, and if, as seems likely, she takes in the Guineas en route, a first six finish should tee her up nicely for Epsom.

The Fillies' Mile runner-up **Maids Causeway** is not as stoutly bred and is likely to find 1m2f about as far as she wants to go, but the third **DASH TO THE TOP** is more interesting.

By Montjeu out of a 1m2f winning daughter of Nashwan, she was too inexperienced to show her true ability at Ascot, running green in the straight, and yet she stayed on well to finish third, beaten under 2l.

She will come into her own this season over middle distances and has bright prospects of reversing the form with the winner if they meet at Epsom. At twice the price of the favourite, she looks worth supporting.

Mona Lisa is still a maiden, but she must be one of the best out there. Unlucky in running in the Fillies' Mile, a race in which she should have probably finished second at least, the following month she was sent over the pond for the Breeders' Cup Juvenile Fillies.

She never got into the race after missing the break and it remains to be seen if the American adventure has left a mark.

The record of Aidan O'Brien's Breeders' Cup two-year-old runners in Europe the following season is pretty dismal, Sophisticat being the one exception, and those notoriously hard races clearly take a lot out of a juvenile.

O'Brien looks to have a better chance with **Silk And Scarlet**, who was progressing nicely before running no sort of race in the Moyglare Stud Stakes.

As the old cliché goes, you can always forgive a horse one bad run, and this daughter of Sadler's Wells, while not short of speed, has decent prospects of getting 1m4f this season.

The Moyglare runner-up **Pictavia** is another who should stay 1m2f this season. You can forget her last run in the C L Weld Park Stakes, as she hated the soft ground.

For a filly who's shown so much speed, **Damson**'s pedigree surprisingly offers hope of her getting middle distances. However, it's probably not worth betting that she'll live up to her breeding.

Magical Romance is another whose stamina will surely run out at 1m2f.

In contrast, there are no stamina doubts regarding **Ayam Zaman**, whose parents both won over 1m4f and whose two wins over 1m2f at two suggest that she will get even farther than that. At this stage she would appeal more as a St Leger candidate than an Oaks filly.

Godolphin have a number of choicely-bred fillies who could develop into Oaks contenders, including a dozen who are currently also entered for the Derby.

One of these is **Saywaan**, who cost $1.5million and is by the Kentucky Derby winner Fusaichi Pegasus out of Sharp Cat, a multiple Grade One winner in the US. She made a pleasing debut when winning a Leicester maiden and could be anything, but 1m2f might turn out to be her ideal trip.

The unraced pair **Anna Wi'Yaak**, who's by Dubai Millennium out of a Caerleon mare, and **Theatre School**, by Sadler's Wells, are two others to note.

Intrigued is another well-bred filly about whom there are no doubts stamina-wise. By Darshaan out of dual Group Two winner Last Second, she must surely have gained valuable experience of Epsom's unique contours when winning her maiden there in September, and she coped well with the step up to Group One company next time when a highly creditable staying-on fourth in the

Oaks

Epsom, 3rd June 2005

	Bet365	*Betfred*	*Chandler*	*Hills*	*Lads*	*PPower*	*SJames*	*Tote*
Playful Act	**10**	8	7	8	8	9	7	8
Intrigued	12	12	12	12	10	**14**	12	12
Silk And Scarlet	**25**	**25**	20	16	**25**	**25**	**25**	**25**
Dash To The Top	**20**	16	14	**20**	16	**20**	16	**20**
Ayam Zaman	20	20	20	20	20	20	**22**	20
Pictavia	**33**	-	25	25	**33**	-	25	25
Her Own Kind	25	25	-	25	**33**	25	22	25
Mona Lisa	33	**40**	33	-	33	25	33	25
Kitty O'Shea	20	25	25	-	**33**	25	25	25
Maids Causeway	25	**33**	25	**33**	**33**	-	25	**33**
Drama	**33**	**33**	**33**	-	-	-	-	**33**
Whazzat	33	**40**	**40**	-	33	33	33	33
Damson	**33**	**33**	**33**	-	-	-	28	25
Saywaan	**33**	-	-	-	-	-	-	-

each-way 1/4 odds, 1-2-3

Others on application, prices correct at time of going to press

PLAYFUL ACT (far left): John Gosden's filly has to be a major player for the Oaks in June

Marcel Boussac. She has strong claims.

Neither **Her Own Kind** nor **Kitty O'Shea** should fail in the Oaks through lack of stamina as they're both related to St Leger winners.

The former is a half-sister to Mutafaweq, while the latter is a sister to Brian Boru. They only have maiden wins to their names so far, but given their connections and pedigrees, they have to be considered for Epsom.

Seven Magicians starts the year a maiden having only run once at two. She shaped with promise that day behind stable companion Quickfire and, being a half-sister to Ocean Silk, who finished runner-up in the Yorkshire Oaks, 1m4f looks likely to be ideal this season.

Having put up **WHAZZAT** for the 1,000 Guineas, it would be stupid not to also recommend backing her for the Oaks, as her breeding suggests she will come into her own over middle-distances.

By Daylami out of a Generous mare, her two-year-old form reads well and her proven ability to handle fast ground is a big plus.

Derby

One horse stands out in the Derby betting and that's DUBAWI. A top-class two-year-old who improved with every outing, his impressive victory in the National Stakes, which he settled with a fine turn of foot, was the highlight, and this from a colt with a middle-distance pedigree.

The National Stakes has had a fine record of producing Classic winners in recent years and I'm convinced that last year's winner will enhance its profile even further.

Having put up **Dubawi** for the 2,000 Guineas as well, it's worth considering backing him in what bookies term a 'special double' to win both events. 25-1 is the best offer at the time of writing, and at that price we're effectively being asked to bet that he's quoted at less than 15-8 for Epsom after he wins at Newmarket.

It sounds unlikely but it's not so long ago that Entrepreneur was quoted at Evens following his Guineas success, and was eventually sent off at 4-6 for the Derby. Another three Guineas winners have been sent off favourite for the Epsom showpiece in the last ten years, although none won.

However, it's not the mug bet some may suggest, and of course we always have the option of laying off the bet if he's successful in the first leg.

Motivator looks like he takes after his father more than his mother, who was a miler, and he's unlikely to be found wanting for stamina. The ground is the worry for him, though, as it cannot be a coincidence that his two starts to date have been on soft ground.

His trainer did well to find a soft-ground maiden for him in August and, impressive though his Racing Post Trophy victory was, conditions clearly played to his strengths that day. If the ground was on the easy side on Derby day he would have as decent a chance as any, but that's a big if, as it's only been good to soft or worse once in the last 21 years.

It's difficult to see **Shamardal** getting 1m4f, although 1m2f shouldn't be a problem. However, Godolphin are entering him for the American Triple Crown races, and if he takes to the dirt in Dubai as his breeding suggests he should, the chances are his stamina won't be being tested at Epsom in the first week of June, but rather at Belmont Park.

Godolphin have other possibles for the race, but the majority would not be in the same league as Dubawi. **Oude** is fairly exposed as below top class, and a doubtful stayer to boot.

Russian Rhythm's half-brother **Perfectperformance** is an admirable type and can be forgiven his disappointing run in the Dewhurst on soft ground at the end of a tough season, but he's another who looks set to struggle to match the best in Group 1 company this season.

Centaurus should have little trouble staying 1m4f, and he looks one of Godolphin's more interesting maiden winners.

Quest For Fame in 1990 was the last Derby winner, apart from Commander In Chief, who didn't run as a juvenile, to fail to win a race at two.

Therefore, despite their promise, recent history is against the likes of **Echo Of Light**, **Hard Top** and **Down Mexico Way**. Echo Of Light was a talking horse last season, even-

PERFECTPERFORMANCE (left): Will the Godolphin colt be up to a Derby bid this season?

tually making his reappearance in the Newmarket maiden won by interesting Derby outsider **Proclamation** at the back-end.

In time he may well turn out to be a star, but the chances are that others will be more forward come June. Incidentally, Jeremy Noseda's charge has plenty of stamina on his dam's side and could make his mark in one of the trials.

Windsor Knot, previously trained by John Gosden, is out of a mare who stayed well, but he's by the sprinter Pivotal, and it would be quite something if he was able to sire a Derby winner.

Andre Fabre trained **Layman** to place in a couple of Group 1s over 6f and 7f last season, which was quite an achievement as the colt is bred for middle-distances.

He's an interesting addition to the Godolphin camp, as is **Berenson**, who was put in his place by Dubawi in the National Stakes but is stoutly bred and should come into his own this year.

Belenus is highly regarded and will surely make his mark in the best company, but 1m2f might be as far as he'll want to go.

As you would expect, Aidan O'Brien's team features a number of potential candidates, but most make only limited appeal.

Grand Central appears quite short in the betting given that he's only won a minor maiden, albeit easily. His dam's side of his pedigree won't see him get farther than a mile so he's relying on Sadler's Wells imparting the stamina. It's an unconvincing profile and I'm happy to take him on.

It's difficult to see **Albert Hall** reversing Racing Post Trophy placings with Motivator, even on quicker ground, and in any case he's not guaranteed to stay 1m4f.

Yehudi appears to thrive in testing conditions and, while his stamina isn't in doubt, it's anyone's guess whether he will replicate his form on a quicker surface, and **Footstepsinthesand**, while clearly an exciting prospect, strikes me as more of a Guineas type than a Derby horse.

I see Aidan O'Brien's strongest hopes as **Gypsy King** and **Almighty**.

The former was at one stage being considered for the Racing Post Trophy, but he didn't make his debut until late October. By Sadler's Wells out of a Darshaan mare, he won his only start easily and is sure to find 1m4f right up his street this year.

Almighty had newcomer Bogside Dancer, who finished a length and a half behind Gypsy King on his following start, 8l back when winning his maiden at Navan.

A half-brother to Arc winner Sagamix, he has the potential to go right to the top.

As I mentioned in the 2,000 Guineas preview, **Rob Roy**'s maiden isn't working out particularly well, although he won it easily of course and, given Sir Michael Stoute's record in the Classics, and the colt's promi-

Derby

Epsom, 4th June 2005

	Bet365	*Chandler*	*Coral*	*Hills*	*Lads*	*PPower*	*SJames*	*Tote*
Dubawi	**8**	6	6	7	6	6	13-2	13-2
Motivator	**10**	**10**	**10**	7	8	**10**	**10**	9
Shamardal	16	**20**	-	**20**	16	**20**	12	**20**
Rob Roy	**25**	20	20	20	20	20	20	**25**
Albert Hall	**25**	**25**	**25**	**25**	**25**	**25**	**25**	20
Echo Of Light	33	33	33	**40**	33	25	33	33
Belenus	**33**	**33**	25	**33**	**33**	**33**	**33**	**33**
Windsor Knot	33	**40**	33	-	**40**	33	33	**40**
Gypsy King	25	-	-	20	33	33	25	**40**
Hard Top	40	40	40	-	33	40	33	**50**
Oude	25	**33**	25	-	**33**	**33**	25	25
Raydan	33	-	-	**40**	33	33	**40**	-
Avalon	33	-	33	33	**40**	33	33	**40**
Berenson	33	-	-	**40**	-	33	**40**	-

each-way 1/4 odds, 1-2-3

Others on application, prices correct at time of going to press

nence in the market, he cannot be dismissed lightly.

This fellow has a chance of staying 1m4f, but a prominent display in the Guineas or one of the Derby trials will tell us a lot more.

Currently unraced, the following half-dozen are worth keeping an eye out for, as they're all bred for the job and have the potential to shorten dramatically in the betting following an impressive maiden victory in the spring.

Kalamkar is from a top Aga Khan family. He is a half-brother to Kalanisi, Champion Stakes and breeders' Cup hero, as well as Kalaman, who was placed in the Eclipse last season.

Raydan is out of an Irish St Leger runner-up, while **Air Commodore** is a brother to an Oaks winner in Love Divine.

Intend To Leave is a half-brother to Henry Cecil's 1999 Derby winner Oath, **Glistening** is a half-brother to Dante winner Tenby, and Aidan O'Brien's **Portsmouth** is out of a half-sister to Derby winner Generous and Oaks winner Imagine. Families don't come much better than that.

Recommended Bets

2,000 Guineas

2pts Dubawi 8-1
(Sean Graham)
1pt Etlaala 16-1
(Bet365)

1,000 Guineas

1pt Damson 12-1
(Bet365, Chandler, Corals)
1pt Whazzat 50-1
(Blue Square)

Oaks

1pt Dash To The Top 20-1
(Bet365, Paddy Power, Totesport, Hills)
1pt Whazzat 40-1
(Betfred, Chandler)

Derby

2pts Dubawi 8-1
(Bet365)

All bets to win.
Prices correct at time of going to press.

GYPSY KING (front, left): a potential dark horse for the Derby from Aidan O' Brien's camp

Outlook's Horses to Follow

ALFONSO 4 ch g

Efisio – Winnebago (Kris)

1702421-

Alfonso has been brought along steadily by Barry Hills, not really showing much until coming second in a Newmarket handicap in August. That race followed a four-month break during which time he was gelded. He returned to Newmarket for a competitive 7f handicap in late October, when he encountered his ideal good to soft ground, and won again. He's been a slow learner but things should come good for him this year.

Barry Hills, Lambourn

AYAM ZAMAN 3 b f

Montjeu – Kardashina (Darshaan)

511-

This filly's sire Montjeu (a son of Sadler's Wells) had an outstanding first season, with Motivator his chief earner. We suspect that Ayam Zaman will enhance Montjeu's reputation. She looked the part when winning the Listed Zetland Stakes over 1m2f at Newmarket in October. It would be no surprise if she made up into an Oaks filly, with stamina aplenty on her dam's side. Her sire, a multiple Group 1 winner over 1m4f and 1m2f, can supply the brilliance.

Michael Jarvis, Newmarket

AZAMOUR 4 b c

Night Shift – Asmara (Lear Fan)

2113-

This colt has a progressive profile and improvement should continue into his four-year-old campaign. His two finest hours last year came at Royal Ascot (the St James's Palace Stakes, 1m) and at Leopardstown (the Irish Champion Stakes, 1m2f). His inexperience was against him in the 2,000 Guineas and he was surprised by Bachelor Duke at The Curragh. He's a big colt and should be even more imposing this season when all the Group 1s over 1m2f are available to him.

John Oxx, Ireland

BAGO 4 b c

Nashwan – Moonlight's Box (Nureyev)

11331-

It may not have been a vintage Arc but that he won, but Bago was palpably best on the day with half a length to spare over Cherry Mix and a length back to Ouija Board. Furthermore there could be better to come and he looks a leading contender to be champion four-year-old. His record is already illustrious. Unbeaten as a two-year-old, he returned as a three-year-old to win the 1m1f Prix Jean Prat and the Grand Prix de Paris - both Group 1s. He only met defeat when there was some cut in the ground.

Jonathan Pease, France

BLUE DAKOTA 3 b c

Namid – Touraya (Tap On Wood)

11116-

Was a precocious two-year-old who ran up a string of four consecutive wins, all over 5f, culminating in the Norfolk Stakes at Royal Ascot. After that he ran in the Richmond Stakes at Glorious Goodwood where he injured himself. Jeremy Noseda reports him to be fully recovered and the King's Stand Stakes (at York this year, not Royal Ascot) has been earmarked as a first target. Precocious two-year-olds sometimes don't train on but this one has plenty of size about him and it is to be hoped that he can return to his devastating two-year-old days.

Jeremy Noseda, Newmarket

BLUE TRAIN 3 b c

Sadler's Wells – Igreja (Southern Halo)

4-

One run is not a lot to go on but there was a lot to like about the way this colt shaped in a 1m York maiden in October. He wasn't quito up for it when the pace quickened and settled for fourth but he had travelled well up to then. The stable seldom do too much with their juveniles and, in any case, this colt is most definitely bred for middle distances and beyond.

Sir Michael Stoute, Newmarket

CAESAR BEWARE 3 b g

Daggers Drawn – Red Shareef (Marju)

1112-

Took the eye when storming home 6l clear in a Windsor conditions race and not surprisingly was made 13-8 favourite for the 22-runner St Leger Yearling Stakes at Doncaster, a race with £173,000 to the winner and big prize-money back to tenth place. Suffice to say, they were all trying that day. Caesar Beware looked a class apart and won by 2l, a performance made all the more meritorious in that he was drawn in the middle of the pack in stall 12 when high numbers dominated. He didn't nearly run up to form when running-up in Redcar's Two-Year-Old Trophy but horses aren't machines. He wintered in Dubai.

Henry Candy, Wantage

CENTIFOLIA 3 gr f

Kendor – Djayapura (Fabulous Dancer)

10111-

This grey filly has yet to race beyond 6f but she could easily take in a 1,000 Guineas, most likely the French version. The time of her last race, the Criterium de Maisons-Laffitte over 6f, was comparatively fast on ground that was very soft. The form is solid and she had 2l to spare at the line. France's champion jockey Ioritz Mendizabal reckons she will not get beyond 6f. In which case, she can fly the flag for France in the sprinting division.

Robert Collet, France

FOOTSTEPSINTHESAND 3 b c

Giant's Causeway – Glatisant (Rainbow Quest)

11-

It may only have been a maiden at Naas but it was the scene of a massive gamble, one in which newspaper favourite Olympic, trained by Aidan O'Brien and ridden by stable jockey Jamie Spencer, was ignored in favour of stablemate Footstepsinthesand. The second-string could not have won more easily, sidling away to score by four and a half lengths. He was brought out eight days later, this time for a 7f Group 3 at Leopardstown, where he won by two and a half lengths. The experience will have done him good and he must be on the shortlist for the Derby. According to O'Brien he resembles his sire Giant's Causeway, but, unlike his sire, he should stay 1m4f. Both his races were on softish ground and, according to Spencer: "When he gets fast ground next year, we will be in business."

Aidan O'Brien, Ireland

FORWARD MOVE 3 ch c

Dr Fong – Kissing Gate (Easy Goer)

21-

The Queen could have plenty to smile about if her home-bred trains on. Forward Move was touched off a short-head on his debut, in a 1m Kempton maiden. He reappeared on the all two-year-old card at Newmarket in September and, with a strong tailwind, knocked a second off the course record. He won by an emphatic 5l, and the fourth horse home boosted the form by winning next time out

Richard Hannon, East Everleigh

FREE TRIP 4 b c

Cadeaux Genereux – Well Away (Sadler's Wells)

1602555217-

Started off 2004 on a mark of 78 and ended up on 94, improving gradually over nine runs. There's every reason to suppose he can find more this term and, with his ability to handle ground from soft to firm, he should find a valuable handicap or two. One of his best efforts was in the Britannia Handicap over a mile when only 2l behind Mandobi. He's also effective at 7f.

John Gosden, Manton

GENTLEMAN'S DEAL 4 b c

Danehill – Sleepytime (Royal Academy)

411-

Here's another four-year-old who, along with Ouija Board and Post And Rail, has been kept in training by Ed Dunlop. Unraced at two, he ran a debut fourth in a Newmarket maiden before hacking up in a much weaker 7f maiden at Chepstow. He went on to land a Wolverhampton 1m1f handicap by 3l under top weight. Dunlop has given this giant of a horse plenty of time. By the late, great sire Danehill and out of 1,000 Guineas winner Sleepytime, he simply has to be talented. Handicaps to start with, Group races later on.

Ed Dunlop, Newmarket

HATHRAH 4 Gr f

Linamix – Zivania (Shernazar)

13-

This filly has the advantage of being a forgotten sort, one who might pop up at a nice price first time out. Second in the May Hill Stakes as a two-year-old, she burst onto the scene at three when winning the 1m Masaka Stakes at Kempton - by 9l, no less. Her second and final run of 2004 came a month afterwards when she was third, beaten 1l, to Attraction in the 1,000 Guineas. That's top-class form and if she can run to that sort of level again, the world is her oyster. Races such as the Falmouth Stakes, Matron Stakes and Sun Chariot Stakes, all now Group 1s, could be on the agenda.

John Dunlop, Arundel

HOME AFFAIRS 3 b c

Dansili – Orford Ness (Selkirk)

510-

Made his debut in a maiden at Newmarket's July meeting and was fourth to Librettist having started 5-2 favourite. Although a fit and good-looking colt in the paddock, he showed no spark when asked to pick up. However, next time at Yarmouth he showed what he was really made of when beating Notability (winner next time). A flop in the Dewhurst, probably on account of the soft ground, he looks sure to pick up some black type.

Sir Michael Stoute, Newmarket

KING MARJU 3 b c

Marju – Katoushka (Hamas)

62123-

This is the kind of horse who could run in the better handicaps between 6f and a mile and also compete in Listed and Group 3s. He had a big problem as a two-year-old in that he ran too freely. He refused to settle in all four of the races that he didn't win, the last of which was the Horris Hill Stakes at Newbury. But for this unfortunate trait, his form figures might have looked very different. In fact he did well to be third at Newbury, where he had no cover and wasn't suited by the soft ground. Rely on Peter Chapple-Hyam to iron out this colt's problem.

Peter Chapple-Hyam, Newmarket

LOCHBUIE 4 b c

Definite Article – Uncertain Affair (Darshaan)

41131443-

Should make up into an above-average staying handicapper with a little improvement. He showed that he had trained on with two quick victories over 1m4f in the spring. His high watermark came with a win at Glorious Goodwood in the 1m6f handicap, where he was always holding Yoshka in the final furlong. He probably felt the effects of that race in the autumn and we can expect to see a fresher, better animal on his return. He has yet to try 2m but should stay that far.

Geoff Wragg, Newmarket

MERGER 3 gr c

Mr Greeley – Toledo Queen (El Gran Senor)

12-

Dermot Weld came good with one grey colt last season, Grey Swallow, and could do the same with another this season. Merger made his debut in a 1m maiden at Thurles and pulverised some good-looking sorts. He then ran second to Albert Hall in the Group 2 Beresford Stakes at The Curragh. He was unlucky in running that day and Albert Hall enforced the form by running second in the Racing Post Trophy. His best trip should be 1m.

Dermot Weld, Ireland

MOTIVATOR 3 b c

Montjeu – Out West (Gone West)

11-

Michael Bell has had a long wait for his first domestic Group 1 winner - 16 years - which came in the Racing Post Trophy, courtesy of Motivator. We suspect that there may be more Group 1s coming his way. Having won a Newmarket maiden on soft ground in August by 6l, Motivator had a two-month break before going to Doncaster, bypassing the Royal Lodge in between. News of an outstanding gallop saw him heavily backed for the Racing Post and he came home two and a half lengths clear of Albert Hall in the soft ground. Motivator should just about get 1m4f but fast ground at Epsom has to be a concern. The Prix du Jockey Club and the Irish Derby, both races won by his sire Montjeu, look better bets.

Michael Bell, Newmarket

MUTAJAMMEL 3 b c

Kingmambo – Irtifa (Lahib)

41-

At 525,000 guineas, he represents a sizeable chunk of change. He made his debut in a Newmarket maiden over 7f in August, running green in fourth. Three weeks later he came home first in a mile maiden at Sandown after which Sir Michael Stoute put him away. He is entered for the Derby and while we don't consider him quite as scopey as the 2004 Derby winner, North Light, we expect him to be a force in Group company.

Sir Michael Stoute, Newmarket

PASTORAL PURSUITS 4 b c

Bahamian Bounty – Star (Most Welcome)

2115-

A promising two-year-old who won the Group 3 Sirenia Stakes at Kempton, Pastoral Pursuits was subsequently injured for the rest of the season. But he trained on all right and won twice as a three-year-old, the second time in the GNER Park Stakes at Doncaster over 7f. His victim was Firebreak, who went on to Group 1 success in Hong Kong. Pastoral Pursuits still has some growing to do and could make up into a high-class four-year-old. Hughie Morrison is convinced that he will get a mile this year and the Queen Anne Stakes is a target. Not as his best on soft.

Hughie Morrison, East Ilsley

POST AND RAIL 4 b c

Silver Hawk – Past The Post (Danzig)

-

Ed Dunlop houses a real champion in Ouija Board but Post And Rail could turn out a worthy stablemate. He never ran last season due to injury, which was a big blow to Dunlop who had him entered in the Derby. And following North Light's victory in the Derby, it would have been a surprise if Dunlop hadn't cursed his luck a second time. The reason is simple. Post And Rail was the only horse to have beaten North Light as a two-year-old. The race was a 7f Sandown maiden on soft and the margin a short-head. It would be fascinating if this colt ran into North Light again, and he shouldn't be forgotten.

Ed Dunlop, Newmarket

REAL QUALITY 3 br g

Elusive Quality – Pleasant Prize (Pleasant Colony)

21-

Made his debut in a 6f Ayr maiden and, whereas the winner Ingleton made all, Real Quality dwelt and did well to be beaten only a head, with the third two and a half lengths back. He duly obliged next time at Newcastle over 7f in the faster of two divisions of the maiden. Ian Semple brings his juveniles along patiently so for this one to show such form is a hint in itself.

Ian Semple, Carluke

SAYWAAN 3 ch f

Fusaichi Pegasus – Sharp Cat (Storm Cat)

1-

Owners don't often run fillies in the Derby. Godolphin did with their 1,000 Guineas winner Cape Verdi in 1998 and, although the exercise was a conspicuous failure, the Arab syndicate has entered Saywaan in the big one at Epsom. She was one of the most impressive maiden winners of 2004, storming away to win the second division of a Leicester maiden fillies event in a much faster time than the first division. A half-sister to the top class Royal Anthem, she could go to the top.

Saeed bin Suroor, Newmarket

SHANGHAI LILY 3 b f

King's Best – Marlene D (Selkirk)

11-

The Cheveley Park Stud-owned filly is unbeaten in two races and is a live contender for the 1,000 Guineas. She made her debut in a 6f Newbury maiden in August and beat Ruby Wine by 4l in a good time. She returned to Newbury for a 7f conditions race and won by two and a half lengths, beating three others. The time was again good. It's difficult to gauge just how useful this filly is. However she is well-bred, is already a decent size and has a trainer with Classic know-how.

Sir Michael Stoute, Newmarket

SONGERIE 3 b f

Hernando – Summer Night (Nashwan)

101-

Sir Mark Prescott is lucky enough to enjoy the patronage of Kirsten Rausing, who came seventh in the Sunday Times 2004 Rich List. Suffice to say, he doesn't make too many mistakes with her horses. This one ploughed through heavy ground to take a Chepstow maiden, came last in the Weld Park Stakes at The Curragh before winning a Deauville soft-ground Group 3. Prescott will race her selectively this year, scouring Europe for black type.

Sir Mark Prescott, Newmarket

STARCRAFT 5 ch h

Soviet Star – Flying Floozie (Pompeii Court)

211123-

Luca Cumani has done well with imported older horses, in particular ex-Italian Falbrav, who won five Group 1s. Now he takes custody of another, the high-class Australian horse Starcraft who won the Australian Derby over 1m4f as a four-year-old (they do things differently down there) and was a narrowly-beaten third in the Cox Plate over 1m2f at Moonee Valley last October. He's a versatile sort distance-wise (has won over 7f), so Cumani has all kinds of possibilities open to him. Former rider Glen Boss describes Starcraft as a "machine".

Luca Cumani, Newmarket

TEEBA 3 ch f

Seeking The Gold – Shadayid (Shadeed)

4-

John Dunlop's stable had a lean time of it last season compared to previous ones and it wasn't until mid-October that Dunlop was able to race Teeba, the two-year-old that work-watchers were shouting up as the best in the yard. Sent to Newmarket for a 6f maiden full of horses from top stables, she was slowly away, squeezed for room when beginning her run and then finished fast once breaking through heavy traffic. It was a promising run from the daughter of 1,000 Guineas winner Shadayid. If the stable hits form, we can expect big things from her.

John Dunlop, Arundel

TUCKER 3 b c

Inchinor – Tender Moment (Caerleon)

01-

One should be cautious of soft-ground maiden form but let's make an exception with Tucker. For a start, six of his dam's seven progeny are winners and his dam won three races herself. Secondly, he had something in hand when winning the first division of a 6f maiden at Newmarket in late October. In addition, the time was 0.73secs quicker than the second division half an hour later. A good-bodied colt, he looks sure to train on and his sire's progeny prefer good ground.

David Elsworth, Whitsbury

VILLARRICA 3 ch f

Selkirk – Melikah (Lammtarra)

43-

Hasn't achieved much thus far, but could be biding her time under the patient tutelage of Sir Michael Stoute. She was slowly away and green on her Salisbury debut, a soft-ground 7f maiden. At Redcar, on her only other start, she didn't show that much more sparkle and afterwards was put away for the season. Her dam, who was placed in the Oaks and Irish Oaks, is a half-sister to Galileo, and All Too Beautiful. Her sire is a proven commodity, while her broodmare sire won the Derby and the Arc de Triomphe.

Sir Michael Stoute, Newmarket

WINDSOR KNOT 3 ch c

Pivotal – Triple Tie (The Minstrel)

411-

John Gosden was surely disappointed to see Windsor Knot whisked away to join Godolphin not long after the colt had landed the Group 3 Solario Stakes at Sandown in August. That was on soft ground but previously Windsor Knot had looked convincing when landing a 7f maiden at Newmarket on good to firm. His sire Pivotal is making a real name for himself and most of his good two-year-olds train on. Group races at around 7f and 1m will be on Windsor Knot's agenda.

Saeed bin Suroor, Newmarket

RFO's top 10 to follow

Alfonso	Merger
Ayam Zaman	Pastoral Pursuits
Bago	Saywaan
Footstepsinthesand	Shanghai Lily
Lochbuie	Starcraft

Outlook

Pedigrees for punters

by Amy Bennett

WHEN placing a bet on the Flat, a horse's pedigree is one of the most important things to consider. Breeding can tell you all kinds of information, from the trip it will favour to the ground that suits, even how early in the season a horse may mature.

Talented trainers and jockeys can make the most of a horse's genetic mix in placing it over a certain trip on particular ground, but the basic ingredients to make a horse a fast-ground sprinter or a mud-loving stayer cannot be trained - they are inherited. Whenever a horse is trying a new trip or venturing out on new going it always pays to study it's pedigree. Breeding isn't an exact science, but the study of a pedigree can still yield valuable information for punters.

The six stallions discussed below were all top-class winners over a variety of trips, and they have all proved themselves equal to the task of siring top-flight performers. Hopefully after reading this you will have an idea of what to look for when their sons and daughters hit the racecourse, and it can be factored into your betting.

PIVOTAL ch 1993
Polar Falcon – Fearless Revival (Cozzene)

The lightly-raced winner of the Nunthorpe and the King's Stand, Pivotal was retired to stud at three to stand for a fee of £6,000. Bred to modest mares in his first few seasons, his fee fell to £5,000 in his third season and remained there for the next three years.

Now, thanks to talented sprinters such as **Kyllachy**, **Somnus** and **Captain Rio**, he commands a fee of £65,000 with a reputation to match his price tag, and attracts a higher class of mare.

Mainly due to the trio already mentioned, Pivotal has acquired a reputation as a sire of sprinters, but several of his daughters have shown his ability to get top-flight winners over longer distances.

Top among these in Britain last year was **Chorist**, winner of the Pretty Polly Stakes over 1m2f at the Curragh. A good performer over a mile at three, William Haggas' charge hit top form over the longer trip, and crowned an impressive five-year-old season with a good second to Haafhd in the Champion Stakes.

Other top-class daughters include Grade 1-winning US fillies **Megahertz** and **Golden Apples**, and **Silvester Lady**, winner of the 2001 Preis der Diana (German Oaks). Of Pivotal's top five earners to date, Golden Apples and Megahertz lead the way, with Chorist in fourth- speedy son Somnus separates them.

Another point to bear in mind with Pivotal's progeny is that they progress with age. While he has got high-class juveniles, his best progeny have all hit top form as three or four-year-olds.

CAPE CROSS b/br 1994
Green Desert – Park Appeal (Ahonoora)

Cape Cross announced his arrival as a top-class miler with victory in the Lockinge Stakes as a four-year-old. Prior to this, he had shown solid rather than spectacular form as a two- and three-year-old, but added to his Group 1 win by taking the Queen Anne Stakes and the Celebration Mile at five.

With only two crops of racing age having represented him to date, he has been marked as a sire to watch, thanks to the exploits of his all-conquering daughter **Ouija Board**.

GIANT'S CAUSEWAY (left) seeing off Kalanisi: the 'Iron Horse' is making an impact at stud

A dual Oaks winner and third in the Prix de l'Arc de Triomphe, she put the seal on a fantastic season with her victory in the Breeders' Cup Filly & Mare Turf.

While Cape Cross never raced beyond 9f, his first crops have shown that he is more than capable of siring top-class middle-distance performers. **Privy Seal**, third in the Italian Derby, is out of a dam with stamina influence, as is Group-placed **Hazyview**, while Ouija Board is from the family of Arlington Million winner Teleprompter.

GIANT'S CAUSEWAY ch 1997

Storm Cat – Mariah's Storm (Rahy)

Already the sire of a Group 1 winner in Dewhurst victor **Shamardal**, he also got high-class duo **Footstepsinthesand** and **Maids Causeway** in his first crop of racing age.

However, the 'Iron Horse' gained his reputation as a tough-as-teak battler when winning five Group 1 contests as a three-year-old, and it is more than likely that the best is yet to come from his progeny.

Winner of the Group 1 Prix de la Salamandre as a juvenile, Giant's Causeway had already stamped himself a top-class horse prior to his superlative three-year-old season, culminating in his narrow defeat by Tiznow in the Breeders' Cup Classic on his first attempt at dirt.

It is too early to draw conclusions about the average trip his progeny will favour after just one season, but Giant's Causeway excelled over a mile to 1m2f and his progeny could be expected to show their best over a similar trip.

Although he is at stud in America, many of his progeny sold to European buyers, and his second crop of two-year-olds will be ones to watch out for from summer onwards.

MONTJEU b 1996

Sadler's Wells – Floripedes (Top Ville)

Like Giant's Causeway, Montjeu retired the winner of six Group 1 contests, and sired a Group 1 winner in his first crop last season.

Montjeu's victories included both the Irish and French Derbys and the Prix de l'Arc de Triomphe, in which he proved himself a true middle-distance performer with brilliant acceleration. Montjeu never raced at under a mile, and his first crop of juveniles who debuted last season look set to emulate the distance preference of their sire.

Most notable among his first progeny is Racing Post Trophy winner **Motivator**, second favourite for the 2005 Derby, who, like his sire, has not raced at under a mile.

The victory of **Ayam Zaman** in the Listed Zetland Stakes over 1m2f last October should come as no surprise, given Montjeu's middle-distance ability.

Kings Quay, winner of the Washington Singer Stakes, from which several Classic performers have emerged, is another colt who represented his sire with distinction last season, as is **Walk In The Park**, placed in the Criterium International over a mile at Saint-Cloud.

ALHAARTH b 93

Unfuwain – Irish Valley (Irish River)

Another sire who rose to prominence last season, following the victories of his son **Haafhd**.

A brilliant juvenile himself, Alhaarth didn't quite live up to expectations as a three-year-old, although he performed consistently in high-class company at four, winning two Group 2 contests over a mile and 1m2f.

Alhaarth's oldest progeny are now six, and although Haafhd is his first Classic winner, the son of Unfuwain has been consistently siring classy performers in each of his crops.

Chief among these are **Bandari** and **Phoenix Reach**, who both progressed well with age to become top-class over 1m4f.

Although **Dominica**, winner of the King's Stand, showed that his sire can get high-class sprinters, Alhaarth's progeny tend to be at their best at distances over a mile, maturing later in the season.

GALILEO b 98

Sadler's Wells – Urban Sea (Miswaki)

Breeders and punters alike will be anxious to see how his first yearlings perform. He is from a hugely talented family, being a brother to **Black Sam Bellamy** and Oaks runner-up **All Too Beautiful**, and his dam is an Arc winner.

Winner of the English and Irish Derbies, Galileo is best remembered for his battles with the year-older Fantastic Light. The son of Sadler's Wells won a ding-dong battle for the King George VI & Queen Elizabeth Diamond Stakes, while the Godolphin horse took the Irish Champion Stakes by a head.

Galileo's retirement denied us the chance to see who would take the best of three, but now we can look to their progeny, as Fantastic Light will also have runners this season.

The first son of Sadler's Wells to win the Derby, Galileo had stamina in abundance but was also blessed with a sharp turn of foot. He raced only once at two and slaughtered his opposition when winning by 14l.

His progeny will likely progress with age and may be at their best as three-year-olds.

However, Sadler's Wells has been a noted source of talented juveniles and it could pay to watch out for Galileo's progeny during the autumn. He might well make an impact on the 2006 Classic scene.

GALILEO (left): plenty will be expected of his progeny, who will appear this season

OUIJA BOARD (left): rounding the home turn en route to a famous Breeders' Cup win

Newmarket by Aborigine

Ouija Board put *ED DUNLOP* on the international stage with her emphatic Breeders' Cup Fillies & Mares Turf triumph under Kieren Fallon and she will again be his flag-bearer this season.

On the home front, she was allowed plenty of time to come to hand before her two Oaks successes, followed by that slightly unlucky-in-running third to Bago in the Arc de Triomphe.

Dunlop told me out on the gallops early in the year: "The plan will be to bring her back for the Hardwicke Stakes at the Royal Ascot meeting run at York.

"However if she showed me that she was coming to hand earlier, I would consider the Coronation Cup, as her win in the Oaks proved that she can handle the Epsom gradients."

SIR MICHAEL STOUTE did well with another HQ filly Russian Rhythm, who has now been retired to stud, but her owner Cheveley Park Stud has a potential 1,000 Guineas replacement in **Shanghai Lily**.

Her two wins were at Newbury and, being by 2,000 Guineas winner King's Best, the mile trip will be ideal for her.

Sir Michael's **Desert Star** has plied his trade mainly in handicaps, but his work indicates that he could step up into pattern-race company.

JAMES FANSHAWE's **Soviet Song** was yet another local filly to hit the 2004 headlines, winning the Group 1 Sussex Stakes and Falmouth Stakes.

She appears to have recovered from the injury, which curtailed her programme, and can continue her winning ways.

Lower down the fillies' social order at Pegasus Stables, **Soldera** and **Fling** are names for the notebook. On the staying front, **Prins Willem** should use his hurdling fitness to winning effect in races like the Queen's Prize and the Chester Cup.

LUCA CUMANI handled the Italian horse Falbrav brilliantly a couple of seasons back and he has been sent the Australian Group 1 winner **Stagecraft**.

Though he has classic form over a mile, his owner Paul Makin wants to land the July Cup with him to emulate the achievement of Choisir - a previous triumphant sprinter from Down Under in 2003.

Cumani also holds out high hopes for **Alkaased**.

The five-year-old Kingmambo colt won two of his four starts last season - following his Old Newton Cup triumph with a Listed race win at Goodwood.

MICHAEL JARVIS' Prince Of Wales's Stakes and Queen Elizabeth II Stakes winner **Rakti** stays in training but backing this brilliant but mercurial character is always a gamble.

Divine Gift is more reliable at a lower level and will pay his way in mile handicaps.

Jarvis holds a high opinion of his Montjeu filly **Ayam Zaman**.

Her fluent 5l win in the 1m2f Zetland Stakes marks her as an Oaks type. **Pearl King** was too backward to run as a juvenile but, being by Daylami, the patient approach could see him become a force in middle-distance events.

MARK TOMPKINS started last season with Babodana's Lincoln win. **St Petersburg** would have landed a notable Tompkins Doncaster double in the Lincoln Silver Mile but for the presence of subsequent Group race winner Autumn Glory.

St Petersburg is capable of continuing his trainer's good record in the season's first big betting handicap.

JAMES EUSTACE did us a good turn with 33-1 winner **Orcadian**, who showed his appreciation of a step up in distance to land his trainer's first Group 3 success in the Stan James St Simon Stakes at Newbury.

ORCADIAN: seen here winning at a soggy Newbury last October at odds of 33-1

SO NEAR AND YET SO FAR: Ashdown Express (right) denied by Frizzante in July Cup

That win saved him from going through the Newmarket sales ring and, when he gets soft ground he will pay further tributes to his capable trainer's talents.

Fancied horses from this well-run small yard always start at real value-for-money odds and a couple of names to keep in mind as they are already looking a picture out on the heath are **Welcome Stranger** and **Considine**.

JEREMY NOSEDA had a quiet domestic season by his own high standards, even though Wilko's brilliant win under Frankie Dettori in the Breeders' Cup Juvenile thrust him deservedly into the international limelight.

He had hoped **Ecomium** would have done just that in Woodbine's Canadian International but an eleventh-hour scare put paid to the plan.

The four-year-old is fully recovered and will use the Winter Derby at Lingfield as the launching pad to what could be a highly rewarding campaign, with the Hardwicke Stakes on the Royal Ascot card at York a possible target.

On the sprinting front, Noseda's Norfolk Stakes winner **Blue Dakota** is over a training setback and could also be appearing at York in the King's Stand Stakes.

MICHAEL BELL is looking to **Motivator** to build on his smart two-year-old success in the Racing Post Trophy.

The Derby is the prime target, but having watched him work throughout the summer and autumn, the speed he showed to go clear of his galloping companions makes me believe he could still use the 2,000 Guineas as a stepping-stone to the big one at Epsom.

CHRIS WALL had a frustrating season, with his Induna team hit by a low-grade virus.

Typical of Wall's frustrations was **Ashdown Express**'s heart-stopping short-head July Cup second to Frizzante.

His long autumn haul to Japan was an-

AFRICAN DREAM (left): powering home to win the Dee Stakes from Putra Sas at Chester

other blow for Wall as he missed the break. He will surely gain the rewards he deserves this year.

Two Wall handicappers sure to pay their way are **Ace Of Hearts** and **Counsel's Opinion**.

DECLAN DALY, a former head lad with Sir Michael Stoute, quickly established himself with some well-fancied winners last year and **Nounou** contributed wins at Folkestone and Epsom.

He was kept on the move over hurdles during the winter and, granted good ground, is one to keep in mind for staying handicaps as he figures on a handy weight.

Derby-winning trainer *PETER CHAPPLE-HYAM* successfully launched the new phase of his career from St Gatien Stables on his return from Hong Kong.

His handling of the cheaply-claimed **African Dream**, who won four races including the Sandown Classic Trial and the Dee Stakes, was exemplary.

The plan is to run him in the Winter Derby on his way to the Flat season proper.

Chapple-Hyam also expects his Richmond Stakes hero **Montgomery's Arch** and July Stakes winner **Captain Hurricane** to make their mark in Group company.

Their early conditioning work on the Al Bahathri Polytrack suggests that this will definitely be the case.

WILLIAM JARVIS was delighted that the executors of Lord Howard de Walden's Plantation Stud decided to keep **La Persiana** in training.

Her three wins followed by two Listed race placings have already increased her paddock value and there is more to come from this impeccably-bred filly.

HUGH COLLINGRIDGE still believes that **Sundance** has the ability to make his mark in Pattern Races.

Last year he failed to build on early promise but, because he was a bit of a lad, he was gelded, which appears to have settled him.

Reaching Out and **Blue Hedges** are two other likely winners from the same source.

JEFF PEARCE always does well with his

modest material but he could have a jewel in **Fantasy Ride**.

After hacking up at Yarmouth, he did his handicap mark no good when second to Ayam Zaman in the Zetland Stakes, but there are still races to be won with him.

ED VAUGHAN, who took over the Clarehaven string after the sad death of Alec Stewart, has rented part of Henry Cecil's Warren Place training complex.

The Newmarket winner **Namroc** could be one of his stars, with races like the Royal Hunt Cup a possible target.

Day To Remember is lightly raced and also has the ability to start a sequence of wins off his current rating.

On the *HENRY CECIL* front the lightly-raced **Sayadaw** has always looked the part in his work but is injury-prone.

If Cecil's' patience pays off, this powerfully built individual could follow in the footsteps of Cecil's previous Ascot Gold Cup winners Le Moss, Buckskin and Ardross.

GREG CHUNG is emerging as a capable smaller trainer and two handicappers to watch out for from his Linden Tree yard are the ex-*SIR MARK PRESCOTT* **Mandarin Spirit** and **Ever Cheerful**.

Talking of Sir Mark, his triple German Group 1 winner Albanova has been retired but her owner-breeder Kirsten Rausing has a serious Classic prospect in the Group 3-winning filly **Songerie**.

Sir Mark will also be aiming **Cupid's Glory** at top races at home and abroad.

Last but not least - the mighty Godolphin empire will indulge in its usual globetrotting exploits.

Keep an eye open for the ex-Australian Group 3 winner **Keep The Faith** and an unraced Green Desert colt **Seven Seas**.

Both of these highly promising individuals could be carrying the familiar royal blue silks to further global glory.

Hot off the Heath

Ayam Zaman
Ouija Board
Songerie

Ireland by Jerry M

IN 2001, *AIDAN O'BRIEN*'s two-year-olds dominated every Group one race in Europe. The Tipperary trainer was untouchable, but such a high level of success could not last forever and it's unfair sometimes to expect him to have the winner of every race in his yard.

That said, he is still the top trainer in this country and, with the backing of John Magnier and Michael Tabor, will continue to turn out our best youngsters.

O'Brien's two year-olds had been a bit hit and miss during the early part of last season, which had also been the case the year before.

However, maybe due to a change in training methods, his horses last season and the year before, seemed to be flourishing in the latter months of the Flat season, with some excellent two year-olds coming to the fore at the end of term.

They have been making their mark on the best races around but it is not easy to assess accurately whether they will improve sufficiently enough for this year's early Classics.

After winning the St Leger in 2003 with Brian Boru, O'Brien admitted: "With all the three-year-olds, we probably over-did them in the spring.

"We gave them a break in the middle of the summer, and they have come on in leaps and bounds for every run. Obviously every year that goes by you wonder whether you could do something different to try and improve things."

FOOTSTEPSINTHESAND: could be about to make a big impression this season

The Ballydoyle master has clearly tried to experiment, which is fair enough considering the success he has achieved over the years.

A few of his better two year-olds have really taken the eye in September and October, not least **Footstepsinthesand**, who stood out at Naas as a colt of some potential. He won his maiden and then a strong-looking Group 3, with such authority that bookies have already made him as short as 16-1 for the season's first Classic, the 2,000 Guineas.

The son of Giant's Causeway (who himself was the top first-season sire, ahead of Dubai Millennium and Montjeu, and the third most successful sire of two year-olds last year in Britain and Ireland) is owned by Michael Tabor and on his debut looked to be Aidan O'Brien's second string on jockey bookings.

However his odds tumbled from 20-1 to 3-1 and it was clear that those close to connections knew something the bookies didn't. He hosed up by four and a half lengths.

With his first run out of the way, the intention was to save him for the year, but the trainer was keen to get a Group race under his belt: "It was a bit of a risk running him again so soon, but it has worked out well. We have always thought that he was a very good horse and Jamie was delighted with him today."

The Group 3 at Leopardstown was contested by five other runners, four of which were previous winners (including a colt of Kevin Prendergast's who had won four races), so the form of his win looks solid enough.

Of Ballydoyle's other two year-olds to impress last year, **Ad Valorem** and **Oratorio** are most likely the two to follow for this coming Flat campaign.

The aforementioned, owned by the Magnier family is unbeaten after three runs - a nice run of wins that culminated in the Middle Park Stakes at Newmarket (usually an informative race for the following season).

Ad Valorem won a decent Listed race at the Curragh prior to Newmarket, and this appeared to entitle him to contest the Group 1 across the water.

The race looked hot on paper, but the son of Danzig gave Aidan O'Brien his first British Group 1 of the season.

With Jamie Spencer in the saddle, the colt showed a good turn of foot and battled to the line, giving the impression that he is wholly genuine.

However, whether he can step up from 6f is questionable. That said, his trainer was delighted with the performance and sounded a hopeful note about the colt getting further: "It didn't look like he was stopping. Jamie thinks he'll stay further than six, but the colt has a lot of natural speed too."

The jockey added: "He's very lazy at home and it's hard to gauge where you are with him, but he certainly does it on the track. He prefers it faster and I'm sure he'll get further."

Oratorio was Ballydoyle's two year-old flag-bearer last year: he contested three Group 1s and two Group 2s within a seven-race stint.

Considering the yard had not been prolific at the highest level last year, Oratorio's performances seem all the more impressive.

The Danehill colt was only beaten half a length when he came up against *DAVID WACHMAN*'s star filly, **Damson** in the Group 1 Phoenix Stakes.

Not deterred, he was later sent over to Longchamp, where he was given a super ride by Jamie Spencer to win the Grand Criterium.

His final race of the season at Newmarket probably offered his stiffest task, as he

DAVID WACHMAN

was sent out to contest the Dewhurst against the best two-year-olds around.

The winner, Shamardal, is probably an excellent prospect, so to finish second (in testing ground) after a tough season bodes well for this Guineas prospect.

Not only has Jamie Spencer had the privilege of riding Aidan O'Brien's best two year-olds, but David Wachman also gave him the ride on board Damson when she went across the sea to England for Royal Ascot.

The Queen Mary Stakes (now a Group 2) looked tough on paper and with last year's winner Attraction raising the crossbar in her three-year-old campaign, the racing public were looking for something special.

The race was run at a quick tempo, but Damson's finishing kick in the last furlong took the breath away, as she won by three lengths (the same as Attraction did).

Spencer, overjoyed at the beating she handed out, cheekily said that the trainer "had one better at home and that she's already won!"

That was her fourth win on the trot and being a filly of some promise, was given a break until the Cheverley Park Stakes over at Newmarket.

On the day, conditions were extremely tacky, which didn't suit Ireland's super filly. The race became something of a lottery and as a result the daughter of Entrepreneur went down by half a length, which was no disgrace.

The filly in question that Spencer was boasting about is called **Intriguing**, and having won her only race to date, must be followed this year.

The daughter of Fasliyev is well thought of at home and went off 4-5 for her maiden. She knew her job, as she broke quickly from the stalls and never saw another horse as she won cozily by two and a half lengths.

It came as no surprise to *Outlook* readers to see **Azamour** and **Grey Swallow** have such fine seasons last year.

They were well tipped up here to have a good time of it at the highest level, and between them won three Group 1s, as well as finishing placed in four.

Azamour, trained by *JOHN OXX*, took the eye when finishing well in the 2,000 Guineas, but it was over 1m2f that he really shone, recording a fantastic time in winning the St James Palace Stakes.

He later franked the form of that win by taking the Irish Champion Stakes, but perhaps it was the way he was defeated in the Champion Stakes at Newmarket that really established him as a top-class,

AZAMOUR: always gives his all, and one to keep on side with in all the top races

versatile colt.

He was staying on in soft conditions when those in the know felt a mile and two furlongs in quick conditions suited best.

We expect him to take top honours again this year, and improve further for Oxx, who knows how to look after the older horses.

Grey Swallow's preparation for the 2,000 Guineas had not been straightforward and *DERMOT WELD* offered a cautious note for punters willing to back the grey (who received rave reviews when he was a two year-old).

The trainer was worried that the Newmarket showpiece would probably "come a bit too soon", and through lack of fitness his horse might not be able to show his best.

The son of Daylami also received a whack on the nose from another jockey's whip when contesting the Guineas trial at Leopardstown - which may have lowered his confidence.

On the day of the Classic, Grey Swallow ran into fourth place, but his trainer remained confident he could still show his true colours in a top race.

He did not disappoint in the Irish Derby, where everything fell right for Pat Smullen. The strong pace seemed to suit the grey and he was nicely positioned to pounce on the Derby winner, North Light. The locally-trained colt won nicely in the end, justifying the trainer's unwavering faith.

JIM BOLGER

Alexander Goldrun has shown great consistency for her trainer *JIM BOLGER*.

As a two year-old, she ran eight times (winning three races) and seven times last year as a three year-old (finally taking the Hong Kong Cup over 10f). The Carlow trainer was not worried about burning out his star filly.

Quite the opposite (with her staying pedigree obviously a benefit), she was stepped up in class at the beginning of the campaign to contest Group races, and duly obliged at Leopardstown over 7f.

Our Guineas was next on the agenda, but Attraction travelling over from Middleham for Mark Johnston was always going to be hard to shift and she had to settle for second.

She again faced a stiff task, this time at the Curragh, where she faced the William Haggas-trained Chorist in the Group 1 Pretty Polly Stakes.

Despite Bolger's charge going off favourite, she never looked like reeling in the four-year-old from England.

Not finished yet, her trainer persisted, and at the next time of asking finally got a Group 1 win to her name, this time at Longchamp in the Prix de l'Opera.

If that wasn't enough, she was kept in training such was her enthusiasm and in December travelled over to the warmer climate of Hong Kong.

Aidan O'Brien's Powerscourt was fancied to lead the way for our boys while high hopes were pinned on Rakti's connections lifting the Cup.

However, Alexander Goldrun, who had a good build-up to the race, spoiled the party, much to the delight of her owner who got their hands on the £733,813 prize money. Kevin Manning rode a perfect race and kicked on after following Rakti in the middle stages.

She won't be underestimated again this year and punters are advised to keep her on side.

Invincible Irish

Azamour
Damson
Footstepsinthesand

Berkshire by Downsman

A YOUNG schoolboy domiciled in the heart of the Lambourn Valley was asked during the course of his English lesson to define the meaning of the phrase "A Curate's Egg." His response, "*BARRY HILLS*' 2004 Flat campaign" was, from all accounts, not greeted with overwhelming enthusiasm by the man under the mortar board.

But not even the feisty Faringdon Place maestro himself would argue with the young pundit's assessment that an undeniably memorable season had only been "good in parts".

The highlights, of course, were the impressive 2,000 Guineas and Champion Stakes victories of Haafhd.

But for much of the campaign the stable's runners were laid low with viral problems.

Even the stable star did not escape. He flopped at both Royal Ascot and Goodwood in mid-summer but his runaway win on his return to Newmarket in October came as a relief to connections as his career at stud beckoned.

With Haafhd gone, the search is now on to find a replacement. Some might say that it is optimistic to find another 2,000 winner so soon, especially as the latest success came 25 years after Hills' only previous victory with Tap On Wood.

However, there is plenty of confidence among the Hills' team that **Etlaala** will at least make up into a credible challenger to his Dewhurst conqueror Shamardal and the other leading players for the first Classic.

He was an impressive winner of the Champagne Stakes at Doncaster and the general consensus of opinion after his flop at Newmarket was that he failed to handle the soft ground.

That was true, but he was a very big horse for a juvenile and connections also feel he had outgrown his strength by the time the Cesarewitch meeting came around.

He has put on some weight during the winter and is doing well, but the Hills team think it's unlikely he will run before the the Guineas.

There are a number of maiden colts to back up Etlaala. **Holiday Camp** is very highly rated and expected to waste no time in building on his solid debut effort at Newbury.

Two more to note are **Astronomical** (who was not right when well beaten at Newmarket on his second start) and **Fortunate Isle** (a good second to Rob Roy at New-

A CLASS APART: Etlaala spreadeagles his opponents at Newbury last August on his debut

THAT WAS SO EASY: Michael Hills explains Whazzat's Chesham win to his connections

market on his only public appearance).

Kenmore has some solid placed form behind him, and an unraced colt to look out for is **Self Discipline**, a son of Dansili.

Shannon Spring has the best placed form of any of the maidens and he is likely to lead the three year-old assault on the Doncaster Lincoln meeting. Hills always does well here and seven furlongs or a mile will be his trip.

On the subject of Doncaster, **Kamanda Laugh**, who did not stop improving last season, and **Alfonso** are the two likely players for the Lincoln – the latter is the preferred option.

Hills has a few aces to play in the distaff division, with Rockfel Stakes winner **Maids Causeway** sure to make her presence felt in the 1,000 Guineas. Her overall form is very good, but cannot match that of lightly raced **Whazzat**.

She beat Maids Causeway in what turned out to be a very hot maiden at Newbury in the spring and went on to thrash Brecon Beacon and subsequent Breeder's Cup winner Wilko in the Chesham at Royal Ascot.

She went wrong after that win and is something of a forgotten horse.

She is now back firing again and her form suggests she has a great chance in the 1,000 Guineas. Neither this filly nor her stablemate are likely to take in a trial.

Of the more unexposed three year-old fillies, **Basserah**, unplaced on her two juvenile outings, is a classy sort at home, and **Dixieanna**, an eye-catching second at Windsor on her only start, look good for this season.

Hills is still the number one trainer in Lambourn and its upper village, but *BRIAN MEEHAN* has done a great job in improving the quality of his team year on year. His progress was further underlined in 2004 with his first domestic Group 1 winner.

Magical Romance looked to have little if any chance going into the Cheveley Park Stakes. Her two victories in a maiden at Kempton and a nursery at Leicester were impressive enough, but she had been beaten out of sight on her first venture into Pattern company at Ascot in July.

The Newlands team were quietly confident of a big run after rain softened the ground and there was certainly no fluke about the way she battled back after looking beaten to see off Suez and Damson by half a length and the same.

It was a great effort in what looked an above-average renewal of the great race and the Meehan team have every right to think she will be a leading player in the 1,000 Guineas, especially if there is a wet spring.

Her trainer is more than happy with her progress during the winter, but he confesses he may fight shy of giving her a preparatory run.

Meehan came very close to landing a second domestic Group 1 with **Rebuttal** in the Middle Park 24 hours later and this performance confirmed that his two year-olds were of a very high calibre indeed.

David Junior, a most impressive winner

of a maiden at Thirsk, is another highly regarded colt and certainly one to note for the mid-season. But the one I look forward to seeing most again from the whole crop is **Maggie Jordan**.

During the summer, rumours were circling within the Valley that the Meehan camp were excited about an unraced filly, but it was not until the backend arrived that she saw the light of day.

Despite some strong whispers for Lambourn rivals Oranmore Castle and Puya, there was considerable stable confidence behind Maggie Jordan and she duly delivered an emphatic win, despite running green. She is likely to see action before the Guineas, but the Newmarket Classic is the target.

Humble Opinion won the second of his two outings as a juvenile and is expected to more than pay his way.

A newcomer to look out for is **A Bientot**, who is unraced but well regarded.

Among the older generation, **Attune** is expected to make up into a Group filly and fill the void of great stable stalwart Silence Is Golden, who has now been packed off to stud.

In sharp contrast to Newlands, *MARCUS TREGONING*'s Kingwood emporium suffered for much of the campaign with health problems and never really got into gear.

Very few of the two year-olds saw action on the racecourse, and stable star **Mubtaker** was unable to take his place in the Prix de l'Arc de Triomphe after sustaining an injury.

HIGH ACCOLADE (left): will be back for more

Tregoning is pleased to have the eight-year-old back for another season, but he has no plans to send him to Dubai for the World Cup meeting in the spring. The Arc will again be the main target.

The trainer was keen to point out, however, that he will be represented in sunny Dubai. **Alkaadhem**'s promotion from talented handicapper to Pattern-race performer was one of the high points of the season and he will take his chance in one of the shoulder races on World Cup day.

He has done very well again during the summer and hopes are high he has improved.

High Accolade will also be back to bolster the powerful team of older horses, as will progressive filly **Tahtheeb**, who did well as a three year-old.

She has taken the darker months particularly well and could have the Winter Derby at Lingfield in March on her early-season agenda.

With so many two-year-olds untried last season, even at home, Tregoning is hoping some stars emerge from the pack.

Three singled out were **Shohrah**, **Night Hour** and the unraced **Mogaamer**.

Shohrah looked a quality filly when she made a winning start at Ascot during the summer and later ran a race full of promise in the Fillies Mile after experiencing trouble in running. She could develop into a Classic filly.

Night Hour appeared to have his limitations exposed in the Houghton Stakes at Newmarket, but he comes from a family that needs time to produce their best and connections are anticipating a much better 2005 from him.

Tregoning makes no secret of his high regard for Mogaamer. The son of Dixieland Band produced some high quality work last season despite not getting to the racecourse, and boasts a first-class middle-distance pedigree.

Whilst the Tregoning team struggled with their juveniles' form for much of the campaign, the *JOHN GOSDEN* youngsters proved much more consistent.

The Manton trainer is not renowned for getting two year-olds in the thick of the action during the opening weeks of the turf campaign, but a number came to hand early this time around.

Three colts, **Prince Charming**, **Mystical Land** and **Iceman** all showed Pattern-race ability.

The latter turned out to be the best and looked to have all the potential in the world when landing the Coventry Stakes.

He went on to show he was a genuine Group 1 operator, even though he did not win at that level, and looks sure to make his presence felt in the spring Classic, given his favoured good or fast ground.

Even though the colts held their end up very well, the Gosden fillies achieved more, with one in particular standing out.

Playful Act had always been highly regarded and, after breaking her duck at the second attempt, went on to beat Maids Causeway in both the May Hill at Doncaster and the Group 1 Fillies Mile at Ascot.

These two victories saw her rocket to the top of the ante-post lists for the Oaks and there seems no reason why she should not train on, even though her half-sister Echoes In Eternity did not really realise her potential under the Godolphin banner in her second campaign.

Playful Act may have stolen the headlines, but **Titian Time** proved more than an able support. She made great strides during the autumn and ended the season with a high class second in the Group 1 Prix Marcel Boussac at Longchamp.

She set out to make all that day and, if she continues on her upward curve, she must have a great chance of making a winning mark at Group 1 level in 2005, especially as there are now so many more opportunities for three-year-old fillies around a mile and a quarter at the highest level.

As you might expect, Gosden has lots of untapped talent housed at the famous Wiltshire establishment. **Alhaadh** was one filly who failed to reproduce her smart home form on her only outing, but she is a must for any notebook.

The same can be said of **Karen's Caper**, who carried plenty of stable confidence on her debut at Lingfield in November, and duly hacked up.

Maria Delfina may not be a star but looks sure to win a race at a lower level. Another filly to show distinct back-end promise was **Paradise Mill**.

Cashier, a half-brother to Azarole and Macadamia, looks sure to add to his illustrious family's role of honour and expect **Golden Feather** to leave his below-par effort at Lingfield behind.

He was made favourite after showing initial promise at Newmarket, but lost all chance when his action went on the home turn. Very well bred, he could well be one to watch out for in handicaps.

MICK CHANNON retained his lofty position in the trainers' list, both for number of races won and for prize money, but, to his great credit, and to the benefit of punters who bothered to listen, he kept those famous footballing feet well on the ground when it came to appraising the quality of his team.

Indeed, he made no secret of the fact that the two year-olds were not as good as he had hoped.

Group-race victories may have been rationed at juvenile level, but Channon still believes there are good races to be won with the 2004 generation, now that they have had a good winter behind them.

Joint Aspiration is one of his best chances of making a show in one of the spring Guineas trials.

She has seen action on three occasions and took the notable scalp of Titian Time when landing the second of her victories at Kempton. Admittedly, she proved no match for the leading players in the Fillies Mile on her final start, but the ground was very quick that day and, being a daughter of Pivotal, she will be much more effective on an easier surface.

A much less exposed member of the fair-

TITIAN TIME (left): leading the way

YAJBILL: Mick Channon's tough colt never stopped improving during an arduous season

er sex is **Desert Move**, who showed her liking for an easy surface when she won her only race at Thirsk in August.

The form of the contest was several rungs below what is required to win at Pattern level, but she had the field well strung out at the line and Channon is more than pleased with the progress she has made during the darker months.

Love Thirty had some solid form behind her before she finally got off the mark at the fourth attempt and it was a feather in her cap to hold off Cape Columbine, who went on to win a valuable sales event at Newmarket and establish herself as a very smart filly.

One of the more interesting colts could be the lightly-raced **Mujazaf**, a colt firmly bred in the apricot of the Lord Howard de Walden empire, being a son of Grand Lodge out of a Diesis mare.

A soundly beaten third on his only public airing to date at Pontefract, he has gone the right way during the winter and connections are more than hopeful he will leave that form well behind. Middle distances might be the best option.

Halhoo was touted throughout the summer as one of West Ilsley's leading three year-old lights and there were jubilant scenes at our local course in August when he also saw off the classy Titian Time.

His subsequent performances failed to build on that success, but Channon is convinced we have not seen the best of him yet.

Yajbill again demonstrated Channon's great skill at keeping a horse on the boil for long periods, whilst still managing to exact improvement along the way.

He won three of his last four starts and has potential to take high rank among the three-year-old sprinters this year if maintaining his upward curve.

Berkshire's Best

Holiday Camp
Mogaamer
Whazzat

The North by Borderer

TWELVE months ago Deirdre Johnston revealed that her husband, *MARK JOHNSTON*, had a serious bunch of three-year-olds to realistically aim at the Guineas. That statement proved spot-on, with **Attraction** going on to complete the English and Irish double in the fillies Classic.

The aims to win two million pounds in prizemoney and train over a hundred winners were also achieved and Mark says of the mighty string for the coming season: "We have more horses rated over 100 than we have under 70." That says much about this trainer's attention to quality control.

The north's leading handler looks set for another super season and all racing fans will benefit from connections' decision to keep Attraction in training as a four-year-old.

Graham and Andrea Wylie's huge investment in racing has brought great excitement to the northern scene and the multi-millionaire owners are hoping **Percussionist** can win a major prize in the summer.

The son of Sadler's Wells won the Lingfield Derby Trial by an impressive ten lengths before finishing a creditable fourth in the Epsom showpiece.

He's joined *HOWARD JOHNSON* from John Gosden and, his new trainer told me: "He was prominent for a long way in the big one and I'm sure he'll be a very good Cup horse.

"He's the most exciting among my older horses."

Rainbow Rising could take advantage of a favourable handicap mark.

The son of Desert King cut little ice in three runs last season but Johnson describes him as "a smashing little horse."

This is a must for the notebook as the train-

PERCUSSIONIST: Howard Johnson will try and get a good tune out of him this season

APPALACHIAN TRAIL (nearside): showing the battling qualities needed to win races

er added: "He was a bit backward last year but ran some fine races. There is a big race in him-without a doubt."

Mephisto won the Ebor last season when trained by Luca Cumani and a repeat bid could be on the cards. But Johnson warned: "He could be a two-miler and this fellow is the classiest horse on my land. I would tell readers to follow him closer than any of mine."

IAN SEMPLE had another highly successful season and the Scotsman reckons **Appalachian Trail** "is a horse to follow".

He said: "This horse won at Wolverhampton in January and we are planning to run in the Lincoln at Doncaster.

"I might even run him in the Lincoln Trial at Wolverhampton on March 12 and you haven't seen the best of him.

"He was gelded in the autumn and I've been impressed with his physical improvement.

"He should have won the Esher Cup at Sandown in April but Richard Hughes held his hands up afterwards after being blocked behind a wall of horses with a double handful.

"He finished fourth to Gatwick and Zonus in the Silver Bowl at Haydock in May and that was probably the best three-year-old handicap form of the season.

"Appalachian Trail handles most types of ground but good going is ideal.

"You've got to stick with him because there is a big handicap to be won with this horse."

Semple continued: "**Real Quality** was a good horse last season and I'm looking forward to him enormously this time around.

"He was a late foal, who took time to come to hand. I'm sure he should have won at Ayr's Western meeting when beaten a head by Ingleton.

"Real Quality went on to win at Newcastle in good style and, although the handicapper has given him a mark of 93, he has always worked extremely well.

"I'll look for one or two early conditions races and the replacement for the Thirsk Classic Trial could be suitable.

"He's not big but he has a very big engine and bags of speed but I reckon he'll stay a mile. The sire, Elusive Quality, is the new kid on the block, having sired a Kentucky Derby winner."

Semple insisted: "Get him in the notebook because he could be anything on the evidence of his homework."

Readers should also look out for an interesting ex-Irish horse called **Defi**.

The Scotsman said: "I bought him out of Kevin Prendergast's yard last backend and this 88-rated gelding is a son of Rainbow Quest.

"He loves top of the ground and although he isn't big, he's a great doer with a superb constitution.

"He's built like an apple, so he's got plenty of strength and I'm sure he'll do well over a mile and a quarter.

"Defi will do well in the summer months because he has a lot of quality."

Kames Park put up an encouraging effort when fourth at Haydock on his debut. Semple said: "That was a good run considering he looked green.

"He didn't handle the track when third at Hamilton on his second start but came back and won at Ayr.

"That was a very good run because he beat Mark Johnston's Alrafidain.

"Kames Park is a good one to look forward to this season and I'm sure he'll improve again from three to four. He will give us a lot of fun off a mark of 84."

Mintlaw also created a favourable impression last season and her trainer told me: "She ran very green when second to Ed Dunlop's Epiphany on her debut - she should have won.

"This filly was due to run at Ayr's Western meeting but pulled a muscle and missed a bit of work.

"I ran her over a mile on very soft ground at Ayr in October but she blew up and probably needed the run.

"I would say she definitely gets a mile, despite quickening stylishly to win over 7f at Musselburgh.

"She was still very green, so there's a lot of improvement to come."

Stable stalwart **Chookie Heiton** is difficult to train but Semple said: "He was brilliant when winning the Listed Beverley Bullet but sustained a foot injury just before the Ayr Gold Cup.

"The ground was very testing and Tom Eaves said he knew going to post that he wouldn't handle the conditions.

CHOOKIE HEITON: Ian Semple's veteran isn't the easiest to train, but has plenty of ability

MARY READ (in front): Bryan Smart's filly just gets beaten, this time by Tournedos (far left)

"Chookie always sustains an injury before the start of each season, so there aren't many miles on the clock.

"There could still be another big win in him when he encounters fast ground. He takes a long time to come to hand but he lets me know when he's buzzing."

Monsieur Bond rewarded Reg Bond and *BRYAN SMART* with a well-deserved Group 2 success in the Duke Of York Stakes in May.

The son of Danehill Dancer has taken up duties at Whitsbury Manor Stud, so connections will be hoping to find an able replacement on the racecourse.

Smart said: "**Bond City** is an exciting horse. He's a great type and very fast.

"I always expected him to show plenty of speed but he was a bit slow coming to hand.

"I probably cocked up when running him over 6f first time in May at Doncaster - he didn't seem to get the trip.

"He won three times last season, including a conditions event at Lingfield.

"Bond City beat a good field very impressively that day and will be aimed at all the top five-furlong races.

"This horse could be special - you look at his form and tell me I'm wrong."

Bond Becks will be back after an 18-month break.

Smart said: "He had surgery for colic but I've always rated him highly.

"He looks fabulous after his long holiday and will be flying the flag for us if he comes back to his best.

"His form in the Listed Field Marshal at Haydock two years ago is very good, so he won't be far away in the better races."

Out Of India finished mid-division at Wolverhampton in December on her only start but Smart told me: "She was struck into, so forget the run - I do like her.

"She has a staying pedigree and was very backward last year but she has come to herself now and looks fantastic.

"Look out for her in the first part of the season."

Rainbow Iris is no superstar at Hambleton House but the Yorkshireman insisted: "She has done particularly well over the winter and, although she takes a long time to come right, this filly will win races."

Mary Read was just touched off in the Group 3 Molecomb Stakes at Glorious Goodwood and Smart revealed: "I'm looking forward to her big-style. If she trains on she could be anything, so I'll aim her at the Listed Silver Bowl at Ripon in April. We won that race with Bonne De Fleur and this filly is just as good."

Northern rocks

Mephisto
Percussionist
Real Quality

The West by Hastings

DAVID ELSWORTH is regarded as one of the best dual-purpose trainers in turf history, and possesses the ammo to keep his Whitsbury Manor Stables in the headlines during 2005.

He netted level-stake profits in all age categories in the last turf Flat season, leaving loyal followers in clover. He's never been afraid to aim high, and is no stranger to saddling big-priced winners.

One of last season's revelations has to be **Spanish Don**, who bagged his third handicap prize of the year when providing one of the biggest shock wins in racing records at 100-1 in the prestigious Cambridgeshire at Newmarket in October.

The gelding stuck his neck out gamely to deny Take A Bow in the fiercely competitive feature at Headquarters, and proved it was no fluke when following up in a Listed race on a return there later in the month.

CAPE COLUMBINE

At seven years of age, he's maturing like a fine wine and could well be up to landing his first Group race before 2005 is over.

Norse Dancer mixed it effectively with some of the best in Europe over a mile and 1m2f last year.

Highlights included a Group 3 win at Salisbury and close seconds to Sulamani in the Juddmonte, and Azamour in the Irish Champion.

His form is rock-solid, and it will be a crying shame if he fails to break his duck in Group 1 company during the months to come.

Although Elsworth enjoyed success with In The Groove in the Irish 1,000 Guineas back in 1990, a first British Classic victory still eludes. However, his luck could well change when smart prospect **Cape Columbine** tackles the 1,000 Guineas at Newmarket on May 1.

She's related to top-class Hong Kong performer Cape Of Good Hope (trained by Elsworth at two), and made an eyecatching debut when finishing with a rare rattle to finish within inches of the 94-rated Love Thirty in a 6f maiden at Goodwood in September.

She duly stepped up on that encouraging debut effort when pulling clear of the very useful hat-trick-seeker Obe Gold under a better-judged ride from Richard Quinn at a soft-ground Newmarket shortly after.

The mountainous filly will have continued to fill her enormous frame during the winter months and will relish every yard of the stiff mile encountered at HQ. Watch her win one of the spring trials before tasting Classic success.

Elsworth's **Massif Centrale** is related to numerous Group 1 performers and, although he'll never make his mark at the very highest level, there is some serious money to be farmed from him this summer.

He was thought highly enough of to earn a crack at the Derby in June, but found maiden company more to his liking when running away with a lesser contest at Newbury the following month.

More recently, he readily defied a 96-rating at Leicester in October. On that evidence, he looks a live contender for the big middle-distance handicaps, like the Duke Of Edinburgh Stakes at Royal Ascot.

A highly progressive type to watch out for is **Nota Bene**.

He made amends for a narrow debut defeat at Salisbury when making all in a back-end Windsor maiden. He then did remarkably well when beating some older, higher rated rivals in a strongly-run conditions race at Newmarket last time (time compared well with Listed race on card).

Further success will be a formality for the exciting son of Zafonic in his second term.

Brecon was too headstrong as a juvenile and will no doubt settle better given age.

She did well to overcome considerable greenness to gamely win a Salisbury maiden.

Then, despite taking a pull early, she proceeded to finish strongly to fill fourth in a Listed prize next time and ran a similar race on better ground at Newmarket a week later. She'll return wiser and stronger this term.

The lightly-raced **Topkat** pounced to win a middle-distance Salisbury handicap in August, and the late developer can continue to defy the official assessor this summer.

Former classy handicapper **Romany Prince** kept on doggedly when fifth in the Group 2 Lonsdale Cup at York and, although he'll never fill the considerable void left by the tragic death of people's champion Persian Punch, there should be some decent staying prizes to be won with him.

With upwards of 180 horses in his care, the *RICHARD HANNON* team continues to boast one of the largest strings in the land, and one of his brightest prospects among the Classic generation is **Grand Marque**.

Pilot Kieren Fallon was impressed with the attitude the Grand Lodge colt showed when gamely landing a conditions stakes over 7f at Newbury in July.

Although that proved to be his last juvenile success, there was plenty to like about a staying-on fifth behind Etlaala in the Group 2 Champagne Stakes at Doncaster.

He may not be up to Classic potential, but that shouldn't prevent him gaining Pattern glory before long.

Another exciting prospect among the three-year-olds is **Kings Quay**, who managed to lower the colours of subsequent Breeders' Cup Juvenile hero Wilko in a Newbury Listed prize previously won by the likes of Haafhd, Lammtarra, Millenary and Mamool.

He may have gone over the top when disappointing in September – an effort worth overlooking. His breeding and lazy attitude suggests a step up to a mile will suit and, giv-

KINGS QUAY: seeing off the subsequent Breeders' Cup Juvenile victor Wilko

en the rock-solid form, he merits a small each-way voucher for the 2,000 Guineas at Newmarket in May 2.

Fantastic View wasn't right for much of last year but it wouldn't surprise to see Hannon bring him back to his best as a four-year-old.

As a juvenile, the chestnut managed to plunder Listed and Group 3 races prior to chasing home American Post in the prestigious Racing Post Trophy at Doncaster.

It would be folly to write off such a quality animal after a couple of defeats last year.

Miss Cassia is an interesting one for handicaps. Trained by Hannon, she more than confirmed her promise shown in maidens when keeping on well to land a sprint nursery at Goodwood.

She handles all ground types and was a tad unlucky when trailing in a bunch finish to a competitive Windsor handicap last time. She's bred to improve with age and distance, so keep her on your side.

The Queen has a promising type to look forward to called **The Coires**. The son of Green Desert opened the account when comfortably landing a 7f maiden at Newmarket in August, and wasn't outclassed in a strong nursery at Doncaster the following month.

He relished some cut in the ground at HQ and, in her second term, could well be one for spring/autumn campaigns for Hannon.

As a two-year-old, the pacey **Baltic Dip** did very well from limited sightings.

She fared best in a bobbing finish to a Goodwood maiden in May, and has run extremely well in defeat against stronger company since.

ROD MILLMAN

Having lost 6l at the start, she did particularly well to pass most of the field in an ultra-competitive sales race at Newbury; an effort sandwiched between two creditable runs in Listed races at Newmarket.

Although speed is her main asset, she's bred to stay further with age.

The remarkable flagbearing speedball **The Tatling** will no doubt more than pay his way for Chepstow trainer *MILTON BRADLEY* in the top sprints.

The popular veteran won the King's Stand at Royal Ascot and suffered a near miss in the Group 1 Nunthorpe at York last term.

Although he flopped at Hong Kong in December, he didn't travel well and can be forgiven the uncharacteristic poor show. Back on home soil, he can recapture peak form.

Another lightning-fast Bradley inmate worth checking out is **Enchantment**.

She won more than her share under varying ground conditions last summer and, given her handler's excellent record with sprinters, expect even greater things from this genuine type during the months ahead.

ROD MILLMAN's younger recruits netted level-stakes profits on turf last year, and the Devonian maestro looks sure to enjoy handicap successes with **Polar Dawn**.

She came up with the goods to land a Warwick maiden and was making some late gains to finish a creditable tenth behind Cape Columbine in the £100,000 Tattersalls race at Newmarket next time.

The consistent **Sergeant Cecil** will no doubt ply a successful trade in staying handicaps.

The chestnut excelled himself when going down by less than a length off a lofty 93-rating in the Old Borough Cup at Haydock and held his form well since. Abundant stamina and a game attitude can help him pick up where he left off, providing the ground rides good or faster.

Best of the West

Cape Columbine
King's Quay
Sergeant Cecil

The South by Southerner

JOHN DUNLOP would be the first to admit that the 2004 season was by no means a vintage one for Castle Stables but he still sent out 55 winners and earned well over £1m in prizemoney for his patrons.

The best of last year's team have been retained and 60 choicely-bred juveniles have joined the strength at Arundel for this term.

Double Agent and **Persian Conqueror** are two of the more interesting newcomers.

Both are sons of the dual Derby and Arc hero Sinndar. The first-named is a half brother to his owner the Earl Of Cadogan's useful handicapper **Jedburgh**, who remains at Arundel despite being unable to add to his three juvenile victories last year.

Persian Conqueror is a half-brother to one of Dunlop's stalwarts, **Persian Lightning**.

A six-year-old now, Persian Lightning, who made his usual contribution to the stable's coffers when landing a £23,000 handicap at Epsom on Oaks day last year, is another older horse still in training at the Sussex yard.

Double Agent and Persian Conqueror will both need time, as will the good looking **Mount Kilimanjaro**.

By perennial champion sire Sadler's Wells out of a mare by the Derby winner Reference Point, the colt has "middle-distance" written all over his pedigree.

Qusoor is expected to be much more precocious. Hamdan Al Maktoum's filly is by the young stallion Fasliyev, who has quickly established himself as an excellent source of speedy two-year-olds.

Cassydora is one of Dunlop's major hopes among the three-year-olds. As a daughter of Darshaan, it was no surprise that she relished the cut in the ground when beating subsequent Fillies Mile winner Playful Act,

PERSIAN LIGHTNING: a regular winner for John Dunlop's Arundel team

who was making her debut, by a comfortable two and a half lengths in a 7f maiden at Newmarket in August on her second start.

She was a shade disappointing when finishing only a 5l fourth to Playful Act in the Group 2 May Hill Stakes over a mile at Doncaster on her third and final outing but the race was run in over four seconds faster than average time and the ground was probably much too quick for her.

Teeba promises to be the best offspring yet of Dunlop's Shadayid, who he saddled to land the 1,000 Guineas at Newmarket in 1991.

The Seeking The Gold filly was introduced in a six furlong maiden at Newmarket last October.

Slowly into her stride and hampered at halfway, she looked set to finish out with the washing until finding her stride entering the final furlong and finishing best of all to be a never-nearer fourth to Tomoohat.

Millenary's sister **Dancingintheclouds** made a highly satisfactory start to her career when making late headway to be eighth to Titian Time in a mile maiden at Newmarket in September. She seems sure to pick up some nice middle-distance prizes this season.

The $8,000 that **In The Lead** cost as a foal looks money very well spent. The Bahri filly showed there are races to be won with her when finishing seventh in a 7f Newbury maiden in September on her sole start as a juvenile.

Tawqeet and **Karlu** are two of the better prospects among the three-year-old colts. The first-named made his racecourse bow in a mile maiden at Newmarket in October.

Although he trailed home near the rear of the field at HQ, he clearly benefited from the experience as he powered through the mud to win another mile maiden at Nottingham in early November on his only other appearance.

Karlu was blooded in a 7f maiden at Lingfield in July. He showed rather more that his stablemate had on his debut when making late headway, after meeting traffic problems, to be a 4l ninth to Minnesota.

He also learned a good deal from his first start, as he demonstrated when handling the heavy ground at Chepstow in September to open his account in a 7f maiden with a ready half a length victory from Spectait.

The unraced **Before Time** is worth noting. By the very successful young stallion Giant's Causeway, the chestnut is out of Original Spin, who was a useful filly and won a couple of handicaps for the stable five years ago.

As usual Dunlop has a team of tried and trusted older horses and pride of place naturally goes to the 2,000 St Leger hero **Millenary**.

He had a terrific campaign last year, winning the Yorkshire Cup and the Jockey Club Cup and dead-heating for the Doncaster Cup.

Millenary shows no sign of losing his enthusiasm at the age of eight and he will follow a similar programme again.

Race The Ace has a long long way to go before he can be mentioned in the same breath as his illustrious stablemate but he started to develop into a useful stayer last term.

He got off the mark with an easy success in a 2m maiden handicap at Goodwood in August and followed up by running away with another 2m handicap at Newmarket in October on his final appearance.

Race The Ace, who is particularly effective when there is juice in the ground, could pick up one of the big handicaps and the Cesarewitch is the obvious long-term target.

WALTER SWINBURN never let the butterflies get to him in his days in the saddle but the former top jockey was a bundle of nerves at Lingfield last November when watching **Grand Show** give him his first success as a trainer since taking over the licence

MILLENARY: old favourite

at Berkhamsted from his father-in-law Peter Harris.

Swinburn says: "My main aim this year is to continue the good name of the stable. I'm not thinking about Derby winners just yet - though one would be nice!"

Grand Show has no pretensions to Classic glory but he should more than continue to pay his way this year in handicap company.

Before his victory in a 6f maiden on the Polytrack he had shown a decent level of ability on turf when finishing fourth to Wise Owl on his debut at Pontefract and fifth to the highly-regarded Tucker in a well-contested maiden at Newmarket.

Swinburn will be extra keen to win races with **Phoebe Woodstock**, as she is owned by his father-in-law.

It shouldn't prove too difficult a task, as this well-related filly showed abundant promise when a strong-finishing third to Fen Shui in a 7f maiden at Kempton last September on her sole appearance as a juvenile.

Biriyani is a similar sort. She too had just one start as a juvenile and also revealed talent when finishing to Halle Bop in a 6f maiden at Kempton the same month.

AMANDA PERRETT has assembled her strongest team ever at her Pulborough base in West Sussex.

Perrett's four-year-old **Corsican Native** should prove well worth following. He managed to win a 1m2f maiden at Goodwood in August from four outings last year when he was just a shell of a horse and he is sure to strengthen up as he gets older.

AMANDA PERRETT

His year-younger sister **Corcoran** is an even more exciting prospect. She overcame greenness to make a winning debut in a 7f maiden at Leicester in October.

Skyscape stayed on well close home to finish a promising third to Mayadeen in a mile two-year-old maiden at Bath in October last year on her only outing.

A big, rangy individual, Skyscape has plenty of stamina in her pedigree and she will come into her own when able to race over 1m4f or further.

Winds Of Time is another with plenty of scope and this daughter of the excellent sire Danehill did well to make a winning start to her career when catching subsequent scorer Unreal in a 6f maiden at Newmarket in July on her debut. Winds Of Time will be suited by a mile this season.

Vodafone Derby entry **Westland** will probably fall short of the standard required to line up for the premier Classic at Epsom in June but there should be plenty of good races to be won with him.

The American-bred grey showed he had a powerful engine when cruising home 3l clear of Stage School in a 6f maiden at Yarmouth in November on the second of his two starts last year.

Epsom trainer *TERRY MILLS* has been in fine form on the All-Weather this winter and his team will be well forward for the start of the turf campaign.

Resplendent Glory won a couple of six furlong events on Lingfield's Polytrack in January in pleasing style.

Mills is confident the chestnut will be just as effective on turf and that he will be very well suited by a straight track.

PAT CHAMINGS expects great things of **Take A Bow** this summer.

The Basingstoke trainer believes the four-year-old, who won three good prizes and finished runner-up in the Cambridgeshire last term, is still improving.

Southern stars

Phoebe Woodstock
Teeba
Westland

The Midlands by John Bull

PIVOTAL FLAME: Ed McMahon has high hopes for the star of his yard

IT'S all change at Woodlands Farm, where, after forty-one years of holding the trainer's licence, *BRYAN MCMAHON* hands over the running of one our region's most consistently successful Flat operations to his son Ed.

McMahon senior will still play a key role as assistant trainer, and his experience is sure to be a tremendous asset to his son as he embarks on his new career.

Last year was a vintage one for the yard: they landed the Group 3 Cornwallis Stakes, the Spring Cup at Newbury, and valuable two year-old races at Chester, York and Doncaster.

Level-stakes followers would have been rewarded with a profit of £66.89 - the second highest figure of any stable which sent out more than 200 runners.

With nine new John Fretwell-owned two year-olds in training, plus the continued services of his more established performers, everything looks set for another fine campaign.

The star of the season is likely to be **Pivotal Flame**. The colt won his maiden over 6f at York in May before finishing a highly promising fifth when stepped up in class and trip for the Group 3 7f Superlative Stakes at Newmarket in July.

The form of that race has worked out a treat, with the third placed-Wilko - who finished only a length and a quarter ahead of McMahon's charge - running Sharmadal to two lengths in the Vintage Stakes before going on to cover himself in glory in the Breeders Cup Juvenile.

Pivotal Flame subsequently found 7f on testing ground beyond him in the Solario Stakes at Sandown but, after landing a novices event at Leicester, ran another fine race in the Two Year-Old Trophy at Redcar, finishing sixth despite dwelling at the start and conceding weight to all those who finished ahead of him.

On his last run of the season, in the October Yearlings Sales Race at Doncaster, the colt was slowly away again, but stayed on powerfully at the business end to overhaul stablemate Hidden Jewel.

Bryan McMahon filled me in with plans for the three-year old: "We've entered him in the 2,000 Guineas - with the Craven Stakes at Newmarket or the Greenham Stakes at Newbury as his first likely target. I think he'll be an even better horse this season - he's filled out a bit now."

When you consider just how much ground Pivotal Flame was conceding his rivals at the start of last season with his slow getaways, it wouldn't need much improvement to put this talented performer right in the top bracket.

Two other horses from the yard to keep close tabs on are **Fictional** and **El Coto**.

"Fictional has turned into a nice horse - he'll be a decent sprinter," predicts McMahon.

"He won first time out at Leicester as a three-year- old, but later we had a little problem with him.

"We gave him a rest so we could sort it out and kept hold of him in the hope that he can now build on what he's already achieved.

"His first target would be one of the early Doncaster sprints - the only thing is that he wouldn't want it too soft - he really likes fast ground."

Seasoned campaigner El Coto will kick off his campaign in the Lincoln (which his stable landed ten years ago with Roving Minstrel), before heading south to Newbury for the Spring Cup - which he won last year at juicy odds of 20-1.

His failure to win again for the rest of the season does mean that he'll start 2005 on a feasible mark but it's worth noting that the five year-old has won on either his first or second starts for each of the last three seasons.

MARK BRISBOURNE surpassed last year's target of 50 winners and the indefatigable master of Great Ness will be going all out to do even better this time round.

The Shropshire shrewdie told John Bull: "An Irishman said to me 'I hope you've just had the worst season you've ever had' and I'd go along with that!"

Brisbourne picks out the ex-Khalid Abdullah owned three year-old **Rapid Flow** as a 'dark' horse for RFO readers to follow.

"He has ticks in all the right boxes. He had two runs last season when trained by Amanda Perrett, finishing eighth of 11 and eighth of 13 - but was not given a hard time.

"Physically we're only getting started on him, but his bloodlines are exceptional.

"He needs one more run to be handi-

EL COTO: Victorious in Newbury's Spring Cup, will be aimed at the Lincoln

capped and I think he could be a real unknown quantity.

"We'll start him off over 7f - he won't be out until April at the earliest."

From his more established inmates, Brisbourne believes both **Roman Maze** and **Merrymaker** are set for profitable campaigns.

"I still don't think we've seen the best of Roman Maze.

"He was only beaten a short-head in a Class C handicap at Chester in July from a bad draw and 4l in a similar event at York despite experiencing trouble in running.

"He's still only a five year-old and I think he can win a big one. He's equally good over 6f or 7f.

"Merrymaker won four races for us last year, and although he's now rated in the 80s I think he could still improve at the age of five - he's by Machiavellian and his progeny often do.

"He'd be our main mile and a half horse and I think he'd be capable of winning a nice race or two.

"In the lower leagues, **Liquid Lover** will be a good fun horse to follow. He's only had four runs and is very well handicapped off 46 - I can see him progressing into the 60s.

He's by Night Shift and his trip would be from 6f to a mile. He's also wintered very well."

REG HOLLINSHEAD kicked off the 2004 turf campaign (his fifty-fourth as a trainer) in grand style, with **Royal Cavalier** and his half-sister **Goldeva** landing a 1,320-1 double on Lincoln Day at Doncaster.

REG HOLLINSHEAD

The latter went on to land another Listed race at Pontefract in August at odds of 20-1 and her handler confirms that the underrated mare will have the race as her mid-season target again.

"She'll have the same sort of programme this year. Although both her wins last year were with cut in the ground, the going won't be important."

Royal Cavalier may be eight years old now, but in the words of his trainer: "his form has not deteriorated", and the 2001 November Handicap winner should still make his presence felt, especially in 1m4f handicaps and conditions races at his beloved Doncaster.

"He wasn't quite right in the second half of last season, which is why we didn't run him," Hollinshead told me, "but he's had his rest now and will probably be back for Doncaster."

IAN WILLIAMS and *JOHN MACKIE* are primarily thought of as two of our region's most skilful National Hunt operators - but it's a big mistake to ignore their runners on the Flat.

Both showed healthy level-stakes profits last season - £39.96 and £17.96 to £1 stakes , with Mackie boasting a strike rate of 19%, the highest of any Midlands trainer.

"I'm hoping to expand my Flat string," the Church Broughton handler told John Bull. "I hope Sheikh Mohammed is reading this - As I would be happy to be sent some of his!"

Mackie ran through some of his likely stars of the new campaign: "**Cantarna** - who comes from the same family as the Pierse Hurdle winner Essex - did well for us on soft ground last season and she'll be out early on, when the ground is right. We'll also be stepping her up in trip.

"**Ne Oublie** is a very nice horse - he was a bit weak and backward as a two-year old last season, but he'll do better this time, while in the staying department **Welkino's Boy** is one to watch out for."

Midlands magic

Pivotal Flame
Rapid Flow
Ne Oublie

Outlook

Morning Mole

by Steve Mellish

Godolphin – too many horses?

2004 was an excellent season on the Flat, especially on the three-year-old front, with the likes of Attraction, North Light and Ouija Board. At the time of writing, they are all set to stay in training, so 2005 should be even better.

One slight cloud on the horizon, in my view at least, is the continuing expansion of the Godolphin Empire.

There is no question that the Boys In Blue have been good for British racing up to now, but I feel the negatives are starting to outweigh the positives.

On the plus side, everything is always trying, they are pretty open and helpful with the media, and, almost single-handedly, have ensured that horses are kept in training longer.

BLUE ARMY: returning from exercise

It's not unusual to see their stars still running as four, five and even six-year-olds. Because of these boons, I was just about prepared to put up with their infuriating policy of "cherry-picking" other peoples' animals, but a couple of things have persuaded me that it's all getting a bit out of hand.

Firstly there was the switch of Shamardal to Godolphin from Mark Johnston, who'd handled him brilliantly. Now this was nothing new and no surprise, but in one fell swoop all interest was removed from the 2,000 Guineas market.

Godolphin now has the first two in the betting, Shamardal and Dubawi, plus several of the lightly-raced, promising maiden winners who are open to improvement. I reckon the chances of the big two making the line-up are remote. France will almost certainly beckon for one of them.

Now, Flat racing has always been something of a rich man's plaything; the likes of the Aga Khan and Khalid Abdulla, not to mention the Coolmore mob, are hardly skint members, but for sheer size they are as nothing compared to Godolphin.

This brings me to the second bit of concerning news. Rumour has it that they will have around 400 horses in Newmarket this year and frankly this is almost obscene. They obviously believe in the great Zero Mostel's maxim: "If you've got it, flaunt it."

Competition is vital for any sport to survive but with all the best horses being in so few hands at present, it's in danger of being stifled.

Anyway, enough of the rant and, with my invite to Dubai firmly on hold it's time to move onto a few horses that it could pay to follow in 2005.

Morning Mole's horses to follow

BAILEY GATE

3yo bay filly
Mister Baileys – Floppie (Law Society)
Richard Hannon

What we have here is a lightly-raced filly - only three runs so far - who is progressing at a rate of knots.

A quick glance at her breeding suggests she'll keep on improving. She's a half-sister to Ringmoor Down, who's got better as she's got older and last season developed into a Pattern race sprinter.

In her first two runs in maidens at Newbury and Kempton, Bailey Gate showed a bit of promise but nothing to get excited about. It was her final start back at Newbury that showed her in an altogether better light.

Looking at the 14 maidens in the paddock beforehand, she struck me as one of the more imposing types, and it was no surprise to see her nibbled at in the market.

In the race itself, she was soon settled, going well and, once produced, strode effortlessly clear of Westland, who went on to score easily at Yarmouth next time.

The ground at Newbury was soft and she has to prove she's as effective on a quicker surface, but I don't see that as a problem.

She showed a nice action going to post and is by Mister Baileys, who loved quick ground. Very much one to follow.

GENTLEMAN'S DEAL

4yo brown colt
Danehill – Sleepytime (Royal Academy)
Ed Dunlop

As an animal that's won his last two races I can hardly claim Gentleman's Deal to be an inspired selection, but I reckon there's every reason to believe we've by no means seen the best of him yet.

He's a massive colt - just the sort to get better as he gets older - and he's been given an easy time of it so far, with just three runs on the board.

After scoring in maiden company at Chepstow on his second appearance, he was stepped up into handicap company for his next outing. That was on the polytrack at Wolverhampton and, on what he'd achieved at Chepstow, his mark of 75 seemed about right.

As it turned out, it underestimated him. He absolutely hacked up and there's no doubt he's capable of winning off much higher marks and in much better company.

Incidentally, due to his size, I'd never be worried about him having to give inferior rivals weight; he's built like a tank!

MASTER OF THE RACE

3yo chestnut colt
Selkirk – Dust Dancer (Suave Dancer)
Sir Michael Stoute

There were a number of interesting juvenile maiden races run at the last Newmarket meeting and two who especially caught my eye are included in this list. First up is this 200,000gns son of Selkirk.

In the paddock, he struck me as quite a tall, somewhat gangly sort and he looked by no means fully wound-up for his debut. In short, he's just the type to do better as a three-year-old.

Given all this, it's to his great credit that he could run such a promising race. Never far away, he showed his inexperience when first asked for his effort before staying on strongly up the hill to chase home a promising, and fitter, Godolphin animal called Centaurus.

At the line, he'd pulled 2l clear of the twice-raced favourite River Royale and it was a long way back to the 4th.

There were three races for youngsters over 7f that day, plus an older horses handicap and this heat was by far the quickest.

This is undeniably decent form, probably up to pattern company, and, with the experience behind him, and the physical scope to improve, Master Of The Race seems a certainty to pick up races, probably good ones.

SHARED DREAMS

3yo bay filly
Seeking The Gold – Coretta (Caerleon)
Luca Cumani

This is the other animal that grabbed my attention on Newmarket's final card of the season.

READY TO SWOOP: North Light (front left) en route to Derby success at Epsom

Like Master Of The Race, she lined up in one of the maidens, in her case one of the fillies' versions. Also like Master Of The Race, she was a taking type, not fully fit and with loads of scope to progress.

She was unfurnished and needed to fill her frame, and I look forward to seeing her after she's had a winter to develop.

During the race, she was very green and got behind early doors, but once the penny dropped in the final couple of furlongs, she really flew and was closing in some style at the finish.

Cumani is a great trainer, one of the best in my view, and Shared Dreams comes from a family he knows well and has excelled with. The likes of Gossamer and Barathea figure in it.

This likeable filly is open to tons of improvement and could develop into a very useful three-year-old.

NORTH LIGHT

4yo bay colt
Danehill – Sought Out (Rainbow Quest)
Sir Michael Stoute

I make no apologies for including last season's Derby winner. "Why didn't you put it up in last years annual?" I hear you cry. Fair comment, but I'm not missing out again, as I believe he'll get even better and be one of the stars of the year.

His relatives, Researched and Cover Up, won as four and six-year-olds respectively, and in fact the whole of North Light's family seem to get better as they age.

Add to this the fact that he's only had six runs so far and is trained by a master who specialises with older horses and everything seems set fair for a big season.

Besides his win in the Derby, he took the Dante and was placed in the Irish Derby. Ironically, though, it was his one unplaced effort, when fifth in the Arc, that makes me most keen.

Up with the pace throughout in a strongly-run race, he did remarkably well to last as long as he did and granted a more orthodox ride, it's easy to see him going close in the 2005 renewal.

Races such as the King George and the Breeders' Cup will no doubt be on his agenda, too. Given a clear run at things another big race will surely come his way.

Quality not quantity for Nev

2004 was a good year for me on the punting front, but when I looked at the breakdown of where I had made my money, it made very interesting reading.

Basically, if it was not for one huge Jackpot win in August, I would have been level on the year and it surprised me how little money I had made on the day-to-day graft at the races.

This doesn't tell the whole story, but it is still worth looking into why it is so difficult to make it at the track these days. I have a few ideas about why it is as hard as it is and will be taking some action in 2005.

This game is very tough and is getting tougher, largely because the fixture list is expanding at such a rate that even the most diligent of form students must struggle to keep ahead of the game.

I have decided to wave the white flag and not even try to stay on top of all the form.

I took the decision halfway through the winter that I must abandon the All-Weather circuit which has been so good to me for the last few years.

I first concentrated on the sand racing when there was only one meeting a day in the winter, which meant I could see every horse in every race and have a bit of an easier time of it than during the summer.

I have not counted, but I would bet big odds-on that last winter more horses ran on the sand than ran over jumps. And the fact that most of them are so moderate that they can barely put one foot in front of the other makes for decidedly dull racing, and makes reading and watching the form mind-numbing.

I have decided that in 2005 I will be playing big at the big meetings, small or not at all at the minor races. Banded racing is an absolute no-no, as I simply cannot make it pay from a punting perspective.

I can see no positive case for having bad horses going around in ever-decreasing circles ad infinitum, and would suggest that anyone who bets on this stuff is either a villain or a problem gambler.

I am intending to start at Doncaster and go all the way through the Grade 1 meetings until things end at the same track in November.

This way, I will see all the very best races and will have concentrated on an appropriate number of high-class horses, who will hopefully run consistently, which in turn should have a positive impact on profits.

Narrowing the field is the only way to make things manageable these days.

I cannot follow everything, even though I am racing full-time, so the chances of punters who have a day job are virtually nil in

"I can see no positive case for bad horses going around in ever-decreasing circles ad infinitum, and would suggest that anyone who bets on this is either a villain or a problem gambler"

ROB ROY: Michael Stoute's charge is the one Dave Nevison likes for the coming season

my opinion.

You simply must specialize in your betting, nowadays, if you want to profit.

I will definitely be looking at pool bets more, as Jackpots and Placepots have been especially kind to me in the last few years.

The pools do seem to be growing and, whereas the money that is available on the betting exchanges is some of the smartest money around (and therefore very difficult to get hold of), those who play on the Tote are not generally as clued-up.

When the mug money in the pool has reached a decent level, it is well worth stepping in, as the value is phenomenal.

My final rule for success in 2005 is not to rely too heavily on the betting exchanges.

I am a high-turnover punter and, as a result, I pay a low level of commision on my bets. However, it still mounts up and I was staggered when I worked out how much I paid to the exchanges last year.

Looking closer at the markets, I have concluded that, at the front-end of the market, the odds available in the betting ring are almost the same as those on the exchanges, and after commission are probably just as good. The middle-pins in the market are where the value lies on the exchanges.

I will be starting the season on the back foot in any case, as I have had a big antepost bet on Shamardal for the 2,000 Guineas and at the time of writing it seems clear that he will be aimed at the Kentucky Derby.

I was singularly impressed with him in the Dewhurst, but I should have realised that, with his strong American dirt pedigree, there was always a chance that he would go for the American race.

Without Shamardal in the race, the early Classic looks wide open, but at this stage I will be going with a horse of Sir Michael Stoute's to fill the gap.

Rob Roy was one of the most impressive-looking two-year-olds of last year and created a massive impression on me when winning his maiden at Newmarket.

Stoute is not hard on his youngsters, possibly to prevent Godolphin from buying them, but the reports are that this horse has strengthened up well over the winter and that great things are expected of him. He is my horse to follow for this year.

As for trainers, I think the championship is a formality, with Godolphin rumoured to have over 400 horses in Newmarket alone.

This means they will have a runner in virtually every two-year-old maiden event all season.

If there are any odds available about the trainers' championship, I would take anything over Even money, as I feel they will dominate fully this year.

There will be those that think Frankie Dettori might take his foot off the gas this season, having won the jockeys' title in 2004.

However, with the vast army of Godolphin horses available to him to ride, he is nigh-on a certainty already. He could ride the horses blindfold and still gag up in what already looks a one-horse race.

Want some speed?

THE dawn of a new Flat racing season is always something special and, if the *Time Test* figures throw up as many Group race winners as they did last season, then 2005 should be a belter.

I'll start by looking back at the fastest juveniles from last season - which will put us in good shape for the first of this year's Classics.

The top-rated juvenile colt on my figures was **Shamardal**. Unbeaten in three starts for Mark Johnston, his best effort against the clock came when landing the Group 1 Dewhurst Stakes at Newmarket on soft ground.

Personally, I've a niggling doubt that this son of Giant's Causeway may have handled the conditions better than his rivals and he undoubtedly had the best of the draw.

That said, it's hard to argue with the figures and there's no doubt about him staying the mile at Newmarket in May. Now with Godolphin, he justifiably heads the market for the 2,000 Guineas.

The boys in blue have an embarrassment of riches for the season ahead, as they have the likes of **Dubawi** and **Librettist** near the top of my juvenile figures too.

I was mightily impressed with the latter when breaking the two-year-old track record at Doncaster. Although beaten by Shamardal in the Dewhurst, he didn't cope with the soft ground and was forced to race a long way off the favoured rail.

It will be interesting to see what campaign Saeed Bin Suroor has in mind for this colt and don't worry if he appears not to be the stable first-string in some of the top events – he'll be worth following.

The fastest two-year-old filly on my figures last season was **Centifolia**, trained in France by Robert Collet.

The speedy grey is reportedly being aimed at the 1,000 Guineas but all evidence to date suggests she is a pure sprinter.

If she could maintain her blistering pace over a mile, she would be worthy of the utmost respect in the fillies' Classic.

The best home-trained fillies on *Time Test* figures are **Magical Romance** and **Suez**.

Only a neck separated them in the Group 1 Cheveley Park Stakes and that really sums up the fillies division. It's close at the top and there doesn't appear to be a standout filly as there was with Attraction last season.

One I may have underestimated is the John Gosden-trained **Playful Act**.

This daughter of Sadler's Wells clocked one of the best times over the round mile at Doncaster all season when successful in the May Hill Stakes in September.

There were plenty of quick times that day and I took the view that the ground was riding faster than the official assessment of 'good' and, as a result, her *Time Test* figure was just below the very best juveniles on my calculations. She remains a smart prospect, nonetheless.

Youngsters aside, it's also worth highlighting some of the better efforts by the older generation last term, as many of these will pay their way in the months ahead.

Enchantment recorded the fastest time over Bath's 5f for the last couple of seasons when successful there last May.

Consistent thereafter, she has developed into a smart handicapper and could easily make her mark in better company in 2005.

I fully expected **Rum Shot** to take a strong hand last year but, for the most part, he disappointed. Yet, on one occasion he showed his true worth when scoring over 6f at Chester in a terrific time - it was one of the fastest times over the 6f at the Roodeye I can remember for a while.

As Henry Candy didn't have one of his best seasons, I'll give Rum Shot another chance to prove that was no flash in the pan.

Although yet to win at the top level, **Pastoral Pursuits** has clocked some first-class times, not least when landing a Group 2 at Doncaster, and recording a new course record in the process.

The tailwind helped the times for most of that meeting but it's hard to knock this four-year-old, who could be destined for the top.

It would be rude not to mention the exploits of **Azamour**, who was among the best three-year-old colts on my figures in 2004.

The fact that he remains in training for 2005 is a credit to the Aga Khan, who should be rewarded with plenty of success over longer distances this term.

Another three-year-old from last year worth following is **New Morning**, judged on her success at Salisbury.

The Michael Jarvis-trained filly dictated what seemed to be a modest pace in the Listed fillies event over ten furlongs, yet still managed to get close to the course record.

Finally, at a lower level, don't overlook **Polish Emperor** when he returns to turf action.

The five-year-old has responded well to the application of an eyeshield and, as if to underline his improvement, he posted the best time Redcar had seen over 5f all season when successful there in October.

So there's plenty to look forward to and don't forget to keep on top of developments as the 2005 season unfolds by following my thoughts in the *Outlook* each week.

Top two-year-olds of 2004

	Horse	*Speed rating*	*Distance in furlongs*	*Going*	*Track*	*Date achieved*
1	**Shamardal**	**67**	**7**	**S**	**Newmarket**	**Oct 16**
2	Motivator	64	8	S	Doncaster	Oct 23
3	Ad Valorem	63	6	G	Newmarket	Oct 1
	Centifolia	63	6	S	Maisons-Laffitte	Oct 2
	Dubawi	63	7	GS	Curragh	Sep 19
	Librettist	63	7	GF	Doncaster	Sep 8
7	Iceman	62	7	GF	Doncaster	Sep 10
	Obe Gold	62	6	S	Newmarket	Oct 14
9	Albert Hall	61	8	GS	Curragh	Oct 10
	Magical Romance	61	6	G	Newmarket	Sep 30
	Speciale	61	6	G	Deauville	Aug 1
12	Cupid's Glory	60	7	S	Newbury	Oct 22
	Rebuttal	60	6	G	Newmarket	Oct 1
	Suez	60	6	G	Newmarket	Sep 30
15	Campo Bueno	59	6	S	Deauville	Oct 20
	Cape Columbine	59	6	S	Newmarket	Oct 14
	Damson	59	6	G	Newmarket	Sep 30
	Dark Cheetah	59	6	GS	Naas	Oct 17
	Early March	59	7	G	Longchamp	Oct 3
	Etlaala	59	7	GF	Doncaster	Sep 10
	Footstepsinthesand	59	7	S	Leopardstown	Oct 25
	Merger	59	8	GS	Curragh	Oct 10
	Oratorio	59	7	S	Newmarket	Oct 16

Going key: VF = very firm, F = firm, GF = good to firm, G = good, GS = good to soft, S = soft

Review of 2004

Outlook

News diary 2004

by Richard Williams

January

3 Wolverhampton stages the first Regional Racing meeting. There are 70 scheduled meetings in the BHB's initiative and most of the races are to be banded stakes for horses rated 45 or less. Despite the low quality of the horses involved, the daily newspapers publish the racecards. Some 77 horses line up for seven races, the first of which is won by Cleveland Way, ridden by David Nolan and trained by Declan Carroll. Gay Kelleway, who earned £87 as her percentage for winning the seller, said: "I'm a supporter of Regional Racing...It's not about the prize-money." But the *Outlook*'s David Nevison swerves the meeting, complaining: "If this is the standard, you can keep it. I won't be attending." One puzzling thing about Regional Racing is the name. Why 'regional'?

7 Richard Quinn and Henry Cecil end their partnership amicably. Their association hadn't proved that successful and Quinn cited the enormous amount of travelling that he had to do. Willie Ryan is favourite to be the new stable jockey.

12 The International Classifications are published and Hawk Wing tops the older horses, 3lb ahead of Mubtaker. The panel of senior handicappers conclude that the colt's 11l Lockinge Stakes win was every bit as good as it looked at first. Falbrav, who won five Group 1s, including the Eclipse and Queen Elizabeth II Stakes, is rated 6lb behind Hawk Wing and level with High Chaparral. Dalakhani tops the three-year-olds, 1lb ahead of Alamshar - a one-two for the Aga Khan. Kris Kin is 10lb below the French Derby winner, and is thus officially the worst Derby winner for the last ten years. Bago is voted the best two-year-old, 2lb ahead of Attraction and Grey Swallow. The position of Hawk Wing in relation to Falbrav evokes memories of a prediction the *Outlook*'s Off The Bit made in his weekly column to the effect that Hawk Wing would never win another race. He didn't.

15 Johnny Murtagh takes the job as David Loder's principal rider, Loder describing him as "extremely good".

26 Peter Chapple-Hyam has his first runner in Britain since returning from a three-and-a-half-year spell in Hong Kong. Although Toronto Heights can only finish second at Wolverhampton, memories are rekindled of the trainer's former glory days with Dr Devious and Rodrigo de Triano, who were prepared at Manton. Chapple-Hyam is now at Newmarket.

28 Gary Stevens takes the job as Andre Fabre's stable jockey.

29 The Dubai International Racing Carnival, carrying £11.5 million in prize-money, gets underway. It will last two months and will culminate with the Dubai World Cup.

30 TO FOLLOW: The RFO gives its list of the best prospects for this season on pages 28-35

February

5 Paddy Power open the betting on the Flat jockeys' title and install Kieren Fallon as 1-3 favourite with Darryll Holland 100-30 and Richard Hughes and Kevin Darley on 12s. The reigning champion singles out Seb Sanders as a potential threat to a seventh title.

25 Coral have Pleasantly Perfect as their 5-2 favourite for the Dubai World Cup, with Medaglia d'Oro and Victory Moon at 7-2. In Britain, the collapse of Attheraces leads to Newmarket reducing prize-money for the 2,000 and 1,000 Guineas. Both races have a sponsor, though, in poker website Ultimatebet.com.

26 Johnny Murtagh and David Loder team up for their first winner with Scotty's Future in a seller at Lingfield.

March

2 Riding in a maiden on the All-Weather at Lingfield, Kieren Fallon attempts to coast home on Ballinger Ridge and is caught on the line by Rye and Chris Catlin. Fallon is 10l clear entering the short straight with Rye, the 8-11 favourite, being hard-ridden. A few strides past the furlong pole, Fallon looks round and, seeing no threat, begins to ease down. He galvanises his mount when he hears Rye coming at him but it is too late. He is roundly booed by punters outside the weighing room.

Fallon is refered to the Jockey Club and could face a 21-day or even 28-day ban. He would be punished on the spot if it weren't for suspicious betting patterns which mean the whole matter has to go to Portman Square. To make things worse for the champion jockey, it transpires Betfair alerted the Jockey Club to these patterns before the race.

Andrew Balding, Ballinger Ridge's trainer, defends Fallon, pointing out that Ballinger Ridge is a tricky ride and still a maiden.

4 Writing in the Daily Mirror, Fallon apologises for Lingfield: "The last 48 hours have been a living hell for me. The ride I gave Ballinger Ridge was a long way from being my finest". We agree.

7 Things now turn nasty for Fallon when he is the front page story in the News Of The World accused of fixing races. In a taped converstion, broadcast widely on television, Fallon is heard telling reporters, purporting to be Middle Eastern punters, that Rye would beat his mount Ballinger Ridge. He could face disrepute charges.

8 Dark days for the champion jockey. Returning from a break in Malaga, he jostles with photographers at Stansted Airport, an incident caught in graphic detail by Sky cameras. Later in the day, he receives a 21-day ban from the Jockey Club.

The dispute between Sir Alex Ferguson and John Magnier over the breeding rights of Rock Of Gibraltar is over. Ferguson drops legal action against Magnier and says that the two men had agreed "an amicable settlement".

9 Ballinger Ridge, ridden by Martin Dwyer, hacks up at Lingfield. That evening, Fallon and his wife Julie appear on ITV News and face down the News Of The World allegations. "I've been very stupid," he says, "but it would be impossible to fix a race because there are other horses and other people involved."

11 Frankie Dettori enters Paddy Power's betting for the Flat jockeys' title at 50-1. Fallon is 4-5, out from 1-3.

25 Turf racing on the Flat resumes amid the news that Godolphin have recruited a second stable jockey - Kerrin McEvoy of Australia. Trainers pick low draws for the Lincoln.

26, 27 High numbers clean up in the Spring mile on Friday and Babodana, drawn highest in the Lincoln, comes home first for trainer Mark Tompkins and jockey

Philip Robinson. Over in Dubai, the American horse Pleasantly Perfect, trained by Richard Mandella and ridden by Alex Solis, wins the World Cup in good fashion.

28 St Leger winner Brian Boru trains on into a four-year-old by taking the Alleged Stakes at Leopardstown but Jamie Spencer receives a two-day ban.

April

4 One Cool Cat leaves Aidan O'Brien purring after a dazzling spin after racing at The Curragh. The colt is a general 5-2 for the 2,000 Guineas. By contrast, Jamie Osborne's long-priced Dewhurst winner Milk It Mick appears to have blown his Guineas chance after a disappointing effort on Lingfield's All-Weather.

7 Kieren Fallon and John Egan are charged with breaking Jockey Club rule 220 (iii) which relates to acting in a manner prejudicial to the sport's integrity and good reputation. Fallon also faces a hearing relating to a charge that he broke rule 243 relating to the communication of information for personal reward.

That evening, Robert Sangster, a leading owner and breeder for over 30 years, dies of cancer, aged 67. His colours were carried to victory in the Derby by The Minstrel and Golden Fleece.

13 Snow Ridge crashes into the 2,000 Guineas betting with a fantastlc workout at Nad Al Sheba, winding up the gallop 10l clear of Duke Of Venice and other Godolphin luminaries. He is cut from 25-1 to 12-1.

15 Haafhd, a son of Al Bahathri, turns the Craven Stakes into a procession winning by 5l under Richard Hills. He is now 6-1 from 25-1 while runner-up Three Valleys is out to 12-1.

18 An eventful day at Leopardstown, where Derby favourite Yeats beats three others to land the Ballysax Stakes, a race which Sinndar, Galileo and High Chaparral all contested. Grey Swallow lands the Leopardstown 2,000 Guineas Trial but in unimpressive style and is pushed out by the layers. Jamie Spencer is handed a one-day ban for misuse of the whip when winning the 1,000 trial on Royal Tigress.

22 Barry Hills makes bullish noises about Haafhd, proclaiming: "He'd be the best miler I've had. He's an uncomplicated colt in every respect."

25, 26 Jamie Spencer is collecting bans faster than Hurricane Higgins used to. The weekend begins with a four-day ban at Navan for careless riding and the very next day the Longchamp stewards slap two one-day bans on him, demoting him from the runner-up position in two Classic trials.

28 There's tragedy at Ascot as Persian Punch dies while racing for the Sagaro Stakes. The indications are that he ruptured an artery attached to his heart. The 11-year-old was undoubtedly the most popular horse in Flat racing.

May

1 Haafhd, which means "proctector" in Arabic, beats Snow Ridge by one and three-quarter lengths in the 2,000 Guineas by making use of Godolphin's pacemaker. Barry Hills also won the race in 1979 with Tap On Wood but he considers Haafhd superior. It's a particularly sweet day for Snowy Outen, Haafhd's 79-year-old groom, who has been with Hills since he started training. The favourite 15-8 One Cool Cat trails in second last and is found to have an irregular heart rhythm.

2 The Duke of Roxburghe's Attraction bounces out of the stalls and sees off all-comers in the 1,000 Guineas. The Mark Johnston-trained filly has had all sorts of comments made about her legs and Channel 4's Jim McGrath can't resist making another: "She's got legs that would make

money at Sotheby's - they stick out in all the right places."

9 Yeats fails to impress when winning the influential Derrinstown Stud Derby Trial and there's no change in the betting for the big one. He remains 3-1.

11 After just three months, David Loder and Johnny Murtagh are splitting because, in the Irish jockey's words, "David decided we weren't clicking together."

15 Frankie Dettori and Kieren Fallon clean up at Newbury on Lockinge day, Dettori landing a treble and Fallon a double, including the Lockinge with Russian Rhythm. Dettori is 13 ahead in the jockey's table.

16 American Post runs out a most fortuitous winner of the Poule d'Essai des Poulains. Antonius Pius, trained by Aidan O'Brien and ridden by Jamie Spencer, hits the front in the closing stages but veers right and crashes into the rail. Basically, the Irish horse gifts the race to the French horse. To cap it all, Jamie Spencer is handed a six-day ban by the French stewards.

22 Things go from bad to worse for the Ballydoyle team. First, One Cool Cat does not even make it to the Irish 2,000 Guineas, which is won by the late Duke of Devonshire's Bachelor Duke. Secondly, Yeats is reported as being a shade stiff after a gallop.

23 Attraction carves out a piece of racing history by becoming the first filly to win both the 1,000 Guineas and its Irish equivalent. The filly completes an Irish Guineas double for the British dukes Roxburghe and Devonshire (posthumous).

June

1 For the first time this year, Yeats, at 7-2, is not favourite for the Derby. He is replaced by Snow Ridge, 11-4.

2 Yeats is ruled out of the Derby by Aidan O 'Brien. His muscle stiffness has not responded to physiotherapy. Estimated antepost bets of £500,000 are lost. Appearing on BBC2's Money Programme the same evening, Ladbrokes chief Chris Bell says: "I believe one race per day in British racing to be fixed." The programme concerns itself with the issue of internet betting exchanges and their impact on the integrity of racing. Bell also says: "The good thing about virtual racing is that you don 't get fallers and that everyone is trying. It is the perfect race."

5, 6 It's the year the British aristocracy reclaims the Classics. With dukes Devonshire and Roxburghe already on the scoreboard, it's the turn of the 19th Earl of Derby, who leads Ouija Board into the winner's enclosure after the Oaks. The next day, the widow of the late Lord Weinstock leads up North Light after the Derby.

10 The BHB publish a document called 'The Modernisation of British Racing' in which plans are outlined to limit many races to a maximum of 14 runners. This looks bad news for each-way punters and raises the question of whether the BHB is in cahoots with the bookmaking industry.

15 On the first day of Royal Ascot, it's a victory for the little man, as The Tatling steals the show by winning the King's Stand Stakes. It provides Milton Bradley with his first Royal Ascot winner. Bradley, 69, had driven the horsebox up from Chepstow himself.

19 Frankie Dettori is top jockey at the Royal meeting, with six winners over the five days. His sixth winner, Doyen, breaks the track record in the Hardwicke Stakes.

27 Grey Swallow beats North Light by half a length in the Irish Derby. It's trainer Dermot Weld's second victory in the race and his 12th Irish Classic.

30 Peter Savill ends a six-year stint as chairman of the BHB. His reign was controversial but he got things done, and left the place in a better state than when he found it. Possibly his worst mistakes were in 2002, when the BHB attempted to raise data charges to national newspapers from £40,000 to over £1 million. The response of the press was to drop sponsors' names and miss out whole racecards. Savill denied it was his idea but he stepped in to withdraw the proposal.

July

1 The Jockey Club are to investigate the admission by Philip Mitchell of Juddmonte Farms that Endless Summer, winner of the Richmond Stakes in 2000, was officially aged three, not two, at the time. Mitchell confirms that the high-class colt had been foaled on December 26 or 27 and not January 2, the date on his passport. The story goes that Endless Summer was nicknamed the 'secret squirrel' by Juddmonte staff. Mitchell says that, because Endless Summer was a premature birth, he took an "operating decision" to falsify his birthdate. Mitchell argues that "there was no form of deception intended." Well, of course. It must have slipped his mind to tell the Jockey Club what he had done.

3 The Jockey Club decide to drop charges against Kieren Fallon for accepting money or benefits for passing on tips to undercover News of the World journalists.

10 Geoff Huffer returns to the training ranks and will operate out of High Havens stables in Newmarket. Huffer had to quit the game when his Kuwait backers went into receivership following the Gulf war in 1991. He later served a prison sentence for duty fraud. His main backer this time is Terry Ramsden, who himself served ten months for fraud.

15 Gary Carter is charged by the Jockey Club with deliberately losing eight races inside eight weeks of 2003. The horses are spread between seven trainers. Trainer Shaun Keightley and jockey Pat McCabe are charged with ensuring that Red Lancer would n't win or be placed when he ran at Wolverhampton in October. Both the Jockey Club and the *Racing Post* were tipped off before the race that the horse wouldn't win.

18 On the day that Ouija Board outclasses her field in the Irish Oaks, One Cool Cat flops in the International Stakes, despite going off at 2-1 on. The colt has a new heart problem according to Aidan O'Brien, because after the race his heart is beating 80 to the minute instead of 120.

21 Neil Graham, who trained Minster Son to win the St Leger in 1988, when Dick Hern was hospitalised, announces a new job with Godolphin. He accepts the post of assistant trainer to Saeed Bin Suroor.

24 Doyen, ridden by Frankie Dettori and trained by Saeed Bin Suroor, looks the part when beating US challenger Hard Buck by a long-looking 3l in the King George VI and Queen Elizabeth Diamond Stakes. "The sky is the limit," says an elated Sheikh Mohammed, who regularly leads up 'horses of the century'.
The same day, in a Newbury courtroom, one of Marcus Tregoning's former grooms is found guilty of assaulting the trainer and is given a conditional discharge. The court hears that Damien Connor walked into Tregoning's office the day after he was sacked and said: "I'm going to hit you". This he did. He also grabbed Tregoning's hair. Connor's version is different but he admits that he and the trainer had been involved in a scuffle.

29 Mark Johnston cleans up again in the Goodwood Cup. This year he saddles a 1-2-4, with the tigerish Darasim leading them home. "I love it here", says Johnston, "and I aim my horses at all the big races."

August

1 Seb Sanders looks back on July with satisfaction. Not only did he win the Stewards' Cup on Pivotal Point but he rode 44 winners and is in the Flat jockeys' title race. Recently as big as 40-1, Ladbrokes make him 10-1 behind 2-7 favourite Kieren Fallon. Sanders is nine behind Fallon and two behind Frankie Dettori. A lot of the success is due to the resurgence of Sir Mark Prescott, by whom he is retained.

4 A four-timer at Kempton's evening meeting sees Dettori draw level with Fallon at the top of the jockeys' championship race. Alec Stewart, 49, dies of cancer at his home in Newmarket. He achieved fame with his handling of dual Eclipse winner Mtoto.

8 One Cool Cat wins a race. It's the 6f Phoenix Sprint at The Curragh and his SP of 3-1 looks rather juicy with the benefit of hindsight. Next stop is the Nunthorpe.

14, 15 A Saturday night of drama in the US where Powerscourt passes the post first in the Arlington Million but is demoted to fourth. Jamie Spencer and Powerscourt hamper Kicken Kris and Kent Desormeaux and the stewards have little option under American rules. It's another setback for Aidan O'Brien and his Ballydoyle owners. Spencer says: "I'm lucky to have the support of Aidan O'Brien, Mr Magnier and Michael Tabor. Others might have flown off the handle in the circumstances."

19 Nine-year-old Bahamian Pirate becomes the oldest horse to win a British Group 1, the Nunthorpe Stakes at York. He has a length and a neck to spare over The Tatling and One Cool Cat. The last-named is not helped by the testing ground.

24 Gary Stevens decides to quit France and return home to the US just five months after accepting a retainer with Andre Fabre. He rode no Group 1 winners for the Frenchman but did ride one for Tim Easterby, Somnus in the Prix Maurice de Gheest.

26 Britain's biggest bookmaker Ladbrokes unveils large profits in the first six months of 2004. Profits are up 51 per cent on the same period in 2003 . One reason is Ladbrokes' 5,864 fixed odds betting terminals. A second reason is some good results such as only five winning favourites at Cheltenham and Greece winning the European Cup.

September

1 Kieren Fallon is arrested in an early-morning raid. He is one of 16 rounded up by the police for alleged conspiracy to defraud. Others caught in the net are jockeys Fergal Lynch and Darren Williams, plus trainer Karl Burke. More than 130 officers, mainly from the City of London force, are involved in the nationwide swoop. All the jockeys and the trainer are released that evening. Fallon's solicitor says: "The circumstances that relate to his arrest relate to a meeting with an individual [reportedly Miles Rodgers] who Kieren Fallon has met on one occasion and whose name Fallon did not even know at the time of the meeting." Rodgers, a former director of Platinum Racing Club, is also arrested.

2 Fallon, writing in the *Daily Mirror*, says: "The whole thing is a complete joke. I'm being treated like a terrorist."

4 One Cool Cat is on the verge of retirement after coming sixth to Tante Rose in the Stanleybet Sprint Cup at Haydock.

11 Godolphin relinquish their grip on the Irish Champion Stakes as Doyen lets them down, coming seventh and beating only his pacemaker Millstreet. The Aga Khan's Azamour wins the race at 8-1. 15 minutes earlier, Sheikh Mohammed had been watching the St Leger on television, seeing Rule Of Law beat Quiff a head when ridden by Godolphin's number two Kerrin McEvoy.

18 The Dermot Weld-trained Vinnie Roe makes history by winning the Irish St Leger for the fourth year running. Jockey Pat Smullen describes it as the easiest of his four wins. The surprising thing is his price, 7-2.

22 The jockeys' title race is the closest it has been for years. Dettori rides a double at Goodwood to pull three clear of Fallon. The Italian is cut to 4-6. Fallon is 11-10.

25 A fantastic card at Ascot, where Rakti is back to his best to land the Queen Elizabeth II Stakes. Extraordinarily, it is the first time the six-year-old has run over any distance less than 1m2f. Trainer Michael Jarvis is thinking in terms of Cups for his stablestar - in places such as Japan and Hong Kong.

27 Ben Hanbury confirms rumours that he is retiring. He says: "I have sold the yard to Stuart Williams." Hanbury trained out of Diomed Stables, Newmarket since 1947,

sending out Midway Lady to win the 1,000 Guineas and Oaks in 1986.

30 Magical Romance, 40-1, pulls off one of the shocks of the season in the Cheveley Park Stakes, beating Suez and Damson. It is Robert Winston 's first Group 1 winner and the jockey was only booked for the rlde the night before.

October

2 Spanish Don, at 100-1, beats Take A Bow a neck in the Cambridgeshire.

3 Some Classic names - North Light, Ouija Board and Grey Swallow - bite the dust in the Prix de l'Arc de Triomphe behind the Jonathan Pease-trained Bago.

10 Lucky Story and Shamardal change colours ahead of Newmarket's Champions Day. Mystery surrounds the transfer of the horses from Abdulla Buhaleeba to Gainsborough Stud, the bloodstock operation of Maktoum Al Maktoum.

12 Willie Ryan decides to hang up his boots after 23 years. His greatest moment came aboard Benny The Dip in the 1997 Derby.

13 News filters out that Dubai businessman Ahmed Buhaleeba has allegedly suffered gambling losses at the roulette tables in London and that is why his brother's horses have been sold to the Maktoum family.

16 The Buhaleebas' losses are the Maktoums' gains as Shamardal runs out an impressive winner of the Dewhurst and propels himself to 2,000 Guineas favouritism. Mark Johnston, the trainer, will have to wait to see if he has charge of the colt in 2005. Haafhd lands the Champions Stakes at odds of 12-1.

23 Motivator puts himself into Derby calculations, a general 14-1 shot, by winning the Racing Post Trophy. It's trainer Michael Bell's first domestic Group 1 victory in a 15-year career.

24 It is confirmed that Shamardal and Lucky Story will leave Mark Johnston to join Saeed Bin Suroor.

30 The Breeders' Cup, which has seen so many English hopes go up in smoke in the past, will have to be viewed differently from this day forth. Newmarket supplies two runners and two winners. Dual Oaks winner Ouija Board wins the Filly & Mare for Ed Dunlop, while Wilko scoops the Juvenile for Jeremy Noseda.

November, December

Nov 2 Frankie Dettori rides Mamool into seventh place in the Melbourne Cup and gets a 31-day ban for careless riding. Fortunately for him the ban only applies in Australia.

6 It's the last day of the Flat turf season and the November Handicap is won by Carte Diamond. Saeed Bin Suroor is champion trainer, Godolphin top owner, and Dettori winningmost jockey.

8 Peter Harris, the trainer who pioneered ownership syndicates, hands over the reins of his Hertfordshire stable to son-in-law Walter Swinburn. The former jockey saddles his first runner at Southwell.

18 Kris, the outstanding miler who went on to become champion sire, dies of suspected heart failure aged 28.

21 Rakti is a disappointment in Japan, beating only two home in the Mile Championship.

23 Plans for the new London City racecourse at Fairlop Water hit a brick wall when the planning application is turned down by 12 votes to one.

Dec 1 The police round up three more suspected racing fraudsters on top of the previous 19. Alan Berry, Paul Bradley and Steve O' Sullivan are read their rights.

Outlook

Group 1 review
by Adam Bull

For two-year-old Group 1s, see 'Two-year-olds of 2004', page 93

1 Ultimatebet.Com 2000 Guineas (Group 1), (1m) Newmarket May 1 (Good)

1 **Haafhd** 9-0 R Hills
2 **Snow Ridge** 9-0 L Dettori
3 **Azamour** 9-0 M J Kinane
11-2, 8-1, 25-1. 1¾l, 1l. 14 ran. 1m 36.7 (b7.18)
Mr Hamdan Al Maktoum (B Hills, Lambourn).

Of the first five finishers only the ill-fated Snow Ridge failed to win a Group 1, indicating that this race was well up to standard. Azamour, Haafhd and **Whipper** have all won all-age Group 1s, which helps give the form a healthy look. Ante-post favourite, **One Cool Cat** was the subject of a major gamble on the day of the season's first Classic, yet trailed home slowly with only one runner behind. Aidan O 'Brien's "stable star", tagged a sprinter after this flop, managed to win a Group 2 over 6f at the Curragh later in the season but that seemed his limit as a three-year-old, as he failed to deliver in four from five outings.

2 Ultimatebet.Com 1000 Guineas (Group 1 Fillies), (1m) Newmarket May 2 (Good)

1 **Attraction** 9-0 K Darley
2 **Sundrop** 9-0 K McEvoy
3 **Hathrah** 9-0 R Hills
11-2, 16-1, 6-1. ½l, ½l. 16 ran. 1m 36.8 (b7.14)
Duke of Roxburghe (M Johnston, Middleham).

Attraction proved many of her doubters wrong by stepping up to a mile, having excelled at 6f as a two-year-old. She was the highest-rated filly in the race and never gave her backers a worry as she did it the hard way from the front - holding off the fast-finishing Sundrop by half a length. The form though has a rather inconclusive look to it; the next three finishers, (Hathrah, **Red Bloom** and **Secret Charm**) all bagged wins later in the season, while the last four home (**Valjarv**, **Incheni**, **Jath** and **Spotlight** did as well. Of the remaining eight horses (finishing midfield) none went on to score at any level.

3 Juddmonte Lockinge Stakes (Group 1), (1m) Newbury May 15 (Good)

1 **Russian Rhythm** 8-11 K Fallon
2 **Salselon** 9-0 J P Murtagh
3 **Norse Dancer** 9-0 T Quinn
3-1f, 66-1, 10-1. ½l, nk. 15 ran. 1m 37.0 (b5.80)
Cheveley Park Stud (Sir M Stoute, Newmarket).

In what was a competitive Group 1, Sir Michael Stoute's Russian Rhythm was installed as the ante-post favourite. Being a filly, the stats were stacked against her, as she faced other proven milers. On a hot afternoon, the daughter of Kingmambo managed to repel the challenge of Salselon and Norse Dancer (who didn't feel inclined to go in front) and bring her Group 1 tally to four. Second favourite and last year's 2,000 Guineas winner, **Refuse to Bend** (who was running under the Godolphin banner by this stage) finished a poor eighth but later went on to win two Group 1s including the Eclipse stakes.

MARK JOHNSTON: trainer of Attraction

4 **Boylesports Irish 2,000 Guineas (Group 1), (1m) Curragh May 22 (Good to Firm)**

1 **Bachelor Duke** 9-0 S Sanders
2 **Azamour** 9-0 M J Kinane
3 **Grey Swallow** 9-0 P J Smullen
12-1, 6-4f, 2-1. 1l, ½l. 8 ran. 1m 40.0 (b4.55)
Exors Late Duke of Devonshire (J Toller, Newmarket).

Bachelor Duke helped out the bookies, as the James Toller maiden winner nudged out the hyped-up Azamour and Grey Swallow. The Miswaki colt has only been seen once on the track since and barring injury may be aimed at the top mile prizes this season. Azamour, owned by the Aga Khan and now placed in both the English and Irish Guineas was later seen at better effect over middle-distances, while Dermot Weld's Grey Swallow won the Irish Derby, giving the form of this Classic a hefty boost.

5 **Tattersalls Gold Cup (Group 1), (1m2f110yds) Curragh May 23 (Good to Firm)**

1 **Powerscourt** 9-0 J P Spencer
2 **Livadiya** 8-11 J A Heffernan
3 **Nysaean** 9-0 M J Kinane
10-3, 16-1, 9-10f. 6l, ½l. 6 ran. 2m 11.0 (b15.03)
Mrs John Magnier (A P O'Brien, IRELAND).

One of last season's weakest Group 1s but stylishly won by Aidan O'Brien's Powerscourt. Contested by only six runners, Powerscourt slammed his rivals by 6l and never broke sweat. Only **Private Charter** and **Naheef** have gone on to record victories (in Listed class), giving rise to questions over the status of this race and the value in which it is held. The best older horses tend to head to the Coronation Cup at Epsom despite the Curragh race offering over £100,000 to the winner.

6 **Boylesports Irish 1,000 Guineas (Group 1), (1m) Curragh May 23 (Good to Firm)**

1 **Attraction** 9-0 K P Darley
2 **Alexander Goldrun** 9-0 K J Manning
3 **Illustrious Miss** 9-0 K Fallon
2-1f, 8-1, 9-2. 1l, 2l. 15 ran. 1m 37.6 (b6.95)
Duke of Roxburghe (M Johnston, Middleham).

A trip across the Irish Sea and the same result for the flying filly as Attraction set out in her trademark manner from the front in an attempt to burn the others off. The trick worked again and only Alexander Goldrun got close as she won by a length. It was her seventh win on the spin and she became the first filly to do the Anglo-Irish Guineas double. Despite her knock-knees, Mark Johnston's multiple Group 1 winner has defied her ungainly conformation and those who judge horses at the sales.

7 **Vodafone Coronation Cup (Group 1), (1m4f10yds) Epsom June 4 (Good)**

1 **Warrsan** 9-0 D Holland
2 **Doyen** 9-0 L Dettori
3 **Vallee Enchantee** 8-11 D Boeuf
7-1, 9-2, 6-1. 1¾l, shd. 11 ran. 2m 36.0 (b10.39)
Mr Saeed Manana (C Brittain, Newmarket).

As you would expect, the form of this race is solid. Both Doyen and Warrsan have gained subsequent success at the highest level, while the eighth-placed, **Dubai Success** has also won a Group race.The gutsy Warrsan showed his liking for this course as he completed his second successive win in the race, taking advantage of the conditions and a couple of horses not getting clear runs. Vallee Enchantee and Doyen looked to have been unlucky. However, for the jockeys to meet trouble in a race of this nature (1m4f) is rather poor. **Magistretti**, who was 4l behind the winner is now trained in the U.S where he has finished first, and runner-up twice in consecutive Grade 1s.

8 **Vodafone Oaks (Group 1), (1m4f10yds) Epsom June 4 (Good)**

1 **Ouija Board** 9-0 K Fallon
2 **All Too Beautiful** 9-0 J P Spencer
3 **Punctilious** 9-0 L Dettori
7-2, 11-4f, 10-3. 7l, 3½l. 7 ran. 2m 35.4 (b10.94)
Lord Derby (E Dunlop, Newmarket).

Runaway winner Ouija Board made a mockery of this field as she came clear to win by an impressive 7l. She came off the bridle and looked unsettled round Tattenham Corner, but was soon back on an even keel and passed her opponents as if they were stood still. Although Ed Dunlop's filly looked something special those who finished behind (Punctilious apart) have done little to support the form. Despite saddling three of the seven runners including All too Beautiful (a full sister to recent Derby winner Galileo) Aidan O' Brien's string could only manage second, fourth and last (**Necklace** and **Kisses For Me** were his other runners).

9 **Vodafone Derby Stakes (Group 1), (1m4f10yds) Epsom June 5 (Good)**

1 **North Light** 9-0 K Fallon

2 **Rule of Law** 9-0 K McEvoy
3 **Let The Lion Roar** 9-0 M J Kinane
7-2j, 20-1, 14-1. 1½l, hd. 14 ran. 2m 33.7 (b12.63)
Ballymacoll Stud (Sir M Stoute, Newmarket).

A not too dissimilar race to the previous year's one. It had the same outcome, as Sir Michael Stoute and Kieren Fallon teamed up again to win an average Derby. North Light was unsure about things before going into the stalls, but was soon settled by the six-times Champion jockey. He let the son of Danehill bowl along up-front before kicking on early in the straight. A half-brother to Cover Up, his stamina began to tell as his rivals were caught out and never able to mount a serious challenge. Unbelievably, the order of the first three finishers was exactly the same as the Dante at York, a month earlier. **Snow Ridge** continued Frankie's drought in the race, finishing seventh, while the upgraded **Pukka** and **Gatwick** found the going too tough. **American Post** didn't appear to stay.

10 St James's Palace Stakes (Group 1), (1m) Ascot June 15 (Good to Firm)

1 **Azamour** 9-0 M J Kinane
2 **Diamond Green** 9-0 Gary Stevens
3 **Antonius Pius** 9-0 J P Spencer
9-2, 10-1, 7-1. nk, ¾l. 11 ran. 1m 39.0 (b8.26)
H H Aga Khan (J Oxx, IRELAND).

A race won by Azamour in a cracking time. The Aga Khan colt put up one of the best speed figures of the season beating off the challenge of three Guineas' winners. The form looks above average - especially when you consider the exploits of the winner later in the season. The ground during the Royal meeting was particularly fast but this didn't appear to compromise the efforts of Azamour who held Diamond Green by a quarter of a length. Antonius Pius flattered to deceive as he was swinging on the bit entering the straight. He soon emptied out and after this disappointment was tagged a likely sprinter - and ran next in the July Cup at Newmarket. 2,000 Guineas winner **Haafhd** was well to the fore, but weakened close home to finish a below-par fourth.

11 Queen Anne Stakes (Group 1), (1m) Ascot June 15 (Good to Firm)

1 **Refuse To Bend** 9-0 L Dettori
2 **Soviet Song** 8-11 J P Murtagh
3 **Salselon** 9-0 D Holland
12-1, 6-1, 12-1. nk, ¾l. 16 ran. 1m 39.1 (b8.14)
Godolphin (S bin Suroor, Newmarket).

An excellent race on paper and even horses finishing down the field (**Alkaadhem, Norse Dancer**, and **Arakan**) were useful yardsticks throughout the season. Godolphin, who thrive at this course and this Royal meeting, took the honours with Refuse To Bend, beating two of the best fillies around - Soviet Song and **Nebraska Tornado** (who finished fourth). Frankie Dettori was winning the race for the second succesive year and produced the Guineas winner at just the right time. Six different countries were represented in this competitive race, which

OUIJA BOARD: Oaks winner and 'Filly of the year'

is clearly regarded now as one of the best mile races on the calendar.

12 **Prince Of Wales's Stakes (Group 1), (1m2f) Ascot June 16 (Good to Firm)**

1 **Rakti** 9-0 P Robinson
2 **Powerscourt** 9-0 J P Spencer
3 **Ikhtyar** 9-0 R Hills
3-1, 9-2, 8-1. 2l, ½l. 10 ran. 2m 4.5 (b11.50)
Mr Gary A Tanaka (M Jarvis, Newmarket).

Rakti was too quick on the day for his competitors, confirming himself a very difficult horse to beat over 1m2f. Phillip Robinson broke well from his stall and got a nice lead from the pacemaker (Godolphin's **Lunar Sovereign**, not really meant for him). The time was quicker than standard and many of those in behind had Group 1s to their name, so the form has to be respected. Beaten favourite **Sulamani** probably found the ground firm enough in fourth, while **Bandari** was outclassed.

13 **Gold Cup (Group 1), (2m4f) Ascot June 17 (Good to Firm)**

1 **Papineau** 9-0 L Dettori
2 **Westerner** 9-2 G Mosse
3 **Darasim** 9-2 J Fanning
5-1, 13-2, 28-1. 1½l, 2½l. 13 ran. 4m 20.9 (b11.10)
Godolphin (S bin Suroor, Newmarket).

Being the most famous race at Royal Ascot, it was quite fitting that the best stayers in Europe fought out a wonderful race. The market was headed by last year's impressive winner **Mr Dinos** but was sadly missing the much-loved, **Persian Punch** (who is now no longer with us). The ground, still riding on the fast side proved too firm for Westerner. The talented French horse has been sweeping up the best staying races across the Channel but even with the illegal use of ear-plugs (in England) was not able to peg back Papineau. The hugely promising Godolphin horse made the step up to 2m4f look easy and should still be kept on side if he is dropped back in trip, even though another shot at the Gold Cup is very likely.

14 **Coronation Stakes (Fillies' Group 1), (1m) Ascot June 18 (Firm)**

1 **Attraction** 9-0 K Darley
2 **Majestic Desert** 9-0 T E Durcan
3 **Red Bloom** 9-0 K Fallon
6-4f, 25-1, 10-3. 2½l, hd. 11 ran. 1m 38.5 (b8.74)
Duke of Roxburghe (M Johnston, Middleham)

Again an impressive display from Mark Johnston's Attraction. It was thought by many that going around a bend before a stiff uphill finish would play into the hands of her rivals, notably Red Bloom, who was expected to give the Johnston filly a better run for her money. The result however was emphatic and the turning track only helped to keep Attraction focused as she powered on up the hill and away from her helpless pursuers. Godolphin's **Cairns** and Barry Hills' **Secret Charm** both disappointed.

15 **Golden Jubilee Stakes (Group 1), (6f) Ascot June 19 (Firm)**

1 **Fayr Jag** 9-4

FAYR JAG (front, left): seen here gamely winning the Golden Jubilee Stakes at Royal Ascot

W Supple
2 **Crystal Castle** 9-4 K Fallon
3 **Cape Of Good Hope** 9-4 M J Kinane
12-1, 8-1, 13-2. hd, hd. 14 ran. 1m 13.4 (b7.47)
Mr Jonathan Gill (T Easterby, Malton).

Hardly a vintage renewal of a race won impressively last year by the Australian import, Choisir. As a result this year's foriegn raider Cape Of Good Hope, trained in Hong Kong by David Oughton was given more respect by the bookies. However, Tim Easterby's Fayr Jag managed to get his head in front on the line ahead of French raider Crystal Castle, but in truth these were an average bunch. The time though was only fractionally faster than standard on lightning-quick ground. The home contingent were going to prove much of a muchness throughout the season, except for **Ashdown Express**, who who ran consistently throughout the year and almost sneaked the July Cup.

16 Audi Pretty Polly Stakes (Fillies Group 1), (1m2f) Curragh June 26 (Good)

1 **Chorist** 9-7 D Holland
2 **Alexander Goldrun** 8-9 K J Manning
3 **Ivowen** 9-7 P J Smullen
7-4, 6-4f, 16-1. ½l, 6l. 6 ran. 2m 2.8 (b8.96)
Cheveley Park Stud (W Haggas, Newmarket).

With the three year-old weight allowance in her favour Alexander Goldrun was backed into 6-4 favouritism. However, Darryll Holland sent Chorist into the lead from the start and she held her advantage throughout the 1m2f trip. She clearly enjoyed the sound of her feet thundering along and she looked relaxed when her jockey got her into a nice rhythm. Although challenged late on, Chorist always looked as though she was going to hold on.

17 Budweiser Irish Derby (Group 1), (1m4f) Curragh June 27 (Good)

1 **Grey Swallow** 9-0 P J Smullen
2 **North Light** 9-0 K Fallon
3 **Tycoon** 9-0 C O'Donoghue
10-1, 8-11f, 150-1. ½l, 1½l. 10 ran. 2m 28.7 (b9.63)
Mrs Rochelle Quinn (D Weld, IRELAND).

Sir Michael Stoute sent his Derby winner over to Ireland in an attempt to follow in the recent successful footsteps of Sinndar, Galileo and High Chaparral who completed the Derby double. Despite the good record of Epsom winners, Fallon and North Light were sent off rather short at 8-11. For the home side, five of the ten runners belonged to Aidan O'Brien's yard, but the best they could manage was third place with 150-1 shot Tycoon. Dermot Weld, who had kept his faith in Grey Swallow (a son of Daylami), travelled nicely and stepped up a gear to go past North Light in the final stages. **Rule of Law** was rather one-paced and claimed fourth but he showed his staying potential when stepped up in trip at Doncaster for the St Leger later in the year.

18 Coral-Eclipse Stakes (Group 1), (1m2f7yds) Sandown July 3 (Good to Soft)

1 **Refuse To Bend** 9-7 L Dettori
2 **Warrsan** 9-7 D Holland
3 **Kalaman** 9-7 K Fallon
15-2, 12-1, 12-1. hd, 4l. 12 ran. 2m 8.3 (b5.82)
Godolphin (S bin Suroor, Newmarket).

Rakti was a warm order (13-8), having won impressively at Royal Ascot a few weeks previously. With all the usual suspects present (Warrsan, **Norse Dancer, Powerscourt, Ikhtyar** amongst others) there seemed little point opposing the long-time favourite. However, the horse had other ideas and looked ill at ease in the loose ground, officially described as 'Good to Soft'. The underestimated Refuse to Bend took advantage of Rakti's failings and surprised many as he stayed-on up the hill to hold the closing Warrsan by a head. Norse Dancer, who finished 12th in the race the year before appears to have improved but not enough to take a Group 1, while Kalaman put up a personal best, and was possibly unlucky-in-running in third.

19 UAE Equestrian Racing Falmouth Stakes (Group 1 Fillies), (1m) Newmarket July 6 (Good to Firm)

1 **Soviet Song** 9-1 J P Murtagh
2 **Attraction** 8-6 K Darley
3 **Baqah** 8-6 D Bonilla
11-4, 4-5f, 33-1. 2½l, 2½l. 7 ran. 1m 36.1 (b7.25)
Elite Racing Club (J Fanshawe, Newmarket).

This race was to be Attraction's first reversal and it came when she tackled older fillies for the first time. Having won her races from the front in all her previous outings the same ploy was put in to effect here, in the hope that she could burn off her rivals once more. However, her front-running tactics only set up the race for Soviet Song, who came past Attraction with plenty left in the tank. Seeing another horse go past seemed to demoralise the Guineas winner, although in her defence she was having her fourth difficult race in under two months.

20 **Darley July Cup (Group 1), (6f) Newmarket July 8 (Good to Soft)**

1 **Frizzante** 9-2 J P Murtagh
2 **Ashdown Express** 9-5 S Sanders
3 **Balmont** 8-13 E Ahern
14-1, 100-1, 25-1. nk, 2l. 20 ran. 1m 11.5 (b4.39)
Mrs Jan Hopper & Mrs Elizabeth Grundy (J Fanshawe, Newmarket).

Without an obvious top-notch sprinter in the line-up, this highly respected Group 1 dash became a mine field for punters. With the ground on the soft side, the chances of finding the winner looked even more difficult and as a result the form looks rather muddling. Much was expected of **Antonius Pius**, and with the drop in trip likely to be in his favour he was sent off the 5-1 second favourite. Australian Import, **Exceed and Excel** arrived with a lofty reputation on the back off Choisir's exploits the previous year, but trailed in almost last thanks to the give in the ground. James Fanshawe showed what a good trainer of fillies he is, as Frizzante came with a great burst to land the cup by a neck from the luckless Ashdown Express. Horses have come out of this race and won Group 1's (**Somnus** in fifth, **Bahamian Pirate** in 17th) so the form is respectable without going down as a vintage renewal.

21 **Darley Irish Oaks (Fillies' Group 1), (1m4f) Curragh July 18 (Good to Firm)**

1 **Ouija Board** 9-0 K Fallon
2 **Punctilious** 9-0 L Dettori
3 **Hazarista** 9-0 M J Kinane
4-7f, 5-1, 20-1. 1l, ¾l. 7 ran. 2m 28.2 (b10.13)
Lord Derby (E Dunlop, Newmarket).

Just like the race at Epsom only seven fillies were turned out here. The first three home in the English classic renewed their rivalry but the winner was the same, as Ouija Board came home a shade cosily. The pace of the race was on the slow side, hence the winning margin being only a length. However we later saw in the Arc and at the Breeders' Cup what terrific speed Lord Derby's filly possesses. She must be followed next year, with many options open to the trainer.

22 **King George VI And Queen Elizabeth Diamond Stakes (Group 1), (1m4f) Ascot July 24 (Good to Firm)**

1 **Doyen** 9-7 L Dettori
2 **Hard Buck** 9-7 Gary Stevens
3 **Sulamani** 9-7 K McEvoy
11-10f, 33-1, 7-1. 3l, hd. 11 ran. 2m 33.2 (b8.34)
Godolphin (S bin Suroor, Newmarket).

With the Arc late in the season, the King George is the real highlight of the summer calendar. Everyone knows the winner has to be a seriously good horse - hence winners such as Swain, Montjeu, Galileo and Alamshar. This year was no exception and as Godolphin always go close with their horses they send out, the star in their yard Doyen was expected to do the business. A stylish winner at Royal Ascot, Doyen quite literally took the race in his stride. Although he unshipped Frankie Dettori in the paddock, he was beautifully relaxed in the race and shot clear of a good field when asked. Rated the best performance of the season by the handicapper, he may well come back for more next year, and might face Ouija Board at some point. The American horse, Hard Buck, who finished second, was a superb each-way shot at 33-1. Multiple group one winner, Sulamani ran his usual good race despite the ground being too fast. Further back in the field were **Gamut**, **Vallee Enchantee**, **Lunar Sovereign**, **Phoenix Reach** and **Warrsan** all previous winners who were disappointing.

23 **Cantor Odds Sussex Stakes (Group 1), (1m) Goodwood July 28 (Good)**

1 **Soviet Song** 9-4 J P Murtagh
2 **Nayyir** 9-7 M J Kinane
3 **Le Vie Dei Colori** 9-7 D Holland
3-1, 12-1, 12-1. nk, 2l. 11 ran. 1m 37.0 (b3.10)
Elite Racing Club (J Fanshawe, Newmarket).

With many proven top milers in the race, opinions varied to who would come out on top. **Antonius Pius** (who was rapidly losing his supporters) has often travelled well, but emptied out far too quickly. The 2003 and 2004 2,000

MICHAEL STOUTE: Excellent trainer of fillies

Guineas winners (**Refuse To Bend** and **Haafhd**) again came face-to-face as they did at the Royal meeting. In addition the old warrior, **Tillerman** would provide us with an angle on how to judge the form of the race, given that he has been in with the best (third to Falbrav last year over a mile). However it was Gerard Butler's Nayyir (who goes well at Goodwood) that laid down the challenge to James Fanshawe's Soviet Song, but even his turn of foot was not enough to prevent the Elite Racing Club's filly gain another sweet victory. As we saw later in the season, the daughter of Marju continued to gain Group 1 successes, showing us that this was to be a great year for fillies.

24 Vodafone Nassau Stakes (Fillies' Group 1), (1m1f192yds) Goodwood July 31 (Good to Firm)

1 **Favourable Terms** 9-2 K Fallon
2 **Silence Is Golden** 9-2 J Fortune
3 **Chorist** 9-2 D Holland
11-2, 12-1, 6-4f. shd, nk. 6 ran. 2m 5.7 (b7.09)
Maktoum Al Maktoum (Sir M Stoute, Newmarket)

This became Sir Michael Stoute's third win on the spin in this race, and the hat-trick was brought up by Favourable Terms, who was sent out a surprising 11-2 shot with just six runners making up the field. Kieren Fallon, who had a poor meeting up to this point, and who admitted publicly that he found Goodwood a hard course to ride, managed to repel Jimmy Fortune on Brian Meehan's fast-finishing filly Silence Is Golden by the shortest of heads.

25 Juddmonte International Stakes (Group 1), (1m2f88yds) York August 17 (Good)

1 **Sulamani** 9-5 L Dettori
2 **Norse Dancer** 9-5 J F Egan
3 **Bago** 8-11 T Gillet
3-1, 16-1, 13-8f. ¾l, ¾l. 9 ran. 2m 11.8 (b8.11)
Godolphin (S bin Suroor, Newmarket)

Bago came over from France to take on some familiar faces for this respected Group 1. He had a huge reputation to uphold and was sent off the 13-8 jolly despite the likes of Sulamani in the race who was coming across his ideal conditions. Good ground with a bit of cut in it over 1m2f is right up his street and with Frankie Dettori on board the pair looked appetising at 3-1. The pair pulled off an excellent win, taking the horse's Group 1 tally to five (six by the end of the season) but only his first in this country. Although now retired, this consistent performer has left us with a good mark on which to judge the form of the races he ran in.

26 Aston Upthorpe Yorkshire Oaks (Fillies' Group 1), (1m3f198yds) York August 18 (Soft)

1 **Quiff** 8-8 K Fallon
2 **Pongee** 9-4 J Fortune
3 **Hazarista** 8-8 M J Kinane
7-2, 10-1, 9-2. 11l, 1½l. 8 ran. 2m 38.3 (b3.60)
Mr K Abdulla (Sir M Stoute, Newmarket).

An emphatic performance from Quiff who destroyed her rivals on the rain-softened ground. The field was well spread-out, so the form cannot be taken too literally. However, the winner looked good next time out aswell (second in the St Leger) and must be one for the shortlist this season. There are certain races Sir Michael Stoute likes to get stuck into and this is one of them. He's claimed six Yorkshire Oaks, including four in the last five years, so don't dismiss him next year as he is sure to have a nice type primed. There were three 33/1 shots in the eight runner field and they filled the last positions. This included Aidan O'Brien's **Royal Tigress**. The yard was clearly not as strong as the Tipperary trainer would have liked during large parts of the season. He will surely be hoping for a major improvement this season.

27 Victor Chandler Nunthorpe Stakes (Group 1), (5f) York August 19 (Soft)

1 **Bahamian Pirate** 9-11 S Sanders
2 **The Tatling** 9-11 R L Moore
3 **One Cool Cat** 9-9 J P Spencer
16-1, 13-2, 3-1f. nk, 1l. 12 ran. 59.9 (b0.11)
Lucayan Stud (D Nicholls, Thirsk).

The ground was soft and as a result the jockey's decided to be cautious about setting off too quickly. **Airwave, Orientor** and One Cool Cat were all expeceted to have reasonable claims (without an outstanding performer in the field), but for different reasons were unable to quicken clear when the going got tough. Bahamian Pirate, who relishes the mud, looked more at home than any of the others and pulled off a small shock. Dandy Nicholls' old boy beat off Jeremy Noseda's well regarded Balmont a month earlier ,so his performance here was not totally unexpected.

28 Stanleybet Sprint Cup (Group 1), (6f) Haydock September 4 (Good)

1 **Tante Rose** 8-11 R Hughes

2 **Somnus** 9-0 M J Kinane
3 **Patavellian** 9-0 S Drowne
10-1, 7-1, 14-1. shd, ¾l. 19 ran. 1m 11.6 (b3.42)
Mr B E Nielsen (R Charlton, Beckhampton).

Again it was a case of all the usual suspects turning up, but without a really top-notch proven sprinter. The punters latched on to Aidan O'Brien's **One Cool Cat**, but again he let his supporters down and was ridiculously short at 6-4. The Storm Cat colt has only won a maiden in this country and like a couple of the yard's expensive horses was over-hyped at the expense of punters' money. Although Tante Rose is a talented filly the race just proved again that Europe is lacking a top-class sprinter.

29 betfair.com St Leger (Group 1), (1m6f132yds) Doncaster September 11 (Good to Firm)

1 **Rule of Law** 9-0 K McEvoy
2 **Quiff** 8-11 K Fallon
3 **Tycoon** 9-0 D Holland
3-1j, 3-1j, 6-1. hd, 1½l. 9 ran. 3m 6.3 (b22.05)
Godolphin (S bin Suroor, Newmarket).

As it's a classic, the bookies always like to put up some early prices and get punters to part with their money. The eventual winner, Rule of Law was always at the top end of the market and landed a fair blow for ante-post players. Kieren Fallon tried to mount a challenge on his Yorkshire Oaks heroine Quiff, but failed to pull her off the rail early enough to get her into gear. By the time she had found a rhythm and built up a bit a speed, the winning post came in time for Godolphin's runner who had led all the way. The remainder were somewhat disappointing and couldn't be backed next year with any confidence at this level.

30 Baileys Irish Champion Stakes (Group 1), (1m2f) Leopardstown September 11 (Good to Firm)

1 **Azamour** 8-11 M J Kinane
2 **Norse Dancer** 9-4 J F Egan
3 **Powerscourt** 9-4 J P Spencer
8-1, 20-1, 11-1. ½l, nk. 8 ran. 2m 1.9 (b12.36)
H H Aga Khan (J Oxx, IRELAND).

Godolphin, who have a great record in this race (four wins in six years) sent out **Doyen** in an attempt to continue their stranglehold on the race. The punters also felt he was a good thing and as a result he was sent off odds-on at 4-5. However, the distance looked to be a touch short for the son of Sadler's Wells and he never seemed to be travelling as well as he did in the King George. Norse Dancer said thank you very much, and decided to kick-on entering the straight. Despite looking likely to land his first Group 1 at the 13th attempt, Mick Kinane arrived with a perfectly timed run on Azamour to take the honours. Despite the favourite's tame effort, the Aga Khan colt is a classy horse and must be kept a close eye on this coming season.

31 Coolmore Fusaichi Pegasus Matron Stakes (Group 1 Fillies), (1m) Leopardstown September 11 (Good to Firm)

1 **Soviet Song** 9-2 J P Murtagh
2 **Attraction** 8-11 K P Darley
3 **Phantom Wind** 8-11 R Hughes
8-13f, 7-2, 9-1. ½l, 5l. 6 ran. 1m 36.8 (b9.56)
Elite Racing Club (J Fanshawe, Newmarket).

This race was billed as a match between Soviet Song and Attraction and the heroines did not disappoint. The trainer and jockey of Attraction decided to persevere with their fronrunning tactics, but again the Johnston-trained filly resented being headed in the final furlong. You feel that she gives her all on the bridle and doesn't save anything for herself. As a result, Johnny Murtagh who timed his run to perfection, seemed to win cleverly. The pair were a long way clear of the third.

32 Irish Field St Leger (Group 1), (1m6f) Curragh September 18 (Good)

1 **Vinnie Roe** 9-8 P J Smullen
2 **Brian Boru** 9-8 J P Spencer
3 **First Charter** 9-8 K Fallon
7-2j, 7-2j, 5-1. 2½l, ½l. 13 ran. 3m 3.9 (a0.72)
Seamus Sheridan (D Weld, IRELAND).

Six years old and a fourth Irish St Leger for Dermot Weld's Vinnie Roe. The son of Definite Article had run well the year before against Westerner in the Prix Royal-Oak, and Dalakhani in the Arc. At the end of the 2004 season he finished runner up in the Melbourne Cup so he is clearly not on the wain. There is no reason why he cannot continue racing at the top level.

33 Queen Elizabeth II Stakes (Group 1), (1m) Ascot September 25 (Good to Firm)

1 **Rakti** 9-1 P Robinson
2 **Lucky Story** 8-11 D Holland
3 **Refuse To Bend** 9-1 L Dettori
9-2, 16-1, 4-1. ½l, 2½l. 11 ran. 1m 39.8 (b7.46)
Mr Gary A Tanaka (M Jarvis, Newmarket).

Just in the same way that Falbrav came back in trip to comfortably beat some excellent milers, so did Rakti, who's performance here was no less inferior. The traditional route for a highly-rated middle distance colt would be the Arc or the Champion stakes, but as we are seeing, a strongly run QE II can play into the hands of a 1m2f horse. Rakti, who usually pulls like a train got a nice tow from the pace-maker **Blatant** (not meant for him) and got settled into a nice rhthym. A bulk of the others cried off entering the straight, including **Norse Dancer** and it was left to Lucky Story to mow him down in the final stages. It was a tough ask and Darryll Holland eventually failed by a head. Lucky Story has now swapped ownership (now with Godolphin) and must be followed over middle distances next year.

34 Kingdom Of Bahrain Sun Chariot Stakes (Fillies' Group 1), (1m) Newmarket October 2 (Good)

1 **Attraction** 8-11 K Darley
2 **Chic** 9-0 K Fallon
3 **Nebraska Tornado** 9-0 R Hughes
11-4, 9-4f, 5-2. nk, 1½l. 5 ran. 1m 36.3 (b7.65)
Duke of Roxburghe (M Johnston, Middleham).

Attraction gained some compensation for two previous defeats. Punters had deserted the filly this time, but the daughter of Efisio put up arguably her best performance so far. This time when faced with a battle in conditions supposedly against her (tacky ground), she battled back to win by a neck. The most pertinent point about this win was the fact that she has retained all her enthusiasm for racing - and winning

35 Emirates Airline Champion Stakes (Group 1), (1m2f) Newmarket October 16 (Soft)

1 **Haafhd** 8-11 R Hills
2 **Chorist** 8-13 K Fallon
3 **Azamour** 8-11 M J Kinane
12-1, 20-1, 6-1. 2½l, 1l. 11 ran. 2m 6.9 (b4.80)
Mr Hamdan Al Maktoum (B Hills, Lambourn).

Barry Hills had his string back to form, for the final end of season surge, but with Haafhd performing below par during the middle part of the campaign he offered great value at a track which suits. Richard Hills was sure this step up in trip would be ideal and just like his display in the 2,000 Guineas he was left to stretch away. Azamour (again like in the Guineas) tried to claw him back, but the damage was already done. John Oxx's colt showed that he can act efficiently on a variety of surfaces and will be another one to watch out for in 2005. Both **Doyen** and **Lucky Story** disappointed, while **Mister Monet** went wrong and tragically had to be destroyed.

36 Prix de L'Arc de Triomphe Lucien Barriere (Group 1) (Colts and Fillies) (1m4f) Longchamp October 3 (Good)

1 **Bago** 8-11 T Gillet
2 **Cherry Mix** 8-11 C Soumillon
3 **Ouija Board** 8-8 J Murtagh
10-1, 33-1, 7-1. ½l, 1l. 20 ran. 2m 25s
Niarchos Family (J Pease, France).

The early entries suggested this was not going to be a vintage renewal. None of the Derby winners looked that appealing, and with the Arc trials producing below-par performances, the race looked more open than had been the case in previous runnings. With both the first (Bago) and third (Ouija Board) coming from well off the pace, it says something about the

PRIX DE L'ARC DE TRIOMPHE: Ouija Board comes with a fast finish but Bago is already home

Group 1 index

All horses placed or commented on in our Group 1 review section, with race numbers

Outlook

Two-year-olds of 2004

by Adam Bull

1 Isabel Morris Memorial Marble Hill Stakes (listed), (5f) Curragh May 22 (Good to Firm)

1 **Russian Blue** 9-0 J P Spencer
2 **Kay Two** 9-0 P J Smullen
2 **L'Altro Mondo** 9-0 T P O'Shea
1-5f, 20-1, 12-1. 1l, dht. 4 ran. 0.0 (b1m2.68)
Exors of the Late R E Sangster (A P O'Brien, IRELAND).

A disappointing turn-out for this Listed event. However the winner, Russian Blue, won more convincingly than the distance of a length suggests. Aidan O'Brien's second string, **Joyce**, who was fancied to make up the forecast, finished last.

2 Vodafone Woodcote Stakes (Listed), (6f) Epsom June 5 (Good)

1 **Screwdriver** 8-11 R Hughes
2 **Royal Island** 9-0 K Dalgleish
3 **Gortumblo** 9-0 T Quinn
7-2, 6-5f, 12-1. nk, 4l. 8 ran. 1m 10.0 (b2.27)
Mr Raymond Tooth (R Hannon, Marlborough).

A fantastic two year-old race for so early in the season. Only a neck could separate the Richard Hannon and Mark Johnston-trained colts as they had a ding-dong battle in the straight, pulling well clear of the remainder. **Obe Gold** who finshed fourth, won two valuable races towards the end of the season. The winner never ran again during the rest of the season.

3 Swordlestown Stud Sprint Stakes (Listed), (6f) Naas June 7 (Good to Firm)

1 **Damson** 8-11 J P Spencer
2 **Pictavia** 8-11 K J Manning
3 **Umniya** 8-11 T E Durcan
15-8, 11-8f, 7-2. 2l, 1½l. 6 ran. 1m 10.8 (b1.87)
Mrs John Magnier (D Wachman, IRELAND).

Five winners took their place in this line-up, and considering the exploits of Damson later in the season, it is a surprise on reflection to see that David Wachman's filly only went off the second favourite at 15-8. The winning trainer remarked that Damson would not go to Royal Ascot. She did turn up though and was one of the highlights of the meeting.

4 Rochestown Stakes (Listed), (6f) Leopardstown June 9 (Firm)

1 **Man O World** 9-0 P J Smullen
2 **Joyce** 9-0 J P Spencer
3 **Clash Of The Ash** 9-0 K J Manning
7-4, 13-8f, 2-1. hd, 2l. 4 ran. 1m 14.1 (b2.09)
Ludolph Heiligbrodt (D Weld, IRELAND).

Joyce, who was disappointing in a Listed race at the Curragh (1) faired a lot better here. She took up the running but was soon headed by Dermot Weld's charge Man O World. Despite putting up a fight, she was held all the way to the line. Only four runners contested this Listed event and the winner has disappointed in his subsequent races.

5 Coventry Stakes (Group 2), (6f) Ascot June 15 (Good to Firm)

1 **Iceman** 8-12 K Fallon
2 **Council Member** 8-12 L Dettori
3 **Capable Guest** 8-12 C Catlin
5-1j, 5-1j, 33-1. ½l, 1¾l. 13 ran. 1m 14.8 (b5.99)
Cheveley Park Stud (J Gosden, Manton).

The first top-class two year-old race of the season and finely contested by the 5-1 joint-favourites. Council Member might not have been in Godolphin's top band of two-year-olds, but Kieren Fallon on Iceman had to pull out all the stops to win by half a length. Capable Guest ran well at a big price for Mick Channon, but could only find a maiden within his grasp for the remainder of the season.

6 Windsor Castle Stakes (Listed), (5f) Ascot June 15 (Good to Firm)

1 **Chateau Istana** 8-13 T P Queally

2 **Tournedos** 8-13 T E Durcan
3 **Safari Sunset** 8-11 P Doe
12-1, 12-1, 12-1. ½l, ½l. 15 ran. 1m 1.5 (b3.60)
Mr Ivan Allan (N Littmoden, Newmarket).

The form of this race hasn't really stood up, although there was nothing wrong with the winner (he took a whack from an opposing jockey's whip) and he went on to win a Group 2 towards the end of the season at Doncaster. Godolphin's two year-olds took the eye this year, but **Satsoof** who contested this one could only manage 10th.

7 Queen Mary Stakes (Fillies' Group 2), (5f) Ascot June 16 (Good to Firm)

1 **Damson** 8-10 J P Spencer
2 **Soar** 8-10 J P Murtagh
3 **Sharplaw Star** 8-10 M Hills
11-2j, 11-2j, 10-1. 3l, 1¼l. 17 ran. 1m 1.1 (b3.95)
Mrs John Magnier & Mr M Tabor (D Wachman, IRELAND).

Having said that Damson would not go to Royal Ascot, David Wachman changed his mind and it was clear why. Connections wanted to look after her, but couldn't refrain from letting loose their star filly. There were a lot of good fillies in behind, but the backers of the Irish-trained winner would have been delighted at the 11-2 SP. Jamie Spencer enthused after the race that the trainer had one better at home (Intriguing). The second, Soar went on to win a couple of Group races to highlight the standard of opposition on the day, while Sharplaw Star back in third proved no slouch either.

8 Norfolk Stakes (Group 3), (5f) Ascot June 17 (Good to Firm)

1 **Blue Dakota** 8-12 E Ahern
2 **Mystical Land** 8-12 K Fallon
3 **Skywards** 8-12 L Dettori
5-4f, 9-1, 4-1. nk, 1l. 9 ran. 1m 2.0 (b3.08)
Mr A F Nolan, Mrs J M Ryan, Mrs P Duffin (J Noseda, Newmarket).

Blue Dakota had three comfortable wins to his name before the Royal meeting and was expected to have no trouble here on fast ground. However, Mystical Land - from the in-form John Gosden yard - made the 5f speedster work hard for his win, and may have turned over the favourite if the race had been over a furlong further. **Cougar Cat**, back in fourth, didn't appear to enjoy the ground.

9 Albany Stakes (Fillies Listed), (6f) Ascot June 18 (Firm)

1 **Jewel In The Sand** 8-11 R Hughes
2 **Spirit of Chester** 8-9 R Havlin
3 **Salsa Brava** 8-11 J-P Guillambert
10-1, 40-1, 14-1. 1½l, 1l. 17 ran. 1m 16.1 (b4.69)
Sand Associates (R Hannon, Marlborough).

Many of these youngsters were in with chances and there was a lot of jostling during the race - some ran green while others couldn't get a run. The winner, Jewel In The Sand (who was an impressive winner of her maiden at Sandown), was blessed with a nice run up the inside rail. The filly quickened sufficiently to win a touch comfortably in the end, giving the impression that the Cherry Hinton at Newmarket would be well within her grasp. Spirit Of Chester continued Nerys Dutfield's great run with two-year-olds at this meeting.

10 Chesham Stakes (Listed), (7f) Ascot June 19 (Firm)

1 **Whazzat** 8-7 M Hills
2 **Brecon Beacon** 9-0 K Fallon
3 **Wilko** 9-0 E Ahern
7-1, 7-1, 16-1. 3½l, hd. 11 ran. 1m 29.6 (b5.02)
Mr W J Gredley (B Hills, Lambourn).

The form of this race was significantly boosted by Wilko's win late in the season at the Breeders' Cup meeting. But despite Whazzat's impressive three and a half length win, a single Listed event was the best the remainder could muster.

11 The Goffs Challenge, (6f63yds) Curragh June 25 (Good)

1 **Kestrel Cross** 9-0 W J Supple
2 **Encanto** 8-9 J F Egan
3 **Nepro** 9-0 K J Manning
14-1, 20-1, 10-1. shd, 1l. 13 ran. 1m 18.2 (b2.01)
Norman Ormiston (K Prendergast, IRELAND).

The first six home all went off at double figure odds, such was the competitive nature of the race. The favourite, **Spirit Of Chester**, disappointed, finishing ninth of 12. Six British trainers tried to raid the cashpot, but the best they could muster was sixth place with Brian Meehan's **Annatalia**.

12 Anheuser Busch Railway Stakes (Group 2), (6f) Curragh June 27 (Good)

1 **Democratic Deficit** 9-0 K J Manning
2 **Russian Blue** 9-0 J P Spencer
3 **L'Altro Mondo** 9-0 T P O'Shea
7-1, 1-2f, 12-1. ¾l, 1l. 7 ran. 1m 11.6 (b4.49)
D H W Dobson (J Bolger, IRELAND).

Russian Blue has proved herself a decent yard stick and she was sent off the odds-on jolly probably because Aidan O'Brien has such a good record in this event. The progressive Democratic Deficit looked a good prospect here, but was given some stiff tasks after this race (notably when he came up against Dubawi).

13 Chippenham Lodge Stud Cherry Hinton Stakes (Group 2), (6f) Newmarket July 6 (Good to Firm)

1 **Jewel In The Sand** 8-9 R Hughes
2 **Salsa Brava** 8-9 J-P Guillambert
3 **Extreme Beauty** 8-9 D Holland
2-1f, 11-2, 25-1. hd, 5l. 10 ran. 1m 11.6 (b4.35)
Sand Associates (R Hannon, Marlborough).

Jewel In The Sand confirmed that her Royal Ascot performance (9) was no fluke by impressively accelerating away from her pursuers. Richard Hannon's filly is out of a Green Desert mare and was always travelling well but it was the fast-finishing Salsa Brava who took the eye. In the end the pair went 5l clear and look good three-year-old prospects for this year.

14 TNT July Stakes (Group 2), (6f) Newmarket July 7 (Good to Firm)

1 **Captain Hurricane** 8-10 J Fortune
2 **Council Member** 8-10 L Dettori
3 **Mystical Land** 8-10 K Fallon
10-1, 7-4f, 15-8. shd, 1¼l. 7 ran. 1m 13.6 (b2.29)
The Comic Strip Heroes (P Chapple-Hyam, Newmarket).

Peter Chapple-Hyam has always liked this two–year-old, and he landed a nice prize here from a couple of good sorts. The winner was only a maiden previous to this, hence his 10-1 SP. Mystical Land has got good form in his own right, while Royal Ascot winner **Chateau Istana** (6) couldn't go the pace. We can assume that there is more to come from Captain Hurricane, and he is worth watching this season.

15 Weatherbys Superlative Stakes (Group 3), (7f) Newmarket July 8 (Good to Soft)

1 **Dubawi** 8-11 L Dettori
2 **Henrik** 8-11 T E Durcan
3 **Wilko** 8-11 E Ahern
15-8f, 14-1, 11-1. ½l, nk. 12 ran. 1m 26.5 (b3.96)
Godolphin (S bin Suroor, Newmarket).

The horse I expect to make the biggest impression this year. Frankie Dettori has famously never won the Derby, but this could be his year. On his debut, the son of Dubai Millennium didn't look an easy ride - described as a bit of monkey by the jockey – but did his job. Here in this Group 2, the colt looked like he needed further, but still obliged. Wilko (third) went on to win the Breeders Cup Juvenile as we know, while **Pivotal Flame** (fifth) is well thought of by his trainer. The form looks very solid.

16 Silver Flash Stakes (Listed), (6f) Leopardstown July 14 (Good to Soft)

1 **Silk And Scarlet** 8-11 J P Spencer
2 **Alexander Icequeen** 8-11 P J Smullen
3 **La Maitresse** 8-11 T P O'Shea
7-2f, 6-1, 10-1. 1½l, 4½l. 12 ran. 1m 15.7 (b0.49)
Mrs John Magnier (A P O'Brien, IRELAND).

Silk and Scarlet (dropping back in distance to 6f from 7f) was held up for this race and came with a promising run from the back, to win going away. The fact that she is by Sadler's Wells makes the performance worthy of note. She could be bundles better this year when she contests middle-distance races. Those in behind looked limited which hasn't done anything for the form.

17 Weatherbys Super Sprint, (5f34yds) Newbury July 17 (Good to Firm)

1 **Siena Gold** 8-1 J F McDonald
2 **Don't Tell Mum** 8-2 R L Moore
3 **Bond City** 8-8 F Lynch
11-2, 9-2f, 33-1. ¾l, ¾l. 24 ran. 1m 1.9 (b1.46)
Mr N Attenborough & Mrs L Mann (B Meehan, Upper Lambourn).

Don't tell Mum was a well fancied favourite, but was beaten by Siena Gold, who had showed promise early in the season. This sprint is always well-contested (24 runners this year) and the race has thrown up plenty of winners including **Tournedos** (Group 3) and **Tagula Sunrise** (St Leger Yearling Stakes).

18 Dubai Duty Free Anglesey Stakes (Group 3), (6f63yds) Curragh July 18 (Good to Firm)

1 **Oratorio** 9-0 J A Heffernan
2 **Cougar Cat** 9-0 J P Spencer
3 **Indesatchel** 9-0 K Fallon
9-1, 9-2, 2-1f. 1l, nk. 8 ran. 1m 15.7 (b4.51)
Mrs John Magnier (A P O'Brien, IRELAND).

If this colt isn't up there in your horses to follow, it should be. Aidan O'Brien really likes this son of Danehill, and despite the trainer not really dominating the big races in Europe, Oratorio did well here against some promising individuals. Runner-up Cougar Cat was supposedly the first string here, but I wouldn't read to much into that.

19 Star Stakes (Fillies' Listed), (7f16yds) Sandown July 22 (Good to Firm)

1 **Queen of Poland** 8-9 T P Queally
2 **Maids Causeway** 8-9 K Fallon
3 **Bentley's Bush** 8-9 R Hughes
13-2, 5-2f, 16-1. hd, 3½l. 9 ran. 1m 29.7 (b3.41)
Sheikh Mohammed (D Loder, Newmarket).

Barry Hills' Maids Causeway was one of the yard's best two-year-olds and is an excellent yardstick from which to judge other juveniles. Queen Of Poland is a lovely sort too, and lightly-raced. She only finished 3l behind Divine Proportions (rated the best two-year-old filly last year) at the Arc meeting, a performance which demands great respect.

20 Princess Margaret Stakes (Group 3 Fillies'), (6f) Ascot July 24 (Good to Firm)

1 **Soar** 8-9 J P Murtagh
2 **Valentin** 8-9 Dane O'Neill
3 **Kissing Lights** 8-9 D Holland
evensf, 9-2, 25-1. 1¾l, nk. 6 ran. 1m 15.6 (b5.22)
Cheveley Park Stud (J Fanshawe, Newmarket).

Soar managed to get closest to Damson at Royal Ascot (7) and that second gave her excellent claims here. Her time was quick as well (over two seconds faster than the colts race). **Magical Romance** was the last to finish - some 13l behind the winner- but in more testing conditions won the Group 1 Cheveley Park Stakes (60) at Newmarket later in the year, which shows what a lottery two year-old races can be.

21 Tyros Stakes (Listed), (7f) Leopardstown July 24 (Good to Firm)

1 **Elusive Double** 9-0 P Shanahan
2 **Lock And Key** 8-11 Catherine Gannon
3 **Amsterdam** 9-0 J P Spencer
11-2, 10-1, 7-4f. 1l, hd. 7 ran. 1m 29.1 (b3.82)
Moyglare Stud Farm (D Weld, IRELAND).

On the same day that Soar prevailed at Ascot, Elusive Double was doing the business on the other side of the water. It has been hard to rate the Irish two-year-old form this year, and this race was no different. Dermot Weld's charge finished well behind Dubawi and Oratorio in his subsequent starts. But if there is more to come from the colt, his trainer will find it.

22 Betfair Molecomb Stakes (Group 3), (5f) Goodwood July 27 (Good)

1 **Tournedos** 8-12 T E Durcan
2 **Mary Read** 8-9 F Lynch
3 **Safari Sunset** 8-12 P Doe
14-1, 25-1, 66-1. nk, 2l. 13 ran. 58.5 (b1.21)
Ridgeway Downs Racing (M Channon, West Ilsley).

Mary Read was ultra consistent last year, finishing placed in six out of eight starts. She also had a long season (started in April, finished in October). It's not easy for juveniles to handle the Goodwood track, but the first and second did well here. **Beckermet**, who was favourite, is better than this and didn't get the best of rides.

23 Veuve Clicquot Vintage Stakes (Group 2), (7f) Goodwood July 28 (Good)

1 **Shamardal** 8-11 J Fanning
2 **Wilko** 8-11 E Ahern
3 **Fox** 8-11 K Fallon
8-13f, 7-1, 10-1. 2½l, 1¼l. 10 ran. 1m 27.4 (b1.98)
Mr Abdulla BuHaleeba (M Johnston, Middleham)

Mark Johnston was winning this for the second consecutive year. Shamardal (now with Godolphin) was well-backed and for good reason. The race was won early on because the

THREE TO FOLLOW: Damson wins, from Oratorio and Russian Blue.

others could not keep tabs on the son of Giants Causeway. Wilko finished the best of the remainder and we know all about his exploits at the Breeders' Cup. Ultimately, the form is good and the horse probably exceptional. He will be very hard to beat in the 2,000 Guineas this year, if he contests it.

24 Richmond Stakes (Group 2), (6f) Goodwood July 30 (Good to Firm)

1 **Montgomery's Arch** 8-11 J Fortune
2 **Mystical Land** 8-11 L Dettori
3 **Silver Wraith** 8-11 J P Murtagh
13-2, 11-4, 9-1. nk, 2l. 8 ran. 1m 12.8 (a1.59)
Franconson Partners (P Chapple-Hyam, Newmarket).

Blue Dakota held the key to this race. Jeremy Noseda's Royal Ascot winner had shown blistering speed over 5f, but the step up to 6f had to be taken at some point. Looking for a five-timer he didn't convince over this distance and trailed home well-beaten. Montgomery's Arch got home by a neck from John Gosden's consistent two-year-old Mystical Land.

25 Irish Stud Farms EBF Premier Nursery Handicap, (7f) Galway July 31 (Good to Firm)

1 **Alayan** 9-5 M J Kinane
2 **Monashee Star** 8-13 F M Berry
3 **Tivoli Fountain** 8-10 J P Spencer
7-2f, 10-1, 9-2. 1l, 1l. 12 ran. 1m 28.9 (b5.93)
H H Aga Khan (J Oxx, IRELAND).

Alayan was quite well fancied in this competitive nursery and despite shouldering the top-weight, was sent off the favourite. Coming out of the John Oxx yard, this two-year-old has to be respected, but to be honest he didn't beat much. The Aidan O'Brien colt in third, Tivoli Fountain, hasn't won in seven attempts (including three maidens) which says something about the standard of opposition.

26 Porthault Shergar Cup Juvenile (Auction Race), (7f) Ascot August 7 (Good)

1 **Justaquestion** 8-10 L Dettori
2 **Beaver Patrol** 9-6 M J Kinane
3 **Lamh Eile** 8-7 D Vargiu
10-1, 14-1, 11-2. hd, nk. 10 ran. 1m 28.3 (b6.27)
Mr Christopher Shankland (I A Wood, Upper Lambourn).

Justaquestion is an admirable individual. She was ready to win a nice race at Glorious Goodwood but Kieren Fallon found enough traffic to prevent her. Frankie Dettori took the ride this time for this Shergar Cup event, and came with a powerful run to beat some nice juveniles. Upped in class after this, she struggled against tougher opponents, but should be followed this season, as should the second, Beaver Patrol.

27 Swynford Paddocks Hotel Sweet Solera Stakes (Fillies' Grp 3), (7f) Newmarket August 7 (Good to Firm)

1 **Maids Causeway** 8-8 S Drowne
2 **Slip Dance** 8-11 J F Egan
3 **Park Romance** 8-8 R L Moore
5-1, 10-1, 10-1. 1¼l, ½l. 11 ran. 1m 25.5 (b4.94)
Lady Richard Wellesley (B Hills, Lambourn).

Maids Causeway proved to be a consistent high-level performer and deserved this success. The Barry Hills' yard was somewhat disappointing for large amounts of the season, but if things can be turned around this year, this battle-hardened youngster will be interesting for the fillies races over a mile.

28 Independent Waterford Wedgwood Phoenix Stakes (Group 1), (6f) Curragh August 8 (Good to Firm)

1 **Damson** 8-11 K Fallon
2 **Oratorio** 9-0 J A Heffernan
3 **Russian Blue** 9-0 J P Spencer
8-11f, 15-2, 9-4. ¾l, ½l. 6 ran. 1m 13.2 (b2.89)
Mrs John Magnier (D Wachman, IRELAND).

An all-Irish event which featured some excellent two year-olds. It's always difficult to assess races that have minimal runners, but the winner looks smart and she didn't let a muddling pace get the better of her. The pair from the Aidan O'Brien stable had to take a back seat to this one.

29 Robert H. Griffin Debutante Stakes (Fillies Group 2), (7f) Curragh August 8 (Good to Firm)

1 **Silk And Scarlet** 8-11 J P Spencer
2 **Luas Line** 8-11 K Fallon
3 **Chelsea Rose** 8-11 P Shanahan
13-8f, 3-1, 7-2. ½l, 2l. 8 ran. 1m 25.4 (b3.59)
Mrs John Magnier (A P O'Brien, IRELAND).

Another group race at the Curragh, and the principles, trained by the 'biggest' trainers again came out best. O'Brien commented that Silk And Scarlet may be an Oaks filly, and being by Sadler's Wells, she should have no trouble with the Oaks trip. One to keep an eye on.

30 Weatherbys Stonehenge Stakes (Listed), (1m) Salisbury August 11 (Good to Firm)

1 **Perfectperformance** 8-11 L Dettori
2 **Grand Marque** 8-11 J Fortune

3 **Minnesota** 8-11 Dane O'Neill
4-5f, 13-8, 13-2. 3l, 5l. 3 ran. 1m 43.5 (b5.59)
Godolphin (S bin Suroor, Newmarket).

Not a race to get too excited about (as there were only three runners) but not for the first time Godolphin presented us with another juvenile with potential to go far. It's hard to place their good two year-olds in a particular pecking order. Related to Nijinsky, and a half-brother to Russian Rhythm, this one should be kept an eye on.

31 Scottish Equitable Gimcrack Stakes (Group 2), (6f) York August 18 (Soft)

1 **Tony James** 8-11 S Sanders
2 **Andronikos** 8-11 K Fallon
3 **Abraxas Antelope** 8-11 R Winston
16-1, 10-1, 10-3f. 1¼l, ½l. 11 ran. 1m 14.3 (b1.30)
Mr A J Richards (C Brittain, Newmarket).

There were some nice sorts on paper in this race. Namely Abraxas Antelope, trained by Howard Johnson and Mick Channon's **Turnkey**. Godolphin were also double-handed with **Crimson Sun** (8th) and **Council Member** (12th). However the ground was quite soft and as a result, there was a shock result, with the winner and runner-up returning double-figure odds.

32 Jaguar Lowther Stakes (Fillies' Group 2), (6f) York August 19 (Soft)

1 **Soar** 9-0 J Murtagh
2 **Salsa Brava** 8-11 K Fallon
3 **Spirit of Chester** 8-11 R Havlin
2-1f, 9-4, 16-1. 1½l, 1½l. 8 ran. 1m 15.9 (a0.30)
Cheveley Park Stud (J Fanshawe, Newmarket).

Royal Ascot winner, Soar, added this Group 2 to her collection with a convincing success. She was well-fancied to do well with the soft ground in her favour, and beat some useful fillies in the process. Even Michael Bell's charge, **Kissing Lights**, who finished last has performed creditably on the big stage in subsequent races. The same can be said of Salsa Brava (2nd) - who has solid form- and **Castelletto** (5th) who has won a Group 3.

33 Tattersalls Ireland Sale Stakes, (6f) Curragh August 21 (Good)

1 **Beaver Patrol** 8-12 M J Kinane
2 **Indesatchel** 8-12 J P Spencer
3 **Visionist** 8-12 P J Smullen
9-2, 6-4f, 11-2. 1l, 1l. 16 ran. 1m 12.8 (b3.29)
G C Stevens (R Johnson Houghton, Didcot).

Beaver Patrol has been runner-up to some respectable individuals; Blue Dakota at Windsor and Justaquestion at Ascot (26). But he gained his third and final victory of the season at the Curragh, despatching Indesatchel who had been running well in Ireland. Fulke Johnson Houghton ran his two-year-old ten times during the season, and it will be interesting to see if this has taken its toll.

34 Galileo EBF Futurity Stakes (Group 2), (7f) Curragh August 21 (Good)

1 **Oratorio** 9-0 J P Spencer
2 **Democratic Deficit** 9-4 M J Kinane
3 **Elusive Double** 9-0 P J Smullen
5-4f, 7-2, 13-2. 2l, 1l. 5 ran. 1m 25.7 (b3.29)
Mrs John Magnier (A P O'Brien, IRELAND).

Oratorio has improved as the season has progressed, but these small fields really don't tell us anything of great significance. The winner looks useful on this evidence, but the jury is still out on the also-rans.

35 Iveco Daily Solario Stakes (Group 3), (7f16yds) Sandown August 21 (Soft)

1 **Windsor Knot** 8-11 L Dettori
2 **Embossed** 8-11 R L Moore
3 **Propinquity** 8-11 D Holland
9-2, 14-1, 12-1. 2½l, nk. 8 ran. 1m 32.1 (b0.96)
Sheikh Mohammed (J Gosden, Manton).

John Gosden's lightly-raced juveniles are always interesting and on last season's evidence this one could come on for the experience. The Pivotal-colt impressed Frankie Dettori when he went past him at Newmarket (Dettori was on the second, Monsoon Rain), but he took the ride here and won comfortably, with a step up in trip looking like it could bring further improvement.

36 Irish Stallion Farms E.B.F. Premier Nursery, (1m) Tralee August 26 (Heavy)

1 **Crystal View** 8-12 C D Hayes (10)
2 **Imperial Rose** 8-8 R P Cleary (5)
3 **Falstaff** 9-5 J A Heffernan
10-1, 14-1, 2-1f. shd, nk. 12 ran. 1m 54.4 (a8.62)
Denis O'Flynn (K Prendergast, IRELAND).

A heavy ground nursery at Tralee is not the sort of race to make too many notes about. Just over a neck separated the first three and another Aidan O'Brien hotpot, Falstaff, was turned over.

37 Citroen C5 Prestige Stakes (Fillies' Group 3), (7f) Goodwood August 29 (Good to Soft)

1 **Dubai Surprise** 8-9 R L Moore
2 **Nanabanana** 8-9 K Darley

3 **Red Peony** 8-9 J Murtagh
16-1, 9-2, 3-1j. ½l, 3l. 12 ran. 1m 32.3 (a2.91)
Dr Ali Ridha (D Loder, Newmarket).

David Loder's youngsters had not been running as well as the previous year, which is probably why this one returned at 16-1.Goodwood's races cannot always be taken too literally as far as form is concerned, because the course has unusual slopes and turns. There was a strong pace set and the two who finished placed look to have a future at this level.

38 E.B.F./Irish Thoroughbred Dick Poole Fillies' Listed Stakes, (6f) Salisbury September 2 (Good)

1 **Suez** 8-9 P Robinson
2 **Castelletto** 8-9 G Gibbons
3 **Roodeye** 8-9 Martin Dwyer
8-11f, 28-1, 25-1. 2½l, 1l. 11 ran. 1m 13.5 (b5.32)
Sheikh Mohammed (M Jarvis, Newmarket).

Suez was again impressive and beat fillies with established form in the book. The big yards were all well represented, but none could handle the speed of Michael Jarvis' top two-year-old. She may well be switched to Godolphin at some point as she is owned by Sheikh Mohammed.

39 Pentax Sirenia Stakes (Group 3), (6f) Kempton September 4 (Good to Firm)

1 **Satchem** 8-11 K Fallon
2 **Council Member** 8-11 L Dettori
3 **Visionist** 8-11 J Fortune
3-1, 15-8f, 7-1. 1½l, 1½l. 8 ran. 1m 10.9 (b7.31)
Sheikh Hamdan Bin Mohammed Al Maktoum (C Brittain, Newmarket).

The time of the race was a little quicker than standard and was won nicely by Clive Brittain's colt who had looked decent when winning at Newmarket previously. Terry Mills' **Tremar** could be the one to take out of the race - he prefers a softer surface but still ran admirably. Look out for him this year when given an easier assignment.

40 Go And Go Round Tower Stakes (Group 3), (6f) Curragh September 5 (Good to Firm)

1 **Cherokee** 8-11 J P Spencer
2 **Lock And Key** 8-11 Catherine Gannon
3 **Indesatchel** 9-0 M J Kinane
5-2, 10-1, 2-1f. shd, 1½l. 11 ran. 1m 12.1 (b3.99)
Mrs John Magnier (A P O'Brien, IRELAND).

Cherokee made her debut a winning one, despite breaking slowly from the stalls. Aidan O'Brien seems to be producing his better two-year-olds quite late in the season. He has high expectations for this one, so we'll have to wait and see what comes his way this year.

41 Moyglare Stud Stakes (Fillies Group 1), (7f) Curragh September 5 (Good to Firm)

1 **Chelsea Rose** 8-11 P Shanahan
2 **Pictavia** 8-11 K J Manning
3 **Saoire** 8-11 P J Smullen
9-1, 8-1, 6-1. ¾l, ¾l. 12 ran. 1m 24.2

A SERIOUS FILLY: Soar wins her second Group race in the space of four weeks

(b4.79)
Mrs A J Donnelly (C Collins, IRELAND).

A Group 1 by name but not by standard. The two at the head of the market, **Silk And Scarlet** (7th) and Royal Ascot winner, **Jewel In The Sand** (11th), disappointed, which left the race wide open. If you ran this race ten times, there would probably be a different result each time.

42 E.B.F. Carrie Red Fillies' Nursery Handicap, (6f110yds) Doncaster September 8 (Good)

1 **Swan Nebula** 8-13 L Dettori
2 **Indiena** 8-5 C Catlin
3 **Bibury Flyer** 8-13 T E Durcan
4 **Dance Flower** 8-8 A Culhane
5-1, 16-1, 20-1, 12-1. 1¾l, hd, 1l. 21 ran. 1m 18.0 (b6.29)
Godolphin (S bin Suroor, Newmarket).

Godolphin rarely run their horses in handicaps and nurseries, so it was a tip in itself when it was declared for the first race of the St Leger festival. The winning time was also quick suggesting that we should keep on the right side of the first four, who all performed well.

43 200000 St Leger Yearling Stakes, (6f) Doncaster September 8 (Good)

1 **Caesar Beware** 8-11 Dane O'Neill
2 **Distinctly Game** 8-11 N Callan
3 **Moscow Music** 8-11 R Hughes
13-8f, 25-1, 33-1. 2l, 1½l. 22 ran. 1m 9.6 (b9.08)
Mill House Partnership (H Candy, Wantage)

Henry Candy is a master at producing speedy youngsters (Airwave last year), and Caesar Beware took his place here in what would normally be a competitive event. He was sent off 13-8 despite the 22 runner field, but with two easy wins in the book he was completely unexposed and won in emphatic style. It was unfortunate for the rest, that the winner was so good. Others to take out of the race are **Dance Night**, who is served better by softer ground and **Josh** who by all accounts needs further.

44 Betfair.com May Hill Stakes (Fillies' Group 2), (1m) Doncaster September 9 (Good)

1 **Playful Act** 8-10 J Fortune
2 **Queen of Poland** 8-10 T P Queally
3 **Maids Causeway** 8-13 M Hills
8-1, 11-4f, 9-2. ¾l, shd. 8 ran. 1m 35.4 (b12.44)
Sangster Family (J Gosden, Manton).

This was a very impressive performance by Playful Act. She is a half-sister to Echoes in Eternity and Percussionist, and looks to be one for the short-list this year. A step up in distance beckons for this daughter of Sadler's Wells, which should show her in an even better light.

45 DBS St Leger Yearling Stakes, (6f) Doncaster September 10 (Good to Firm)

1 **Tagula Sunrise** 8-6 P Hanagan
2 **Royal Orissa** 8-11 L Dettori
3 **My Gacho** 8-11 R Havlin
8-1, 14-1, 33-1. nk, shd. 21 ran. 1m 11.9 (b6.81)
Mr David M Knaggs & Mel Roberts (R Fahey, Malton).

This is the poorer relation of the two "Yearling Sales" races and was a more competitive event. There were many bunched together on the rails and hard-luck-stories a plenty by the end. A length separated the first three home and it is unlikely that many will be contesting the top races this year.

46 SGB Champagne Stakes (Group 2), (7f) Doncaster September 10 (Good to Firm)

1 **Etlaala** 8-10 R Hills
2 **Iceman** 9-1 K Fallon
3 **Oude** 8-10 L Dettori
6-1, 5-2j, 5-2j. ½l, 2½l. 10 ran. 1m 23.3 (b9.49)
Mr Hamdan Al Maktoum (B Hills, Lambourn)

Etlaala was very impressive here, quickening up off what was already a searching pace. Iceman had the stands rail to help but the winner did it the hard way, coming past them on the far side, having encountered traffic problems.This son of Selkirk is a smart prospect, and this effort is all the better considering the stable was out of form for most of the season. Our expert at Lambourn expects him to go great guns this year.

47 Polypipe Flying Childers Stakes (Group 2), (5f) Doncaster September 11 (Good to Firm)

1 **Chateau Istana** 8-12 S Sanders
2 **Tournedos** 9-1 T Quinn
3 **Kissing Lights** 8-9 D Holland
11-1, 11-2, 20-1. 2l, ¾l. 11 ran. 1m 0.4 (b5.09)
Mr Ivan Allan (N Littmoden, Newmarket).

Chateau Istana gained her third victory adding to her Listed success at Ascot. The race looks quite strong (**Beckermet** who has good form finished last) but it is debatable whether any have superstar status.

48 Irish Stallion Farms EBF Premier Nursery Handicap, (7f) Leopardstown September 11 (Good to Firm)

1 **Kestrel Cross** 8-11 C P Geoghegan (7)

2 **Lord Nelson** 8-0 W M Lordan
3 **Alayan** 9-7 M J Kinane
9-2, 7-1, 9-4f. ½l, shd. 6 ran. 1m 30.7 (b2.22)
Norman Ormiston (K Prendergast, IRELAND).

With some good prize-money on offer one might expect a better turnout, especially as it's a nursery. About the only point of note was the third win on the spin for Kevin Prendergast's colt who appears to be progressing nicely.

49 Aon Consulting Harry Rosebery Stakes (Listed), (5f) Ayr September 17 (Soft)

1 **Prince Charming** 8-11 J Fanning
2 **Mary Read** 8-9 F Lynch
3 **Dance Night** 9-2 G Gibbons
6-1, 10-1, 6-1. 1l, 2l. 12 ran. 1m 0.9 (a0.85)
Sheikh Mohammed (J Gosden, Manton).

Another second for Mary Read, whose middle name surely is consistency. There were some good performers in the field; Dance Night and **Beckermet** who have already been mentioned. I expect one or two of these in the field to step up a notch this year.

50 TSG Firth Of Clyde Stakes (Group 3), (6f) Ayr September 18 (Soft)

1 **Golden Legacy** 8-8 P Hanagan
2 **Nufoos** 8-8 W Supple
3 **Castelletto** 8-8 G Gibbons
7-1, 13-2, 15-8f. nk, ¾l. 9 ran. 1m 17.4 (a3.38)
Mr P N Devlin (R Fahey, Malton).

Godolphin's **Swan Nebula** was impressive on his latest start, but was probably none too keen on the soft ground here. The three that pulled away were only separated by a length and may go on to better things this season.

51 Watership Down Stud Sales Race (Fillies), (6f110yds) Newbury September 18 (Good)

1 **Salamanca** 8-9 L Dettori
2 **Arabian Dancer** 7-12 C Catlin
3 **Umniya** 8-8 T Quinn
5-1f, 13-2, 8-1. shd, shd. 26 ran. 1m 20.1
Wood Street Syndicate (S Kirk, Upper Lambourn)

A huge field, and the favourite with Frankie Dettori on board, obliged for favourite backers. Mick Channon was desperately unlucky, he fielded four runners and they filled the next four places. Five in the race went off at odds of 100-1, while those drawn high benefited from an advantageous stalls position. There is always good prize money on offer for these sales events, but they are not the best form guides.

52 Dubai Duty Free Mill Reef Stakes (Group 2), (6f8yds) Newbury September 18 (Good to Soft)

1 **Galeota** 8-12 R L Moore
2 **Mystical Land** 8-12 L Dettori
3 **Rebuttal** 8-12 J Fortune
7-1, 10-3, 8-1. 1l, shd. 9 ran. 1m 13.8 (b3.18)
Mr J A Lazzari (R Hannon, Marlborough).

The *Racing Post* analysis of the race said that this was a weak Group 2. I would disagree with that, given hindsight. A handful of the runners had excellent form (including Mystical Land) and the time of the race was only a second slower than standard on softish ground. Galeota is probably Richard Hannon's best two-year-old and he looks capable of performing at the highest level this year.

53 Dunnes Stores National Stakes (Group 1), (7f) Curragh September 19 (Good)

1 **Dubawi** 9-0 L Dettori
2 **Berenson** 9-0 W M Lordan
3 **Russian Blue** 9-0 J P Spencer
8-13f, 12-1, 5-1. 3l, 1½l. 7 ran. 1m 24.8 (b4.19)
Godolphin (S Suroor).

Normally a very informative race for this year's top prizes and frequently won by Aidan O'Brien. Not this year however, as Godolphin sent Dubawi across the water to stamp his authority on this year's two-year-old division. His price was skinny but he won well and now heads the ante-post market for the Derby.

54 St. Bernard Blenheim Stakes (Listed), (6f) Curragh September 19 (Good)

1 **Ad Valorem** 9-0 J P Spencer
2 **Indesatchel** 9-0 M J Kinane
3 **Cupid's Glory** 9-0 D P McDonogh
9-4j, 9-4j, 5-2. 1l, ½l. 6 ran. 1m 13.9 (b2.19)
Mrs John Magnier (A P O'Brien, IRELAND).

The form of this race was boosted when Cupid's Glory won the Horris Hill Stakes at Newbury (77). He won on that occasion in convincing fashion. Ad Valorem his conqueror in this Listed event is held in high regard by his trainer, and, if the stable starts to dominate again, this one should lead the way.

55 Irish Breeders Foal Levy Stakes, (6f63yds) Curragh September 19 (Good)

1 **Slip Dance** 8-10 J F Egan
2 **All Night Dancer** 8-4 W M Lordan
3 **Makuti** 8-4 N G McCullagh
11-4, 14-1, 14-1. 2l, ¾l. 10 ran. 1m 18.4 (b1.81)
M McLoughlin (E Tyrrell, IRELAND).

Another tricky race to consider, but its relevance in terms of form questionable. The ground was described as yielding, the time was slow, and the winner came away to win by 2l. Slip Dance, already a Listed winner and runner-up in a Group 1, looks decent, while those behind have average form in relation to what we consider to be useful for this new season.

56 Irish Stallion Farms EBF Premier Nursery Handicap, (1m) Listowel September 20 (Good to Soft)

1 **Crystal View** 9-7 C D Hayes (7)
2 **Brogue Lanterns** 9-5C P Geoghegan (7)
3 **Lord Nelson** 9-6 J P Spencer
7-1, 11-1, 9-2. 4½l, 1½l. 14 ran. 1m 49.7 (a3.44)
Denis O'Flynn (K Prendergast, IRELAND).

Not the strongest race to evaluate. But the point to reflect on is the manner in which the winner came away to win after such a bad start, that confirms her as useful.

57 Hackney Empire Royal Lodge Stakes (Group 2), (1m) Ascot September 25 (Good to Firm)

1 **Perfectperformance** 8-11 L Dettori
2 **Scandinavia** 8-11 J P Spencer
3 **Wilko** 8-11 E Ahern
4-6f, 8-1, 7-1. 1½l, 1¼l. 8 ran. 1m 41.9 (b5.39)
Godolphin (S bin Suroor, Newmarket).

Perfectperformance looked short enough in terms of price at the off, but won all the same. He is beautifully bred - by Rahy and related to Russian Rhythm - and made it three wins from four, edging out some good performers. Sixth placed **Kandidate**, came out and beat some of the best All-Weather performers in February and has been running well in Dubai.

58 Meon Valley Stud Fillies' Mile (Group 1), (1m) Ascot September 25 (Good to Firm)

1 **Playful Act** 8-10 J Fortune
2 **Maids Causeway** 8-10 M Hills
3 **Dash To The Top** 8-10 D Holland
11-4, 7-1, 16-1. 1l, ¾l. 9 ran. 1m 42.2 (b5.06)
Sangster Family (J Gosden, Manton).

Playful Act is beginning to thrive on her racing and is getting to know her job. By taking this Group 1 she has rewarded her trainer who has thought a lot of her - the win would have delighted the late Robert Sangster. Whatever she wins this season will be a bonus. Apart from Maids Causeway, the others are very lightly-raced, so keep an eye out for them, especially Sir Michael Stoute's **Shohrah**, Mick Channon's **Joint Aspiration** and Luca Cumani's **Dash To The Top**.

59 El Gran Senor Stakes (Listed), (7f) Fairyhouse September 29 (Good to Soft)

1 **Gaff** 9-0 P J Smullen
2 **Zelkova** 9-0 F M Berry
3 **Ridder** 9-0 J A Heffernan
6-1, 4-1, 20-1. ½l, shd. 7 ran. 1m 30.0 (a0.78)
Ludolph Heiligbrodt (D Weld, IRELAND).

Gaff's path to the winning post was not a straight-forward one, but he overcame trouble to win. There was not a lot to separate the field and the form has been franked since.

60 Sky Bet Cheveley Park Stakes (Group 1), (6f) Newmarket September 30 (Good to Firm)

1 **Magical Romance** 8-11 R Winston
2 **Suez** 8-11 P Robinson
3 **Damson** 8-11 K Fallon
40-1, 4-1, 10-11f. nk, nk. 7 ran. 1m 12.6 (b2.45)
Mr F C T Wilson (B Meehan, Upper Lambourn).

The highlight of the two-year-old calendar for fillies, and the rain came in time to scupper the chances of the fancied runners. Magical Romance showed that a rain-softened surface was to her liking and she won in a tight finish. Suez and Damson look to have good futures, with the latter sure to be suited by a step up to a mile. **Slip Dance**, in fifth, looked very unlucky as she was repeatedly denied room close home.

61 Somerville Tattersall Stakes (Group 3), (7f) Newmarket September 30 (Good to Firm)

1 **Diktatorial** 8-9 Martin Dwyer
2 **Crimson Sun** 8-9 R Hills
3 **Mister Genepi** 8-9 P Hanagan
3-1, 12-1, 33-1. nk, shd. 9 ran. 1m 26.0 (b5.21)
Tweenhills Thurloe (A Balding, Kingsclere).

A few winners went to post, but not a race one could pick a "Classic" contender from. The meeting on the whole was noted for its sticky ground and jockey's undecided about which parts of the straight were riding quickest.

62 Shadwell Stud Middle Park Stakes (Group 1), (6f) Newmarket October 1 (Good)

1 **Ad Valorem** 8-11 J P Spencer
2 **Rebuttal** 8-11 P J Smullen
3 **Iceman** 8-11 K Fallon
9-2, 9-1, 9-4f. ¾l, 2½l. 9 ran. 1m 12.2 (b2.87)
Mrs John Magnier (A P O'Brien, IRELAND).

Ad Valorem clearly has ability, but it is questionable whether he will step up from 6f, as, by Danzig he does have strong sprinting lines. Corals made him 14-1 for the Guineas after this performance. Take nothing away from Rebuttal who ran a game race, or Iceman, who maintained his form well despite a long season.

63 C.L.Weld Park Stakes (Group 3), (7f) Curragh October 2 (Good to Soft)

1 **Jazz Princess** 8-11 N G McCullagh
2 **Saoire** 8-11 M J Kinane
3 **Virginia Waters** 8-11 J A Heffernan
12-1, 10-3, 5-1. 3l, 1½l. 9 ran. 1m 26.7 (b2.29)
T Curran (Mrs J Harrington, IRELAND).

Jessica Harrington doesn't have many Flat performers, but Jazz Princess won well, with daylight to spare. Of the nine runners, only two were sent off at a bigger price, which was a surprise considering Jazz Princess had won her previous two contests and looked to be improving. She could be a 1,000 Guineas contender, and it will be interesting to see how the trainer of Moscow Flyer places this one.

64 E.B.F. Jersey Lily Fillies' Nursery Handicap, (7f) Newmarket October 2 (Good)

1 **Wedding Party** 9-5 J Murtagh
2 **Love Affair** 8-11 K Darley
3 **Catch A Star** 9-6 N Mackay (3)
4 **Musical Day** 9-4 S Sanders
9-1, 20-1, 7-1, 25-1. 1¾l, shd, hd. 16 ran. 1m 27.2 (b4.03)
Cheveley Park Stud (Mrs A Perrett, Pulborough)

A very competitive affair, and in essence a race for trainers and owners to get their hands on some good prize money. Unsurprisingly the race was a touch slow, the reason being the ground conditions (on the soft side). There could be better to come from Richard Hannon's **Godsend** (8th) and Neville Callaghan's Catch A Star when stepped up in trip.

65 Betfair.com Two-year-old Trophy (Listed), (6f) Redcar October 2 (Good to Firm)

1 **Obe Gold** 8-3 C Catlin
2 **Caesar Beware** 8-9 Dane O'Neill
3 **Dario Gee Gee** 8-7 N Callan
15-2, 4-7f, 33-1. 1l, 1½l. 24 ran. 1m 8.8 (b4.96)
BDR Partnership (M Channon, West Ilsley).

Mick Channon is not afraid to run his horses often and Obe Gold gained due reward. It is always hard for youngsters who had a hard campaign at two, to reproduce their form the following season. Thus it may be best to concentrate on the second home, Caesar Beware, for future reference.

66 Danehill Dancer Tipperary Stakes (Listed), (5f) Tipperary October 3 (Heavy)

1 **Kay Two** 9-0 D P McDonogh
2 **Tournedos** 9-7 S Hitchcott
3 **Dancing Duchess** 8-11 C O'Donoghue
3-1f, 4-1, 6-1. 2l, hd. 9 ran. 1m 3.4 (a3.78)
Hugh B McGahon (Ms F M Crowley, IRELAND).

Kay Two has not been disgraced against some higher class individuals and duly claimed this Listed contest as his form entitled him to. The remainder were quite well strung out, although Tournedos again ran well.

67 Irish Stallion Farms EBF Premier Nursery, (1m) Gowran Park October 7 (Good to Soft)

1 **Lough Gem** 8-0 R P Cleary (5)
2 **Sky High Flyer** 8-8 T P O'Shea
3 **Full Victory** 8-8 J A Heffernan
4 **Starling** 8-2 M C Hussey (3)
14-1, 4-1f, 14-1, 20-1. ½l, 1½l, ¾l. 16 ran. 1m 43.3 (a1.91)
Lough Gem Syndicate (Ms J Morgan, IRELAND).

Joanna Morgan is only a small-time trainer but trumped some of the glitzy yards. Lough Gem was to win four races for the County Meath trainer during the season.

68 Juddmonte Beresford Stakes (Group 2), (1m) Curragh October 10 (Good to Soft)

1 **Albert Hall** 9-0 J P Spencer
2 **Merger** 9-0 P J Smullen
3 **Sant Jordi** 9-0 M J Kinane
4-5f, 9-2, 16-1. ½l, 4½l. 5 ran. 1m 43.8 (b0.75)
Mrs John Magnier (A P O'Brien, IRELAND).

Albert Hall was turned over at short odds-on on his debut, but made amends here. He is clearly well-thought of at home but didn't look a world-beater on this occasion either. Time will tell if he has Classic potential.

69 Flame Of Tara E.B.F. Stakes (Listed), (6f) Curragh October 10 (Good to Soft)

1 **Bibury Flyer** 8-11 A Culhane
2 **Virginia Waters** 8-11 J P Spencer
3 **Gouache** 8-11 D P McDonogh
12-1, 9-4, 20-1. ½l, 4½l. 10 ran. 1m 17.3 (a1.21)
Ridgeway Downs Racing (M Channon, West Ilsley).

Bibury Flyer was kept very busy last season running 22 times in total, and he's kicked off this campaign already by running at Nad Al Sheba. The home contingent had some decent sorts in the race but only Virginia Waters could keep tabs on the winner.

70 **100000 Tattersalls Autumn Auction Stakes, (6f) Newmarket October 14 (Soft)**

1 **Cape Columbine** 8-8 T Quinn
2 **Obe Gold** 9-5 A Culhane
3 **Gifted Gamble** 8-9 N Callan
5-1j, 5-1j, 14-1. 2l, shd. 29 ran. 1m 13.8 (b1.30)
Mrs R F Lowe (D Elsworth, Whitsbury).

A huge field, but quite a few 100-1 shots on the card. Many had form in the book, but Cape Columbine was still able to put sufficient daylight between herself and the field. We already know about some of the others who are more exposed (Obe Gold for example) so we should concentrate on the winner, who is very lightly-raced, and showed a high-level of performance on only her second visit to the racecourse. It will be interesting to see what races David Elsworth aims her at this year, although she might continue to race over 6f.

71 **Cornwallis Stakes (Group 3), (5f) Newmarket October 16 (Soft)**

1 **Castelletto** 8-9 G Gibbons
2 **Cornus** 8-12 R L Moore
3 **Kay Two** 9-1 M J Kinane
15-2, 12-1, 5-1. ¾l, 1¼l. 11 ran. 1m 1.8 (a0.29)
Mr J C Fretwell (B McMahon, Tamworth).

Bryan McMahon's horses have a knack of going well in soft conditions. His son, Ed, is taking over the yard this year and Castelletto should provide him with some fun, now she has a Group race under her belt. Most of the others were quite disappointing including **Prince Charming** who had contested the Middle Park Stakes.

72 **Owen Brown Rockfel Stakes (Fillies' Group 2), (7f) Newmarket October 16 (Soft)**

1 **Maids Causeway** 8-12 M Hills
2 **Penkenna Princess** 8-9 S Sanders
3 **Favourita** 8-9 T Quinn
3-1f, 7-1, 7-1. shd, ¾l. 8 ran. 1m 28.9 (b2.28)
Mr Martin S Schwartz (B Hills, Lambourn).

Maids Causeway continues to run well at this level and deservedly gained another success. The "never say die" attitude that marked her sire (Giants Causeway) has clearly rubbed off on her. It wasn't a great renewal of the Rockfel all the same and she would be the only filly to take out of the race when considering this year's 1,000 Guineas.

73 **Darley Dewhurst Stakes (Group 1), (7f) Newmarket October 16 (Soft)**

1 **Shamardal** 9-0 K Darley
2 **Oratorio** 9-0 J P Spencer
3 **Montgomery's Arch** 9-0 M J Kinane
9-2, 15-2, 10-1. 2½l, nk. 9 ran. 1m 27.2 (b4.05)
Gainsborough Stud (M Johnston, Middleham)

Shamardal produced arguably the two best performances by a two year-old in 2004. We have already noted how easily he beat the Breeders' Cup Juvenile winner, Wilko at Goodwood (23), but he bettered that with a superb exhibition at HQ in the Dewhurst. Strangely not the favourite on the day, he was soon propelled to the top of the ante-post market for the first classic in 2005 after seeing off what was supposedly a strong field. Now with Godolphin, there has been talk of him tackling the US Triple Crown. Oratorio ran a game race in second, but the winner was different gear.

74 **Derrinstown Stud EBF Birdcatcher Premier Nursery, (6f) Naas October 17 (Good to Soft)**

1 **Dark Cheetah** 9-7 J P Spencer
2 **Dipterous** 8-0 T P O'Shea
3 **Cairlinn** 8-6 M J Kinane
5-1, 16-1, 3-1f. 2½l, ½l. 13 ran. 1m 12.8 (a0.13)
Mrs John Magnier (A P O'Brien, IRELAND).

Aidan O'Brien's string are saving their best for late on in the season. Dark Cheetah improved on his previous run and returned a good speed figure. There were some promising youngsters in behind, and we should keep an eye on Dipterous who ran well from out of the handicap.

75 **Totesport Silver Tankard Stakes (Listed), (1m4yds) Pontefract October 18 (Good)**

1 **Comic Strip** 8-11 S Sanders
2 **Wise Dennis** 8-11 K Darley
3 **Haunting Memories** 8-11 P Robinson
4-5f, 14-1, 10-1. 3½l, 4l. 9 ran. 1m 46.5 (b2.60)
Neil Greig - Osborne House (Sir M Prescott, Newmarket).

Sir Mark Prescott's charge made it five wins from six starts and handed out a good beating in the process to nine previous winners. The Newmarket trainer will surely place this one expertly with a big handicap in mind this season.

76 **DBS October Yearling Stakes, (6f) Doncaster October 22 (Soft)**

1 **Pivotal Flame** 8-11 G Carter
2 **Hidden Jewel** 8-11 G Gibbons
3 **Dispol Isle** 8-6 K Darley
6-4f, 100-1, 50-1. hd, 1½l. 21 ran. 1m 17.9 (b0.80)

Mr R L Bedding (B McMahon, Tamworth).

Bryan McMahon trains the first and second (6-4 and 100-1 respectively) and regards the winner as a good prospect for this coming season. 13 of the 21 runners were priced at 50-1 or bigger, so there may not have been much strength in depth to the race.

77 **Stan James Horris Hill Stakes (Group 3), (7f) Newbury October 22 (Soft)**

1 **Cupid's Glory** 8-9 S Sanders
2 **Johnny Jumpup** 8-9 J F Egan
3 **King Marju** 8-9 T Quinn
2-1f, 12-1, 11-1. 4l, 2½l. 13 ran. 1m 29.0 (b1.98)

Hesmonds Stud (Sir M Prescott, Newmarket).

Another progressive youngster trained by Prescott and this was a bloodless victory. He went on to race at Saint-Cloud after this, and the handler may well decide to place him in a few more across the Channel. King Marju (3rd) and **Brecon Beacon** (4th) look to have good futures and more can be expected from them.

78 **Gerrardstown House Stud Silken Glider Stks (Fillies Listed), (1m) Curragh October 23 (Soft)**

1 **Allexina** 8-11 F M Berry
2 **Adaala** 8-11 D P McDonogh
3 **Alexander Icequeen** 8-11 P J Smullen
14-1, 9-2j, 6-1. 2l, 3½l. 13 ran. 1m 48.5 (a3.95)

J Higgins (J Oxx, IRELAND).

Allexina, a lightly-raced filly by Barathea took advantage of a falsely-run race. John Oxx's first-string could only manage tenth, while the other joint favourite, Adaala, finished second. It may be wise to watch these when they return before any punting money is parted with.

79 **Racing Post Trophy (Group 1), (1m) Doncaster October 23 (Soft)**

1 **Motivator** 9-0 K Fallon
2 **Albert Hall** 9-0 J P Spencer
3 **Henrik** 9-0 T E Durcan
6-4f, 5-2, 12-1. 2½l, 1l. 8 ran. 1m 42.6 (b5.22)

The Royal Ascot Racing Club (M Bell, Newmarket).

On only his second lifetime start, Motivator gave a performance which suggests he can go well in this year's Derby. Michael Bell, who is an excellent trainer of two year-olds, picked Kieren Fallon to ride in what looked a weak renewal. However, the Racing Post Trophy is a reliable race when pinpointing Epsom contenders. Aidan O'Brien has an incredible record, having trained the winner and runner-up in three of the last six renewals. Albert Hall doesn't look up to the standard to win a Derby, nor do those who finished behind him, including Henrik, supposedly the best of a weak bunch of Channon two-year-olds in 2004.

80 **Killavullan Stakes (Group 3), (7f) Leopardstown October 25 (Soft)**

1 **Footstepsinthesand** 9-0 J P Spencer
2 **Gaff** 9-0 P J Smullen
3 **Clash Of The Ash** 9-0 K J Manning
4-5f, 10-3, 12-1. 2l, 7l. 6 ran. 1m 32.9 (b0.02)

Michael Tabor (A P O'Brien, IRELAND).

Footstepsinthesand should have a big year. The money was down when he won his maiden and the bookies were taken to the cleaners, expecting him to be the second string on the day. Giant's Causeway's progeny have shown progression and durability in 2004 and Aidan O'Brien will be doing his best to see that this one can show his best in the 2,000 Guineas.

81 **E.B.F. Bosra Sham Fillies' Stakes (Listed), (6f) Newmarket October 29 (Soft)**

1 **Bahia Breeze** 8-8 C Catlin
2 **Nanabanana** 8-8 K Darley
3 **Siena Gold** 8-8 J Fortune
11-1, 4-5f, 11-1. hd, ¾l. 8 ran. 1m 16.4 (a1.35)

Mr F Nowell (R Guest, Newmarket).

Jeremy Noseda's **Bibury Flyer** (finished last) was disappointing having shown form in group and listed contests. Most of these were tightly matched and we weren't expecting to see a superstar so late in the season.

82 **Irish Stallion Farms EBF Premier Nursery Handicap, (7f) Leopardstown October 31 (Heavy)**

1 **Lough Gem** 9-6 R P Cleary (5)
2 **All Woman** 8-5 T P O'Shea
3 **Dipterous** 8-12 J P Spencer
4 **Fuerta Ventura** 8-13 D P McDonogh
11-2, 12-1, 7-1, 25-1. hd, 2l, ¾l. 16 ran. 1m 34.8 (a1.88)

Lough Gem Syndicate (Ms J Morgan, IRELAND).

Lough Gem was noted before in race 67 and has now racked up four handicap wins. A great achievement, but the handicapper may not be kind and he may be hard to place this year.

83 **Eyrefield Stakes (Listed), (1m1f) Leopardstown October 31 (Heavy)**

1 **Yehudi** 9-0 J P Spencer
2 **Imperial Brief** 9-0 D P McDonogh
3 **In The Ribbons** 8-11 D M Grant
7-4j, 7-4j, 33-1. 3l, 2½l. 9 ran. 2m 2.2 (a3.31)

Mrs John Magnier (A P O'Brien, IRELAND).

Aidan O'Brien is definitely saving his best

Two-year-olds index

All horses placed or commented on in our two-year-old review section, with race numbers

Trainer Statistics

DARASIM: Usually guaranteed to contribute to the Johnston numerical tally through the year

Mark Johnston

Carlisle, Musselburgh and Newmarket are three tracks where Mark Johnston shows a very healthy level-stakes profit. Surprisingly, at Ascot, only 10% of his runners are successful, which seems low bearing in mind the success he has enjoyed at the Royal fixture.

In numerical terms, Joe Fanning rides the majority of Johnston winners, but it is Richard Hills who is the most profitable - the pair teamed up with Bandari last season to win the Princess Of Wales's Stakes at Newmarket.

By month

2004

	Overall			Two-year-olds			Three-year-olds			Older horses		
	W-R	%	£1	W-R	%	£1	W-R	%	£1	W-R	%	£1
January	1-5	20	-2.50	0-0		0.00	1-4	25	-1.50	0-1		-1.00
February	1-10	10	-6.00	0-0		0.00	1-6	16	-2.00	0-4		-4.00
March	4-21	19	-9.47	0-0		0.00	4-15	26	-3.47	0-6		-6.00
April	11-74	14	-11.96	2-7	28	-0.64	4-40	10	-21.05	5-27	18	+9.73
May	21-112	18	-22.62	6-19	31	+5.50	12-61	19	-9.46	3-32	9	-18.67
June	17-126	13	-22.51	4-36	11	-26.01	9-60	15	-21.50	4-30	13	+25.00
July	21-125	16	+8.90	9-39	23	+24.75	7-55	12	-13.56	5-31	16	-2.29
August	11-82	13	-35.22	8-36	22	-11.72	3-29	10	-6.50	0-17		-17.00
September	13-107	12	-46.34	9-56	16	-29.09	4-30	13	+3.75	0-21		-21.00
October	14-100	14	-3.28	7-61	11	-18.00	6-28	21	+8.72	1-11	9	+6.00
November	5-28	17	+3.25	3-18	16	+5.00	2-6	33	+2.25	0-4		-4.00
December	0-9		-9.00	0-7		-7.00	0-2		-2.00	0-0		0.00

2003

	Overall			Two-year-olds			Three-year-olds			Older horses		
	W-R	%	£1	W-R	%	£1	W-R	%	£1	W-R	%	£1
January	3-16	18	+0.41	0-0			2-12	16	-0.09	1-4	25	+0.50
February	3-16	18	-9.10	0-0			3-15	20	-8.10	0-1		-1.00
March	1-22	4	-10.00	0-0			0-14		-14.00	1-8	12	+4.00
April	12-57	21	+27.12	2-7	28	-1.83	8-34	23	+30.85	2-16	12	-1.90
May	25-135	18	-13.41	9-22	40	-0.35	14-87	16	-1.05	2-26	7	-12.00
June	29-137	21	-15.61	13-34	38	+12.11	13-59	22	+1.24	3-44	6	-28.96
July	28-113	24	+45.97	8-27	29	-7.49	15-59	25	+32.46	5-27	18	+21.00
August	16-102	15	-13.37	6-33	18	-8.55	9-49	18	+13.35	1-20	5	-18.17
September	14-84	16	-13.41	10-45	22	-5.01	3-28	10	+0.50	1-11	9	-8.90
October	7-53	13	+4.13	6-38	15	+6.13	0-10		-10.00	1-5	20	+8.00
November	2-24	8	-7.00	1-17	5	-9.00	0-5		-5.00	1-2	50	+7.00
December	0-3		-3.00	0-3		-3.00	0-0			0-0		

2002

	Overall			Two-year-olds			Three-year-olds			Older horses		
	W-R	%	£1	W-R	%	£1	W-R	%	£1	W-R	%	£1
January	4-28	14	-17.89	0-0			3-20	15	-12.89	1-8	12	-5.00
February	3-15	20	-2.30	0-0			3-12	25	+0.70	0-3		-3.00
March	8-21	38	+8.43	0-0			6-16	37	+9.14	2-5	40	-0.70
April	9-43	20	-10.86	0-1		-1.00	6-30	20	-15.36	3-12	25	+5.50
May	19-109	17	-9.05	8-21	38	+12.82	8-66	12	-6.75	3-22	13	-15.13
June	19-121	15	+6.47	4-22	18	+11.63	12-66	18	-9.55	3-33	9	+4.40
July	25-110	22	-0.96	7-30	23	+3.97	11-56	19	-16.68	7-24	29	+11.75
August	16-103	15	-19.01	3-32	9	-16.50	9-49	18	-10.14	4-22	18	+7.63
September	18-81	22	+5.39	4-38	10	-18.59	9-26	34	+18.25	5-17	29	+5.73
October	8-65	12	-22.28	1-28	3	-22.00	4-24	16	+0.62	3-13	23	-0.90
November	4-43	9	-7.50	2-25	8	-18.50	1-9	11	-1.00	1-9	11	+12.00
December	2-15	13	-6.25	2-12	16	-3.25	0-2		-2.00	0-1		-1.00

All runners

2004	Wins	Runs	%	2nd	3rd	rest	Win prize	Total prize	£1 Stake
2yo	48	279	17	49	21	33	457,837.70	596,500.95	-57.20
3yo	53	336	16	43	40	24	840,950.99	1,138,060.55	-66.31
4yo+	18	184	10	19	16	15	428,147.90	703,101.15	-33.23
TOTAL	119	799	15	111	77	72	1,726,936.59	2,437,662.65	-156.74

2003	Wins	Runs	%	2nd	3rd	rest	Win prize	Total prize	£1 Stake
2yo	54	223	24	34	19	20	551,614.84	654,310.17	-16.26
3yo	67	372	18	57	34	23	544,026.44	806,894.87	+40.17
4yo+	18	163	11	14	19	21	315,131.50	581,586.39	-29.42
TOTAL	139	758	18	105	72	64	1,410,772.78	2,042,791.43	-5.51

2002	Wins	Runs	%	2nd	3rd	rest	Win prize	Total prize	£1 Stake
2yo	31	208	15	31	32	22	194,065.40	309,170.75	-50.42
3yo	72	375	19	49	42	37	775,035.38	1,026,254.58	-44.64
4yo+	31	165	19	20	21	8	668,635.57	964,406.04	+20.77
TOTAL	134	748	18	100	95	67	1,637,736.35	2,299,831.37	-74.29

By race type

2004

	Overall			Two-year-olds			Three-year-olds			Older horses		
	W-R	%	£1	W-R	%	£1	W-R	%	£1	W-R	%	£1
Handicap	35-365	9	-107.26	6-41	14	-15.97	25-204	12	-25.13	4-120	3	-66.17
Group 1,2,3	11-63	17	-13.76	2-14	14	-6.89	4-13	30	+1.75	5-36	13	-8.63
Maiden	51-262	19	-25.63	31-184	16	-26.17	17-72	23	-18.68	3-6	50	+19.23
1st time out	15-114	13	-22.60	10-84	11	-21.90	4-21	19	-1.70	1-9	11	+1.00

2003

	Overall			Two-year-olds			Three-year-olds			Older horses		
	W-R	%	£1	W-R	%	£1	W-R	%	£1	W-R	%	£1
Handicap	56-372	15	+46.82	2-31	6	-19.75	43-233	18	+74.07	11-108	10	-7.50
Group 1,2,3	8-42	19	-13.50	5-15	33	-0.60	1-7	14	-2.50	2-20	10	-10.40
Maiden	46-233	19	-44.65	32-132	24	+0.26	14-98	14	-41.91	0-3		-3.00
1st time out	14-96	14	-24.28	12-68	17	-9.12	1-25	4	-14.00	1-3	33	-1.17

2002

	Overall			Two-year-olds			Three-year-olds			Older horses		
	W-R	%	£1	W-R	%	£1	W-R	%	£1	W-R	%	£1
Handicap	44-336	13	-62.38	1-32	3	-30.33	31-205	15	-23.92	12-99	12	-8.12
Group 1,2,3	12-53	22	+11.55	0-9		-9.00	6-18	33	-0.08	6-26	23	+20.63
Maiden	38-227	16	-63.96	20-127	15	-26.83	18-99	18	-36.13	0-1		-1.00
1st time out	12-96	12	-35.11	6-63	9	-26.34	6-30	20	-5.77	0-3		-3.00

By jockey

2004

	Overall			Two-year-olds			Three-year-olds			Older horses		
	W-R	%	£1	W-R	%	£1	W-R	%	£1	W-R	%	£1
J Fanning	50-269	18	-36.05	19-96	19	-22.31	26-110	23	+23.16	5-63	7	-36.90
K Dalgleish	16-113	14	-38.73	5-22	22	-8.37	6-59	10	-44.35	5-32	15	+14.00
K Darley	13-93	13	-37.30	7-49	14	-20.80	5-23	21	+1.00	1-21	4	-17.50
R Ffrench	13-119	10	-36.84	7-47	14	-9.70	5-58	8	-30.14	1-14	7	+3.00
S Chin	11-83	13	+5.99	3-24	12	+17.53	6-47	12	-9.89	2-12	16	-1.67
R Hills	9-33	27	+15.53	4-17	23	+1.78	3-10	30	+2.41	2-6	33	+11.33
D Holland	2-23	8	-18.33	2-10	20	-5.33	0-8		-8.00	0-5		-5.00
L Dettori	1-1	100	+3.00	1-1	100	+3.00	0-0		0.00	0-0		0.00
N Mackay	1-2	50	+15.00	0-0		0.00	1-2	50	+15.00	0-0		0.00
J F Egan	1-3	33	+23.00	0-0		0.00	0-0		0.00	1-3	33	+23.00

By jockey ctd

2003

	Overall			Two-year-olds			Three-year-olds			Older horses		
	W-R	%	£1	W-R	%	£1	W-R	%	£1	W-R	%	£1
J Fanning	49-249	19	+35.05	14-83	16	-26.36	28-130	21	+39.36	7-36	19	+22.04
K Dalgleish	41-213	19	+9.29	20-65	30	+17.29	17-97	17	+25.57	4-51	7	-33.57
K Darley	14-70	20	-8.18	6-15	40	+10.20	6-33	18	-10.48	2-22	9	-7.90
R Ffrench	13-75	17	+18.08	2-20	10	-11.25	10-48	20	+23.33	1-7	14	+6.00
D Holland	8-44	18	-21.04	6-13	46	-0.66	1-17	5	-14.38	1-14	7	-6.00
G Duffield	3-15	20	-1.92	1-3	33	-1.92	1-8	12	-5.00	1-4	25	+5.00
S Chin	2-3	66	-0.39	2-2	100	+0.61	0-1		-1.00	0-0		
L Dettori	2-5	40	+3.33	2-4	50	+4.33	0-1		-1.00	0-0		
J F Egan	2-9	22	-1.50	0-0			2-7	28	+0.50	0-2		-2.00
W Hogg	2-16	12	+4.00	0-0			1-10	10	+1.00	1-6	16	+3.00

2002

	Overall			Two-year-olds			Three-year-olds			Older horses		
	W-R	%	£1	W-R	%	£1	W-R	%	£1	W-R	%	£1
K Darley	47-230	20	-45.54	13-76	17	-32.92	25-106	23	-2.22	9-48	18	-10.40
K Dalgleish	35-222	15	-14.94	10-64	15	+21.46	19-109	17	-13.65	6-49	12	-22.75
J Fanning	24-153	15	-64.20	6-37	16	-14.47	13-90	14	-41.46	5-26	19	-8.27
R Hills	5-12	41	+31.70	0-0			4-9	44	+19.30	1-3	33	+12.40
D Holland	4-12	33	+11.50	0-1		-1.00	3-6	50	+10.00	1-5	20	+2.50
R Ffrench	3-41	7	-23.75	1-16	6	-14.00	2-19	10	-3.75	0-6		-6.00
W Hogg	2-13	15	-3.00	0-0			1-8	12	-3.00	1-5	20	
D Corby	1-1	100	+4.50	0-0			0-0			1-1	100	+4.50
K Fallon	1-1	100	+0.50	0-0			1-1	100	+0.50	0-0		
J Quinn	1-1	100	+4.50	0-0			1-1	100	+4.50	0-0		

By class

2004

	Overall			Two-year-olds			Three-year-olds			Older horses		
	W-R	%	£1	W-R	%	£1	W-R	%	£1	W-R	%	£1
A	17-102	16%	-26.76	4-28	14%	-13.05	5-26	19%	-6.92	8-48	16%	-6.79
B	6-74	8%	-18.13	0-8		-8.00	4-36	11%	-2.63	2-30	6%	-7.50
C	12-143	8%	-46.39	4-19	21%	-4.96	6-73	8%	-26.43	2-51	3%	-15.00
D	62-311	19%	-34.28	26-147	17%	-46.96	30-129	23%	-3.38	6-35	17%	+16.06
E	18-126	14%	-5.54	10-57	17%	+18.41	8-56	14%	-10.95	0-13		-13.00
F	3-21	14%	-7.64	3-10	30%	+3.36	0-9		-9.00	0-2		-2.00
G	0-5		-5.00	0-1		-1.00	0-1		-1.00	0-3		-3.00

2003

	Overall			Two-year-olds			Three-year-olds			Older horses		
	W-R	%	£1	W-R	%	£1	W-R	%	£1	W-R	%	£1
A	16-86	18	-18.70	10-29	34	+8.10	2-18	11	-8.50	4-39	10	-18.30
B	8-82	9	-22.50	1-9	11	-7.00	5-43	11	-3.50	2-30	6	-12.00
C	17-114	14	-14.44	3-13	23	-1.34	12-61	19	+17.37	2-40	5	-30.46
D	58-290	20	+8.19	25-120	20	-8.11	27-141	19	-0.54	6-29	20	+16.83
E	29-132	21	+43.44	9-42	21	-16.64	16-75	21	+35.58	4-15	26	+24.50
F	8-40	20	+0.77	3-6	50	+1.02	5-27	18	+6.75	0-7		-7.00
G	3-14	21	-2.29	3-4	75	+7.71	0-7		-7.00	0-3		-3.00

2002

	Overall			Two-year-olds			Three-year-olds			Older horses		
	W-R	%	£1	W-R	%	£1	W-R	%	£1	W-R	%	£1
A	22-92	23	+44.76	3-22	13	+8.21	9-31	29	+7.93	10-39	25	+28.62
B	14-83	16	-7.59	0-5		-5.00	7-37	18	-3.39	7-41	17	+0.79
C	18-112	16	-18.23	1-17	5	-13.50	11-57	19	+3.04	6-38	15	-7.77
D	47-281	16	-69.37	19-117	16	-19.16	28-148	18	-34.21	0-16		-16.00
E	21-127	16	-20.49	7-38	18	-13.22	11-76	14	-23.77	3-13	23	+16.50
F	8-40	20	-8.63	1-7	14	-5.75	3-19	15		4-14	28	-2.87
G	4-13	30	+5.25	0-2		-2.00	3-7	42	+5.75	1-4	25	+1.50

DOUBLE OBSESSION: wins the Ascot Stakes and augments Mark Johnston's Royal record

By course

2004

	Overall			Two-year-olds			Three-year-olds			Older horses		
	W-R	%	£1	W-R	%	£1	W-R	%	£1	W-R	%	£1
Ascot	6-57	10	+3.88	0-11		-11.00	4-22	18	+6.38	2-24	8	+8.50
Ayr	5-31	16	-11.03	4-18	22	-6.03	1-7	14	+1.00	0-6		-6.00
Bath	1-9	11	-3.50	0-4		-4.00	1-4	25	+1.50	0-1		-1.00
Beverley	4-37	10	-11.25	3-10	30	+0.75	1-23	4	-8.00	0-4		-4.00
Brighton	0-2		-2.00	0-0		0.00	0-2		-2.00	0-0		0.00
Carlisle	5-11	45	+43.50	4-4	100	+45.00	1-6	16	-0.50	0-1		-1.00
Catterick	6-20	30	+3.00	3-11	27	+1.75	3-7	42	+3.25	0-2		-2.00
Chepstow	2-6	33	-0.58	1-4	25	-2.33	1-1	100	+2.75	0-1		-1.00
Chester	2-10	20	-2.17	0-1		-1.00	0-2		-2.00	2-7	28	+0.83
Doncaster	4-49	8	-35.47	2-21	9	-13.09	2-16	12	-10.38	0-12		-12.00
Epsom	1-23	4	-20.00	0-9		-9.00	1-9	11	-6.00	0-5		-5.00
Goodwood	4-37	10	-17.68	2-11	18	-5.05	1-15	6	-4.00	1-11	9	-8.63
Hamilton	6-46	13	-32.42	2-15	13	-11.72	4-21	19	-10.70	0-10		-10.00
Haydock	1-28	3	-26.00	0-3		-3.00	1-14	7	-12.00	0-11		-11.00
Kempton	2-11	18	-1.50	0-0		0.00	1-7	14	-3.50	1-4	25	+2.00
Leicester	1-16	6	-14.17	1-8	12	-6.17	0-7		-7.00	0-1		-1.00
Lingfield	1-10	10	-6.75	0-3		-3.00	1-6	16	-2.75	0-1		-1.00
Musselburgh	10-36	27	+16.65	3-12	25	-0.97	5-18	27	+6.89	2-6	33	+10.73
Newbury	0-14		-14.00	0-3		-3.00	0-3		-3.00	0-8		-8.00
Newcastle	5-28	17	-15.82	3-14	21	-5.53	2-11	18	-7.29	0-3		-3.00
Newmarket	12-66	18	+24.01	1-20	5	-14.50	6-29	20	+11.68	5-17	29	+26.83
Nottingham	4-16	25	+4.48	3-8	37	+10.86	1-8	12	-6.39	0-0		0.00
Pontefract	8-34	23	+3.02	3-14	21	-8.98	3-11	27	+8.50	2-9	22	+3.50
Redcar	2-23	8	-9.50	1-11	9	-4.50	1-11	9	-4.00	0-1		-1.00
Ripon	4-24	16	+11.55	2-5	40	+5.80	1-14	7	-10.25	1-5	20	+16.00
Salisbury	0-3		-3.00	0-1		-1.00	0-2		-2.00	0-0		0.00
Sandown	5-28	17	-6.25	2-6	33	+0.75	2-14	14	-3.50	1-8	12	-3.50
Southwell	0-8		-8.00	0-2		-2.00	0-5		-5.00	0-1		-1.00
Thirsk	5-17	29	+1.25	2-9	22	-2.75	3-5	60	+7.00	0-3		-3.00
Warwick	2-10	20	+5.50	1-3	33	+6.00	1-5	20	+1.50	0-2		-2.00
Windsor	2-9	22	-1.50	1-2	50	+2.00	0-4		-4.00	1-3	33	+0.50
Wolver	3-22	13	-11.50	0-8		-8.00	3-9	33	+1.50	0-5		-5.00
Yarmouth	1-12	8	-6.50	1-8	12	-2.50	0-3		-3.00	0-1		-1.00
York	5-46	10	-13.00	3-20	15	-1.00	2-15	13	-1.00	0-11		-11.00

Saeed bin Suroor

The combination of Godolphin and Frankie Dettori was unstoppable last season. Dettori won on 29% of his mounts for the 'boys in blue' and showed a whopping £44.13 level-stakes profit.

The most amazing statistic is the advance of the Godolphin two-year-old operation. 58 won last season, as opposed to three the season before.

The legacy of wonder horse Dubai Millennium bore fruit last term in the juvenile category. June was the best month to follow this team.

By month

2004

	Overall			Two-year-olds			Three-year-olds			Older horses		
	W-R	%	£1	W-R	%	£1	W-R	%	£1	W-R	%	£1
January	0-0			0-0			0-0			0-0		
February	0-0			0-0			0-0			0-0		
March	1-1	100	+1.50	0-0		0.00	1-1	100	+1.50	0-0		0.00
April	0-1		-1.00	0-0		0.00	0-1		-1.00	0-0		0.00
May	14-57	24	-9.61	3-6	50	+5.73	5-25	20	-15.00	6-26	23	-0.33
June	19-72	26	+16.20	7-18	38	+7.43	7-32	21	+3.96	5-22	22	+4.80
July	19-78	24	+7.04	12-38	31	-4.89	4-22	18	+13.83	3-18	16	-1.90
August	15-62	24	+0.59	8-38	21	-0.87	3-11	27	-1.87	4-13	30	+3.33
September	30-104	28	+9.20	18-57	31	+3.92	7-28	25	-1.72	5-19	26	+7.00
October	17-80	21	-12.03	10-50	20	-8.94	4-18	22	-4.93	3-12	25	+1.83
December	0-0			0-0			0-0			0-0		

2003

	Overall			Two-year-olds			Three-year-olds			Older horses		
	W-R	%	£1	W-R	%	£1	W-R	%	£1	W-R	%	£1
January	0-0			0-0			0-0			0-0		
February	0-0			0-0			0-0			0-0		
March	0-0			0-0			0-0			0-0		
April	0-0			0-0			0-0			0-0		
May	4-19	21	+1.25	0-0		0.00	2-12	16	-6.25	2-7	28	+7.50
June	5-23	21	-10.66	0-0		0.00	1-7	14	-5.20	4-16	25	-5.46
July	2-15	13	-11.50	0-0		0.00	1-3	33	-1.00	1-12	8	-10.50
August	2-13	15	-6.71	1-2	50	-0.71	1-6	16	-1.00	0-5		-5.00
September	5-12	41	+9.88	1-3	33	-1.09	2-4	50	+10.38	2-5	40	+0.60
October	4-12	33	+10.04	1-4	25	+3.50	3-7	42	+7.54	0-1		-1.00
November	1-4	25	-0.50	0-1		-1.00	1-3	33	+0.50	0-0		0.00
December	0-0			0-0			0-0			0-0		

2002

	Overall			Two-year-olds			Three-year-olds			Older horses		
	W-R	%	£1	W-R	%	£1	W-R	%	£1	W-R	%	£1
January	0-0			0-0			0-0			0-0		
February	0-0			0-0			0-0			0-0		
March	0-0			0-0			0-0			0-0		
April	0-0			0-0			0-0			0-0		
May	6-21	28	+19.92	0-0		0.00	4-14	28	+15.25	2-7	28	+4.67
June	4-21	19	+5.33	0-0		0.00	2-9	22	+5.33	2-12	16	0.00
July	3-11	27	-6.02	0-0		0.00	3-4	75	+0.98	0-7		-7.00
August	3-9	33	-3.69	0-0		0.00	2-5	40	-1.36	1-4	25	-2.33
September	4-14	28	+0.42	0-0		0.00	3-9	33	+0.92	1-5	20	-0.50
October	1-10	10	-8.39	0-0		0.00	1-6	16	-4.39	0-4		-4.00
November	0-2		-2.00	0-0		0.00	0-2		-2.00	0-0		0.00
December	0-0			0-0			0-0			0-0		

All runners

2004	Wins	Runs	%	2nd	3rd	rest	Win prize	Total prize	£1 Stake
2yo	58	207	28	39	20	14	422,685.30	594,033.75	+2.38
3yo	31	138	22	17	15	12	804,735.64	1,463,907.96	-5.23
4yo+	26	110	24	19	7	13	1,830,500.76	2,266,159.61	+14.73
TOTAL	115	455	25	75	42	39	3,057,921.70	4,324,101.32	+11.88

2003	Wins	Runs	%	2nd	3rd	rest	Win prize	Total prize	£1 Stake
2yo	3	10	30	4	1	1	12,210.25	21,563.15	+0.70
3yo	11	42	26	8	2	3	156,623.50	261,510.20	+4.96
4yo+	9	46	20	5	5	2	360,597.60	700,737.40	-13.86
TOTAL	23	98	23	17	8	6	529,431.35	983,810.75	-8.20

2002	Wins	Runs	%	2nd	3rd	rest	Win prize	Total prize	£1 Stake
2yo	0	0							
3yo	15	49	31	11	4	5	645,014.79	1,010,861.79	+14.74
4yo+	6	39	15	6	8	2	250,254.00	643,650.70	-9.17
TOTAL	21	88	24	17	12	7	895,268.79	1,654,512.49	+5.57

By race type

2004	Overall			Two-year-olds			Three-year-olds			Older horses		
	W-R	%	£1	W-R	%	£1	W-R	%	£1	W-R	%	£1
Handicap	6-41	14	-10.67	1-7	14	-1.00	3-23	13	-9.67	2-11	18	0.00
Group 1,2,3	23-108	21	+9.79	2-18	11	-13.46	7-32	21	+11.10	14-58	24	+12.15
Maiden	57-188	30	+23.76	47-153	30	+23.91	9-34	26	-5.15	1-1	100	+5.00
1st time out	37-149	24	-7.04	23-91	25	-6.66	11-40	27	+0.12	3-18	16	-0.50

2003	Overall			Two-year-olds			Three-year-olds			Older horses		
	W-R	%	£1	W-R	%	£1	W-R	%	£1	W-R	%	£1
Group 1,2,3	5-50	10	-16.50	0-0		0.00	1-17	5	-7.00	4-33	12	-9.50
Maiden	7-14	50	+4.16	3-8	37	+2.70	4-6	66	+1.46	0-0		0.00
1st time out	11-36	30	-1.87	2-7	28	+1.79	6-19	31	-5.29	3-10	30	+1.64

2002	Overall			Two-year-olds			Three-year-olds			Older horses		
	W-R	%	£1	W-R	%	£1	W-R	%	£1	W-R	%	£1
Handicap	0-1		-1.00	0-0		0.00	0-0		0.00	0-1		-1.00
Group 1,2,3	9-48	18	+10.25	0-0		0.00	7-21	33	+22.25	2-27	7	-12.00
Maiden	3-8	37	-3.02	0-0		0.00	3-8	37	-3.02	0-0		0.00
1st time out	7-29	24	+8.62	0-0		0.00	5-20	25	+5.62	2-9	22	+3.00

By jockey

2004	Overall			Two-year-olds			Three-year-olds			Older horses		
	W-R	%	£1	W-R	%	£1	W-R	%	£1	W-R	%	£1
L Dettori	77-263	29	+44.13	41-126	32	+20.44	20-76	26	+9.53	16-61	26	+14.15
K McEvoy	28-120	23	-11.96	13-44	29	-10.06	8-42	19	-1.65	7-34	20	-0.25
R Hills	3-12	25	-1.72	0-3		-3.00	2-3	66	+1.78	1-6	16	-0.50
J P Murtagh	2-2	100	+13.10	1-1	100	+12.00	1-1	100	+1.10	0-0		0.00
J Carroll	2-15	13	-6.50	1-8	12	-5.50	0-6		-6.00	1-1	100	+5.00
T P Queally	1-3	33	+6.50	1-2	50	+7.50	0-1		-1.00	0-0		0.00
W Supple	1-6	16	-1.67	0-3		-3.00	0-1		-1.00	1-2	50	+2.33
T E Durcan	1-15	6	-11.00	1-6	16	-2.00	0-5		-5.00	0-4		-4.00
C Catlin	0-1		-1.00	0-1		-1.00	0-0		0.00	0-0		0.00
S Sanders	0-1		-1.00	0-0		0.00	0-1		-1.00	0-0		0.00

By jockey ctd

2003

	Overall			Two-year-olds			Three-year-olds			Older horses		
	W-R	%	£1	W-R	%	£1	W-R	%	£1	W-R	%	£1
L Dettori	17-64	26	+2.08	0-4		-4.00	9-30	30	+5.68	8-30	26	+0.41
J P Spencer	5-24	20	-2.20	2-4	50	+4.79	2-9	22	+2.29	1-11	9	-9.27
R Hills	1-5	20	-3.09	1-2	50	-0.09	0-1		-1.00	0-2		-2.00
W Supple	0-1		-1.00	0-0		0.00	0-1		-1.00	0-0		0.00
M J Kinane	0-1		-1.00	0-0		0.00	0-0		0.00	0-1		-1.00
K Darley	0-1		-1.00	0-0		0.00	0-0		0.00	0-1		-1.00
T Quinn	0-1		-1.00	0-0		0.00	0-0		0.00	0-1		-1.00

2002

	Overall			Two-year-olds			Three-year-olds			Older horses		
	W-R	%	£1	W-R	%	£1	W-R	%	£1	W-R	%	£1
L Dettori	15-51	29	+10.99	0-0		0.00	12-28	42	+22.82	3-23	13	-11.83
J P Spencer	5-21	23	+6.83	0-0		0.00	2-11	18	-1.83	3-10	30	+8.67
R Hills	1-7	14	-3.25	0-0		0.00	1-4	25	-0.25	0-3		-3.00
R Hughes	0-1		-1.00	0-0		0.00	0-1		-1.00	0-0		0.00
T E Durcan	0-1		-1.00	0-0		0.00	0-1		-1.00	0-0		0.00
D O'Donohoe	0-1		-1.00	0-0		0.00	0-1		-1.00	0-0		0.00
K Darley	0-3		-3.00	0-0		0.00	0-1		-1.00	0-2		-2.00
W Supple	0-3		-3.00	0-0		0.00	0-2		-2.00	0-1		-1.00

By class

2004

	Overall			Two-year-olds			Three-year-olds			Older horses		
	W-R	%	£1	W-R	%	£1	W-R	%	£1	W-R	%	£1
A	31-165	18	-19.95	3-26	11	-19.66	10-57	17	-5.52	18-82	21	+5.23
B	6-27	22	+5.33	1-2	50	+4.00	1-12	8	-3.00	4-13	30	+4.33
C	13-54	24	-6.56	3-14	21	-7.50	8-28	28	+0.44	2-12	16	+0.50
D	56-174	32	+48.38	44-134	32	+41.28	10-37	27	+2.44	2-3	66	+4.67
E	1-9	11	-7.20	1-9	11	-7.20	0-0			0-0		
F	1-2	50	-0.67	1-2	50	-0.67	0-0			0-0		
G	0-0			0-0			0-0			0-0		

2003

	Overall			Two-year-olds			Three-year-olds			Older horses		
	W-R	%	£1	W-R	%	£1	W-R	%	£1	W-R	%	£1
A	12-72	16	-10.01	0-0		0.00	5-30	16	+2.75	7-42	16	-12.76
B	1-3	33	-1.50	0-1		-1.00	0-1		-1.00	1-1	100	+0.50
C	3-8	37	+0.15	0-1		-1.00	2-4	50	+2.75	1-3	33	-1.60
D	7-14	50	+4.16	3-8	37	+2.70	4-6	66	+1.46	0-0		0.00
E	0-0			0-0			0-0			0-0		
F	0-0			0-0			0-0			0-0		
G	0-0			0-0			0-0			0-0		

2002

	Overall			Two-year-olds			Three-year-olds			Older horses		
	W-R	%	£1	W-R	%	£1	W-R	%	£1	W-R	%	£1
A	14-72	19	+6.33	0-0		0.00	9-35	25	+18.00	5-37	13	-11.67
B	1-2	50	+2.50	0-0		0.00	0-1		-1.00	1-1	100	+3.50
C	3-4	75	+1.76	0-0		0.00	3-3	100	+2.76	0-1		-1.00
D	3-10	30	-5.02	0-0		0.00	3-10	30	-5.02	0-0		0.00
E	0-0			0-0			0-0			0-0		
F	0-0			0-0			0-0			0-0		
G	0-0			0-0			0-0			0-0		

By course

2004

	Overall			Two-year-olds			Three-year-olds			Older horses		
	W-R	%	£1	W-R	%	£1	W-R	%	£1	W-R	%	£1
Ascot	12-42	28	+25.22	2-8	25	-1.33	6-15	40	+22.25	4-19	21	+4.30
Ayr	3-6	50	+0.12	1-4	25	-2.39	2-2	100	+2.50	0-0		0.00
Bath	1-4	25	-2.56	1-4	25	-2.56	0-0		0.00	0-0		0.00
Beverley	1-3	33	+0.50	1-3	33	+0.50	0-0		0.00	0-0		0.00
Catterick	0-2		-2.00	0-1		-1.00	0-1		-1.00	0-0		0.00
Chepstow	0-1		-1.00	0-0		0.00	0-1		-1.00	0-0		0.00
Chester	0-4		-4.00	0-2		-2.00	0-1		-1.00	0-1		-1.00
Doncaster	13-32	40	+25.03	6-12	50	+8.03	4-12	33	+9.17	3-8	37	+7.83
Epsom	3-14	21	-0.90	1-1	100	+8.00	0-7		-7.00	2-6	33	-1.90
Folkestone	1-5	20	-3.67	1-4	25	-2.67	0-1		-1.00	0-0		0.00
Goodwood	8-33	24	+20.50	1-6	16	-2.25	4-13	30	+19.00	3-14	21	+3.75
Hamilton	0-2		-2.00	0-0		0.00	0-1		-1.00	0-1		-1.00
Haydock	4-14	28	+0.78	2-4	50	+2.83	1-3	33	-1.56	1-7	14	-0.50
Kempton	6-19	31	+1.15	4-11	36	+1.40	1-7	14	-3.25	1-1	100	+3.00
Leicester	6-15	40	-3.79	4-12	33	-3.90	1-2	50	-0.56	1-1	100	+0.67
Lingfield	5-20	25	-3.47	4-15	26	-0.97	1-4	25	-1.50	0-1		-1.00
Newbury	4-20	20	-4.00	3-8	37	+4.00	0-3		-3.00	1-9	11	-5.00
Newcastle	2-4	50	+3.50	2-4	50	+3.50	0-0		0.00	0-0		0.00
Newmarket	15-93	16	-32.40	10-43	23	+1.12	4-32	12	-22.03	1-18	5	-11.50
Nottingham	2-11	18	-4.13	2-7	28	-0.13	0-3		-3.00	0-1		-1.00
Pontefract	1-2	50	+1.50	0-1		-1.00	0-0		0.00	1-1	100	+2.50
Redcar	2-9	22	-4.27	1-7	14	-5.27	0-1		-1.00	1-1	100	+2.00
Ripon	1-2	50	+4.00	0-1		-1.00	0-0		0.00	1-1	100	+5.00
Salisbury	5-14	35	+5.90	3-8	37	+3.80	2-4	50	+4.10	0-2		-2.00
Sandown	2-17	11	-5.25	0-5		-5.00	0-7		-7.00	2-5	40	+6.75
Southwell	1-1	100	+0.10	1-1	100	+0.10	0-0		0.00	0-0		0.00
Thirsk	3-5	60	+2.03	1-2	50	+0.50	2-3	66	+1.53	0-0		0.00
Warwick	1-4	25	+0.50	1-1	100	+3.50	0-2		-2.00	0-1		-1.00
Windsor	2-11	18	-0.67	0-5		-5.00	0-2		-2.00	2-4	50	+6.33
Yarmouth	4-19	21	+4.75	4-14	28	+9.75	0-4		-4.00	0-1		-1.00
York	7-27	25	-9.60	2-13	15	-8.20	3-7	42	-0.90	2-7	28	-0.50

PAPINEAU (left): seeing off Mr Dinos at Sandown

Richard Hannon

It's no shock to find out that this is a stable that deals primarily with raw two-year-old talent. They contributed 55 successes to the tally last season, compared with just five from the four-year-old and upwards division.

First time out, handicap and Group winners were scarce last term, but maidens were where it's at with a £64.08 level-stakes profit.

This suggests that the time to back a Hannon horse is as a two-year-old, in a maiden after it has had an initial outing.

By month

2004

	Overall			Two-year-olds			Three-year-olds			Older horses		
	W-R	%	£1	W-R	%	£1	W-R	%	£1	W-R	%	£1
January	0-0			0-0			0-0			0-0		
February	0-0			0-0			0-0			0-0		
March	0-9		-9.00	0-2		-2.00	0-4		-4.00	0-3		-3.00
April	9-80	11	-13.77	4-12	33	+8.10	3-49	6	-31.75	2-19	10	+9.88
May	18-162	11	+92.13	6-39	15	+27.25	11-97	11	+80.88	1-26	3	-16.00
June	27-195	13	+11.24	11-57	19	+8.62	14-118	11	-2.37	2-20	10	+5.00
July	19-218	8	-63.14	12-100	12	-7.83	7-105	6	-42.31	0-13		-13.00
August	17-174	9	-80.94	12-91	13	-25.19	5-67	7	-39.75	0-16		-16.00
September	8-183	4	-108.50	4-101	3	-64.00	4-73	5	-35.50	0-9		-9.00
October	6-86	6	-52.00	2-50	4	-37.00	4-35	11	-14.00	0-1		-1.00
November	0-0			0-0			0-0			0-0		
December	0-0			0-0			0-0			0-0		

2003

	Overall			Two-year-olds			Three-year-olds			Older horses		
	W-R	%	£1	W-R	%	£1	W-R	%	£1	W-R	%	£1
January	0-12		-12.00	0-0			0-12		-12.00	0-0		
February	0-0			0-0			0-0			0-0		
March	7-31	22	+5.82	3-3	100	+6.07	4-20	20	+7.75	0-8		-8.00
April	9-87	10	-41.94	4-20	20	-9.30	3-50	6	-32.25	2-17	11	-0.38
May	16-147	10	-69.85	10-46	21	-0.38	5-87	5	-61.47	1-14	7	-8.00
June	18-146	12	-11.68	10-64	15	-23.93	6-72	8	+15.50	2-10	20	-3.25
July	26-178	14	+1.28	16-96	16	-7.98	8-68	11	-4.25	2-14	14	+13.50
August	23-137	16	-4.69	14-86	16	-33.28	9-43	20	+36.58	0-8		-8.00
September	12-133	9	-65.85	10-91	10	-35.60	2-37	5	-25.25	0-5		-5.00
October	11-127	8	-46.41	9-88	10	-18.51	2-32	6	-20.90	0-7		-7.00
November	2-39	5	-27.75	1-25	4	-17.00	0-13		-13.00	1-1	100	+2.25
December	1-6	16	-2.25	1-3	33	+0.75	0-2		-2.00	0-1		-£1.00

2002

	Overall			Two-year-olds			Three-year-olds			Older horses		
	W-R	%	£1	W-R	%	£1	W-R	%	£1	W-R	%	£1
January	1-17	5	-14.38	0-0			1-14	7	-11.38	0-3		-3.00
February	0-4		-4.00	0-0			0-2		-2.00	0-2		-2.00
March	1-14	7	-10.50	0-1		-1.00	1-12	8	-8.50	0-1		-1.00
April	13-94	13	-20.25	4-15	26	+1.75	7-57	12	-9.75	2-22	9	-12.25
May	23-152	15	-36.21	12-45	26	-0.19	9-83	10	-23.40	2-24	8	-12.63
June	25-166	15	-38.65	16-71	22	-4.98	7-72	9	-23.17	2-23	8	-10.50
July	25-188	13	-43.93	14-94	14	-10.14	7-62	11	-24.92	4-32	12	-8.87
August	11-177	6	-121.20	5-90	5	-62.50	3-57	5	-41.50	3-30	10	-17.20
September	13-123	10	-41.35	9-73	12	-22.85	3-37	8	-10.50	1-13	7	-8.00
October	9-115	7	-32.54	7-75	9	-4.79	1-29	3	-23.25	1-11	9	-4.50
November	1-29	3	-12.00	1-19	5	-2.00	0-9		-9.00	0-1		-1.00
December	4-28	14	-12.45	1-16	6	-12.75	0-5		-5.00	3-7	42	+5.30

All runners

2004	Wins	Runs	%	2nd	3rd	rest	Win prize	Total prize	£1 Stake
2yo	55	492	11	54	49	54	391,480.33	661,606.13	-89.06
3yo	53	590	9	60	65	61	311,755.57	623,177.21	-92.63
4yo+	5	119	4	9	13	4	92,706.79	179,342.39	-55.13
TOTAL	113	1201	9	123	127	119	795,942.69	1,464,125.73	-236.82

2003	Wins	Runs	%	2nd	3rd	rest	Win prize	Total prize	£1 Stake
2yo	78	522	14	75	52	73	558,392.70	944,748.08	-139.14
3yo	39	436	8	37	42	32	308,849.05	547,540.88	-111.29
4yo+	8	85	9	8	7	6	258,783.47	332,417.80	-24.88
TOTAL	125	1043	11	120	101	111	1,126,025.22	1,824,706.76	-275.31

2002	Wins	Runs	%	2nd	3rd	rest	Win prize	Total prize	£1 Stake
2yo	69	499	13	77	71	53	637,488.57	1,046,494.30	-119.44
3yo	39	439	8	49	46	34	258,552.87	551,365.46	-192.36
4yo+	18	169	10	21	14	12	196,968.64	353,258.54	-75.65
TOTAL	126	1107	11	147	131	99	1,093,010.08	1,951,118.30	-387.45

By race type

2004

	Overall			Two-year-olds			Three-year-olds			Older horses		
	W-R	%	£1	W-R	%	£1	W-R	%	£1	W-R	%	£1
Handicap	28-479	5	-193.38	5-92	5	-37.00	21-317	6	-111.38	2-70	2	-45.00
Group 1,2,3	3-58	5	-21.00	2-25	8	-14.00	0-18		-18.00	1-15	6	+11.00
Maiden	53-389	13	+64.08	33-284	11	-26.28	20-105	19	+90.34	0-0		0.00
1st time out	13-114	11	+9.50	12-100	12	+10.50	1-14	7	-1.00	0-0		0.00

2003

	Overall			Two-year-olds			Three-year-olds			Older horses		
	W-R	%	£1	W-R	%	£1	W-R	%	£1	W-R	%	£1
Handicap	31-393	7	-147.59	10-102	9	-40.13	19-243	7	-69.22	2-48	4	-38.25
Group 1,2,3	7-57	12	-7.68	2-23	8	-13.38	2-25	8	-10.67	3-9	33	+16.37
Maiden	50-321	15	-84.70	41-259	15	-71.95	9-59	15	-9.75	0-3		-3.00
1st time out	12-119	10	-59.87	12-113	10	-53.87	0-4		-4.00	0-2		-2.00

2002

	Overall			Two-year-olds			Three-year-olds			Older horses		
	W-R	%	£1	W-R	%	£1	W-R	%	£1	W-R	%	£1
Handicap	32-463	6	-186.87	8-93	8	-1.92	16-269	5	-129.00	8-101	7	-55.95
Group 1,2,3	6-66	9	-31.75	3-27	11	-7.75	1-14	7	-8.00	2-25	8	-16.00
Maiden	42-323	13	-121.18	33-249	13	-81.11	9-72	12	-38.07	0-2		-2.00
1st time out	18-108	16	+4.60	17-99	17	+4.60	0-7		-7.00	1-2	50	+7.00

By jockey

2004

	Overall			Two-year-olds			Three-year-olds			Older horses		
	W-R	%	£1	W-R	%	£1	W-R	%	£1	W-R	%	£1
R L Moore	43-298	14	+85.28	18-127	14	-15.63	25-158	15	+113.90	0-13		-13.00
R Hughes	27-235	11	-51.25	15-110	13	-5.79	11-102	10	-30.45	1-23	4	-15.00
Dane O'Neill	14-175	8	-51.00	10-73	13	+21.50	3-80	3	-60.50	1-22	4	-12.00
P Dobbs	8-205	3	-101.17	4-80	5	-47.65	3-93	3	-47.52	1-32	3	-6.00
K Fallon	6-36	16	-12.13	2-12	16	-2.00	3-21	14	-10.00	1-3	33	-0.12
R Smith	5-80	6	-22.00	3-33	9	-7.00	1-39	2	-24.00	1-8	12	+9.00
F Norton	2-10	20	+4.44	0-3		-3.00	2-7	28	+7.44	0-0		0.00
R Thomas	1-5	20	+1.00	1-3	33	+3.00	0-2		-2.00	0-0		0.00
J F McDonald	1-5	20	+12.00	0-1		-1.00	1-4	25	+13.00	0-0		0.00
Paul Eddery	1-5	20	+6.00	0-3		-3.00	1-2	50	+9.00	0-0		0.00

By jockey ctd

2003

	Overall			Two-year-olds			Three-year-olds			Older horses		
	W-R	%	£1	W-R	%	£1	W-R	%	£1	W-R	%	£1
R Hughes	42-204	20	-15.66	29-110	26	+16.86	10-74	13	-24.14	3-20	15	-8.38
R L Moore	18-151	11	-10.85	8-67	11	-22.85	10-72	13	+24.00	0-12		-12.00
P Dobbs	18-170	10	-74.28	13-94	13	-36.53	4-67	5	-43.75	1-9	11	+6.00
Dane O'Neill	16-217	7	-138.86	13-128	10	-63.61	2-79	2	-68.50	1-10	10	-6.75
Pat Eddery	8-67	11	-9.80	6-30	20	+1.70	1-23	4	-18.50	1-14	7	+7.00
R Smith	6-80	7	-9.13	2-27	7	-20.63	4-45	8	+19.50	0-8		-8.00
P Gallagher	5-30	16	+21.50	1-9	11	-4.50	3-16	18	+24.50	1-5	20	+1.50
D Holland	3-18	16	-9.40	0-7		-7.00	3-11	27	-2.40	0-0		
K Fallon	2-7	28	+16.00	1-3	33	+3.00	1-4	25	+13.00	0-0		
J Fortune	2-13	15	-0.25	0-2		-2.00	1-8	12	+2.00	1-3	33	-0.25

2002

	Overall			Two-year-olds			Three-year-olds			Older horses		
	W-R	%	£1	W-R	%	£1	W-R	%	£1	W-R	%	£1
Dane O'Neill	34-264	12	-102.46	22-143	15	-48.13	6-83	7	-41.37	6-38	15	-12.95
R Hughes	32-227	14	-80.75	22-107	20	-0.21	10-92	10	-52.54	0-28		-28.00
Pat Eddery	10-70	14	-14.93	4-27	14	-3.30	1-24	4	-16.50	5-19	26	+4.88
R Smith	7-86	8	-36.25	3-37	8	-13.25	4-38	10	-12.00	0-11		-11.00
D Holland	6-44	13	-15.50	2-14	14	-4.00	4-28	14	-9.50	0-2		-2.00
P Dobbs	6-74	8	-37.72	2-33	6	-22.50	3-34	8	-13.27	1-7	14	-1.95
R L Moore	5-81	6	-23.75	3-26	11	+12.25	2-32	6	-13.00	0-23		-23.00
P Fitzsimons	4-34	11	-8.18	3-19	15	-2.18	0-7		-7.00	1-8	12	+1.00
E Ahern	3-12	25	+13.50	2-8	25	+4.50	1-4	25	+9.00	0-0		
K Fallon	3-17	17	+8.25	0-4		-4.00	3-12	25	+13.25	0-1		-1.00

By class

2004

	Overall			Two-year-olds			Three-year-olds			Older horses		
	W-R	%	£1	W-R	%	£1	W-R	%	£1	W-R	%	£1
A	10-133	7	-50.50	5-39	12	-8.50	3-67	4	-51.00	2-27	7	+9.00
B	1-74	1	-53.00	1-35	2	-14.00	0-31		-31.00	0-8		-8.00
C	11-134	8	-71.03	5-32	15	-10.40	5-87	5	-48.50	1-15	6	-12.13
D	50-515	9	-92.48	22-244	9	-69.04	28-242	11	+5.56	0-29		-29.00
E	28-251	11	+26.29	13-94	13	-10.83	13-122	10	+47.13	2-35	5	-10.00
F	9-61	14	-2.62	7-33	21	+20.71	2-24	8	-19.33	0-4		-4.00
G	3-17	17	+7.50	1-5	20	-2.00	2-12	16	+9.50	0-0		0.00

2003

	Overall			Two-year-olds			Three-year-olds			Older horses		
	W-R	%	£1	W-R	%	£1	W-R	%	£1	W-R	%	£1
A	10-113	8	-43.88	7-49	14	-15.38	2-51	3	-36.50	1-13	7	+8.00
B	6-84	7	-46.47	3-37	8	-12.00	2-34	5	-27.47	1-13	7	-7.00
C	11-121	9	-66.84	8-41	19	-16.09	3-59	5	-29.75	0-21		-21.00
D	56-447	12	-130.19	38-264	14	-87.04	18-165	10	-25.15	0-18		-18.00
E	30-196	15	+34.43	18-99	18	-0.33	10-84	11	+26.25	2-13	15	+8.50
F	8-58	13	-9.68	3-24	12	-2.93	3-29	10	-9.00	2-5	40	+2.25
G	1-12	8	-9.38	1-4	25	-1.38	0-8		-8.00	0-0		

2002

	Overall			Two-year-olds			Three-year-olds			Older horses		
	W-R	%	£1	W-R	%	£1	W-R	%	£1	W-R	%	£1
A	11-122	9	-63.33	3-45	6	-26.25	3-36	8	-18.50	5-41	12	-18.58
B	12-92	13	-19.45	9-46	19	+8.17	1-26	3	-21.50	2-20	10	-6.12
C	20-163	12	-59.86	7-48	14	-17.32	10-88	11	-31.54	3-27	11	-11.00
D	47-452	10	-214.47	30-235	12	-98.15	17-185	9	-84.32	0-32		-32.00
E	22-207	10	-53.20	12-94	12	+0.25	6-76	7	-35.50	4-37	10	-17.95
F	8-52	15	+15.00	3-20	15	+3.00	2-24	8	+3.00	3-8	37	+9.00
G	1-11	9	-1.00	1-5	20	+5.00	0-3		-3.00	0-3		-3.00

SCREWDRIVER: Woodcote Stakes winner for Richard's Hannon and Hughes

By course

2004

	Overall			Two-year-olds			Three-year-olds			Older horses		
	W-R	%	£1	W-R	%	£1	W-R	%	£1	W-R	%	£1
Ascot	3-63	4	-30.00	3-21	14	+12.00	0-37		-37.00	0-5		-5.00
Bath	6-50	12	+1.50	3-25	12	-5.00	3-21	14	+10.50	0-4		-4.00
Beverley	0-1		-1.00	0-0		0.00	0-1		-1.00	0-0		0.00
Brighton	3-22	13	-8.13	1-8	12	-5.13	2-12	16	-1.00	0-2		-2.00
Chepstow	2-35	5	-21.50	0-16		-16.00	2-14	14	-0.50	0-5		-5.00
Chester	1-10	10	-8.56	0-4		-4.00	1-6	16	-4.56	0-0		0.00
Doncaster	1-30	3	-25.00	1-20	5	-15.00	0-9		-9.00	0-1		-1.00
Epsom	4-28	14	-11.75	1-8	12	-3.50	3-17	17	-5.25	0-3		-3.00
Folkestone	6-20	30	+8.81	4-10	40	+11.93	2-8	25	-1.12	0-2		-2.00
Goodwood	10-83	12	+57.50	6-30	20	-2.00	4-41	9	+71.50	0-12		-12.00
Haydock	3-14	21	+25.00	1-7	14	+14.00	1-6	16	+2.00	1-1	100	+9.00
Kempton	6-75	8	-25.76	3-25	12	+12.61	2-39	5	-30.25	1-11	9	-8.13
Leicester	2-44	4	-36.50	0-14		-14.00	2-27	7	-19.50	0-3		-3.00
Lingfield	10-110	9	-37.08	2-39	5	-28.00	8-58	13	+3.93	0-13		-13.00
Musselburgh	0-1		-1.00	0-1		-1.00	0-0		0.00	0-0		0.00
Newbury	9-114	7	-46.00	5-52	9	-22.50	2-56	3	-42.50	2-6	33	+19.00
Newmarket	10-146	6	-46.90	8-69	11	+14.10	2-66	3	-50.00	0-11		-11.00
Nottingham	1-21	4	-19.27	0-10		-10.00	1-10	10	-8.27	0-1		-1.00
Pontefract	0-8		-8.00	0-3		-3.00	0-5		-5.00	0-0		0.00
Redcar	0-2		-2.00	0-1		-1.00	0-1		-1.00	0-0		0.00
Ripon	1-4	25	+6.50	0-0		0.00	1-4	25	+6.50	0-0		0.00
Salisbury	4-88	4	-50.60	2-37	5	-28.00	2-39	5	-10.60	0-12		-12.00
Sandown	9-62	14	+6.50	5-17	29	+11.50	3-37	8	-23.00	1-8	12	+18.00
Southwell	0-1		-1.00	0-0		0.00	0-1		-1.00	0-0		0.00
Warwick	6-24	25	+10.29	2-9	22	-4.08	4-13	30	+16.37	0-2		-2.00
Windsor	12-104	11	+20.13	6-42	14	-11.00	6-49	12	+44.13	0-13		-13.00
Wolver	2-24	8	+8.00	2-16	12	+16.00	0-6		-6.00	0-2		-2.00
Yarmouth	2-4	50	+12.00	0-1		-1.00	2-3	66	+13.00	0-0		0.00
York	0-13		-13.00	0-7		-7.00	0-4		-4.00	0-2		-2.00

Mick Channon

It's interesting to note that Wolverhampton was Mick Channon's most profitable track last season - seven out of 28 (25%) were victorious.

The most successful class category for the stable last season was 'G', indicating that last season wasn't a great one in terms of quality for the Lambourn outfit, but that the lesser lights weighed in with their share. First time out isn't the time to be backing a horse from this stable. Expect a resurgence this season, particularly with the juveniles.

By month

2004

	Overall			Two-year-olds			Three-year-olds			Older horses		
	W-R	%	£1	W-R	%	£1	W-R	%	£1	W-R	%	£1
January	3-8	37	+2.75	0-0		0.00	3-6	50	+4.75	0-2		-2.00
February	0-5		-5.00	0-0		0.00	0-3		-3.00	0-2		-2.00
March	1-34	2	-29.00	0-3		-3.00	1-19	5	-14.00	0-12		-12.00
April	5-69	7	-15.50	1-9	11	+2.00	4-38	10	+4.50	0-22		-22.00
May	13-126	10	-57.20	7-32	21	-6.95	4-55	7	-26.25	2-39	5	-24.00
June	15-156	9	-68.72	6-48	12	-27.35	7-71	9	-23.37	2-37	5	-18.00
July	6-154	3	-122.75	5-71	7	-43.00	1-42	2	-38.75	0-41		-41.00
August	13-159	8	-84.80	9-79	11	-36.63	2-35	5	-22.50	2-45	4	-25.67
September	18-149	12	-3.57	12-77	15	+6.93	2-29	6	-9.50	4-43	9	-1.00
October	15-118	12	-1.00	3-53	5	-36.50	6-32	18	+20.50	6-33	18	+15.00
November	6-46	13	+19.00	3-26	11	+14.00	0-12		-12.00	3-8	37	+17.00
December	3-15	20	+2.00	0-8		-8.00	3-7	42	+10.00	0-0		0.00

2003

	Overall			Two-year-olds			Three-year-olds			Older horses		
	W-R	%	£1	W-R	%	£1	W-R	%	£1	W-R	%	£1
January	3-20	15	-5.00	0-0			2-7	28	+4.50	1-13	7	-9.50
February	0-6		-6.00	0-0			0-2		-2.00	0-4		-4.00
March	1-24	4	-22.20	1-2	50	-0.20	0-13		-13.00	0-9		-9.00
April	15-83	18	+15.51	5-15	33	+1.73	6-35	17	+25.16	4-33	12	-11.38
May	19-148	12	-40.22	7-35	20	-12.45	7-59	11	-28.57	5-54	9	+0.80
June	12-136	8	-32.45	3-35	8	-22.63	5-49	10	+15.55	4-52	7	-25.38
July	27-190	14	+5.37	14-70	20	+13.24	9-62	14	-9.63	4-58	6	+1.75
August	21-187	11	-80.85	8-85	9	-47.63	8-51	15	-14.97	5-51	9	-18.25
September	21-155	13	+4.45	7-80	8	-26.92	5-36	13	-5.79	9-39	23	+37.17
October	21-151	13	-12.72	6-78	7	-47.33	7-36	19	+26.00	8-37	21	+8.61
November	4-41	9	-15.90	2-17	11	+0.50	2-12	16	-4.40	0-12		-12.00
December	2-7	28	+1.75	1-3	33	-0.25	1-4	25	+2.00	0-0		

2002

	Overall			Two-year-olds			Three-year-olds			Older horses		
	W-R	%	£1	W-R	%	£1	W-R	%	£1	W-R	%	£1
January	1-5	20	-0.50	0-0			0-0			1-5	20	-0.50
February	0-9		-9.00	0-0			0-4		-4.00	0-5		-5.00
March	6-28	21	+20.20	1-3	33	-0.80	2-15	13	+2.50	3-10	30	+18.50
April	9-87	10	-25.83	4-17	23	-2.75	3-49	6	-41.08	2-21	9	+18.00
May	18-140	12	-7.84	6-36	16	-16.59	7-67	10	+7.25	5-37	13	+1.50
June	16-134	11	-23.31	7-46	15	-16.31	4-41	9		5-47	10	-7.00
July	23-143	16	-21.13	11-58	18	-13.99	4-48	8	-25.90	8-37	21	+18.75
August	16-166	9	-58.98	6-70	8	-51.53	2-57	3	-23.00	8-39	20	+15.55
September	22-141	15	+33.79	9-63	14	-1.27	10-48	20	+37.56	3-30	10	-2.50
October	9-117	7	-33.50	5-61	8	-23.50	1-31	3	-23.00	3-25	12	+13.00
November	2-27	7	+5.00	1-11	9	-5.00	0-10		-10.00	1-6	16	+20.00
December	3-16	18	-2.50	2-10	20	-2.50	0-3		-3.00	1-3	33	+3.00

All runners

2004	Wins	Runs	%	2nd	3rd	rest	Win prize	Total prize	£1 Stake
2yo	46	406	11	70	44	41	374,910.80	780,975.95	-138.49
3yo	33	349	9	34	25	37	345,744.88	580,899.56	-109.62
4yo+	19	284	7	20	31	24	179,093.46	375,852.92	-115.67
TOTAL	98	1039	9	124	100	102	899,749.14	1,737,728.43	-363.78

2003	Wins	Runs	%	2nd	3rd	rest	Win prize	Total prize	£1 Stake
2yo	54	420	12	57	70	39	442,294.77	770,230.84	-141.93
3yo	52	366	14	33	38	35	481,057.75	770,039.39	-5.14
4yo+	40	362	11	37	46	36	391,978.05	649,220.13	-41.17
TOTAL	146	1148	12	127	154	110	1,315,330.57	2,189,490.36	-188.24

2002	Wins	Runs	%	2nd	3rd	rest	Win prize	Total prize	£1 Stake
2yo	52	375	13	57	56	51	368,590.67	617,943.12	-134.23
3yo	33	373	8	47	49	47	193,105.59	409,904.87	-82.67
4yo+	40	265	15	24	29	22	442,304.94	659,819.82	+93.30
TOTAL	125	1013	12	128	134	120	1,004,001.20	1,687,667.81	-123.60

By race type

2004

	Overall			Two-year-olds			Three-year-olds			Older horses		
	W-R	%	£1	W-R	%	£1	W-R	%	£1	W-R	%	£1
Handicap	30-474	6	-200.33	4-74	5	-34.25	15-185	8	-57.92	11-215	5	-108.17
Group 1,2,3	5-61	8	-4.00	1-19	5	-4.00	2-16	12	+12.50	2-26	7	-12.50
Maiden	39-288	13	-91.39	33-219	15	-50.89	6-67	8	-38.50	0-2		-2.00
1st time out	5-97	5	-64.00	4-82	4	-52.50	1-11	9	-7.50	0-4		-4.00

2003

	Overall			Two-year-olds			Three-year-olds			Older horses		
	W-R	%	£1	W-R	%	£1	W-R	%	£1	W-R	%	£1
Handicap	67-579	11	-15.36	8-81	9	-28.34	31-219	14	+15.87	28-279	10	-2.89
Group 1,2,3	4-55	7	-22.00	1-25	4	-12.00	1-14	7	-5.00	2-16	12	-5.00
Maiden	39-275	14	-65.57	26-189	13	-56.34	12-78	15	-2.89	1-8	12	-6.33
1st time out	9-110	8	-69.15	9-87	10	-46.15	0-22		-22.00	0-1		-1.00

2002

	Overall			Two-year-olds			Three-year-olds			Older horses		
	W-R	%	£1	W-R	%	£1	W-R	%	£1	W-R	%	£1
Handicap	50-493	10	-26.05	10-91	10	-16.13	12-189	6	-58.27	28-213	13	+48.35
Group 1,2,3	5-41	12	-21.19	2-18	11	-7.27	1-7	14	-5.67	2-16	12	-8.25
Maiden	37-250	14	-64.38	27-154	17	-61.82	10-92	10	+1.44	0-4		-4.00
1st time out	11-105	10	-51.13	8-71	11	-40.47	3-32	9	-8.67	0-2		-2.00

By jockey

2004

	Overall			Two-year-olds			Three-year-olds			Older horses		
	W-R	%	£1	W-R	%	£1	W-R	%	£1	W-R	%	£1
T E Durcan	24-275	8	-95.27	15-123	12	-38.27	6-88	6	-25.50	3-64	4	-31.50
S Hitchcott	23-250	9	-99.48	9-77	11	-17.90	8-89	8	-38.92	6-84	7	-42.67
A Culhane	16-133	12	-33.18	11-61	18	-0.98	3-43	6	-25.20	2-29	6	-7.00
C Catlin	13-179	7	-89.25	4-78	5	-54.00	3-60	5	-48.75	6-41	14	+13.50
T O'Brien	6-40	15	+14.00	0-6		-6.00	6-19	31	+35.00	0-15		-15.00
T Quinn	3-11	27	+6.25	0-2		-2.00	2-7	28	+1.25	1-2	50	+7.00
K Fallon	3-13	23	-5.20	2-9	22	-3.70	1-2	50	+0.50	0-2		-2.00
D Allan	2-3	66	+12.00	0-1		-1.00	1-1	100	+5.00	1-1	100	+8.00
J Fanning	2-4	50	+7.25	2-4	50	+7.25	0-0		0.00	0-0		0.00
J Quinn	2-6	33	+0.10	2-4	50	+2.10	0-1		-1.00	0-1		-1.00

By jockey ctd

2003

	Overall			Two-year-olds			Three-year-olds			Older horses		
	W-R	%	£1	W-R	%	£1	W-R	%	£1	W-R	%	£1
S Hitchcott	36-189	19	+78.04	6-45	13	-25.59	18-63	28	+71.38	12-81	14	+32.25
A Culhane	34-152	22	+35.33	15-75	20	+5.83	10-34	29	+25.51	9-43	20	+3.98
C Catlin	24-220	10	-59.16	12-97	12	-8.92	5-61	8	-46.59	7-62	11	-3.66
S Drowne	22-184	11	-79.57	11-75	14	-35.87	8-83	9	-43.45	3-26	11	-0.25
T E Durcan	15-133	11	-26.38	8-69	11	-27.13	3-35	8	+15.00	4-29	13	-14.25
D Corby	3-87	3	-64.25	0-18		-18.00	1-29	3	-25.00	2-40	5	-21.25
E Creighton	2-59	3	-37.00	0-5		-5.00	1-21	4	-4.00	1-33	3	-28.00
M J Kinane	1-1	100	+1.25	1-1	100	+1.25	0-0			0-0		
J F McDonald	1-2	50	+4.50	0-0			1-2	50	+4.50	0-0		
R L Moore	1-2	50	+19.00	0-0			0-1		-1.00	1-1	100	+20.00

2002

	Overall			Two-year-olds			Three-year-olds			Older horses		
	W-R	%	£1	W-R	%	£1	W-R	%	£1	W-R	%	£1
S Drowne	40-325	12	-29.71	20-139	14	-42.88	14-130	10	+24.67	6-56	10	-11.50
C Catlin	26-256	10	-67.90	10-101	9	-53.93	6-99	6	-39.22	10-56	17	+25.25
A Culhane	21-91	23	+27.67	10-42	23	+1.04	4-33	12	-4.00	7-16	43	+30.63
D Corby	20-162	12	+23.18	6-30	20	+6.43	2-45	4	-37.17	12-87	13	+53.92
T E Durcan	6-41	14	-6.81	2-10	20	-4.56	2-15	13	-8.25	2-16	12	+6.00
J Carroll	3-10	30	+2.48	1-4	25	-2.09	1-4	25	-2.43	1-2	50	+7.00
J F McDonald	3-17	17	-2.27	1-6	16	-1.00	2-3	66	+6.73	0-8		-8.00
W Ryan	2-5	40	+16.00	0-1		-1.00	2-4	50	+17.00	0-0		
L Dettori	2-11	18	+3.00	0-5		-5.00	0-1		-1.00	2-5	40	+9.00
M Tebbutt	1-8	12	-5.25	1-3	33	-0.25	0-4		-4.00	0-1		-1.00

By class

2004

	Overall			Two-year-olds			Three-year-olds			Older horses		
	W-R	%	£1	W-R	%	£1	W-R	%	£1	W-R	%	£1
A	9-101	8	-15.50	3-37	8	-9.50	4-32	12	+12.50	2-32	6	-18.50
B	5-80	6	-32.25	1-19	5	+2.00	3-23	13	-5.25	1-38	2	-29.00
C	7-135	5	-91.17	2-31	6	-23.50	2-40	5	-25.67	3-64	4	-42.00
D	37-347	10	-131.09	22-182	12	-67.17	9-100	9	-49.25	6-65	9	-14.67
E	18-214	8	-113.83	11-78	14	-21.63	6-85	7	-44.70	1-51	1	-47.50
F	10-96	10	-18.05	3-28	10	-21.80	4-44	9	-13.25	3-24	12	+17.00
G	6-37	16	+23.10	2-17	11	+2.10	2-15	13	+5.00	2-5	40	+16.00

2003

	Overall			Two-year-olds			Three-year-olds			Older horses		
	W-R	%	£1	W-R	%	£1	W-R	%	£1	W-R	%	£1
A	8-106	7	-49.15	3-46	6	-14.00	3-35	8	-17.90	2-25	8	-17.25
B	16-119	13	+19.17	3-23	13	-6.83	5-33	15	+9.50	8-63	12	+16.50
C	16-188	8	-46.38	2-40	5	-32.25	6-60	10	-7.38	8-88	9	-6.75
D	53-401	13	-99.63	27-197	13	-75.60	17-138	12	-16.25	9-66	13	-7.78
E	27-196	13	+10.55	10-68	14	+1.37	10-63	15	+19.68	7-65	10	-10.50
F	17-94	18	-16.05	4-25	16	-11.38	9-32	28	+3.70	4-37	10	-8.39
G	6-32	18	-5.75	3-14	21	-1.25	2-4	50	+4.50	1-14	7	-9.00

2002

	Overall			Two-year-olds			Three-year-olds			Older horses		
	W-R	%	£1	W-R	%	£1	W-R	%	£1	W-R	%	£1
A	7-83	8	-35.44	1-32	3	-30.27	2-23	8	-19.42	4-28	14	+14.25
B	8-107	7	-4.50	1-21	4	-9.00	0-31		-31.00	7-55	12	+35.50
C	19-189	10	-44.19	7-46	15	-12.07	2-66	3	-53.00	10-77	12	+20.88
D	48-365	13	+7.21	23-164	14	-45.12	17-151	11	+47.26	8-50	16	+5.07
E	28-172	16	-15.50	11-65	16	-29.44	9-70	12	-2.67	8-37	21	+16.60
F	9-65	13	-30.44	4-23	17	-10.59	3-28	10	-19.85	2-14	14	
G	4-27	14	-9.75	4-20	20	-2.75	0-4		-4.00	0-3		-3.00

GATWICK: flying home at Goodwood for Channon

By course

2004

	Overall			Two-year-olds			Three-year-olds			Older horses		
	W-R	%	£1	W-R	%	£1	W-R	%	£1	W-R	%	£1
Ascot	1-43	2	-39.00	0-12		-12.00	1-15	6	-11.00	0-16		-16.00
Ayr	1-23	4	-21.20	0-9		-9.00	1-8	12	-6.20	0-6		-6.00
Bath	5-48	10	-26.50	4-20	20	-1.00	1-21	4	-18.50	0-7		-7.00
Beverley	3-20	15	-4.38	2-6	33	+1.63	1-11	9	-3.00	0-3		-3.00
Brighton	6-35	17	+23.25	3-9	33	+17.75	1-17	5	-4.00	2-9	22	+9.50
Carlisle	0-3		-3.00	0-1		-1.00	0-1		-1.00	0-1		-1.00
Catterick	3-20	15	+4.75	2-10	20	-0.25	0-6		-6.00	1-4	25	+11.00
Chepstow	3-24	12	-13.45	3-11	27	-0.45	0-5		-5.00	0-8		-8.00
Chester	0-22		-22.00	0-5		-5.00	0-8		-8.00	0-9		-9.00
Doncaster	4-34	11	-12.25	1-11	9	-7.25	2-9	22	+1.50	1-14	7	-6.50
Epsom	3-23	13	-4.00	1-7	14	-3.00	2-4	50	+11.00	0-12		-12.00
Folkestone	1-13	7	-7.50	1-5	20	+0.50	0-7		-7.00	0-1		-1.00
Goodwood	7-71	9	-20.92	3-29	10	-0.17	2-21	9	-0.75	2-21	0	5.00
Hamilton	3-10	30	-2.15	2-5	40	-0.40	1-3	33	+0.25	0-2		-2.00
Haydock	2-31	6	-22.40	1-10	10	-7.90	1-11	9	-4.50	0-10		-10.00
Kempton	3-34	8	-19.00	2-13	15	-5.50	1-7	14	+0.50	0-14		-14.00
Leicester	2-15	13	-8.25	1-5	20	-2.75	1-8	12	-3.50	0-2		-2.00
Lingfield	8-72	11	-27.35	2-21	9	-8.60	5-34	14	-9.75	1-17	5	-9.00
Musselburgh	2-16	12	+14.00	1-4	25	+17.00	0-4		-4.00	1-8	12	+1.00
Newbury	4-84	4	-63.50	3-38	7	-20.00	1-23	4	-20.50	0-23		-23.00
Newcastle	3-20	15	+8.00	0-9		-9.00	2-5	40	+14.00	1-6	16	+3.00
Newmarket	6-85	7	+2.50	1-36	2	-15.00	3-28	10	+25.00	2-21	9	-7.50
Nottingham	1-24	4	-9.00	0-7		-7.00	1-14	7	+1.00	0-3		-3.00
Pontefract	2-16	12	-5.17	0-4		-4.00	0-7		-7.00	2-5	40	+5.83
Redcar	3-19	15	-2.70	2-10	20	+0.30	1-6	16	0.00	0-3		-3.00
Ripon	3-20	15	-6.50	1-8	12	-5.50	1-9	11	-5.00	1-3	33	+4.00
Salisbury	5-38	13	-10.67	4-17	23	+6.00	1-12	8	-7.67	0-9		-9.00
Sandown	0-25		-25.00	0-10		-10.00	0-6		-6.00	0-9		-9.00
Southwell	0-11		-11.00	0-8		-8.00	0-2		-2.00	0-1		-1.00
Thirsk	1-14	7	-8.50	1-7	14	-1.50	0-5		-5.00	0-2		-2.00
Warwick	2-12	16	+2.50	2-5	40	+9.50	0-5		-5.00	0-2		-2.00
Windsor	0-21		-21.00	0-11		-11.00	0-3		-3.00	0-7		-7.00
Wolver	7-28	25	+26.50	1-14	7	-6.00	2-9	22	+4.50	4-5	80	+28.00
Yarmouth	4-38	10	-1.90	2-17	11	-11.90	1-9	11	+1.00	1-12	8	+9.00
York	0-27		-27.00	0-12		-12.00	0-6		-6.00	0-9		-9.00

Sir Michael Stoute

May and August were the best months to catch Sir Michael last season, but he is pretty consistent in all months from May onwards.

It was a great season for Group success too, with 25% of Stoute inmates triumphing. This was characterised by yet another Derby win with North Light. Once again though, the St Leger proved elusive with Quiff just losing out to Godolphin's Rule Of Law. Nicky Mackay doesn't get many chances, but has impressive stable stats.

By month

2004

	Overall			Two-year-olds			Three-year-olds			Older horses		
	W-R	%	£1	W-R	%	£1	W-R	%	£1	W-R	%	£1
January	0-0			0-0			0-0			0-0		
February	0-0			0-0			0-0			0-0		
March	1-2	50	+2.50	0-0		0.00	0-0		0.00	1-2	50	+2.50
April	3-28	10	-15.06	0-0		0.00	2-20	10	-10.56	1-8	12	-4.50
May	15-51	29	+32.66	0-0		0.00	10-39	25	+16.51	5-12	41	+16.15
June	13-60	21	-0.17	2-4	50	+5.13	8-45	17	-7.55	3-11	27	+2.25
July	11-69	15	-26.32	0-9		-9.00	8-43	18	-15.15	3-17	17	-2.17
August	23-60	38	+51.55	5-21	23	+8.10	14-28	50	+28.95	4-11	36	+14.50
September	10-65	15	-30.84	7-38	18	-13.04	2-20	10	-14.30	1-7	14	-3.50
October	9-63	14	+13.08	7-43	16	+19.75	2-16	12	-2.67	0-4		-4.00
November	2-2	100	+3.55	2-2	100	+3.55	0-0		0.00	0-0		0.00
December	0-0			0-0			0-0			0-0		

2003

	Overall			Two-year-olds			Three-year-olds			Older horses		
	W-R	%	£1	W-R	%	£1	W-R	%	£1	W-R	%	£1
January	0-0			0-0			0-0			0-0		
February	0-0			0-0			0-0			0-0		
March	0-0			0-0			0-0			0-0		
April	8-20	40	-2.85	0-0			7-18	38	-3.85	1-2	50	+1.00
May	31-80	38	+58.69	1-1	100	+0.83	19-55	34	+27.60	11-24	45	+30.26
June	16-72	22	-25.63	0-4		-4.00	12-41	29	-3.43	4-27	14	-18.20
July	12-75	16	-31.26	3-13	23	-8.26	6-43	13	-26.75	3-19	15	+3.75
August	25-101	24	-22.66	6-25	24	-8.69	14-54	25	-9.25	5-22	22	-4.72
September	16-71	22	+19.63	8-36	22	+1.12	5-24	20	-1.48	3-11	27	+20.00
October	8-61	13	-25.95	6-39	15	-14.45	2-17	11	-6.50	0-5		-5.00
November	0-8		-8.00	0-6		-6.00	0-1		-1.00	0-1		-1.00
December	0-0			0-0			0-0			0-0		

2002

	Overall			Two-year-olds			Three-year-olds			Older horses		
	W-R	%	£1	W-R	%	£1	W-R	%	£1	W-R	%	£1
January	0-0			0-0			0-0			0-0		
February	0-0			0-0			0-0			0-0		
March	0-0			0-0			0-0			0-0		
April	7-35	20	+8.24	0-0		+0.00	7-35	20	+8.24	0-0		+0.00
May	19-77	24	+22.24	0-1		-1.00	19-68	27	+31.24	0-8		-8.00
June	18-84	21	-19.11	1-6	16	-2.75	14-67	20	-20.61	3-11	27	+4.25
July	13-58	22	+3.12	4-12	33	+3.75	8-42	19	-3.13	1-4	25	+2.50
August	21-89	23	-19.92	4-22	18	-9.76	17-60	28	-3.17	0-7		-7.00
September	14-72	19	-22.03	10-39	25	+1.23	4-30	13	-20.27	0-3		-3.00
October	13-63	20	-5.33	10-40	25	+7.75	3-20	15	-10.08	0-3		-3.00
November	1-10	10	-7.62	0-5		-5.00	1-5	20	-2.62	0-0		+0.00
December	0-2		-2.00	0-2		-2.00	0-0		+0.00	0-0		+0.00

All runners

2004	Wins	Runs	%	2nd	3rd	rest	Win prize	Total prize	£1 Stake
2yo	23	117	20	14	11	14	128,011.90	170,325.95	+14.49
3yo	46	211	22	29	23	30	1,439,075.54	1,769,742.77	-4.76
4yo+	18	72	25	6	12	6	749,842.80	1,002,156.80	+21.23
TOTAL	87	400	22	49	46	50	2,316,930.24	2,942,225.52	+30.96

2003	Wins	Runs	%	2nd	3rd	rest	Win prize	Total prize	£1 Stake
2yo	24	124	19	21	12	19	237,922.08	353,334.28	-39.45
3yo	65	253	25	41	38	21	1,934,014.71	2,477,145.58	-24.66
4yo+	27	111	24	12	21	9	643,699.22	1,049,521.95	+26.09
TOTAL	116	488	23	74	71	49	2,815,636.01	3,880,001.81	-38.02

2002	Wins	Runs	%	2nd	3rd	rest	Win prize	Total prize	£1 Stake
2yo	29	127	22	22	19	18	221,774.35	404,548.30	-7.78
3yo	73	327	22	48	46	40	793,731.64	1,281,815.17	-20.42
4yo+	4	36	11	2	4	9	563,047.85	791,416.74	-14.25
TOTAL	106	490	21	72	69	67	1,578,553.84	2,477,780.21	-42.45

By race type

2004

	Overall			Two-year-olds			Three-year-olds			Older horses		
	W-R	%	£1	W-R	%	£1	W-R	%	£1	W-R	%	£1
Handicap	18-109	16	+12.13	1-6	16	+2.00	13-84	15	-4.38	4-19	21	+14.50
Group 1,2,3	14-56	25	+9.08	0-3		-3.00	5-22	22	-0.75	9-31	29	+12.83
Maiden	39-170	22	+20.01	17-94	18	+16.25	22-76	28	+3.76	0-0		0.00
1st time out	13-82	15	+20.30	11-64	17	+28.30	2-18	11	-8.00	0-0		0.00

2003

	Overall			Two-year-olds			Three-year-olds			Older horses		
	W-R	%	£1	W-R	%	£1	W-R	%	£1	W-R	%	£1
Handicap	24-127	18	+22.53	0-2		-2.00	13-74	17	-5.30	11-51	21	+29.83
Group 1,2,3	10-71	14	-4.30	1-8	12	-4.00	7-34	20	+17.97	2-29	6	-18.27
Maiden	54-195	27	-46.15	15-94	15	-38.62	38-99	38	-8.53	1-2	50	+1.00
1st time out	11-83	13	-27.86	6-61	9	-27.83	5-21	23	+0.98	0-1		-1.00

2002

	Overall			Two-year-olds			Three-year-olds			Older horses		
	W-R	%	£1	W-R	%	£1	W-R	%	£1	W-R	%	£1
Handicap	12-107	11	-56.38	1-4	25	+0.50	11-98	11	-51.88	0-5		-5.00
Group 1,2,3	10-71	14	-33.22	2-11	18	-7.39	5-35	14	-18.83	3-25	12	-7.00
Maiden	68-242	28	+45.47	23-91	25	+9.13	45-151	29	+36.33	0-0		+0.00
1st time out	21-107	19	+25.47	13-61	21	+8.25	8-46	17	+17.22	0-0		+0.00

By jockey

2004

	Overall			Two-year-olds			Three-year-olds			Older horses		
	W-R	%	£1	W-R	%	£1	W-R	%	£1	W-R	%	£1
K Fallon	51-228	22	-21.57	11-53	20	-12.72	26-122	21	-17.58	14-53	26	+8.73
N Mackay	6-12	50	+28.70	2-6	33	+10.00	4-6	66	+18.70	0-0		0.00
B Doyle	5-27	18	+4.63	0-5		-5.00	5-22	22	+9.63	0-0		0.00
R Winston	4-13	30	+16.43	4-9	44	+20.43	0-4		-4.00	0-0		0.00
R Hills	4-23	17	-8.03	1-10	10	-7.38	2-9	22	-3.65	1-4	25	+3.00
D Holland	3-12	25	+16.62	3-9	33	+19.63	0-2		-2.00	0-1		-1.00
F Lynch	3-16	18	-4.78	0-3		-3.00	3-11	27	+0.23	0-2		-2.00
J P Murtagh	2-4	50	+9.50	0-0		0.00	1-2	50	+7.00	1-2	50	+2.50
M J Kinane	1-1	100	+12.00	0-0		0.00	0-0		0.00	1-1	100	+12.00
F Norton	1-2	50	+7.00	0-0		0.00	1-2	50	+7.00	0-0		0.00

By jockey ctd

2003

	Overall			Two-year-olds			Three-year-olds			Older horses		
	W-R	%	£1	W-R	%	£1	W-R	%	£1	W-R	%	£1
K Fallon	64-243	26	-21.88	15-59	25	-13.39	30-124	24	-20.35	19-60	31	+11.84
B Doyle	15-57	26	-9.50	2-19	10	-15.39	11-32	34	+4.39	2-6	33	+1.50
R Hills	5-20	25	-6.97	2-6	33	+3.00	3-9	33	-4.97	0-5		-5.00
W Supple	4-13	30	+4.29	0-0		+0.00	3-11	27	-4.71	1-2	50	+9.00
J P Murtagh	4-16	25	-8.64	0-0		+0.00	3-8	37	-2.89	1-8	12	-5.75
R Hughes	4-26	15	-11.68	1-11	9	-9.43	2-11	18	-3.25	1-4	25	+1.00
J P Spencer	3-9	33	+16.50	2-5	40	+9.50	0-3		-3.00	1-1	100	+10.00
Pat Eddery	3-22	13	-8.75	1-9	11	-5.25	1-4	25	+3.00	1-9	11	-6.50
F Lynch	3-24	12	+2.08	0-3		-3.00	3-17	17	+9.08	0-4		-4.00
F Norton	2-4	50	+1.25	0-1		-1.00	2-3	66	+2.25	0-0		+0.00

2002

	Overall			Two-year-olds			Three-year-olds			Older horses		
	W-R	%	£1	W-R	%	£1	W-R	%	£1	W-R	%	£1
K Fallon	36-151	23	-30.25	11-44	25	-9.93	23-90	25	-13.56	2-17	11	-6.75
F Lynch	22-72	30	-0.63	9-22	40	+12.90	13-49	26	-12.53	0-1		-1.00
Pat Eddery	11-43	25	-5.34	1-7	14	-4.00	10-34	29	+0.67	0-2		-2.00
J Fortune	7-30	23	+33.00	2-10	20	-0.25	5-20	25	+33.25	0-0		
J P Murtagh	7-36	19	-1.88	1-7	14	-0.50	5-22	22	-1.89	1-7	14	+0.50
R Hughes	7-43	16	-10.22	2-11	18	+4.25	5-32	15	-14.47	0-0		
R Hills	6-30	20	-7.47	3-9	33	+6.75	3-16	18	-9.22	0-5		-5.00
J P Spencer	2-7	28	-1.00	0-2		-2.00	2-5	40	+1.00	0-0		
S W Kelly	2-19	10	-6.50	0-2		-2.00	2-16	12	-3.50	0-1		-1.00
K Dalgleish	1-1	100	+4.00	0-0			1-1	100	+4.00	0-0		

By class

2004

	Overall			Two-year-olds			Three-year-olds			Older horses		
	W-R	%	£1	W-R	%	£1	W-R	%	£1	W-R	%	£1
A	22-89	24	+4.23	0-4		-4.00	7-36	19	-9.00	15-49	30	+17.23
B	5-28	17	+6.57	1-1	100	+0.57	2-17	11	-4.00	2-10	20	+10.00
C	7-52	13	-6.38	0-4		-4.00	7-37	18	+8.63	0-11		-11.00
D	48-207	23	+28.06	20-95	21	+25.30	27-110	24	-2.24	1-2	50	+5.00
E	3-10	30	+8.75	1-3	33	+5.00	2-7	28	+3.75	0-0		0.00
F	0-1		-1.00	0-0		0.00	0-1		-1.00	0-0		0.00
G	0-0			0-0			0-0			0-0		

2003

	Overall			Two-year-olds			Three-year-olds			Older horses		
	W-R	%	£1	W-R	%	£1	W-R	%	£1	W-R	%	£1
A	22-128	17	-17.43	3-14	21	-0.50	10-66	15	-5.72	9-48	18	-11.21
B	11-60	18	+4.65	0-3		-3.00	4-24	16	-12.40	7-33	21	+20.05
C	21-72	29	+20.54	2-6	33	+1.90	9-42	21	-1.61	10-24	41	+20.25
D	60-214	28	-37.88	19-98	19	-34.85	40-113	35	-3.03	1-3	33	
E	1-7	14	-3.00	0-3		-3.00	1-4	25		0-0		
F	0-1		-1.00	0-0			0-1		-1.00	0-0		
G	0-0			0-0			0-0			0-0		

2002

	Overall			Two-year-olds			Three-year-olds			Older horses		
	W-R	%	£1	W-R	%	£1	W-R	%	£1	W-R	%	£1
A	13-100	13	-49.18	3-15	20	-4.39	8-57	14	-30.79	2-28	7	-14.00
B	6-37	16	-12.91	1-5	20	-3.27	4-27	14	-8.38	1-5	20	-1.25
C	12-64	18	-23.68	1-9	11	-6.75	11-54	20	-15.93	0-1		-1.00
D	71-270	26	+45.07	23-96	23	+4.63	48-174	27	+40.43	0-0		
E	2-8	25	+1.25	0-1		-1.00	2-7	28	+2.25	0-0		
F	1-5	20	-1.00	1-1	100	+3.00	0-4		-4.00	0-0		
G	0-0			0-0			0-0			0-0		

By course

2004

	Overall			Two-year-olds			Three-year-olds			Older horses		
	W-R	%	£1	W-R	%	£1	W-R	%	£1	W-R	%	£1
Ascot	3-28	10	-8.00	0-1		-1.00	2-17	11	-4.50	1-10	10	-2.50
Ayr	1-2	50	-0.17	0-0		0.00	0-0		0.00	1-2	50	-0.17
Bath	1-6	16	-4.09	0-2		-2.00	1-4	25	-2.09	0-0		0.00
Beverley	1-2	50	+7.00	0-1		-1.00	1-1	100	+8.00	0-0		0.00
Brighton	3-4	75	+9.83	0-0		0.00	3-4	75	+9.83	0-0		0.00
Catterick	2-3	66	+1.00	1-1	100	+1.88	1-2	50	-0.88	0-0		0.00
Chepstow	0-3		-3.00	0-0		0.00	0-3		-3.00	0-0		0.00
Chester	2-5	40	+8.00	0-0		0.00	2-3	66	+10.00	0-2		-2.00
Doncaster	2-20	10	-12.00	0-8		-8.00	0-6		-6.00	2-6	33	+2.00
Epsom	2-10	20	+1.00	0-2		-2.00	2-7	28	+4.00	0-1		-1.00
Folkestone	1-3	33	+8.00	1-2	50	+9.00	0-1		-1.00	0-0		0.00
Goodwood	5-20	25	+1.65	0-1		-1.00	2-10	20	-1.25	3-9	33	+3.90
Hamilton	2-3	66	+4.10	0-0		0.00	2-3	66	+4.10	0-0		0.00
Haydock	0-4		-4.00	0-0		0.00	0-4		-4.00	0-0		0.00
Kempton	1-18	5	-16.39	1-9	11	-7.39	0-8		-8.00	0-1		-1.00
Leicester	1-11	9	-3.00	1-8	12	0.00	0-3		-3.00	0-0		0.00
Lingfield	7-18	38	+11.08	3-9	33	+5.62	4-9	44	+5.45	0-0		0.00
Musselburgh	1-1	100	+0.44	0-0		0.00	1-1	100	+0.44	0-0		0.00
Newbury	5-22	22	+2.07	2-5	40	+0.57	1-11	9	-2.00	2-6	33	+3.50
Newmarket	16-75	21	+29.10	4-23	17	+18.00	6-33	18	-1.90	6-19	31	+13.00
Nottingham	2-9	22	-3.13	2-6	33	-0.13	0-3		-3.00	0-0		0.00
Pontefract	3-15	20	-3.45	1-3	33	+3.50	2-11	18	-5.95	0-1		-1.00
Redcar	0-1		-1.00	0-1		-1.00	0-0		0.00	0-0		0.00
Ripon	0-4		-4.00	0-0		0.00	0-4		-4.00	0-0		0.00
Salisbury	2-11	18	-4.93	0-6		-6.00	2-4	50	+2.07	0-1		-1.00
Sandown	7-25	28	+5.16	2-3	66	+1.16	4-16	25	+3.00	1-6	16	+1.00
Southwell	0-1		-1.00	0-0		0.00	0-1		-1.00	0-0		0.00
Thirsk	1-5	20	-2.37	0-1		-1.00	1-4	25	-1.37	0-0		0.00
Warwick	1-6	16	+9.00	0-4		-4.00	1-2	50	+13.00	0-0		0.00
Windsor	4-28	14	-18.72	0-5		-5.00	4-23	17	-13.72	0-0		0.00
Wolver	2-4	50	+1.55	2-3	66	+2.55	0-1		-1.00	0-0		0.00
Yarmouth	4-17	23	+9.22	3-12	25	+12.72	1-4	25	-2.50	0-1		-1.00
York	5-16	31	+12.00	0-1		-1.00	3-8	37	+5.50	2-7	28	+7.50

FIRST CHARTER (centre): wins the Lonsdale for Stoute

Barry Hills

Last season was a veritable curate's egg for Barry Hills - it started and ended with a bang courtesy of Haafhd winning the 2,000 Guineas and the Champion Stakes, but it was a little 'iffy' in between times.

Son Michael rode the vast majority of winners from this yard, but Tony Culhane emerges with credit too. He won on 17% of his mounts for the stable, generating a £39.87 profit. Although they are a long way from home, Haydock and Redcar are the best courses to follow this stable.

By month

2004

	Overall			**Two-year-olds**			**Three-year-olds**			**Older horses**		
	W-R	%	£1	W-R	%	£1	W-R	%	£1	W-R	%	£1
January	2-7	28	-2.81	0-0		0.00	2-5	40	-0.81	0-2		-2.00
February	2-4	50	-0.72	0-0		0.00	2-3	66	+0.28	0-1		-1.00
March	3-16	18	-6.59	0-0		0.00	3-11	27	-1.59	0-5		-5.00
April	8-59	13	-4.46	0-0		0.00	6-45	13	-4.46	2-14	14	0.00
June	14-99	14	-43.54	4-10	40	+10.90	9-73	12	-42.44	1-16	6	-12.00
July	5-79	6	-60.60	1-28	3	-26.20	4-42	9	-25.40	0-9		-9.00
August	6-65	9	-27.25	3-20	15	-4.75	3-36	8	-13.50	0-9		-9.00
September	15-114	13	+22.88	5-56	8	-35.85	8-50	16	+53.98	2-8	25	+4.75
October	10-81	12	+2.00	3-33	9	-16.50	6-45	13	+4.50	1-3	33	+14.00
November	2-18	11	-9.50	1-6	16	-2.00	1-12	8	-7.50	0-0		0.00
December	3-3	100	+6.16	0-0		0.00	3-3	100	+6.16	0-0		0.00

2003

	Overall			**Two-year-olds**			**Three-year-olds**			**Older horses**		
	W-R	%	£1	W-R	%	£1	W-R	%	£1	W-R	%	£1
January	4-15	26	-0.64	0-0			3-9	33	-2.14	1-6	16	+1.50
February	1-8	12	-3.00	0-0			0-4		-4.00	1-4	25	+1.00
March	8-22	36	+5.18	0-1		-1.00	5-16	31	-1.57	3-5	60	+7.75
April	10-45	22	-5.07	2-3	66	+3.79	7-33	21	-5.86	1-9	11	-3.00
May	11-81	13	-18.33	2-14	14	-9.25	8-50	16	+2.42	1-17	5	-11.50
June	7-74	9	-36.53	0-14		-14.00	6-50	12	-16.53	1-10	10	-6.00
July	19-105	18	+13.83	11-34	32	+33.00	5-55	9	-32.17	3-16	18	+13.00
August	13-89	14	-26.59	9-43	20	-2.17	4-36	11	-14.42	0-10		-10.00
September	17-94	18	+16.46	9-54	16	-1.17	6-28	21	+22.63	2-12	16	-5.00
October	12-77	15	+24.00	4-43	9	-25.00	5-25	20	+37.50	3-9	33	+11.50
November	5-33	15	+14.50	2-18	11	+7.00	3-13	23	+9.50	0-2		-2.00
December	0-2		-2.00	0-1		-1.00	0-1		-1.00	0-0		

2002

	Overall			**Two-year-olds**			**Three-year-olds**			**Older horses**		
	W-R	%	£1	W-R	%	£1	W-R	%	£1	W-R	%	£1
January	0-9		-9.00	0-0			0-5		-5.00	0-4		-4.00
February	1-5	20	-3.00	0-0			1-4	25	-2.00	0-1		-1.00
March	3-28	10	-8.63	0-0			2-21	9	-12.63	1-7	14	+4.00
April	6-61	9	-24.65	0-6		-6.00	4-44	9	-21.15	2-11	18	+2.50
May	8-93	8	-51.75	0-11		-11.00	8-62	12	-20.75	0-20		-20.00
June	6-80	7	-56.39	3-19	15	-7.50	2-44	4	-39.39	1-17	5	-9.50
July	22-137	16	-10.05	9-52	17	-9.74	10-61	16	-4.82	3-24	12	+4.50
August	16-98	16	-35.00	13-44	29	+6.25	1-39	2	-33.00	2-15	13	-8.25
September	11-98	11	-6.56	3-46	6	-39.31	5-37	13	+18.75	3-15	20	+14.00
October	10-98	10	-38.80	6-44	13	-14.52	2-39	5	-19.50	2-15	13	-4.78
November	6-33	18	+20.15	3-19	15	+4.65	3-12	25	+17.50	0-2		-2.00
December	2-11	18	-3.25	2-6	33	+1.75	0-3		-3.00	0-2		-2.00

All runners

2004	Wins	Runs	%	2nd	3rd	rest	Win prize	Total prize	£1 Stake
2yo	17	160	11	26	17	11	219,938.50	345,426.40	-81.40
3yo	58	392	15	41	41	39	794,065.33	1,055,450.25	-49.20
4yo+	7	84	8	9	3	5	85,563.20	155,886.95	-31.75
TOTAL	82	636	13	76	61	55	1,099,567.03	1,556,763.60	-162.35

2003	Wins	Runs	%	2nd	3rd	rest	Win prize	Total prize	£1 Stake
2yo	39	225	17	33	24	28	255,538.95	439,907.90	-9.81
3yo	52	320	16	28	42	25	410,311.35	653,862.77	-5.63
4yo+	16	100	16	11	10	9	265,566.88	367,524.24	-2.75
TOTAL	107	645	16	72	76	62	931,417.18	1,461,294.91	-18.19

2002	Wins	Runs	%	2nd	3rd	rest	Win prize	Total prize	£1 Stake
2yo	39	247	15	44	29	22	266,014.40	439,187.55	-75.4
3yo	38	371	10	48	44	40	314,627.41	601,032.08	-124.97
4yo+	14	133	10	14	12	10	491,430.35	744,880.22	-26.54
TOTAL	91	751	12	106	85	72	1,072,072.16	1,785,099.85	-226.92

By race type

2004

	Overall			Two-year-olds			Three-year-olds			Older horses		
	W-R	%	£1	W-R	%	£1	W-R	%	£1	W-R	%	£1
Handicap	19-248	7	-68.00	1-11	9	-6.50	16-179	8	-16.50	2-58	3	-45.00
Group 1,2,3	7-43	16	+8.83	3-10	30	+7.00	3-26	11	-2.17	1-7	14	+4.00
Maiden	39-266	14	-110.06	11-125	8	-79.15	28-139	20	-28.91	0-2		-2.00
1st time out	3-75	4	-59.75	2-62	3	-50.75	1-13	7	-9.00	0-0		0.00

2003

	Overall			Two-year-olds			Three-year-olds			Older horses		
	W-R	%	£1	W-R	%	£1	W-R	%	£1	W-R	%	£1
Handicap	24-251	9	-96.76	5-30	16	-3.51	8-140	5	-86.25	11-81	13	-7.00
Group 1,2,3	3-48	6	-9.50	0-15		-15.00	2-29	6	+4.00	1-4	25	+1.50
Maiden	58-260	22	+62.78	26-149	17	+6.12	31-109	28	+56.41	1-2	50	+0.25
1st time out	13-98	13	+6.25	10-83	12	-1.75	3-15	20	+8.00	0-0		

2002

	Overall			Two-year-olds			Three-year-olds			Older horses		
	W-R	%	£1	W-R	%	£1	W-R	%	£1	W-R	%	£1
Handicap	25-318	7	-117.26	4-29	13	-16.86	14-186	7	-60.15	7-103	6	-40.25
Group 1,2,3	6-47	12	-17.15	2-13	15	-3.00	1-18	5	-15.25	3-16	18	+1.10
Maiden	45-290	15	-88.14	27-162	16	-49.05	17-127	13	-55.08	1-1	100	+16.00
1st time out	3-91	3	-74.75	3-78	3	-61.75	0-13		-13.00	0-0		

By jockey

2004

	Overall			Two-year-olds			Three-year-olds			Older horses		
	W-R	%	£1	W-R	%	£1	W-R	%	£1	W-R	%	£1
M Hills	40-308	12	-108.65	7-81	8	-51.40	29-183	15	-48.00	4-44	9	-9.25
R Hughes	8-39	20	-5.75	3-16	18	-0.50	5-22	22	-4.25	0-1		-1.00
R Hills	8-47	17	+2.83	2-12	16	-1.75	5-27	18	+3.58	1-8	12	+1.00
A Culhane	6-34	17	+39.87	1-9	11	-4.50	4-23	17	+41.87	1-2	50	+2.50
Martin Dwyer	5-24	20	-2.40	0-3		-3.00	5-20	25	+1.60	0-1		-1.00
P Hanagan	2-5	40	+28.50	0-0		0.00	2-5	40	+28.50	0-0		0.00
E Ahern	2-16	12	-8.25	1-4	25	0.00	1-9	11	-5.25	0-3		-3.00
D Holland	2-20	10	-16.29	0-4		-4.00	2-15	13	-11.29	0-1		-1.00
K May	2-26	7	-1.75	1-7	14	-3.75	1-15	6	+6.00	0-4		-4.00
R Winston	1-2	50	+3.50	1-1	100	+4.50	0-1		-1.00	0-0		0.00

By jockey ctd

2003

	Overall			Two-year-olds			Three-year-olds			Older horses		
	W-R	%	£1	W-R	%	£1	W-R	%	£1	W-R	%	£1
M Hills	48-297	16	-31.22	24-119	20	+10.86	17-131	12	-37.33	7-47	14	-4.75
R Hills	9-42	21	+3.42	6-20	30	+9.25	3-18	16	-1.83	0-4		-4.00
A Culhane	8-34	23	+30.94	1-7	14	-1.50	6-20	30	+34.44	1-7	14	-2.00
R Hughes	8-44	18	-7.56	1-10	10	-7.00	5-27	18	-6.06	2-7	28	+5.50
W Supple	6-24	25	+20.13	1-5	20	+0.50	5-19	26	+19.63	0-0		
Pat Eddery	5-22	22	-0.22	0-3		-3.00	3-11	27	+0.78	2-8	25	+2.00
K Darley	3-9	33	+9.33	1-4	25	-2.67	2-5	40	+12.00	0-0		
D McKeown	3-16	18	-2.25	1-6	16	-2.00	1-8	12	-4.25	1-2	50	+4.00
P Hanagan	2-4	50	+1.16	1-3	33	+0.25	1-1	100	+0.91	0-0		
G Duffield	2-8	25	-1.67	0-1		-1.00	2-5	40	+1.33	0-2		-2.00

2002

	Overall			Two-year-olds			Three-year-olds			Older horses		
	W-R	%	£1	W-R	%	£1	W-R	%	£1	W-R	%	£1
M Hills	43-301	14	-54.68	18-119	15	-32.21	14-119	11	-32.42	11-63	17	+9.97
R Hills	9-58	15	-15.38	4-27	14	-16.38	5-27	18	+5.00	0-4		-4.00
R Hughes	7-60	11	-24.65	2-12	16	-4.75	5-38	13	-9.90	0-10		-10.00
A Culhane	6-17	35	+34.28	2-2	100	+6.53	3-13	23	+12.75	1-2	50	+15.00
Pat Eddery	5-23	21	+16.50	3-5	60	+19.75	1-14	7	-10.25	1-4	25	+7.00
D Holland	5-54	9	-38.99	4-22	18	-9.74	1-23	4	-20.25	0-9		-9.00
K Darley	3-12	25	+0.10	0-2		-2.00	3-9	33	+3.10	0-1		-1.00
D McKeown	3-19	15	+13.75	1-4	25	-1.25	2-12	16	+18.00	0-3		-3.00
W Supple	2-22	9	-16.50	1-9	11	-5.50	1-13	7	-11.00	0-0		
J D Smith	2-34	5	-23.00	1-11	9	-2.00	1-18	5	-16.00	0-5		-5.00

By class

2004

	Overall			Two-year-olds			Three-year-olds			Older horses		
	W-R	%	£1	W-R	%	£1	W-R	%	£1	W-R	%	£1
A	13-88	14	+6.78	4-15	26	+10.00	7-56	12	-14.22	2-17	11	+11.00
B	2-56	3	-41.50	0-4		-4.00	1-27	3	-21.50	1-25	4	-16.00
C	9-78	11	-16.06	0-3		-3.00	8-56	14	+2.94	1-19	5	-16.00
D	43-320	13	-161.18	12-115	10	-69.40	30-193	15	-83.53	1-12	8	-8.25
E	7-60	11	+54.37	1-16	6	-8.00	6-38	15	+68.37	0-6		-6.00
F	3-17	17	-4.75	0-0		0.00	3-15	20	-2.75	0-2		-2.00
G	4-7	57	+5.99	0-1		-1.00	2-3	66	+1.49	2-3	66	+5.50

2003

	Overall			Two-year-olds			Three-year-olds			Older horses		
	W-R	%	£1	W-R	%	£1	W-R	%	£1	W-R	%	£1
A	15-86	17	+25.33	4-26	15	-12.67	9-53	16	+32.50	2-7	28	+5.50
B	6-78	7	-35.50	1-7	14	-1.00	1-30	3	-26.50	4-41	9	-8.00
C	13-104	12	-48.13	4-18	22	-8.84	5-57	8	-33.29	4-29	13	-6.00
D	62-307	20	+66.83	26-158	16	+13.58	33-142	23	+44.99	3-7	42	+8.25
E	10-44	22	-5.72	4-12	33	+3.12	4-23	17	-8.34	2-9	22	-0.50
F	1-19	5	-14.00	0-2		-2.00	0-12		-12.00	1-5	20	
G	0-2		-2.00	0-1		-1.00	0-0			0-1		-1.00

2002

	Overall			Two-year-olds			Three-year-olds			Older horses		
	W-R	%	£1	W-R	%	£1	W-R	%	£1	W-R	%	£1
A	10-91	10	-26.04	3-30	10	-3.00	4-42	9	-19.75	3-19	15	-3.29
B	5-78	6	-23.50	0-11		-11.00	1-22	4	-11.00	4-45	8	-1.50
C	14-115	12	-44.39	6-20	30	-1.99	5-58	8	-23.40	3-37	8	-19.00
D	50-358	13	-105.65	25-163	15	-52.83	22-177	12	-61.08	3-18	16	+8.25
E	9-70	12	-12.85	5-22	22	-5.60	4-43	9	-2.25	0-5		-5.00
F	1-29	3	-12.00	0-0			1-25	4	-8.00	0-4		-4.00
G	1-5	20	-0.50	0-1		-1.00	1-3	33	+1.50	0-1		-1.00

MAIDS CAUSEWAY (right): winning at Newmarket

By course

2004

	Overall			Two-year-olds			Three-year-olds			Older horses		
	W-R	%	£1	W-R	%	£1	W-R	%	£1	W-R	%	£1
Ascot	1-27	3	-19.00	1-4	25	+4.00	0-16		-16.00	0-7		-7.00
Ayr	1-6	16	-1.50	1-2	50	+2.50	0-4		-4.00	0-0		0.00
Bath	3-25	12	-7.00	1-6	16	+1.00	2-19	10	-8.00	0-0		0.00
Beverley	2-4	50	+2.63	0-1		-1.00	2-3	66	+3.63	0-0		0.00
Brighton	1-5	20	-2.75	0-0		0.00	1-5	20	-2.75	0-0		0.00
Catterick	1-5	20	+4.00	0-3		-3.00	1-2	50	+7.00	0-0		0.00
Chepstow	1-7	14	-3.00	0-3		-3.00	1-4	25	0.00	0-0		0.00
Chester	6-25	24	+5.07	2-3	66	+4.40	4-19	21	+3.67	0-3		-3.00
Doncaster	5-42	11	-14.84	1-9	11	-2.00	3-24	12	-12.84	1-9	11	0.00
Epsom	0-10		-10.00	0-0		0.00	0-8		-8.00	0-2		-2.00
Folkestone	0-4		-4.00	0-1		-1.00	0-1		-1.00	0-2		-2.00
Goodwood	1-19	5	-13.50	0-8		-8.00	1-10	10	-4.50	0-1		-1.00
Haydock	5-30	16	+31.15	0-4		-4.00	5-19	26	+42.15	0-7		-7.00
Kempton	1-18	5	-16.60	1-8	12	-6.60	0-7		-7.00	0-3		-3.00
Leicester	2-10	20	-3.25	0-2		-2.00	2-7	28	-0.25	0-1		-1.00
Lingfield	3-32	9	-21.63	0-3		-3.00	3-27	11	-16.63	0-2		-2.00
Newbury	3-56	5	-33.75	2-19	10	-7.75	0-28		-28.00	1-9	11	+2.00
Newcastle	0-5		-5.00	0-1		-1.00	0-4		-4.00	0-0		0.00
Newmarket	13-97	13	+9.83	2-32	6	-22.00	10-55	18	+24.83	1-10	10	+7.00
Nottingham	0-12		-12.00	0-3		-3.00	0-8		-8.00	0-1		-1.00
Pontefract	2-11	18	-3.77	0-2		-2.00	2-7	28	+0.23	0-2		-2.00
Redcar	3-10	30	+26.00	1-3	33	+2.50	2-7	28	+23.50	0-0		0.00
Ripon	4-16	25	+1.53	1-1	100	+2.25	3-15	20	-0.72	0-0		0.00
Salisbury	1-10	10	-8.56	0-6		-6.00	1-4	25	-2.56	0-0		0.00
Sandown	1-24	4	-20.00	1-5	20	-1.00	0-12		-12.00	0-7		-7.00
Southwell	3-7	42	+0.52	0-1		-1.00	2-5	40	-1.47	1-1	100	+3.00
Thirsk	0-4		-4.00	0-0		0.00	0-4		-4.00	0-0		0.00
Warwick	4-24	16	-11.25	1-8	12	-4.50	2-12	16	-5.75	1-4	25	-1.00
Windsor	1-30	3	-28.20	1-14	7	-12.20	0-14		-14.00	0-2		-2.00
Wolver	11-29	37	+21.82	1-1	100	+3.00	9-22	40	+20.32	1-6	16	-1.50
Yarmouth	1-6	16	-4.56	0-4		-4.00	1-2	50	-0.56	0-0		0.00
York	2-26	7	-16.75	0-3		-3.00	1-18	5	-12.50	1-5	20	-1.25

Richard Fahey

Any entries from this stable in handicaps, and ridden by Paul Hanagan are worthy of a second glance. Last season Hanagan showed a healthy profit for the stable on such animals, who contributed the vast majority of stable successes.

Runners in class 'C' handicaps made good returns, while Group runners were thin on the ground, indicating that Fahey knows the merit of his runners and doesn't overface them. Beverley, Chester, Ripon and York were the four best courses for Fahey runners.

By month

2004

	Overall			Two-year-olds			Three-year-olds			Older horses		
	W-R	%	£1	W-R	%	£1	W-R	%	£1	W-R	%	£1
January	2-16	12	-6.75	0-0		0.00	0-3		-3.00	2-13	15	-3.75
February	2-15	13	-2.67	0-0		0.00	0-0		0.00	2-15	13	-2.67
March	1-19	5	-10.00	0-0		0.00	0-1		-1.00	1-18	5	-9.00
April	0-6		-6.00	0-1		-1.00	0-0		0.00	0-5		-5.00
May	2-47	4	-26.25	0-3		-3.00	1-9	11	-5.25	1-35	2	-18.00
June	9-85	10	-0.62	1-8	12	+3.00	5-25	20	+30.00	3-52	5	-33.63
July	12-108	11	+4.11	2-22	9	-12.56	3-28	10	+25.50	7-58	12	-8.83
August	22-110	20	+43.37	4-27	14	-3.75	3-25	12	-16.33	15-58	25	+63.45
September	12-114	10	-39.47	3-32	9	-9.50	2-24	8	-13.75	7-58	12	-16.22
October	8-68	11	-10.87	0-13		-13.00	5-22	22	+24.50	3-33	9	-22.37
November	6-38	15	+16.00	2-10	20	+16.00	3-7	42	+11.00	1-21	4	-11.00
December	1-23	4	-17.00	0-3		-3.00	0-4		-4.00	1-16	6	-10.00

2003

	Overall			Two-year-olds			Three-year-olds			Older horses		
	W-R	%	£1	W-R	%	£1	W-R	%	£1	W-R	%	£1
January	3-14	21	-0.12	0-0		0.00	0-4		-4.00	3-10	30	+3.88
February	1-5	20	-3.00	0-0		0.00	0-2		-2.00	1-3	33	-1.00
March	3-14	21	+13.00	0-0		0.00	2-6	33	+18.50	1-8	12	-5.50
April	1-38	2	-35.00	0-2		-2.00	0-7		-7.00	1-29	3	-26.00
May	4-66	6	-49.25	0-3		-3.00	1-16	6	-10.50	3-47	6	-35.75
June	11-76	14	-17.32	0-7		-7.00	0-13		-13.00	11-56	19	+2.68
July	10-73	13	-22.25	0-10		-10.00	2-13	15	-5.50	8-50	16	-6.75
August	8-63	12	-12.08	1-15	6	-13.33	2-12	16	+4.50	5-36	13	-3.25
September	4-61	6	-46.24	3-20	15	-12.24	0-12		-12.00	1-29	3	-22.00
October	3-40	7	+41.20	2-10	20	+64.70	0-8		-8.00	1-22	4	-15.50
November	0-9		-9.00	0-2		-2.00	0-2		-2.00	0-5		-5.00
December	0-7		-7.00	0-4		-4.00	0-2		-2.00	0-1		-1.00

2002

	Overall			Two-year-olds			Three-year-olds			Older horses		
	W-R	%	£1	W-R	%	£1	W-R	%	£1	W-R	%	£1
January	1-7	14	-1.00	0-0		0.00	0-2		-2.00	1-5	20	+1.00
February	1-7	14	-1.00	0-0		0.00	0-2		-2.00	1-5	20	+1.00
March	1-14	7	-3.00	0-0		0.00	0-0		0.00	1-14	7	-3.00
April	2-35	5	-17.00	0-1		-1.00	1-10	10	+3.00	1-24	4	-19.00
May	6-58	10	-15.25	0-3		-3.00	2-21	9	-1.50	4-34	11	-10.75
June	11-55	20	+15.25	0-2		-2.00	3-17	17	-3.75	8-36	22	+21.00
July	13-64	20	+52.38	0-7		-7.00	8-29	27	+46.67	5-28	17	+12.71
August	5-48	10	-2.10	0-5		-5.00	2-22	9	-3.10	3-21	14	+6.00
September	4-39	10	+1.50	1-7	14	-2.00	0-11		-11.00	3-21	14	+14.50
October	2-23	8	+13.00	0-3		-3.00	1-9	11	+6.00	1-11	9	+10.00
November	0-16		-16.00	0-6		-6.00	0-5		-5.00	0-5		-5.00
December	0-4		-4.00	0-1		-1.00	0-0		0.00	0-3		-3.00

All runners

2004	Wins	Runs	%	2nd	3rd	rest	Win prize	Total prize	£1 Stake
2yo	12	119	10	11	18	6	126,356.75	181,743.20	-26.81
3yo	22	148	15	18	13	16	99,270.75	153,227.39	+47.67
4yo+	43	382	11	32	41	32	279,186.92	405,670.42	-77.02
TOTAL	77	649	12	61	72	54	504,814.42	740,641.01	-56.16

2003	Wins	Runs	%	2nd	3rd	rest	Win prize	Total prize	£1 Stake
2yo	6	73	8	6	16	10	23,020.40	54,683.30	+11.13
3yo	7	97	7	5	5	12	34,290.50	49,786.75	-43.00
4yo+	35	296	12	31	24	18	282,096.30	416,577.73	-115.20
TOTAL	48	466	10	42	45	40	339,407.20	521,047.78	-147.07

2002	Wins	Runs	%	2nd	3rd	rest	Win prize	Total prize	£1 Stake
2yo	1	35	3	0	4	5	8,450.00	13,793.45	-30.00
3yo	17	128	13	15	6	10	79,940.90	114,696.10	+27.32
4yo+	28	207	14	17	16	18	314,737.33	377,441.51	+25.46
TOTAL	46	370	12	32	26	33	403,128.23	505,931.06	+22.78

By race type

2004

	Overall			Two-year-olds			Three-year-olds			Older horses		
	W-R	%	£1	W-R	%	£1	W-R	%	£1	W-R	%	£1
Handicap	59-431	13	+33.27	8-30	26	+32.75	16-96	16	+44.42	35-305	11	-43.90
Group 1,2,3	1-2	50	+6.00	1-2	50	+6.00	0-0		0.00	0-0		0.00
Maiden	4-110	3	-76.81	1-71	1	-69.56	3-37	8	-5.25	0-2		-2.00
1st time out	4-48	8	+31.50	1-27	3	-16.00	2-8	25	+54.00	1-13	7	-6.50

2003

	Overall			Two-year-olds			Three-year-olds			Older horses		
	W-R	%	£1	W-R	%	£1	W-R	%	£1	W-R	%	£1
Handicap	28-321	8	-165.20	0-12		-12.00	3-76	3	-57.00	25-233	10	-96.20
Group 1,2,3	0-1		-1.00	0-0		0.00	0-0		0.00	0-1		-1.00
Maiden	5-72	6	+20.28	3-46	6	+21.28	2-22	9	+3.00	0-4		-4.00
1st time out	3-47	6	+45.70	1-25	4	+38.70	1-9	11	+12.00	1-13	7	-5.00

2002

	Overall			Two-year-olds			Three-year-olds			Older horses		
	W-R	%	£1	W-R	%	£1	W-R	%	£1	W-R	%	£1
Handicap	38-284	13	+54.11	0-13		-13.00	14-94	14	+38.15	24-177	13	+28.96
Group 1,2,3	0-0			0-0			0-0			0-0		
Maiden	2-51	3	-31.00	1-21	4	-16.00	1-26	3	-11.00	0-4		-4.00
1st time out	2-27	7	-1.00	0-8		-8.00	1-13	7	+2.00	1-6	16	+5.00

By jockey

2004

	Overall			Two-year-olds			Three-year-olds			Older horses		
	W-R	%	£1	W-R	%	£1	W-R	%	£1	W-R	%	£1
P Hanagan	42-277	15	+35.61	11-63	17	+25.44	12-66	18	+25.42	19-148	12	-15.25
T Hamilton	18-213	8	-81.60	1-33	3	-29.25	5-46	10	+16.25	12-134	8	-68.60
G Parkin	4-39	10	-1.50	0-5		-5.00	3-13	23	+16.50	1-21	4	-13.00
R Ffrench	2-9	22	+2.50	0-2		-2.00	1-4	25	+2.00	1-3	33	+2.50
S Sanders	1-1	100	+29.70	0-0		0.00	0-0		0.00	1-1	100	+29.70
L Vickers	1-1	100	+9.00	0-0		0.00	0-0		0.00	1-1	100	+9.00
F P Ferris	1-1	100	+5.50	0-0		0.00	0-0		0.00	1-1	100	+5.50
P Dobbs	1-1	100	+1.75	0-0		0.00	0-0		0.00	1-1	100	+1.75
M Hills	1-1	100	+5.50	0-0		0.00	1-1	100	+5.50	0-0		0.00
R Stephens	1-2	50	+4.00	0-0		0.00	0-0		0.00	1-2	50	+4.00

By jockey ctd

2003

	Overall			Two-year-olds			Three-year-olds			Older horses		
	W-R	%	£1	W-R	%	£1	W-R	%	£1	W-R	%	£1
P Hanagan	26-216	12	-12.29	5-43	11	+37.38	4-46	8	-12.50	17-127	13	-37.17
R Ffrench	6-19	31	+16.00	1-3	33	+0.75	2-6	33	+8.00	3-10	30	+7.25
C Poste	6-59	10	-29.40	0-3		-3.00	0-14		-14.00	6-42	14	-12.40
F Norton	2-2	100	+11.50	0-0		0.00	0-0		0.00	2-2	100	+11.50
A Nicholls	2-5	40	+6.25	0-2		-2.00	0-0		0.00	2-3	66	+8.25
A Culhane	2-7	28	-0.62	0-2		-2.00	0-1		-1.00	2-4	50	+2.38
Miss V Tunnicliffe	1-1	100	+4.50	0-0		0.00	0-0		0.00	1-1	100	+4.50
G Duffield	1-2	50	+4.50	0-0		0.00	1-1	100	+5.50	0-1		-1.00
P Fessey	1-7	14	-3.00	0-3		-3.00	0-1		-1.00	1-3	33	+1.00
D Swift	1-49	2	-45.50	0-4		-4.00	0-11		-11.00	1-34	2	-30.50

2002

	Overall			Two-year-olds			Three-year-olds			Older horses		
	W-R	%	£1	W-R	%	£1	W-R	%	£1	W-R	%	£1
P Hanagan	28-190	14	+41.92	1-19	5	-14.00	12-79	15	+14.17	15-92	16	+41.75
C Poste	4-64	6	-33.20	0-6		-6.00	0-12		-12.00	4-46	8	-15.20
R Ffrench	3-13	23	+3.25	0-1		-1.00	1-5	20	-1.25	2-7	28	+5.50
A Culhane	2-3	66	+29.00	0-0		0.00	0-1		-1.00	2-2	100	+30.00
Miss S Brotherton	2-4	50	+2.91	0-0		0.00	0-0		0.00	2-4	50	+2.91
K Dalgleish	1-2	50	+19.00	0-1		-1.00	1-1	100	+20.00	0-0		0.00
G Carter	1-3	33	+2.50	0-0		0.00	0-1		-1.00	1-2	50	+3.50
C Catlin	1-3	33	+3.00	0-0		0.00	0-0		0.00	1-3	33	+3.00
W Woods	1-4	25	+8.40	0-0		0.00	1-3	33	+9.40	0-1		-1.00
F Lynch	1-5	20	+16.00	0-1		-1.00	1-2	50	+19.00	0-2		-2.00

By class

2004

	Overall			Two-year-olds			Three-year-olds			Older horses		
	W-R	%	£1	W-R	%	£1	W-R	%	£1	W-R	%	£1
A	1-9	11	-1.00	1-7	14	+1.00	0-0		0.00	0-2		-2.00
B	4-46	8	-2.50	2-8	25	+12.00	0-8		-8.00	2-30	6	-6.50
C	10-62	16	+20.70	4-11	36	+11.75	1-15	6	-11.25	5-36	13	+20.20
D	20-170	11	-8.22	4-31	12	+1.44	6-50	12	-1.33	10-89	11	-8.33
E	23-212	10	-72.25	1-42	2	-33.00	5-39	12	0.00	17-131	12	-39.25
F	14-109	12	+20.53	0-14		-14.00	8-29	27	+65.50	6-66	9	-30.97
G	1-12	8	-5.50	0-1		-1.00	1-3	33	+3.50	0-8		-8.00

2003

	Overall			Two-year-olds			Three-year-olds			Older horses		
	W-R	%	£1	W-R	%	£1	W-R	%	£1	W-R	%	£1
A	1-8	12	-5.75	0-1		-1.00	0-0		0.00	1-7	14	-4.75
B	2-27	7	-8.00	0-6		-6.00	0-0		0.00	2-21	9	-2.00
C	4-58	6	-45.12	0-2		-2.00	0-8		-8.00	4-48	8	-35.12
D	14-115	12	+37.40	2-19	10	+46.80	4-35	11	-1.00	8-61	13	-8.40
E	20-172	11	-79.59	3-31	9	-23.67	2-32	6	-15.50	15-109	13	-40.42
F	4-68	5	-43.00	1-12	8	-1.00	1-21	4	-17.50	2-35	5	-24.50
G	3-18	16	-3.00	0-2		-2.00	0-1		-1.00	3-15	20	0.00

2002

	Overall			Two-year-olds			Three-year-olds			Older horses		
	W-R	%	£1	W-R	%	£1	W-R	%	£1	W-R	%	£1
A	0-4		-4.00	0-0		0.00	0-0		0.00	0-4		-4.00
B	4-20	20	+23.25	0-3		-3.00	0-1		-1.00	4-16	25	+27.25
C	9-64	14	+24.00	0-2		-2.00	1-18	5	-3.00	8-44	18	+29.00
D	11-119	9	-34.84	0-10		-10.00	3-49	6	-26.75	8-60	13	+1.91
E	14-115	12	-7.13	1-15	6	-10.00	10-45	22	+39.57	3-55	5	-36.70
F	8-46	17	+23.50	0-5		-5.00	3-15	20	+18.50	5-26	19	+10.00
G	0-2		-2.00	0-0		0.00	0-0		0.00	0-2		-2.00

By course

2004

	Overall			Two-year-olds			Three-year-olds			Older horses		
	W-R	%	£1	W-R	%	£1	W-R	%	£1	W-R	%	£1
Ascot	0-7		-7.00	0-2		-2.00	0-2		-2.00	0-3		-3.00
Ayr	4-30	13	-6.33	1-3	33	+5.00	1-6	16	-4.33	2-21	9	-7.00
Beverley	7-47	14	+35.50	1-10	10	+1.00	1-15	6	+26.00	5-22	22	+8.50
Brighton	1-3	33	+14.00	0-0		0.00	1-2	50	+15.00	0-1		-1.00
Carlisle	3-22	13	-7.22	0-7		-7.00	1-3	33	+4.50	2-12	16	-4.72
Catterick	5-28	17	-4.06	1-8	12	-6.56	1-5	20	+1.00	3-15	20	+1.50
Chester	5-20	25	+25.75	2-5	40	+7.75	0-2		-2.00	3-13	23	+20.00
Doncaster	3-21	14	+17.00	2-6	33	+20.00	0-4		-4.00	1-11	9	+1.00
Epsom	0-5		-5.00	0-0		0.00	0-1		-1.00	0-4		-4.00
Goodwood	1-5	20	+1.50	0-0		0.00	0-0		0.00	1-5	20	+1.50
Hamilton	5-25	20	-6.71	0-0		0.00	2-6	33	+1.25	3-19	15	-7.96
Haydock	2-29	6	-20.00	1-3	33	+2.50	1-11	9	-7.50	0-15		-15.00
Kempton	0-3		-3.00	0-0		0.00	0-0		0.00	0-3		-3.00
Leicester	2-15	13	-0.50	0-0		0.00	1-6	16	+0.50	1-9	11	-1.00
Lingfield	0-18		-18.00	0-0		0.00	0-2		-2.00	0-16		-16.00
Musselburgh	2-23	8	-9.00	0-3		-3.00	1-2	50	+6.00	1-18	5	-12.00
Newbury	0-3		-3.00	0-1		-1.00	0-1		-1.00	0-1		-1.00
Newcastle	2-30	6	-17.50	0-9		-9.00	1-8	12	-1.00	1-13	7	-7.50
Newmarket	2-14	14	-5.00	0-4		-4.00	0-3		-3.00	2-7	28	+2.00
Nottingham	1-18	5	-12.00	0-3		-3.00	1-6	16	0.00	0-9		-9.00
Pontefract	3-31	9	-0.50	0-6		-6.00	1-7	14	+6.00	2-18	11	-0.50
Redcar	2-33	6	-14.50	1-9	11	-3.50	1-10	10	+3.00	0-14		-14.00
Ripon	4-20	20	+17.25	1-6	16	-1.00	2-8	25	+16.25	1-6	16	+2.00
Salisbury	0-2		-2.00	0-1		-1.00	0-0		0.00	0-1		-1.00
Sandown	2-4	50	+5.75	0-1		-1.00	1-1	100	+6.00	1-2	50	+0.75
Southwell	4-37	10	-3.50	0-3		-3.00	0-4		-4.00	4-30	13	+3.50
Thirsk	2-29	6	-14.50	1-10	10	-2.00	1-11	9	-4.50	0-8		-8.00
Warwick	0-3		-3.00	0-1		-1.00	0-0		0.00	0-2		-2.00
Wolver	11-71	15	-17.79	1-8	12	+1.00	4-16	25	+4.50	6-47	12	-23.30
Yarmouth	0-9		-9.00	0-0		0.00	0-1		-1.00	0-8		-8.00
York	4-44	9	+16.20	0-10		-10.00	0-5		-5.00	4-29	13	+31.20

SUALDA (left): winning a competitive handicap at 33-1 at York's Ebor meeting

John Gosden

No Oasis Star last season to act as flagbearer, although the filly Playful Act put in some mighty performances and looks a likely Oaks winner even at this stage.

In the last three years, September has proved to be the best month to follow Gosden horses, with pleasing returns made in consecutive years.

In the last two seasons, the stable has made a slow start to the campaign, so it may be worth waiting until the yard proves conclusively that it has struck some form.

By month

2004

	Overall			Two-year-olds			Three-year-olds			Older horses		
	W-R	%	£1	W-R	%	£1	W-R	%	£1	W-R	%	£1
January	0-0			0-0			0-0			0-0		
February	0-0			0-0			0-0			0-0		
March	2-6	33	+8.00	0-0		0.00	2-4	50	+10.00	0-2		-2.00
April	8-46	17	-2.79	2-4	50	+0.54	5-37	13	-9.33	1-5	20	+6.00
May	10-73	13	-32.96	2-8	25	-3.21	8-53	15	-17.75	0-12		-12.00
June	12-66	18	-21.91	2-10	20	+2.00	9-46	19	-17.41	1-10	10	-6.50
July	4-53	7	-16.50	2-20	10	-13.50	1-25	4	-8.00	1-8	12	+5.00
August	6-46	13	-31.77	4-18	22	-7.17	2-25	8	-21.61	0-3		-3.00
September	11-68	16	+34.24	9-41	21	+51.24	2-25	8	-15.00	0-2		-2.00
October	10-67	14	-13.51	5-40	12	-14.95	5-23	21	+5.44	0-4		-4.00
November	2-25	8	-7.50	0-15		-15.00	2-7	28	+10.50	0-3		-3.00
December	0-8		-8.00	0-7		-7.00	0-1		-1.00	0-0		0.00

2003

	Overall			Two-year-olds			Three-year-olds			Older horses		
	W-R	%	£1	W-R	%	£1	W-R	%	£1	W-R	%	£1
January	0-0			0-0			0-0			0-0		
February	0-0			0-0			0-0			0-0		
March	1-1	100	+10.00	0-0			1-1	100	+10.00	0-0		
April	2-24	8	-15.25	0-0			1-20	5	-17.25	1-4	25	+2.00
May	7-57	12	-13.95	1-7	14	+6.00	5-41	12	-13.95	1-9	11	-6.00
June	14-72	19	-26.39	3-9	33	+0.88	10-52	19	-18.78	1-11	9	-8.50
July	9-45	20	+10.38	1-10	10	-7.50	6-25	24	-1.00	2-10	20	+18.88
August	11-62	17	-30.63	1-16	6	-13.63	10-41	24	-12.01	0-5		-5.00
September	18-69	26	+15.89	12-38	31	-1.86	5-26	19	-3.25	1-5	20	+21.00
October	7-50	14	-30.54	6-27	22	-10.54	1-21	4	-18.00	0-2		-2.00
November	4-18	22	-1.50	3-8	37	+5.88	1-10	10	-7.38	0-0		
December	0-0			0-0			0-0			0-0		

2002

	Overall			Two-year-olds			Three-year-olds			Older horses		
	W-R	%	£1	W-R	%	£1	W-R	%	£1	W-R	%	£1
January	0-0			0-0			0-0			0-0		
February	0-0			0-0			0-0			0-0		
March	0-0			0-0			0-0			0-0		
April	11-34	32	+14.80	0-0			11-33	33	+15.80	0-1		-1.00
May	10-46	21	+27.95	1-6	16	+28.00	8-37	21	-9.45	1-3	33	+9.40
June	7-47	14	-5.29	1-7	14	-4.38	3-35	8	-27.83	3-5	60	+26.91
July	4-35	11	-22.88	2-7	28	-0.88	1-24	4	-22.00	1-4	25	
August	18-64	28	+18.63	4-21	19	+1.58	12-37	32	+15.43	2-6	33	+1.62
September	17-63	26	+17.69	9-20	45	+14.44	5-31	16	+2.25	3-12	25	+1.00
October	13-68	19	-5.17	10-42	23	-8.17	2-21	9	+4.50	1-5	20	-1.50
November	5-17	29	+13.50	4-15	26	+11.50	1-2	50	+2.00	0-0		
December	0-4		-4.00	0-4		-4.00	0-0			0-0		

All runners

2004	Wins	Runs	%	2nd	3rd	rest	Win prize	Total prize	£1 Stake
2yo	26	163	16	26	23	10	358,183.25	524,618.90	-7.05
3yo	36	246	15	35	27	19	321,659.70	591,021.58	-64.15
4yo+	3	49	6	4	9	3	44,125.50	148,305.80	-21.50
TOTAL	65	458	14	65	59	32	723,968.45	1,263,946.28	-92.70

2003	Wins	Runs	%	2nd	3rd	rest	Win prize	Total prize	£1 Stake
2yo	27	115	23	13	12	11	268,580.45	315,228.45	-20.77
3yo	40	237	16	48	35	26	526,247.18	901,241.14	-81.61
4yo+	6	46	13	9	2	7	108,059.60	177,703.04	+20.38
TOTAL	73	398	18	70	49	44	902,887.23	1,394,172.63	-82.00

2002	Wins	Runs	%	2nd	3rd	rest	Win prize	Total prize	£1 Stake
2yo	31	122	25	12	15	14	342,490.60	407,550.27	+38.11
3yo	43	220	19	33	28	22	260,175.50	527,205.88	-19.30
4yo+	11	36	30	3	1	4	270,232.85	396,328.60	+36.42
TOTAL	85	378	22	48	44	40	872,898.95	1,331,084.75	+55.23

By race type

2004

	Overall			Two-year-olds			Three-year-olds			Older horses		
	W-R	%	£1	W-R	%	£1	W-R	%	£1	W-R	%	£1
Handicap	8-99	8	-46.00	1-6	16	-1.50	5-69	7	-35.00	2-24	8	-9.50
Group 1,2,3	7-48	14	+10.00	4-15	26	+9.25	2-19	10	+1.75	1-14	7	-1.00
Maiden	41-259	15	-57.36	18-132	13	-15.96	23-125	18	-39.40	0-2		-2.00
1st time out	9-106	8	-62.33	3-72	4	-55.33	6-32	18	-5.00	0-2		-2.00

2003

	Overall			Two-year-olds			Three-year-olds			Older horses		
	W-R	%	£1	W-R	%	£1	W-R	%	£1	W-R	%	£1
Handicap	11-73	15	-12.50	3-7	42	-0.50	8-53	15	+1.00	0-13		-13.00
Group 1,2,3	3-33	9	-0.06	0-5		-5.00	2-18	11	-11.06	1-10	10	+16.00
Maiden	44-218	20	-68.73	19-90	21	-17.64	25-124	20	-47.08	0-4		-4.00
1st time out	8-83	9	-22.84	4-46	8	-19.67	3-36	8	-28.18	1-1	100	+25.00

2002

	Overall			Two-year-olds			Three-year-olds			Older horses		
	W-R	%	£1	W-R	%	£1	W-R	%	£1	W-R	%	£1
Handicap	13-68	19	-0.07	2-7	28	+3.00	9-53	16	-11.58	2-8	25	+8.50
Group 1,2,3	4-37	10	-2.50	3-12	25	+5.50	0-14		-14.00	1-11	9	+6.00
Maiden	55-214	25	+57.29	22-89	24	+33.34	30-121	24	+7.93	3-4	75	+16.02
1st time out	15-94	15	+13.25	6-53	11	+7.75	8-40	20	+0.50	1-1	100	+5.00

By jockey

2004

	Overall			Two-year-olds			Three-year-olds			Older horses		
	W-R	%	£1	W-R	%	£1	W-R	%	£1	W-R	%	£1
J Fortune	20-135	14	-50.20	13-68	19	-14.04	6-56	10	-38.16	1-11	9	+2.00
L Dettori	15-62	24	+3.32	7-16	43	+2.19	6-38	15	-5.37	2-8	25	+6.50
R Hughes	5-37	13	-18.50	0-7		-7.00	5-26	19	-7.50	0-4		-4.00
R Havlin	5-67	7	-31.63	1-24	4	-12.00	4-40	10	-16.63	0-3		-3.00
R Hills	4-28	14	-7.50	0-7		-7.00	4-14	28	+6.50	0-7		-7.00
Dane O'Neill	2-9	22	+12.00	0-3		-3.00	2-4	50	+17.00	0-2		-2.00
J P Murtagh	2-15	13	-9.70	1-6	16	-4.20	1-8	12	-4.50	0-1		-1.00
K Fallon	2-15	13	-6.63	1-8	12	-2.00	1-7	14	-4.63	0-0		0.00
K Darley	2-16	12	+36.67	1-3	33	+48.00	1-8	12	-6.33	0-5		-5.00
W Supple	2-19	10	-9.00	1-2	50	+4.00	1-15	6	-11.00	0-2		-2.00

By jockey ctd

2003

	Overall W-R	%	£1	Two-year-olds W-R	%	£1	Three-year-olds W-R	%	£1	Older horses W-R	%	£1
J Fortune	22-109	20	-27.90	5-21	23	+4.38	13-75	17	-33.65	4-13	30	+1.38
L Dettori	14-41	34	+2.44	11-25	44	+10.06	3-13	23	-4.62	0-3		-3.00
R Hughes	8-64	12	-37.97	3-21	14	-9.67	5-36	13	-21.31	0-7		-7.00
R Havlin	7-55	12	+4.69	1-12	8	-6.00	5-35	14	-7.31	1-8	12	+18.00
R Hills	6-18	33	+27.75	1-2	50	+2.00	4-10	40	+5.75	1-6	16	+20.00
F Norton	5-24	20	-1.60	0-3		-3.00	5-20	25	+2.40	0-1		-1.00
W Supple	4-16	25	-6.13	2-4	50	+0.38	2-10	20	-4.50	0-2		-2.00
Dane O'Neill	2-13	15	-9.09	2-7	28	-3.09	0-5		-5.00	0-1		-1.00
K Darley	2-16	12	-10.75	1-8	12	-5.63	1-8	12	-5.13	0-0		
C Catlin	1-1	100	+12.00	0-0			1-1	100	+12.00	0-0		

2002

	Overall W-R	%	£1	Two-year-olds W-R	%	£1	Three-year-olds W-R	%	£1	Older horses W-R	%	£1
J Fortune	34-134	25	+20.91	15-53	28	+9.43	19-74	25	+18.48	0-7		-7.00
R Hughes	12-44	27	+25.23	3-9	33	+7.63	6-28	21	-4.80	3-7	42	+22.40
R Hills	10-33	30	+0.92	3-5	60	+5.43	4-17	23	-3.12	3-11	27	-1.38
L Dettori	7-25	28	+6.08	3-9	33	+2.25	3-15	20	+1.33	1-1	100	+2.50
R Havlin	6-49	12	+1.28	3-13	23	+25.16	3-35	8	-22.88	0-1		-1.00
K Fallon	3-8	37	+5.21	2-5	40	+1.71	0-2		-2.00	1-1	100	+5.50
W Supple	3-11	27	-1.59	0-5		-5.00	1-4	25	-1.00	2-2	100	+4.41
Dane O'Neill	2-5	40	+8.50	0-1		-1.00	2-4	50	+9.50	0-0		
P Robinson	2-6	33	+10.50	0-0			2-5	40	+11.50	0-1		-1.00
J Carroll	2-8	25	-1.56	0-0			2-7	28	-0.56	0-1		-1.00

By class

2004

	Overall W-R	%	£1	Two-year-olds W-R	%	£1	Three-year-olds W-R	%	£1	Older horses W-R	%	£1
A	13-88	14	+12.00	5-20	25	+11.25	7-49	14	+6.75	1-19	5	-6.00
B	0-15		-15.00	0-1		-1.00	0-9		-9.00	0-5		-5.00
C	3-35	8	-15.13	1-3	33	-0.13	1-15	6	-9.00	1-17	5	-6.00
D	42-262	16	-52.11	17-114	14	+1.54	24-142	16	-51.15	1-6	16	-2.50
E	3-33	9	-21.71	2-10	20	-6.71	1-21	4	-13.00	0-2		-2.00
F	2-9	22	+1.25	0-2		-2.00	2-7	28	+3.25	0-0		0.00
G	0-0			0-0			0-0			0-0		

2003

	Overall W-R	%	£1	Two-year-olds W-R	%	£1	Three-year-olds W-R	%	£1	Older horses W-R	%	£1
A	8-65	12	-12.93	1-10	10	-7.25	4-34	11	-16.56	3-21	14	+10.88
B	5-25	20	+25.50	1-2	50	+3.00	2-14	14	-0.50	2-9	22	+23.00
C	5-41	12	-21.97	0-1		-1.00	4-32	12	-15.47	1-8	12	-5.50
D	43-229	18	-72.30	18-92	19	-25.48	25-132	18	-41.83	0-5		-5.00
E	7-20	35	+2.92	3-3	100	+3.58	4-16	25	+0.34	0-1		-1.00
F	3-10	30	+1.15	2-4	50	+5.75	1-6	16	-4.60	0-0		
G	1-1	100	+0.13	1-1	100	+0.13	0-0			0-0		

2002

	Overall W-R	%	£1	Two-year-olds W-R	%	£1	Three-year-olds W-R	%	£1	Older horses W-R	%	£1
A	8-63	12	+8.00	3-15	20	+2.50	2-30	6	-4.00	3-18	16	+9.50
B	5-25	20	+0.12	0-0			2-17	11	-10.38	3-8	37	+10.50
C	9-39	23	-3.09	2-6	33	+0.83	5-27	18	-4.32	2-6	33	+0.41
D	60-236	25	+60.56	25-98	25	+36.44	32-134	23	+8.11	3-4	75	+16.02
E	1-9	11	-7.43	0-1		-1.00	1-8	12	-6.43	0-0		
F	0-1		-1.00	0-0			0-1		-1.00	0-0		
G	2-2	100	+1.06	1-1	100	+0.33	1-1	100	+0.73	0-0		

PRIVY SEAL: (right) winning the Easter Stakes at Kempton

By course

2004

	Overall			Two-year-olds			Three-year-olds			Older horses		
	W-R	%	£1	W-R	%	£1	W-R	%	£1	W-R	%	£1
Ascot	4-25	16	-3.37	3-5	60	+7.63	1-16	6	-7.00	0-4		-4.00
Ayr	1-4	25	+3.00	1-1	100	+6.00	0-1		-1.00	0-2		-2.00
Bath	1-17	5	-14.13	1-5	20	-2.13	0-12		-12.00	0-0		0.00
Beverley	0-3		-3.00	0-0		0.00	0-3		-3.00	0-0		0.00
Brighton	0-6		-6.00	0-1		-1.00	0-5		-5.00	0-0		0.00
Chepstow	1-8	12	+5.00	0-2		-2.00	0-5		-5.00	1-1	100	12.00
Chester	1-8	12	-4.00	0-1		-1.00	1-6	16	-2.00	0-1		-1.00
Doncaster	3-28	10	-13.71	2-12	16	-1.71	1-10	10	-6.00	0-6		-6.00
Epsom	0-6		-6.00	0-1		-1.00	0-5		-5.00	0-0		0.00
Folkestone	2-4	50	+9.75	0-2		-2.00	2-2	100	+11.75	0-0		0.00
Goodwood	5-27	18	+1.16	2-7	28	-1.14	3-17	17	+5.30	0-3		-3.00
Hamilton	0-1		-1.00	0-0		0.00	0-0		0.00	0-1		-1.00
Haydock	1-9	11	-6.00	0-2		-2.00	1-5	20	-2.00	0-2		-2.00
Kempton	4-21	19	+1.67	3-11	27	+1.67	1-9	11	+1.00	0-1		-1.00
Leicester	1-11	9	+1.00	1-9	11	+3.00	0-2		-2.00	0-0		0.00
Lingfield	5-43	11	-10.95	2-21	9	-14.70	3-20	15	+5.75	0-2		-2.00
Newbury	4-42	9	-23.50	2-8	25	-0.75	2-27	7	-15.75	0-7		-7.00
Newcastle	1-2	50	+3.00	0-0		0.00	1-2	50	+3.00	0-0		0.00
Newmarket	8-46	17	+33.12	4-20	20	+38.08	3-21	14	-10.96	1-5	20	+6.00
Nottingham	1-18	5	-15.38	0-6		-6.00	1-11	9	-8.38	0-1		-1.00
Pontefract	2-10	20	-2.63	1-5	20	-0.50	1-5	20	-2.13	0-0		0.00
Redcar	2-7	28	+2.67	0-4		-4.00	2-3	66	+6.67	0-0		0.00
Ripon	0-4		-4.00	0-0		0.00	0-3		-3.00	0-1		-1.00
Salisbury	2-24	8	-14.33	0-10		-10.00	2-13	15	-3.33	0-1		-1.00
Sandown	8-25	32	+10.23	2-9	22	+2.50	5-12	41	+8.23	1-4	25	-0.50
Southwell	0-2		-2.00	0-2		-2.00	0-0		0.00	0-0		0.00
Thirsk	1-2	50	+1.25	0-0		0.00	1-2	50	+1.25	0-0		0.00
Windsor	3-24	12	-18.56	1-2	50	0.00	2-18	11	-14.56	0-4		-4.00
Wolver	1-15	6	-8.50	0-11		-11.00	1-4	25	+2.50	0-0		0.00
Yarmouth	1-12	8	-9.00	1-6	16	-3.00	0-5		-5.00	0-1		-1.00
York	2-4	50	+1.50	0-0		0.00	2-2	100	+3.50	0-2		-2.00

Michael Jarvis

Although Philip Robinson rides the majority of the stable winners (and very well he does it too) both Neil Callan and Kevin Darley are predatory when assuming the reins.

Although Ameerat won the 1,000 Guineas there in 2001, Newmarket wasn't a happy hunting ground for the Jarvis stable last season, with only a solitary win from 64 attempts. Folkestone, Lingfield and Ascot were the three best courses in terms of success, for the stable, while September was the best month.

By month

2004

	Overall			Two-year-olds			Three-year-olds			Older horses		
	W-R	%	£1	W-R	%	£1	W-R	%	£1	W-R	%	£1
January	1-6	16	+1.00	0-0		0.00	0-5		-5.00	1-1	100	+6.00
February	1-7	14	+0.50	0-0		0.00	0-3		-3.00	1-4	25	+3.50
March	4-11	36	+13.00	0-0		0.00	2-8	25	+7.50	2-3	66	+5.50
April	9-32	28	+13.25	0-0		0.00	5-20	25	+7.75	4-12	33	+5.50
May	10-45	22	-15.04	0-5		-5.00	5-21	23	-7.54	5-19	26	-2.50
June	6-54	11	-19.27	0-5		-5.00	4-31	12	-7.27	2-18	11	-7.00
July	7-55	12	-20.64	3-13	23	+0.25	2-19	10	-8.89	2-23	8	-12.00
August	7-48	14	-15.17	4-18	22	+3.83	2-15	13	-8.50	1-15	6	-10.50
September	13-51	25	+14.93	6-28	21	+1.26	4-15	26	+1.92	3-8	37	+11.75
October	4-48	8	-32.25	3-25	12	-13.75	0-11		-11.00	1-12	8	-7.50
November	3-13	23	+1.78	1-6	16	+4.00	1-4	25	-1.12	1-3	33	-1.09
December	0-1		-1.00	0-1		-1.00	0-0		0.00	0-0		0.00

2003

	Overall			Two-year-olds			Three-year-olds			Older horses		
	W-R	%	£1	W-R	%	£1	W-R	%	£1	W-R	%	£1
January	1-3	33	+4.00	0-0		0.00	0-2		-2.00	1-1	100	+6.00
February	1-5	20	-2.00	0-0		0.00	1-2	50	+1.00	0-3		-3.00
March	1-7	14	+0.50	0-0		0.00	1-3	33	+4.50	0-4		-4.00
April	5-21	23	+5.78	0-0		0.00	3-14	21	-2.05	2-7	28	+7.83
May	5-47	10	-23.38	1-3	33	-0.38	2-28	7	-19.25	2-16	12	-3.75
June	9-43	20	+21.46	3-7	42	+7.21	4-22	18	+14.00	2-14	14	+0.25
July	14-49	28	+53.34	4-8	50	+19.63	8-31	25	+26.21	2-10	20	+7.50
August	4-31	12	-11.00	0-8		-8.00	3-17	17	+0.50	1-6	16	-3.50
September	9-40	22	-8.23	5-15	33	-0.76	1-14	7	-9.67	3-11	27	+2.20
October	6-33	18	-3.83	2-14	14	-7.95	3-13	23	-1.88	1-6	16	+6.00
November	1-17	5	-14.13	1-9	11	-6.13	0-5		-5.00	0-3		-3.00
December	1-2	50	+1.25	1-2	50	+1.25	0-0		0.00	0-0		0.00

2002

	Overall			Two-year-olds			Three-year-olds			Older horses		
	W-R	%	£1	W-R	%	£1	W-R	%	£1	W-R	%	£1
January	1-6	16	+3.00	0-0		0.00	0-1		-1.00	1-5	20	+4.00
February	2-5	40	+6.33	0-0		0.00	1-1	100	+6.00	1-4	25	+0.33
March	0-0			0-0			0-0			0-0		
April	1-22	4	-18.75	0-0		0.00	1-19	5	-15.75	0-3		-3.00
May	16-62	25	+21.49	2-6	33	+0.50	9-42	21	-3.69	5-14	35	+24.67
June	6-49	12	-28.96	1-4	25	-2.39	5-30	16	-11.58	0-15		-15.00
July	7-48	14	-16.63	1-13	7	-9.50	5-21	23	+2.38	1-14	7	-9.50
August	3-38	7	-12.50	1-12	8	-2.00	2-17	11	-1.50	0-9		-9.00
September	6-43	13	-5.96	2-14	14	+0.54	3-18	16	+0.75	1-11	9	-7.25
October	9-54	16	+22.69	5-26	19	+9.35	3-19	15	+16.33	1-9	11	-3.00
November	3-26	11	-15.13	2-14	14	-6.00	0-8		-8.00	1-4	25	-1.12
December	0-1		-1.00	0-1		-1.00	0-0		0.00	0-0		0.00

All runners

2004	Wins	Runs	%	2nd	3rd	rest	Win prize	Total prize	£1 Stake
2yo	17	101	17	7	12	11	132,965.75	215,353.40	-15.41
3yo	25	152	16	32	17	15	185,335.11	327,268.06	-35.16
4yo+	23	118	19	10	15	9	625,070.29	768,045.19	-8.34
TOTAL	65	371	18	49	44	35	943,371.15	1,310,666.65	-58.91

2003	Wins	Runs	%	2nd	3rd	rest	Win prize	Total prize	£1 Stake
2yo	17	66	26	6	8	4	77,803.45	147,677.95	+4.87
3yo	26	151	17	23	13	11	117,801.73	200,213.91	+6.37
4yo+	14	81	17	8	10	5	409,026.40	561,258.30	+12.53
TOTAL	57	298	19	37	31	20	604,631.58	909,150.16	+23.77

2002	Wins	Runs	%	2nd	3rd	rest	Win prize	Total prize	£1 Stake
2yo	14	90	16	10	11	11	62,720.25	111,534.70	-10.49
3yo	29	176	16	18	21	18	182,577.25	280,246.45	-16.05
4yo+	11	88	13	16	10	14	95,218.84	200,556.56	-18.87
TOTAL	54	354	15	44	42	43	340,516.34	592,337.71	-45.41

By race type

2004

	Overall			Two-year-olds			Three-year-olds			Older horses		
	W-R	%	£1	W-R	%	£1	W-R	%	£1	W-R	%	£1
Handicap	19-150	12	-42.00	1-9	11	-3.50	5-62	8	-28.50	13-79	16	-10.00
Group 1,2,3	2-21	9	-11.50	0-4		-4.00	0-6		-6.00	2-11	18	-1.50
Maiden	30-135	22	+8.12	13-75	17	-4.97	16-57	28	+9.09	1-3	33	+4.00
1st time out	6-49	12	-4.67	4-35	11	-2.00	1-10	10	-5.67	1-4	25	+3.00

2003

	Overall			Two-year-olds			Three-year-olds			Older horses		
	W-R	%	£1	W-R	%	£1	W-R	%	£1	W-R	%	£1
Handicap	24-146	16	+8.70	1-4	25	-0.75	15-91	16	-1.25	8-51	15	+10.70
Group 1,2,3	1-15	6	-3.00	0-9		-9.00	0-0		0.00	1-6	16	+6.00
Maiden	21-92	22	+17.29	11-42	26	+11.83	8-46	17	+0.62	2-4	50	+4.83
1st time out	8-46	17	+2.33	7-28	25	+13.83	1-13	7	-6.50	0-5		-5.00

2002

	Overall			Two-year-olds			Three-year-olds			Older horses		
	W-R	%	£1	W-R	%	£1	W-R	%	£1	W-R	%	£1
Handicap	15-131	11	-34.54	0-11		-11.00	11-74	14	-14.87	4-46	8	-8.67
Group 1,2,3	0-13		-13.00	0-1		-1.00	0-7		-7.00	0-5		-5.00
Maiden	23-130	17	+16.65	12-63	19	+11.10	11-64	17	+8.55	0-3		-3.00
1st time out	5-49	10	-14.00	3-29	10	-9.50	1-17	5	-6.00	1-3	33	+1.50

By jockey

2004

	Overall			Two-year-olds			Three-year-olds			Older horses		
	W-R	%	£1	W-R	%	£1	W-R	%	£1	W-R	%	£1
P Robinson	46-254	18	-65.25	15-77	19	-9.91	14-98	14	-48.00	17-79	21	-7.34
N Callan	8-34	23	+17.44	2-8	25	+10.50	3-15	20	+0.44	3-11	27	+6.50
K Darley	4-9	44	+18.90	0-0		0.00	3-6	50	+10.90	1-3	33	+8.00
M Henry	3-37	8	-6.50	0-8		-8.00	3-21	14	+9.50	0-8		-8.00
S Sanders	2-4	50	+2.50	0-0		0.00	1-3	33	-1.00	1-1	100	+3.50
L Dettori	1-2	50	0.00	0-0		0.00	1-2	50	0.00	0-0		0.00
K Fallon	1-5	20	0.00	0-1		-1.00	0-1		-1.00	1-3	33	+2.00
M Tebbutt	0-1		-1.00	0-0		0.00	0-0		0.00	0-1		-1.00
B Doyle	0-1		-1.00	0-0		0.00	0-0		0.00	0-1		-1.00
N Mackay	0-1		-1.00	0-1		-1.00	0-0		0.00	0-0		0.00

By jockey ctd

2003

	Overall			Two-year-olds			Three-year-olds			Older horses		
	W-R	%	£1	W-R	%	£1	W-R	%	£1	W-R	%	£1
P Robinson	38-199	19	+21.79	13-50	26	+8.50	15-86	17	+2.25	10-63	15	+11.03
M Henry	7-22	31	+10.58	1-6	16	-2.75	4-10	40	+9.83	2-6	33	+3.50
M Tebbutt	5-31	16	-16.15	1-3	33	-1.43	3-24	12	-15.22	1-4	25	+0.50
K Fallon	2-2	100	+4.50	0-0		0.00	2-2	100	+4.50	0-0		0.00
D Holland	1-1	100	+2.55	1-1	100	+2.55	0-0		0.00	0-0		0.00
J Tate	1-2	50	+11.00	0-0		0.00	1-2	50	+11.00	0-0		0.00
S Drowne	1-2	50	+19.00	0-0		0.00	1-2	50	+19.00	0-0		0.00
J F Egan	1-2	50	+3.50	0-0		0.00	0-0		0.00	1-2	50	+3.50
N Callan	1-22	4	-18.00	1-5	20	-1.00	0-15		-15.00	0-2		-2.00
Miss E Ramsden	0-1		-1.00	0-0		0.00	0-0		0.00	0-1		-1.00

2002

	Overall			Two-year-olds			Three-year-olds			Older horses		
	W-R	%	£1	W-R	%	£1	W-R	%	£1	W-R	%	£1
P Robinson	36-228	15	-28.69	12-61	19	+11.01	17-111	15	-31.40	7-56	12	-8.30
M Tebbutt	5-32	15	-2.75	2-6	33	+1.50	3-19	15	+2.75	0-7		-7.00
N Callan	4-26	15	+14.60	0-5		-5.00	3-13	23	+25.50	1-8	12	-5.90
M Henry	4-30	13	-8.57	0-14		-14.00	1-11	9	-8.90	3-5	60	+14.33
L Dettori	2-7	28	-1.84	0-2		-2.00	2-4	50	+1.16	0-1		-1.00
P Shea	1-1	100	+5.50	0-0		0.00	1-1	100	+5.50	0-0		0.00
J P Spencer	1-3	33	+1.33	0-0		0.00	1-3	33	+1.33	0-0		0.00
Pat Eddery	1-7	14	-5.00	0-1		-1.00	1-2	50	0.00	0-4		-4.00
G Duffield	0-1		-1.00	0-0		0.00	0-0		0.00	0-1		-1.00
M Savage	0-1		-1.00	0-0		0.00	0-1		-1.00	0-0		0.00

By class

2004

	Overall			Two-year-olds			Three-year-olds			Older horses		
	W-R	%	£1	W-R	%	£1	W-R	%	£1	W-R	%	£1
A	9-46	19	-2.02	2-8	25	-2.27	2-17	11	-2.50	5-21	23	+2.75
B	2-44	4	-37.50	0-2		-2.00	0-9		-9.00	2-33	6	-26.50
C	12-64	18	-13.34	1-7	14	-1.50	3-23	13	-8.50	8-34	23	-3.34
D	36-169	21	-0.14	11-66	16	-13.23	19-79	24	+3.84	6-24	25	+9.25
E	4-31	12	-3.90	1-10	10	-3.40	1-16	6	-11.00	2-5	40	+10.50
F	0-9		-9.00	0-1		-1.00	0-7		-7.00	0-1		-1.00
G	0-1		-1.00	0-1		-1.00	0-0		0.00	0-0		0.00

2003

	Overall			Two-year-olds			Three-year-olds			Older horses		
	W-R	%	£1	W-R	%	£1	W-R	%	£1	W-R	%	£1
A	1-34	2	-22.00	0-13		-13.00	0-5		-5.00	1-16	6	-4.00
B	6-35	17	+37.50	0-1		-1.00	1-9	11	+12.00	5-25	20	+26.50
C	9-52	17	-13.17	2-4	50	+4.13	2-27	7	-13.00	5-21	23	-4.30
D	21-120	17	-31.31	12-41	29	+6.20	8-71	11	-31.35	1-8	12	-6.17
E	14-44	31	+13.27	3-6	50	+9.55	10-28	35	+9.21	1-10	10	-5.50
F	6-13	46	+39.50	0-1		-1.00	5-11	45	+34.50	1-1	100	+6.00
G	0-0			0-0			0-0			0-0		

2002

	Overall			Two-year-olds			Three-year-olds			Older horses		
	W-R	%	£1	W-R	%	£1	W-R	%	£1	W-R	%	£1
A	4-39	10	-13.22	0-2		-2.00	2-18	11	-6.09	2-19	10	-5.13
B	3-50	6	-22.75	0-5		-5.00	1-14	7	-10.75	2-31	6	-7.00
C	9-70	12	-36.37	0-10		-10.00	6-32	18	-5.79	3-28	10	-20.58
D	29-159	18	+18.02	10-61	16	-4.03	17-93	18	+13.55	2-5	40	+8.50
E	9-27	33	+17.90	4-12	33	+10.54	3-13	23	-0.97	2-2	100	+8.33
F	0-9		-9.00	0-0		0.00	0-6		-6.00	0-3		-3.00
G	0-0			0-0			0-0			0-0		

AYAM ZAMAN: passes the post in glorious isolation at Newmarket

By course

2004

	Overall			Two-year-olds			Three-year-olds			Older horses		
	W-R	%	£1	W-R	%	£1	W-R	%	£1	W-R	%	£1
Ascot	5-20	25	+13.50	0-0		0.00	1-8	12	+4.00	4-12	33	+9.50
Ayr	1-8	12	-6.60	0-1		-1.00	1-5	20	-3.60	0-2		-2.00
Bath	1-4	25	+1.00	1-2	50	+3.00	0-2		-2.00	0-0		0.00
Beverley	0-3		-3.00	0-1		-1.00	0-2		-2.00	0-0		0.00
Brighton	1-6	16	-1.50	0-2		-2.00	0-2		-2.00	1-2	50	+2.50
Catterick	1-1	100	+3.50	0-0		0.00	1-1	100	+3.50	0-0		0.00
Chepstow	0-1		-1.00	0-0		0.00	0-0		0.00	0-1		-1.00
Chester	2-8	25	0.00	0-1		-1.00	1-3	33	+2.00	1-4	25	-1.00
Doncaster	1-15	6	-9.50	0-3		-3.00	1-5	20	+0.50	0-7		-7.00
Epsom	1-8	12	-2.50	0-0		0.00	0-2		-2.00	1-6	16	-0.50
Folkestone	1-5	20	+16.00	0-1		-1.00	1-4	25	+17.00	0-0		0.00
Goodwood	1-8	12	-2.50	1-2	50	+3.50	0-1		1.00	0-5		-5.00
Hamilton	3-7	42	+1.94	0-0		0.00	3-6	50	+2.94	0-1		-1.00
Haydock	7-25	28	+9.18	2-4	50	+9.10	2-10	20	-4.17	3-11	27	+4.25
Kempton	2-18	11	-9.25	0-5		-5.00	1-8	12	-2.50	1-5	20	-1.75
Leicester	3-17	17	-10.19	0-7		-7.00	3-6	50	+0.81	0-4		-4.00
Lingfield	7-31	22	+13.75	1-10	10	0.00	2-14	14	+1.00	4-7	57	+12.75
Musselburgh	1-1	100	+1.00	0-0		0.00	1-1	100	+1.00	0-0		0.00
Newbury	1-10	10	-8.60	1-3	33	-1.60	0-5		-5.00	0-2		-2.00
Newcastle	3-9	33	+3.25	1-1	100	+4.50	1-4	25	-2.75	1-4	25	+1.50
Newmarket	1-64	1	-60.00	1-26	3	-22.00	0-22		-22.00	0-16		-16.00
Nottingham	3-10	30	+11.41	1-5	20	+3.50	0-3		-3.00	2-2	100	10.91
Pontefract	2-7	28	-3.50	2-5	40	-1.50	0-1		-1.00	0-1		-1.00
Redcar	1-6	16	-3.13	0-2		-2.00	1-4	25	-1.13	0-0		0.00
Ripon	2-3	66	+1.42	0-0		0.00	1-2	50	-0.33	1-1	100	+1.75
Salisbury	4-5	80	+7.76	2-2	100	+3.93	2-3	66	+3.83	0-0		0.00
Sandown	3-12	25	+2.23	0-1		-1.00	2-5	40	+5.73	1-6	16	-2.50
Southwell	0-5		-5.00	0-0		0.00	0-5		-5.00	0-0		0.00
Thirsk	0-2		-2.00	0-0		0.00	0-2		-2.00	0-0		0.00
Warwick	0-4		-4.00	0-2		-2.00	0-2		-2.00	0-0		0.00
Windsor	2-14	14	-7.42	1-4	25	+0.33	0-5		-5.00	1-5	20	-2.75
Wolver	0-5		-5.00	0-1		-1.00	0-1		-1.00	0-3		-3.00
Yarmouth	3-11	27	+3.33	1-6	16	-1.67	0-3		-3.00	2-2	100	+8.00
York	2-18	11	-3.50	2-4	50	+10.50	0-5		-5.00	0-9		-9.00

Tim Easterby

Amazingly, runners from this stable showed a level-stakes loss all the way through the summer until October, where the figures improved.

Stable runners are worth looking out for at Ayr, as they show a £35 level-stakes profit, but Doncaster last season proved to be an unlucky track. Out of 59 starters only one was successful, while Haydock didn't fare much better. Group success was once again provided by the hardy Somnus, but it is handicaps that this stable are best waited for.

By month

2004

	Overall			Two-year-olds			Three-year-olds			Older horses		
	W-R	%	£1	W-R	%	£1	W-R	%	£1	W-R	%	£1
January	1-5	20	-0.67	0-0		0.00	0-1		-1.00	1-4	25	+0.33
February	1-2	50	+3.50	0-0		0.00	1-1	100	+4.50	0-1		-1.00
March	0-20		-20.00	0-0		0.00	0-11		-11.00	0-9		-9.00
April	4-65	6	-49.00	2-11	18	-0.50	2-34	5	-28.50	0-20		-20.00
May	10-122	8	-40.75	2-33	6	-9.75	2-49	4	-39.00	6-40	15	+8.00
June	8-138	5	-75.13	3-55	5	-32.13	3-51	5	-28.50	2-32	6	-14.50
July	12-143	8	-66.38	4-42	9	-29.00	6-57	10	-19.38	2-44	4	-18.00
August	9-93	9	-22.87	3-38	7	-14.50	3-30	10	-8.87	3-25	12	+0.50
September	8-93	8	-34.50	1-40	2	-33.50	4-23	17	+7.00	3-30	10	-8.00
October	5-38	13	+24.50	2-14	14	+30.00	0-12		-12.00	3-12	25	+6.50
November	2-14	14	-7.75	2-7	28	-0.75	0-2		-2.00	0-5		-5.00
December	2-5	40	+4.50	2-2	100	+7.50	0-2		-2.00	0-1		-1.00

2003

	Overall			Two-year-olds			Three-year-olds			Older horses		
	W-R	%	£1	W-R	%	£1	W-R	%	£1	W-R	%	£1
January	1-8	12	-1.00	0-0			0-3		-3.00	1-5	20	+2.00
February	0-4		-4.00	0-0			0-2		-2.00	0-2		-2.00
March	3-21	14	+22.00	0-2		-2.00	2-13	15	+25.00	1-6	16	-1.00
April	5-60	8	-19.50	0-7		-7.00	2-35	5	-22.50	3-18	16	+10.00
May	5-145	3	-101.50	1-31	3	-27.50	3-66	4	-32.00	1-48	2	-42.00
June	19-161	11	-66.52	5-34	14	+5.05	6-71	8	-48.19	8-56	14	-23.38
July	9-133	6	-65.25	0-33		-33.00	6-57	10	-11.25	3-43	6	-21.00
August	10-125	8	-81.07	2-37	5	-31.38	4-50	8	-31.67	4-38	10	-18.02
September	4-100	4	-62.00	0-34		-34.00	3-30	10	+3.50	1-36	2	-31.50
October	2-56	3	-50.33	0-19		-19.00	2-22	9	-16.33	0-15		-15.00
November	1-20	5	-15.50	1-7	14	-2.50	0-9		-9.00	0-4		-4.00
December	0-0			0-0			0-0			0-0		

2002

	Overall			Two-year-olds			Three-year-olds			Older horses		
	W-R	%	£1	W-R	%	£1	W-R	%	£1	W-R	%	£1
January	0-0			0-0			0-0			0-0		
February	1-1	100	+10.00	0-0			1-1	100	+10.00	0-0		
March	1-22	4	-5.00	0-1		-1.00	1-15	6	+2.00	0-6		-6.00
April	4-72	5	-39.88	1-17	5	-5.00	3-42	7	-21.87	0-13		-13.00
May	9-114	7	-71.00	3-26	11	-17.25	3-54	5	-34.00	3-34	8	-19.75
June	23-165	13	-13.33	6-52	11	-31.85	6-71	8	-23.68	11-42	26	+42.20
July	17-151	11	-62.69	7-53	13	-19.44	8-55	14	-16.25	2-43	4	-27.00
August	9-115	7	-46.13	6-55	10	-14.50	3-38	7	-9.63	0-22		-22.00
September	8-94	8	-15.45	5-45	11	+11.75	2-23	8	-13.20	1-26	3	-14.00
October	6-61	9	-10.00	3-27	11	-3.50	2-18	11	-1.50	1-16	6	-5.00
November	3-24	12	-6.50	1-11	9	-7.00	0-4		-4.00	2-9	22	+4.50
December	0-7		-7.00	0-1		-1.00	0-0			0-6		-6.00

All runners

2004	Wins	Runs	%	2nd	3rd	rest	Win prize	Total prize	£1 Stake
2yo	21	242	9	22	19	23	138,758.10	201,349.85	-82.62
3yo	21	273	8	34	32	23	101,364.40	192,473.30	-140.75
4yo+	20	223	9	30	20	16	321,661.15	525,229.01	-61.17
TOTAL	62	738	8	86	71	62	561,783.65	919,052.16	-284.54

2003	Wins	Runs	%	2nd	3rd	rest	Win prize	Total prize	£1 Stake
2yo	9	204	4	17	27	35	43,115.95	150,748.21	-151.33
3yo	28	358	7	41	37	32	370,341.21	531,897.17	-147.44
4yo+	22	271	8	23	23	28	294,957.11	550,307.10	-145.90
TOTAL	59	833	7	81	87	95	708,414.27	1,232,952.48	-444.67

2002	Wins	Runs	%	2nd	3rd	rest	Win prize	Total prize	£1 Stake
2yo	32	288	11	28	42	36	443,583.75	561,400.93	-88.79
3yo	29	321	9	26	33	24	435,954.80	629,336.25	-112.13
4yo+	20	217	9	27	23	17	154,706.67	270,735.07	-66.05
TOTAL	81	826	9	81	98	77	1,034,245.22	1,461,472.25	-266.97

By race type

2004

	Overall			Two-year-olds			Three-year-olds			Older horses		
	W-R	%	£1	W-R	%	£1	W-R	%	£1	W-R	%	£1
Handicap	35-413	8	-122.87	7-50	14	+20.00	11-175	6	-91.37	17-188	9	-51.50
Group 1,2,3	1-18	5	-5.00	0-4		-4.00	0-0		0.00	1-14	7	-1.00
Maiden	16-236	6	-170.01	11-151	7	-112.62	5-81	6	-53.39	0-4		-4.00
1st time out	2-70	2	-44.50	2-52	3	-26.50	0-16		-16.00	0-2		-2.00

2003

	Overall			Two-year-olds			Three-year-olds			Older horses		
	W-R	%	£1	W-R	%	£1	W-R	%	£1	W-R	%	£1
Handicap	36-530	6	-292.42	1-40	2	-37.38	18-254	7	-126.02	17-236	7	-129.03
Group 1,2,3	3-16	18	+4.25	0-1		-1.00	1-4	25	+9.00	2-11	18	-3.75
Maiden	12-201	5	-105.43	6-129	4	-86.45	5-69	7	-19.83	1-3	33	+0.85
1st time out	3-64	4	-0.50	2-48	4	-18.50	1-13	7	+21.00	0-3		-3.00

2002

	Overall			Two-year-olds			Three-year-olds			Older horses		
	W-R	%	£1	W-R	%	£1	W-R	%	£1	W-R	%	£1
Handicap	46-472	9	-132.22	6-55	10	-8.67	21-223	9	-73.50	19-194	9	-50.05
Group 1,2,3	1-6	16	+2.00	0-2		-2.00	1-4	25	+4.00	0-0		
Maiden	22-216	10	-81.35	17-158	10	-51.73	5-56	8	-27.63	0-2		-2.00
1st time out	4-68	5	-13.50	3-60	5	-16.50	1-7	14	+4.00	0-1		-1.00

By jockey

2004

	Overall			Two-year-olds			Three-year-olds			Older horses		
	W-R	%	£1	W-R	%	£1	W-R	%	£1	W-R	%	£1
D Allan	27-304	8	-112.16	11-106	10	-25.29	10-123	8	-53.87	6-75	8	-33.00
W Supple	5-66	7	-29.39	1-23	4	-18.50	1-20	5	-18.39	3-23	13	+7.50
P M Quinn	4-18	22	+36.00	3-11	27	+37.00	1-6	16	0.00	0-1		-1.00
G Gibbons	4-25	16	+5.50	1-10	10	-3.50	2-9	22	+7.00	1-6	16	+2.00
K Darley	4-45	8	-24.75	1-13	7	-8.00	3-20	15	-4.75	0-12		-12.00
R Winston	4-50	8	-21.90	1-12	8	-9.90	0-14		-14.00	3-24	12	+2.00
Dale Gibson	3-18	16	+5.00	0-4		-4.00	1-7	14	-1.50	2-7	28	+10.50
A Mullen	3-42	7	-18.17	0-8		-8.00	1-19	5	-12.50	2-15	13	+2.33
M Fenton	2-7	28	+9.00	0-1		-1.00	0-2		-2.00	2-4	50	+12.00
T Quinn	2-11	18	-4.93	1-5	20	-3.43	0-0		0.00	1-6	16	-1.50

By class

2004	Overall			Two-year-olds			Three-year-olds			Older horses		
	W-R	%	£1	W-R	%	£1	W-R	%	£1	W-R	%	£1
A	4-31	12	+20.00	2-11	18	+19.00	0-1		-1.00	2-19	10	+2.00
B	0-37		-37.00	0-7		-7.00	0-3		-3.00	0-27		-27.00
C	13-99	13	+16.80	2-11	18	+1.50	2-23	8	-0.20	9-65	13	+15.50
D	24-259	9	-84.29	11-87	12	+8.60	8-99	8	-51.39	5-73	6	-41.50
E	16-199	8	-112.14	6-85	7	-63.72	7-84	8	-42.92	3-30	10	-5.50
F	2-90	2	-79.17	0-33		-33.00	1-51	1	-44.50	1-6	16	-1.67
G	1-11	9	-6.00	0-5		-5.00	1-4	25	+1.00	0-2		-2.00

2003	Overall			Two-year-olds			Three-year-olds			Older horses		
	W-R	%	£1	W-R	%	£1	W-R	%	£1	W-R	%	£1
A	4-33	12	-8.88	0-1		-1.00	2-16	12	+3.00	2-16	12	-10.88
B	3-82	3	-68.25	0-8		-8.00	1-27	3	-22.00	2-47	4	-38.25
C	17-139	12	-6.38	0-13		-13.00	8-53	15	+13.75	9-73	12	-7.13
D	16-256	6	-154.31	6-72	8	-51.63	5-111	4	-58.18	5-73	6	-44.50
E	14-231	6	-155.77	1-74	1	-72.20	10-103	9	-41.92	3-54	5	-41.65
F	3-78	3	-46.09	1-30	3	-4.00	2-44	4	-38.09	0-4		-4.00
G	1-10	10	-5.50	1-5	20	-0.50	0-3		-3.00	0-2		-2.00

By course

2004	Overall			Two-year-olds			Three-year-olds			Older horses		
	W-R	%	£1	W-R	%	£1	W-R	%	£1	W-R	%	£1
Ascot	1-9	11	+4.00	0-2		-2.00	0-0		0.00	1-7	14	+6.00
Ayr	3-16	18	+35.00	1-6	16	+28.00	1-4	25	+4.00	1-6	16	+3.00
Beverley	12-74	16	+9.67	3-25	12	-4.33	7-38	18	+9.50	2-11	18	+4.50
Carlisle	2-20	10	+2.00	0-7		-7.00	1-10	10	-1.00	1-3	33	+10.00
Catterick	1-27	3	-23.00	1-9	11	-5.00	0-12		-12.00	0-6		-6.00
Chester	2-12	16	+2.00	1-4	25	-1.00	1-3	33	+8.00	0-5		-5.00
Doncaster	1-59	1	-56.63	1-21	4	-18.63	0-14		-14.00	0-24		-24.00
Epsom	0-2		-2.00	0-1		-1.00	0-0		0.00	0-1		-1.00
Goodwood	0-3		-3.00	0-0		0.00	0-0		0.00	0-3		-3.00
Hamilton	1-10	10	-5.67	0-1		-1.00	1-4	25	+0.33	0-5		-5.00
Haydock	4-59	6	-30.87	2-20	10	-9.17	1-21	4	-9.20	1-18	5	-12.50
Leicester	1-5	20	0.00	0-1		-1.00	1-3	33	+2.00	0-1		-1.00
Lingfield	0-1		-1.00	0-0		0.00	0-0		0.00	0-1		-1.00
Musselburgh	1-18	5	-13.00	0-5		-5.00	0-7		-7.00	1-6	16	-1.00
Newbury	1-1	100	+9.00	1-1	100	+9.00	0-0		0.00	0-0		0.00
Newcastle	3-41	7	-27.50	1-15	6	-10.50	2-14	14	-5.00	0-12		-12.00
Newmarket	0-14		-14.00	0-2		-2.00	0-4		-4.00	0-8		-8.00
Nottingham	2-21	9	-4.00	0-8		-8.00	0-6		-6.00	2-7	28	+10.00
Pontefract	6-37	16	+2.50	2-11	18	-1.50	0-12		-12.00	4-14	28	+16.00
Redcar	4-69	5	-49.25	1-21	4	-18.75	1-30	3	-26.00	2-18	11	-4.50
Ripon	2-59	3	-43.75	2-19	10	-3.75	0-27		-27.00	0-13		-13.00
Sandown	0-1		-1.00	0-0		0.00	0-0		0.00	0-1		-1.00
Southwell	2-31	6	-23.42	0-7		-7.00	1-21	4	-17.75	1-3	33	+1.33
Thirsk	4-71	5	-30.39	1-28	3	-7.00	1-24	4	-22.39	2-19	10	-1.00
Warwick	1-6	16	-3.75	0-2		-2.00	1-4	25	-1.75	0-0		0.00
Wolver	3-10	30	+5.00	2-4	50	+5.50	1-3	33	+2.50	0-3		-3.00
Yarmouth	0-2		-2.00	0-0		0.00	0-0		0.00	0-2		-2.00
York	5-60	8	-19.50	2-22	9	-9.50	1-12	8	-2.00	2-26	7	-8.00

For Borderer's best Northern prospects of the season, see pages 53-57

Top trainers by winners (Turf)

All runs				First time out			Horses*		
Won	Ran	%	Trainer	Won	Ran	%	Won	Ran	%
115	759	15	M Johnston	20	170	12	76	170	45
110	439	25	S bin Suroor	35	166	21	79	166	48
104	1107	9	R Hannon	17	187	9	79	187	42
84	938	9	M Channon	11	141	8	63	141	45
81	382	21	Sir M Stoute	26	145	18	62	145	43
66	575	11	B Hills	10	146	7	43	146	29
62	523	12	R Fahey	5	81	6	36	81	44
61	405	15	J Gosden	16	135	12	48	135	36
59	335	18	M Jarvis	13	73	18	40	73	55
57	699	8	T Easterby	2	120	2	39	120	33
55	506	11	J Dunlop	14	135	10	42	135	31
54	646	8	D Nicholls	3	78	4	39	78	50
49	381	13	M Bell	5	73	7	33	73	45
49	462	11	P Evans	3	32	9	22	32	69
45	159	28	Sir M Prescott	3	37	8	19	37	51
44	331	13	K Ryan	3	48	6	23	48	48
43	391	11	B Meehan	7	87	8	33	87	38
39	255	15	J Fanshawe	9	66	14	29	66	44
39	339	12	Mrs A Perrett	7	93	8	27	93	29
37	259	14	L Cumani	3	55	5	24	55	44
36	301	12	P Harris	6	67	9	21	67	31
36	414	9	A Balding	5	66	8	27	66	41
35	241	15	W Haggas	12	57	21	27	57	47
35	303	12	K R Burke	5	36	14	15	36	42
35	312	11	P Cole	8	70	11	21	70	30
35	326	11	T Barron	4	55	7	20	55	36
35	541	6	J Bradley	1	54	2	20	54	37
34	296	11	D Loder	12	93	13	28	93	30
33	191	17	R Charlton	8	56	14	21	56	38
33	285	12	M Tompkins	3	53	6	23	53	43
33	325	10	E Dunlop	4	62	6	26	62	42
31	262	12	D Elsworth	3	47	6	22	47	47
31	471	7	W Brisbourne	1	53	2	18	53	34
30	243	12	N Callaghan	1	43	2	20	43	47
29	175	17	J Noseda	5	49	10	19	49	39
29	409	7	A Berry	4	48	8	16	48	33
27	276	10	M Dods	2	31	6	17	31	55
25	197	13	B McMahon	3	30	10	16	30	53
25	253	10	I Semple	6	34	18	20	34	59
25	262	10	H Morrison	6	50	12	16	50	32
25	265	9	J J Quinn	3	37	8	17	37	46
25	394	6	M W Easterby	2	63	3	15	63	24
24	176	14	M Tregoning	9	62	15	20	62	32
24	266	9	A Carroll	0	32	0	13	32	41
24	306	8	N Littmoden	2	39	5	11	39	28
23	134	17	P Chapple-Hyam	6	41	15	16	41	39
23	154	15	S C Williams	0	26	0	9	26	35
23	187	12	H Candy	8	45	18	21	45	47
23	194	12	J R Best	4	21	19	15	21	71
23	293	8	S Kirk	2	45	4	17	45	38
23	403	6	J Given	3	86	3	16	86	19

*Shows how many individual horses ran last season, how many won at least once, and percentage.

Top trainers by prizemoney (Turf)

Total prizemoney	Trainer	Win prizemoney	Wins	Class A-C Won	Class A-C Ran	Class A-C %	Class D-G Won	Class D-G Ran	Class D-G %
4,224,495	**S bin Suroor**	2,993,708	110	49	245	20	60	191	31
2,907,834	**Sir M Stoute**	2,305,635	81	34	168	20	46	213	22
2,415,353	**M Johnston**	1,709,468	115	35	312	11	79	441	18
1,656,125	**M Channon**	858,923	84	21	310	7	62	619	10
1,472,600	**B Hills**	1,044,632	66	24	219	11	42	355	12
1,419,767	**R Hannon**	761,621	104	21	334	6	83	770	11
1,263,167	**M Jarvis**	917,101	59	22	149	15	36	183	20
1,222,406	**J Gosden**	714,521	61	17	135	13	44	270	16
1,185,292	**J Dunlop**	654,338	55	24	163	15	31	342	9
1,162,115	**J Fanshawe**	847,756	39	17	111	15	22	144	15
1,033,839	**L Cumani**	622,836	37	17	93	18	20	165	12
892,049	**T Easterby**	543,268	57	17	167	10	38	524	7
875,235	**D Nicholls**	618,489	54	18	240	8	36	405	9
781,695	**A P O'Brien**	240,297	4	4	59	7	0	1	0
742,733	**B Meehan**	470,293	43	10	145	7	32	245	13
728,560	**D Elsworth**	412,115	31	14	103	14	17	159	11
717,399	**E Dunlop**	508,076	33	8	86	9	25	237	11
672,785	**R Fahey**	459,132	62	15	111	14	45	402	11
661,737	**Mrs A Perrett**	378,770	39	15	118	13	24	219	11
648,047	**C Brittain**	371,920	19	6	113	5	13	147	9
604,777	**A Balding**	355,833	36	10	157	6	25	255	10
599,571	**P Cole**	294,470	35	11	114	10	24	196	12
594,891	**M Bell**	406,721	49	9	87	10	39	290	13
580,441	**R Charlton**	445,283	33	10	61	16	23	130	18
567,631	**M Tregoning**	319,056	24	11	69	16	13	107	12
544,384	**W Haggas**	282,038	35	9	76	12	26	164	16
521,285	**J Bradley**	288,580	35	8	87	9	26	429	6
474,280	**M Tompkins**	276,959	33	8	92	9	25	191	13
470,889	**P Harris**	352,000	36	15	79	19	21	221	10
470,235	**K Ryan**	281,656	44	8	100	8	36	226	16
467,742	**H Morrison**	300,226	25	9	59	15	15	193	8
466,756	**H Candy**	317,150	23	6	50	12	17	136	13
460,082	**J Noseda**	252,379	29	6	69	9	22	104	21
446,804	**Sir M Prescott**	354,810	45	10	32	31	35	126	28
406,437	**N Littmoden**	271,155	24	9	98	9	15	208	7
403,454	**D Loder**	234,920	34	6	96	6	28	198	14
401,676	**G A Butler**	139,226	21	3	75	4	18	142	13
396,579	**G Wragg**	215,606	18	8	74	11	10	75	13
384,946	**S Kirk**	283,250	23	4	46	9	19	245	8
364,738	**T Barron**	242,238	35	7	80	9	26	238	11
340,158	**P Evans**	222,313	49	4	54	7	43	400	11
331,096	**P Chapple-Hyam**	248,579	23	5	34	15	17	99	17
327,867	**W Muir**	177,142	17	6	59	10	11	171	6
318,995	**J J Quinn**	179,456	25	5	62	8	20	193	10
311,605	**B McMahon**	211,983	25	11	77	14	14	120	12
310,014	**N Callaghan**	185,509	30	7	96	7	23	147	16
295,577	**A Berry**	179,076	29	5	89	6	24	312	8
288,069	**C Wall**	136,962	18	6	61	10	12	125	10
287,239	**J Oxx**	169,042	3	2	10	20	1	1	100
276,128	**J Bethell**	195,646	19	6	50	12	13	135	10
273,746	**J Given**	121,466	23	3	92	3	19	304	6

Top trainers by winners (AW)

All runs				First time out			Horses*		
Won	Ran	%	Trainer	Won	Ran	%	Won	Ran	%
36	235	15	P Blockley	7	65	11	21	65	32
29	180	16	K R Burke	7	36	19	17	36	47
26	120	22	T Barron	5	25	20	16	25	64
26	232	11	Miss G Kelleway	4	42	10	16	42	38
24	157	15	P Howling	2	19	11	12	19	63
22	148	15	W Brisbourne	4	30	13	11	30	37
22	225	10	R Hollinshead	1	35	3	12	35	34
21	75	28	Sir M Prescott	4	21	19	13	21	62
21	151	14	K Ryan	5	32	16	15	32	47
21	214	10	G L Moore	3	56	5	17	56	30
19	163	12	J A Osborne	2	33	6	13	33	39
19	211	9	N Littmoden	3	46	7	14	46	30
18	114	16	P Haslam	4	28	14	12	28	43
18	213	8	D Chapman	1	30	3	10	30	33
17	154	11	J R Best	1	23	4	7	23	30
17	233	7	D Shaw	0	33	0	12	33	36
16	161	10	A Carroll	3	27	11	9	27	33
16	221	7	P Evans	5	43	12	11	43	26
15	77	19	E Dunlop	4	30	13	8	30	27
14	99	14	B Meehan	5	27	19	12	27	44
14	110	13	R Fahey	1	23	4	6	23	26
14	139	10	A Reid	1	27	4	10	27	37
14	151	9	M Polglase	3	24	13	7	24	29
13	50	26	Mrs A Perrett	1	11	9	11	11	100
13	60	22	B Hills	5	14	36	12	14	86
13	92	14	M Channon	2	26	8	6	26	23
12	89	13	B Powell	1	16	6	6	16	38
11	46	24	D Loder	3	14	21	8	14	57
11	86	13	G A Butler	4	31	13	9	31	29
11	106	10	R Cowell	1	24	4	8	24	33
11	108	10	W Musson	2	30	7	6	30	20
11	113	10	Stef Liddiard	3	20	15	9	20	45
11	123	9	B Smart	2	25	8	7	25	28
11	127	9	A Balding	5	45	11	9	45	20
10	59	17	C Brittain	1	11	9	10	11	91
10	59	17	E Alston	2	13	15	6	13	46
10	59	17	W Haggas	2	11	18	8	11	73
10	62	16	P D'Arcy	2	17	12	6	17	35
10	71	14	S C Williams	2	18	11	6	18	33
10	79	13	P Mitchell	2	18	11	5	18	28
10	88	11	J Given	3	25	12	7	25	28
10	127	8	J Balding	3	21	14	9	21	43
10	130	8	P Hiatt	2	19	11	7	19	37
10	176	6	Mrs N Macauley	2	25	8	6	25	24
9	53	17	Miss J Feilden	3	13	23	4	13	31
9	65	14	H Morrison	3	17	18	9	17	53
9	83	11	R Hannon	4	24	17	8	24	33
9	107	8	J C Poulton	3	20	15	6	20	30
8	43	19	W Jarvis	2	9	22	4	9	44
8	45	18	D Elsworth	4	15	27	5	15	33
8	51	16	T Mills	3	19	16	6	19	32

**Shows how many individual horses ran last season, how many won at least once, and percentage.*

Top trainers by prizemoney (AW)

Total prizemoney	Trainer	Win prizemoney	Wins	Class A-C Won	Ran	%	Class D-G Won	Ran	%
168,418	Miss G Kelleway	111,453	26	4	35	11	16	171	9
143,266	N Littmoden	81,980	19	2	28	7	15	174	9
140,175	P Blockley	96,728	36	0	12	0	31	195	16
118,981	K R Burke	90,739	29	1	6	17	21	144	15
114,240	T Barron	94,905	26	3	15	20	22	101	22
112,564	K Ryan	81,912	21	3	19	16	17	117	15
109,094	G L Moore	66,145	21	2	12	17	13	159	8
97,451	B Meehan	74,877	14	1	8	13	11	82	13
93,085	J A Osborne	63,397	19	0	4	0	17	138	12
88,908	E Dunlop	59,132	15	0	4	0	15	71	21
84,943	R Hollinshead	56,253	22	0	2	0	16	164	10
82,896	W Brisbourne	61,299	22	1	6	17	13	118	11
82,869	Sir M Prescott	71,712	21	0	1	0	20	73	27
77,428	J R Best	51,489	17	0	6	0	15	130	12
77,192	A Balding	37,422	11	0	18	0	9	90	10
74,887	C Brittain	37,884	10	1	10	10	7	44	16
74,515	P Howling	55,609	24	0	0	0	15	112	13
73,943	P Evans	42,720	16	0	12	0	15	185	8
73,687	M Channon	48,761	13	2	8	25	11	83	13
72,172	A Reid	52,597	14	1	4	25	12	119	10
71,770	Mrs A Perrett	55,881	13	0	9	0	13	38	34
69,892	M Polglase	51,553	14	2	14	14	7	114	6
68,691	G A Butler	47,347	11	1	8	13	9	75	12
68,170	B Hills	42,967	13	0	2	0	12	54	22
67,879	S bin Suroor	58,805	5	1	2	50	4	14	29
67,085	D Chapman	47,959	18	1	8	13	10	131	8
64,922	A Carroll	42,083	16	0	4	0	13	118	11
64,622	P Haslam	52,645	18	1	4	25	13	93	14
61,393	B Smart	33,676	11	1	14	7	7	93	8
61,248	G Wragg	51,545	6	3	7	43	3	21	14
60,469	R Fahey	45,599	14	0	6	0	12	91	13
58,855	D Shaw	35,470	17	0	0	0	8	173	5
57,104	P D'Arcy	40,251	10	1	7	14	8	50	16
56,791	Stef Liddiard	31,895	11	0	9	0	10	98	10
55,732	B Powell	35,921	12	0	7	0	11	66	17
55,182	W Haggas	41,111	10	0	10	0	10	49	20
54,720	J Balding	28,233	10	1	9	11	6	93	6
53,974	D Loder	39,934	11	1	8	13	9	36	25
53,732	D Elsworth	32,002	8	1	7	14	7	38	18
52,426	R Hannon	34,925	9	0	6	0	9	74	12
50,193	P Mitchell	35,026	10	1	6	17	7	59	12
49,048	Mrs N Macauley	34,538	10	2	7	29	8	132	6
48,772	E Alston	34,691	10	0	11	0	9	43	21
48,499	P Harris	21,821	6	0	7	0	6	31	19
46,865	H Morrison	31,345	9	0	7	0	8	52	15
46,447	A Newcombe	28,535	5	2	12	17	3	56	5
45,359	S Dow	31,126	8	1	4	25	5	104	5
45,096	M Jarvis	35,975	7	1	3	33	6	34	18
44,660	S Kirk	23,575	8	0	3	0	7	75	9
44,339	J Jenkins	17,433	6	0	8	0	5	90	6
43,521	S C Williams	30,653	10	0	1	0	9	62	15

Profiles for punters: Nerys Dutfield, Mark Polglase and Geraldine Rees: see pages 6-16

Top jockeys (Turf)

W	R	%	Jockey	Best Trainer	W	R	%
174	777	22%	**L Dettori**	S bin Suroor	74	255	29
159	930	17%	**K Fallon**	Sir M Stoute	49	223	22
143	861	17%	**S Sanders**	Sir M Prescott	34	99	34
114	881	13%	**R L Moore**	R Hannon	43	288	15
106	925	11%	**D Holland**	L Cumani	13	70	19
88	774	11%	**R Winston**	J J Quinn	13	107	12
83	625	13%	**P Hanagan**	R Fahey	35	228	15
82	797	10%	**K Darley**	M Johnston	13	93	14
72	782	9%	**S Drowne**	R Charlton	13	98	13
70	538	13%	**J Fanning**	M Johnston	46	246	19
66	530	12%	**P Robinson**	M Jarvis	45	244	18
65	574	11%	**N Callan**	K Ryan	27	181	15
62	434	14%	**R Hills**	M Tregoning	10	59	17
62	676	9%	**E Ahern**	J Noseda	23	124	19
61	538	11%	**T Quinn**	D Elsworth	10	56	18
59	612	10%	**A Culhane**	M Channon	15	120	13
56	451	12%	**M Hills**	B Hills	35	287	12
56	495	11%	**J Fortune**	J Gosden	18	103	17
56	557	10%	**R Hughes**	R Hannon	22	208	11
53	587	9%	**Martin Dwyer**	A Balding	12	156	8
52	679	8%	**Dane O'Neill**	H Candy	17	125	14
51	391	13%	**J P Murtagh**	J Fanshawe	14	64	22
50	561	9%	**T P Queally**	D Loder	17	140	12
49	452	11%	**F Norton**	A Berry	10	86	12
48	595	8%	**W Supple**	E Dunlop	8	57	14
47	534	9%	**J F Egan**	S Kirk	11	113	10
44	317	14%	**N Mackay**	L Cumani	10	87	11
43	316	14%	**K McEvoy**	S bin Suroor	27	119	23
40	477	8%	**R Ffrench**	M Johnston	13	117	11
39	587	7%	**J Quinn**	P Chapple-Hyam	6	23	26
38	474	8%	**D Allan**	T Easterby	25	287	9
38	565	7%	**T E Durcan**	M Channon	23	271	8
37	339	11%	**F Lynch**	B Smart	14	157	9
34	478	7%	**S W Kelly**	M Dods	6	50	12
33	576	6%	**C Catlin**	M Channon	8	155	5
32	460	7%	**T Eaves**	B Ellison	9	91	10
32	474	7%	**M Fenton**	J Given	10	175	6
31	397	8%	**I Mongan**	M Bell	8	69	12
30	266	11%	**W Ryan**	H Cecil	15	95	16
30	319	9%	**Darren Williams**	K R Burke	20	164	12
27	249	11%	**P Makin**	T Barron	11	98	11
27	259	10%	**F P Ferris**	P Evans	16	93	17
27	268	10%	**Hayley Turner**	M Bell	8	40	20
26	249	10%	**R Thomas**	G Balding	8	69	12
26	315	8%	**J F McDonald**	B Meehan	12	77	16
26	360	7%	**P Mulrennan**	M W Easterby	8	118	7
26	402	6%	**Dale Gibson**	M W Easterby	6	151	4
25	336	7%	**D Sweeney**	H Candy	5	26	19
25	359	7%	**Lisa Jones**	J Toller	4	61	7
24	320	8%	**J Mackay**	M Bell	8	72	11
22	165	13%	**O Urbina**	J Fanshawe	8	55	15

Top jockeys (AW)

W	R	%	Jockey	Best Trainer	W	R	%
52	429	12%	**N Callan**	K Ryan	17	87	20
52	437	12%	**A Culhane**	D Chapman	15	121	12
50	337	15%	**E Ahern**	E Dunlop	10	26	38
46	253	18%	**D Holland**	N Littmoden	6	27	22
39	162	24%	**K Fallon**	P Howling	4	9	44
38	404	9%	**I Mongan**	J Jay	3	6	50
31	233	13%	**R Winston**	P Howling	9	47	19
31	277	11%	**M Fenton**	Miss G Kelleway	15	93	16
30	380	8%	**J Quinn**	E Alston	5	16	31
27	238	11%	**D Sweeney**	M Blanshard	6	33	18
26	157	17%	**B Reilly**	Miss J Feilden	7	27	26
26	210	12%	**Martin Dwyer**	A Balding	10	59	17
26	354	7%	**C Catlin**	M Channon	6	24	25
25	276	9%	**Dane O'Neill**	Mrs L Stubbs	2	2	100
23	218	11%	**J Fanning**	P Howling	4	17	24
22	142	15%	**S Sanders**	Sir M Prescott	11	33	33
22	308	7%	**S Whitworth**	G L Moore	7	46	15
22	320	7%	**Lisa Jones**	P Blockley	4	6	67
21	75	28%	**L Dettori**	S bin Suroor	4	9	44
21	76	28%	**J P Spencer**	D Loder	6	13	46
21	194	11%	**Darren Williams**	K R Burke	11	73	15
21	276	8%	**S Drowne**	H Morrison	3	13	23
20	143	14%	**B Swarbrick**	W Brisbourne	11	72	15
20	177	11%	**N Pollard**	J R Best	10	73	14
19	137	14%	**J Mackay**	Sir M Prescott	9	28	32
19	325	6%	**S W Kelly**	J A Osborne	5	56	9
18	126	14%	**R L Moore**	G L Moore	5	34	15
16	160	10%	**G Baker**	K R Burke	3	20	15
15	181	8%	**L Fletcher**	M Polglase	4	45	9
14	59	24%	**G Faulkner**	P Haslam	7	26	27
14	82	17%	**R Hughes**	R Hannon	5	23	22
14	121	12%	**R Miles**	T Mills	4	16	25
14	147	10%	**Dale Gibson**	R Hollinshead	6	32	19
14	176	8%	**Dean McKeown**	P Blockley	5	45	11
13	54	24%	**D Mernagh**	T Barron	11	39	28
13	93	14%	**F Norton**	A Berry	3	18	17
13	120	11%	**T P Queally**	W Haggas	2	4	50
12	111	11%	**P Hanagan**	R Fahey	7	30	23
12	149	8%	**J F Egan**	T J FitzGerald	2	3	67
11	104	11%	**M Savage**	B Baugh	3	6	50
11	109	10%	**F Lynch**	B Smart	4	42	10
11	112	10%	**T Quinn**	E Vaughan	1	1	100
11	132	8%	**D Nolan**	P Blockley	4	37	11
11	139	8%	**P Doe**	B Pearce	2	4	50
10	58	17%	**M Hills**	B Hills	5	21	24
10	131	8%	**Paul Eddery**	C Horgan	3	16	19
10	137	7%	**N Chalmers**	Ms Deborah J Evans	2	7	29
9	82	11%	**Derek Nolan**	P Blockley	5	26	19
9	109	8%	**S Carson**	A Reid	4	19	
9	140	6%	**T Hamilton**	R Fahey	4	54	21
8	71	11%	**P Fitzsimons**	D Elsworth	2	3	67

Top apprentices

W	R		Jockey	Best Trainer	W	R	%
52	383	14	**N Mackay**	L Cumani	14	117	12
49	589	8	**D Allan**	T Easterby	27	303	9
47	666	7	**Lisa Jones**	J Toller	6	80	8
45	606	7	**T Eaves**	I Semple	10	72	14
42	423	10	**P Makin**	T Barron	16	140	11
39	468	8	**B Swarbrick**	W Brisbourne	22	239	9
35	359	10	**R Miles**	R J Price	6	21	29
35	457	8	**S Hitchcott**	M Channon	23	250	9
34	351	10	**R Thomas**	G Balding	8	73	11
34	354	10	**Hayley Turner**	M Bell	9	47	19
32	363	9	**F P Ferris**	P Evans	16	111	14
31	422	7	**P Mulrennan**	M W Easterby	11	139	8
31	447	7	**J F McDonald**	B Meehan	15	107	14
27	294	9	**B Reilly**	Miss J Feilden	8	82	10
26	435	6	**T Hamilton**	R Fahey	18	211	9
24	296	8	**D Nolan**	P Blockley	7	65	11
22	246	9	**C Haddon**	W G M Turner	15	108	14
22	306	7	**J-P Guillambert**	N Littmoden	6	107	6
21	300	7	**L Fletcher**	H Morrison	7	65	11
19	322	6	**N Chalmers**	A Balding	5	55	9
19	430	4	**L Keniry**	D Elsworth	7	45	16
18	315	6	**L Enstone**	D Barker	8	76	11
17	185	9	**A Quinn**	P Makin	4	6	67
16	186	9	**M Savage**	B Baugh	3	7	43
15	211	7	**D Fox**	C Dwyer	4	35	11
14	170	8	**Rory Moore**	P Haslam	8	64	13
12	203	6	**D Corby**	M Wallace	2	13	15
11	157	7	**M Lawson**	J Parkes	5	39	13
11	157	7	**Natalia Gemelova**	I McInnes	4	57	7
10	109	9	**L Treadwell**	D Nicholls	3	38	8
9	103	9	**Dean Williams**	Miss J Feilden	2	6	33

NICKY MACKAY: top of the pile

AMIR QUINN: good percentages

Outlook

Group One records

2,000 Guineas (1m) Newmarket

Year	Winner	Age (if appropriate)	Trainer	Jockey	SP	draw/ran
1995	**Pennekamp**		A Fabre	T Jarnet	9-2	11/11
1996	**Mark Of Esteem**		S bin Suroor	L Dettori	8-1	2/13
1997	**Entrepreneur**		Sir M Stoute	M Kinane	11-2	4/16
1998	**King Of Kings**		A O'Brien	M Kinane	7-2	17/18
1999*	**Island Sands**		S bin Suroor	L Dettori	10-1	3/16
						*(*run on July course)*
2000	**King's Best**		Sir M Stoute	K Fallon	13-2	12/27
2001	**Golan**		Sir M Stoute	K Fallon	11-1	19/18
2002	**Rock Of Gibraltar**		A O'Brien	J Murtagh	9-1	22/22
2003	**Refuse To Bend**		D Weld	P Smullen	9-2	18/20
2004	**Haafhd**		B Hills	R Hills	11-2	4/14

THE FIRST colts' Classic was first run in 1809 and is usually held on the first Saturday in May. It's often a specialist miler's race. As with the 1,000 Guineas, you don't get many winners who haven't earned themselves a high place in the International Classifications, although Island Sands bucked that trend. King Of Kings was rated 111 and was already a Group 1 winner at two, as was Rock Of Gibraltar, who had won the Dewhurst, which has proved the best of the two-year-old trials. The race currently known as the Racing Post Trophy has produced only one winner, High Top. Newmarket's Craven Stakes has proved a far better guide than Newbury's Greenham in recent years. It appears that horses having their seasonal debut in the race are not disadvantaged, with Rock Of Gibraltar, Golan, King Of Kings, Entrepreneur, Mark Of Esteem and Mister Baileys all making their seasonal reappearances when triumphing here.

1,000 Guineas (1m) Newmarket

Year	Winner	Age (if appropriate)	Trainer	Jockey	SP	draw/ran
1995	**Harayir**		W Hern	R Hills	5-1	2/14
1996	**Bosra Sham**		H Cecil	Pat Eddery	10-11f	11/13
1997	**Sleepytime**		H Cecil	K Fallon	5-1	3/15
1998	**Cape Verdi**		S bin Suroor	L Dettori	10-3	7/16
1999*	**Wince**		H Cecil	K Fallon	4-1	19/22
						*(*run on July course)*
2000	**Lahan**		J Gosden	R Hills	14-1	10/18
2001	**Ameerat**		M Jarvis	P Robinson	11-2	10/18
2002	**Kazzia**		S bin Suroor	L Dettori	9-2	12/17
2003	**Russian Rhythm**		Sir M Stoute	K Fallon	12-1	2/19
2004	**Attraction**		M Johnston	K Darley	11-2	8/16

FIRST RUN in 1814, since 1995 the first fillies' Classic has been run on a Sunday. A high place in the International Classifications has been critical – very few winners register less than 112. Ameerat (106) and Cape Verdi (109) count against this theory but the latter was campaigned at distances short of her best at two, which may explain the extent of her apparent improvement. The Marcel Boussac and the Cheveley Park are the races to study from the previous year. Two key trials are Newbury's Fred Darling and Newmarket's Nell Gwyn, but don't necessarily be put off by horses beaten in those. Cape Verdi was an unusual winner at the time, not having had a prep-run, but the last five winners have all been making their seasonal reappearances.

Lockinge (1m) Newbury

1995	**Soviet Line**	*5*	Sir M Stoute	W Swinburn	2-1f	4/5
1996	**Soviet Line**	*6*	Sir M Stoute	T Quinn	13-2	1/7
1997	**First Island**	*5*	G Wragg	M Hills	11-4	1/10
1998	**Cape Cross**	*4*	S bin Suroor	D O'Donohoe	20-1	8/10
1999	**Fly To The Stars**	*5*	S bin Suroor	W Supple	9-1	6/6
2000	**Aljabr**	*4*	S bin Suroor	L Dettori	8-13f	1/7
2001	**Medicean**	*4*	Sir M Stoute	K Fallon	3-1	5/7
2002	**Keltos**	*4*	C Laffon-Parias	O Peslier	9-1	7/10
2003	**Hawk Wing**	*4*	A O'Brien	M Kinane	2-1f	4/6
2004	**Russian Rhythm**	*4*	Sir M Stoute	K Fallon	3-1f	3/15

Formerly Group 2, Group 1 from 1995.

OFTEN QUITE weak for a Group 1, the Lockinge was a Godolphin benefit in the late 1990s. It's worth noting, however, that both Cape Cross and Fly To The Stars were perceived to be their second-strings, with their Intikhab getting turned over at 4-7 in the 1999 race. Godolphin's Noverre was also beaten at odds-on behind Keltos. Four-year-olds seem to have the call over their older rivals. This race is often run on ground with plenty of give, and can therefore provide a rare chance at this level for horses who like to get their toe in. Last year, Russian Rhythm bucked a strong trend and became the first filly to win the race for twenty years.

Coronation Cup (1m4f) Epsom

1995	**Sunshack**	*4*	A Fabre	Pat Eddery	10-1	2/7
1996	**Swain**	*4*	A Fabre	L Dettori	11-10f	2/4
1997	**Singspiel**	*5*	Sir M Stoute	L Dettori	5-4f	3/5
1998	**Silver Patriarch**	*4*	J Dunlop	Pat Eddery	7-2	2/7
1999	**Daylami**	*5*	S bin Suroor	L Dettori	9-2	3/7
2000	**Daliapour**	*4*	Sir M Stoute	K Fallon	11-8f	2/4
2001	**Mutafaweq**	*5*	S bin Suroor	L Dettori	11-2	1/6
2002	**Boreal**	*4*	P Schiergen	K Fallon	4-1	3/6
2003	**Warrsan**	*5*	C Brittain	P Robinson	9-2	4/9
2004	**Warrsan**	*5*	C Brittain	D Holland	7-1	5/11

IT'S HARD to escape the conclusion that this race is suffering a fall from grace, with the quality of winner dropping markedly, even within the last ten years. Almost always featuring a small field, the combination of a false pace and the tricky course have produced some funny results, including when Silver Patriarch beat Swain in 1998.

The Oaks (1m4f) Epsom

1995	**Moonshell**	S bin Suroor	L Dettori	3-1	9/10
1996	**Lady Carla**	H Cecil	Pat Eddery	100-30	9/11
1997	**Reams Of Verse**	H Cecil	K Fallon	5-6f	6/12
1998	**Shahtoush**	A O'Brien	M Kinane	12-1	5/8
1999	**Ramruma**	H Cecil	K Fallon	3-1	5/10
2000	**Love Divine**	H Cecil	T Quinn	9-4f	3/16
2001	**Imagine**	A O'Brien	M Kinane	3-1f	10/14
2002	**Kazzia**	S bin Suroor	L Dettori	100-30f	13/14
2003	**Casual Look**	A Balding	Martin Dwyer	10-1	7/15
2004	**Ouija Board**	E Dunlop	K Fallon	7/2	3/7

FIRST RUN in 1779, the Oaks is one year older then the Derby. Breeding is just as important as in the Derby, particularly since so few three-year-old fillies stay so far at this time of the year. The 1,000 Guineas has provided the best guide, followed by the Musidora at York. In 1998, Shahtoush kept up the good record of 1,000 Guineas runners – she had finished second in the first fillies' Classic, while Kazzia provided a further boost by winning the Newmarket feature. Casual Look was sixth in the Guineas on her only previous outing that season. Ramruma won the Lingfield Oaks Trial, while Imagine was the first filly to do the Irish Guineas/Oaks double since 1966. Ouija Board went on to complete the Oaks double.

The Derby (1m4f) Epsom

1995	**Lammtarra**	S bin Suroor	W Swinburn	14-1	7/15
1996	**Shaamit**	W Haggas	M Hills	12-1	9/20
1997	**Benny The Dip**	J Gosden	W Ryan	11-1	8/13
1998	**High-Rise**	L Cumani	O Peslier	20-1	14/15
1999	**Oath**	H Cecil	K Fallon	13-2	1/16
2000	**Sinndar**	J Oxx	J Murtagh	7-1	15/15
2001	**Galileo**	A O'Brien	M Kinane	11-4j	10/12
2002	**High Chaparral**	A O'Brien	J Murtagh	7-2	9/12
2003	**Kris Kin**	Sir M Stoute	K Fallon	6-1	4/20
2004	**North Light**	Sir M Stoute	K Fallon	7-2jf	6/14

MANY HIGH-CLASS colts are beaten here due to lack of stamina. It's important to have a top-class sire (Sadler's Wells took an age to get a Derby winner but produced two in succession) plus a staying pedigree on the dam's side. Since the golden years of Nijinsky and Mill Reef (1970 and 1971) only one horse, Nashwan, has won both the 2,000 Guineas and Derby, although Dancing Brave was unlucky at Epsom having landed the Newmarket race. Key races include York's Dante Stakes (especially last year, as the first three home at York filled the same places in last year's renewel) and the Lingfield Derby Trial, High-Rise winning the latter. In three of the last five years, Leopardstown's Derby Trial has been the key pointer. Oath warmed up by winning a Listed race at Chester, while Kris Kin's final prep was in a Group 3 race at the same track. Generally this is a race for fancied runners in the first four in the betting – 20-1 winner High-Rise was the biggest priced winner for 25 years. Having said that, outright favourites don't have a strong record. Kris Kin was the subject of a huge gamble on the morning of the race, and punters stuck with the same jockey-trainer combination last year.

Queen Anne Stakes (1m) Royal Ascot

1995	**Nicolotte**	4	G Wragg	M Hills	16-1	2/7
1996	**Charnwood Forest**	4	S bin Suroor	M Kinane	10-11	6/9
1997	**Allied Forces**	4	S bin Suroor	L Dettori	10-1	11/11
1998	**Intikhab**	4	S bin Suroor	L Dettori	9-4	6/9
1999	**Cape Cross**	5	S bin Suroor	G Stevens	7-1	2/8
2000	**Kalanisi**	4	Sir M Stoute	K Fallon	11-2	11/11
2001	**Medicean**	4	Sir M Stoute	K Fallon	11-2	8/10
2002	**No Excuse Needed**	4	Sir M Stoute	J Murtagh	13-2	11/12
2003	**Dubai Destination**	4	S bin Suroor	L Dettori	9-2	10/10
2004	**Refuse To Bend**	4	S bin Suroor	L Dettori	12-1	1/16

Formerly Group 3. Group 2 from 1985, Group 1 from 2003.

THE FIRST race of the Royal Ascot meeting, usually run at a furious pace, and won by Saeed Bin Suroor or Sir Michael Stoute. Four-year-olds who were once considered Classic contenders fit the bill and this age group has taken ten of the last 11 runnings. Three-year-olds have a dreadful record and few of them attempt the race these days – only one in the last five years. Godolphin won the race four times in a row before Kalanisi's success in 2000 and they again hit the target in 2003; Sir Michael Stoute won all three renewals in the intervening years. The Lockinge Stakes is a key race; Medicean won both races, while No Excuse Needed ran a feeble race behind Keltos in the Lockinge before landing this. Dubai Destination was given a low-key warm-up at Nottingham in 2003, when Lockinge winner Hawk Wing let down the record of the Newbury race by beating only three home.

Prince Of Wales's Stakes (1m2f) Royal Ascot

1995	**Muhtarram**	6	J Gosden	W Carson	5-1	5/6
1996	**First Island**	4	G Wragg	M Hills	9-1	3/12
1997	**Bosra Sham**	4	H Cecil	K Fallon	4-11f	1/6
1998	**Faithful Son**	4	S bin Suroor	J Reid	11-2	7/8
1999	**Lear Spear**	4	D Elsworth	M Kinane	20-1	5/8
2000	**Dubai Millennium**	4	S bin Suroor	J Bailey	5-4	7/6
2001	**Fantastic Light**	5	S bin Suroor	L Dettori	100-30	8/9
2002	**Grandera**	4	S bin Suroor	L Dettori	4-1	3/12
2003	**Nayef**	5	M Tregoning	R Hills	5-1	6/10
2004	**Rakti**	5	M Jarvis	P Robinson	3-1	10/10

FIRST RUN in 1968 and now one of the races of the week. Four and five-year-olds have proved most successful in recent years. Three-year-olds have won only twice since the inception of the race. The Brigadier Gerard Stakes, won by Bosra Sham, the Gordon Richards Stakes and the Tattersalls Gold Cup (won by Fantastic Light in 2001) are other key pointers. Grandera came into the race from a spring international campaign taking in Dubai, Hong Kong and Singapore, while Nayef's only prep-run was also in Dubai.

St James's Palace Stakes (1m) Royal Ascot

1995	**Bahri**	J Dunlop	W Carson	11-4f	7/9
1996	**Bijou d'Inde**	M Johnston	J Weaver	9-1	7/9
1997	**Starborough**	D Loder	L Dettori	11-2	5/8
1998	**Dr Fong**	H Cecil	K Fallon	4-1	4/8
1999	**Sendawar**	A de Royer-Dupre	G Mosse	2-1f	11/11
2000	**Giant's Causeway**	A O'Brien	M Kinane	7-2f	3/11

2001	**Black Minnaloushe**	A O'Brien	J Murtagh	8-1	1/11
2002	**Rock Of Gibraltar**	A O'Brien	M Kinane	4-5f	4/9
2003	**Zafeen**	M Channon	D Holland	8-1	5/11
2004	**Azamour**	J Oxx	M Kinane	9-2	1/11

FIRST RUN in 1925, this is restricted to three-year-olds. Winners and also-rans from the Irish, French and English Guineas often line up for this valuable prize. The last five winners all ran in the Irish Guineas, Black Minnaloushe and Rock Of Gibraltar having won on the Curragh, Giant's Causeway and last year's winner, Azamour had been second, while Zafeen was a dismal fourteenth. Seven of the last eight winners had made the frame in the English version. Less exposed types such as Persian Heights and Shavian can make a breakthrough. Derby runners have a mixed record; Marju was second in the Derby and won, but Rodrigo De Triano flopped in both races.

Coronation Stakes (1m) Royal Ascot

1995	**Ridgewood Pearl**	J Oxx	J Murtagh	9-2	8/10
1996	**Shake The Yoke**	E Lellouche	O Peslier	Evensf	4/7
1997	**Rebecca Sharp**	G Wragg	M Hills	25-1	3/6
1998	**Exclusive**	Sir M Stoute	W Swinburn	5-1	10/9
1999	**Balisada**	G Wragg	M Roberts	16-1	8/9
2000	**Crimplene**	C Brittain	P Robinson	4-1j	6/9
2001	**Banks Hill**	A Fabre	O Peslier	4-1j	4/13
2002	**Sophisticat**	A O'Brien	M Kinane	11-2	3/11
2003	**Russian Rhythm**	Sir M Stoute	K Fallon	4-7f	11/9
2004	**Attraction**	M Johnston	K Darley	6-4f	10/11

A CHAMPIONSHIP race for three-year-old fillies, first run in 1870. Winners and runners from all the Guineas races fare well, but Irish 1,000 Guineas winners have the best record through Ridgewood Pearl, Kooyonga and Crimplene. Up untill last year, English 1,000 Guinness winners had been worth opposing – failures include Harayir, Las Meninas, Shadayid and Sleepytime. Russian Rhythm was the first Newmarket winner to take this since 1979, now Attraction has followed her up.

Golden Jubilee Stakes (6f) Royal Ascot

1995	**So Factual**	5	S bin Suroor	L Dettori	9-2	9/11
1996	**Atraf**	3	D Morley	W Carson	12-1	2/17
1997	**Royal Applause**	4	B Hills	M Hills	11-2f	16/23
1998	**Tomba**	4	B Meehan	M Tebbutt	4-1	13/12
1999	**Bold Edge**	4	R Hannon	D O'Neill	16-1	16/19
2000	**Superior Premium**	6	R Fahey	J Murtagh	20-1	17/16
2001	**Harmonic Way**	6	R Charlton	S Drowne	10-1	1/21
2002	**Malhub**	4	J Gosden	K Darley	16-1	12/12
2003	**Choisir**	4	P Perry	J Murtagh	13-2	20/17
2004	**Fayr Jag**	4	T Easterby	W Supple	12-1	9/14

AKA 'The Cork And Orrery'. Formerly Group 3. Group 2 from 1999, Group 1 from 2002.

ALWAYS A fiercely competitive race and one that has thrown up more than its share of shocks in recent seasons. Four-year-olds have won most often, but then they usually make up most of the field. By contrast, three-year-olds haven't won since 1996 but one or two often run well at big prices, notably Baron's Pit (third at 50-1 last year), Indian Country (fourth at the same price the year before) and Freud (third at 25-1 in 2001).

Gold Cup (2m4f) Royal Ascot

1995	**Double Trigger**	4	M Johnston	J Weaver	9-4	6/7
1996	**Classic Cliche**	4	S bin Suroor	M Kinane	3-1	7/7
1997	**Celeric**	5	D Morley	Pat Eddery	11-2	2/13
1998	**Kayf Tara**	4	S bin Suroor	L Dettori	11-1	17/16
1999	**Enzeli**	4	J Oxx	J Murtagh	20-1	16/17
2000	**Kayf Tara**	6	S bin Suroor	M Kinane	11-8f	6/11
2001	**Royal Rebel**	5	M Johnston	J Murtagh	8-1	10/12
2002	**Royal Rebel**	6	M Johnston	J Murtagh	16-1	8/15
2003	**Mr Dinos**	4	P Cole	K Fallon	3-1	6/12
2004	**Papineau**	4	S bin Suroor	L Dettori	5-1	4/13

ROYAL ASCOT'S most famous race and the only British Group 1 race run over 2m4f. Many winners, including most recently Royal Rebel, have followed up from the year before -this is due to the fact that winners have to possess a blend of speed and stamina which is very rare in modern racing stock. Previous to the 2003 renewal, the key races were the St Leger and Sandown's Henry II Stakes. Mr Dinos had been fifth in the Leger and warmed up for this by landing the Sandown race. Papineau was an excellent winner last year and since the horse fits the bill for the race so well, should come back next year for another dose.

Eclipse (1m2f) Sandown

1995	**Halling**	4	S bin Suroor	W Swinburn	7-1	3/8
1996	**Halling**	5	S bin Suroor	J Reid	100-30	1/7
1997	**Pilsudski**	5	Sir M Stoute	M Kinane	11-2	1/5
1998	**Daylami**	4	S bin Suroor	L Dettori	6-4f	5/7
1999	**Compton Admiral**	3	G Butler	D Holland	20-1	7/8
2000	**Giant's Causeway**	3	A O'Brien	G Duffield	8-1	4/8
2001	**Medicean**	4	Sir M Stoute	K Fallon	7-2	7/8
2002	**Hawk Wing**	3	A O'Brien	M Kinane	8-15f	6/5
2003	**Falbrav**	5	L Cumani	D Holland	8-1	14/15
2004	**Refuse To Bend**	4	S bin Suroor	L Dettori	15-2	9/12

CHANGES IN the weight-for-age scale meant that, from 1990 onwards, three-year-olds became 2lb worse off with their elders, but that didn't stop Environment Friend, Compton Admiral, Giant's Causeway or Hawk Wing (though the latter won a very weak renewal). Derby winners and fillies have a poor record. Pebbles, in the mid-Eighties, was the first filly to succeed since the nineteenth century. Proven Group 1 form is a major asset. Daylami and Falbrav, both beaten in the Prince of Wales's Stakes, kept up the good record of runners from that race and Royal Ascot form in general is a key to this race; Giant's Causeway won the St James's Palace, while Medicean and Refuse To Bend won the Queen Anne.

July Cup (6f) Newmarket

1995	**Lake Coniston**	4	G Lewis	Pat Eddery	13-8f	9/9
1996	**Anabaa**	4	C Head	F Head	11-4	2/10
1997	**Compton Place**	3	J Toller	S Sanders	50-1	1/9
1998	**Elnadim**	4	J Dunlop	R Hills	3-1f	18/17
1999	**Stravinsky**	3	A O'Brien	M Kinane	8-1	6/17
2000	**Agnes World**	5	H Mori	Y Take	4-1f	6/10
2001	**Mozart**	3	A O'Brien	M Kinane	4-1f	19/18
2002	**Continent**	5	D Nicholls	D Holland	12-1	2/14
2003	**Oasis Dream**	3	J Gosden	R Hughes	9-2	11/16
2004	**Frizzante**	5	J Fanshawe	J Murtagh	14-1	18/20

THE BLUE RIBAND event of Newmarket's July meeting, it was first staged in 1876. Horses dropping down in distance succeeded in 1987, 1988, 1999 and 2001. Mozart had won the 7f Jersey Stakes and finished second in the Irish Guineas. However, in the main over the last 10 years it is specialist sprinters who have been doing well in this race. The Cork and Orrery (Royal Ascot, June), the King's Stand (also Royal Ascot), the Duke of York (York, May), the 2,000 Guineas (Newmarket, May) and the 1,000 Guineas (also Newmarket, May) give the most helpful clues.

King George VI and Queen Elizabeth Diamond Stakes (1m4f) Ascot

1995	**Lammtarra**	3	S bin Suroor	L Dettori	9-4f	3/7
1996	**Pentire**	4	G Wragg	M Hills	100-30	7/8
1997	**Swain**	5	S bin Suroor	J Reid	16-1	5/8
1998	**Swain**	6	S bin Suroor	L Dettori	11-2	5/8
1999	**Daylami**	5	S bin Suroor	L Dettori	3-1	8/8
2000	**Montjeu**	4	J Hammond	M Kinane	1-3f	5/7
2001	**Galileo**	3	A O'Brien	M Kinane	1-2f	7/12
2002	**Golan**	4	Sir M Stoute	K Fallon	11-2	8/9
2003	**Alamshar**	3	J Oxx	J Murtagh	13-2	5/12
2004	**Doyen**	4	S bin Suroor	L Dettori	11/10f	5/11

ALTHOUGH IT has less prestige than the Arc, the King George is always won by a top-class horse. It was first run in 1951. Lammtarra and Galileo came into this race as Derby winners, while King's Theatre had been second at Epsom and Alamshar third. Although a top-class older horse, trained by an established handler, best fits the bill. A seriously good three-year-old is almost given a head-start by the weight-for-age scale – but note that no three-year-old has won this in the last decade without having made the frame in the Derby. The Eclipse is also a big influence, while, for the older horses, the Coronation Cup is a good pointer. Golan was the first horse ever to win this on his seasonal debut, though few serious contenders will have attempted such a feat. Also note that Godolphin have had the winner five times in ten years.

Sussex Stakes (1m) Goodwood

1995	**Sayyedati**	*5*	C Brittain	B Doyle	11-2	4/6
1996	**First Island**	*4*	G Wragg	M Hills	5-1	9/10
1997	**Ali-Royal**	*4*	H Cecil	K Fallon	13-2	3/9
1998	**Among Men**	*4*	Sir M Stoute	M Kinane	4-1	10/10
1999	**Aljabr**	*3*	S Bin Suroor	L Dettori	11-10f	6/8
2000	**Giant's Causeway**	*3*	A O'Brien	M Kinane	3-1j	6/10
2001	**Noverre**	*3*	S Bin Suroor	L Dettori	9-2	11/10
2002	**Rock Of Gibraltar**	*3*	A O'Brien	M Kinane	8-13f	3/5
2003	**Reel Buddy**	*5*	R Hannon	Pat Eddery	20-1	7/9
2004	**Soviet Song**	*5*	J Fanshawe	J Murtagh	3-1	5/11

THIS GENERALLY features a glamorous three-year-old, who is sent off a well-backed favourite. As well as winners Rock Of Gibraltar, Aljabr and Giant's Causeway, losing jollies Trade Fair, Lend A Hand, Starborough, Bahri and Mister Baileys would fall into this category. This race is dominated by the big-league yards and big-name jockeys.The trends of the afore mentioned were bucked last year, with James Fanshawe's filly Soviet Song just succeeding, also hinting that, after the success of Reel Buddy the previous year,ve year-olds now have a shout.

Nassau Stakes (1m1f192yds) Goodwood

1995	**Caramba**	*3*	R Hannon	M Roberts	5-2f	3/6

1996	**Last Second**	*3*	Sir M Prescott	G Duffield	7-4f	1/8
1997	**Ryafan**	*3*	J Gosden	M Hills	9-4f	5/7
1998	**Alborada**	*3*	Sir M Prescott	G Duffield	4-1	5/9
1999	**Zahrat Dubai**	*3*	S bin Suroor	G Stevens	5-1	3/8
2000	**Crimplene**	*3*	C Brittain	P Robinson	7-4f	3/7
2001	**Lailani**	*3*	E Dunlop	L Dettori	5-4f	5/7
2002	**Islington**	*3*	Sir M Stoute	K Fallon	100-30	6/10
2003	**Russian Rhythm**	*3*	Sir M Stoute	K Fallon	4-5f	7/8
2004	**Favourable Terms**	*4*	Sir M Stoute	K Fallon	11-2	2/6

AN AMAZINGLY good race for favourites, pointing up a real lack of strength in depth among fillies at this distance and at this level. Russian Rhythm was the first Guineas winner to add this for many a year. Three-year-olds have dominated to the exclusion of their elders. Michael Stoute has won it three times on the trot and his winner last year was surprisingly allowed to go off at 11-2.

Juddmonte International Stakes (1m2f85yds) York

1995	**Halling**	4	S bin Suroor	W Swinburn	9-4f	2/6
1996	**Halling**	5	S bin Suroor	L Dettori	6-4f	1/6
1997	**Singspiel**	5	Sir M Stoute	L Dettori	4-1	2/4
1998	**One So Wonderful**	4	L Cumani	Pat Eddery	6-1	5/8
1999	**Royal Anthem**	4	H Cecil	G Stevens	3-1f	9/12
2000	**Giant's Causeway**	3	A O'Brien	M Kinane	10-11f	5/6
2001	**Sakhee**	4	S bin Suroor	L Dettori	7-4f	5/8
2002	**Nayef**	4	M Tregoning	R Hills	6-4f	5/7
2003	**Falbrav**	5	L Cumani	D Holland	5-2	2/8
2004	**Sulamani**	5	S bin Suroor	L Dettori	3-1	9/9

FAMOUS FOR its many upsets since its first running in 1972 when Roberto beat Grundy. Bosra Sham in 1997 was one of many hot favourites to be beaten in this race when she finished last of four at 4-5. That said, favourites won four on the reel before 2003. Older horses, especially lightly-raced ones (Sakhee) have mostly kept on top of the three-year-olds, though Giant's Causeway bucked the trend in 2000. Note the previous year's running and the Eclipse.

Yorkshire Oaks (1m3f195yds) York

1995	**Pure Grain**	*3*	Sir M Stoute	J Reid	11-10f	2/8
1996	**Key Change**	*3*	J Oxx	J Murtagh	7-1	1/9
1997	**My Emma**	*4*	R Guest	D Holland	7-1	7/8
1998	**Catchascatchcan**	*3*	H Cecil	K Fallon	2-1f	7/6
1999	**Ramruma**	*3*	H Cecil	Pat Eddery	5-6f	9/11
2000	**Petrushka**	*3*	Sir M Stoute	J Murtagh	5-4f	1/6
2001	**Super Tassa**	*5*	V Valiani	K Darley	25-1	7/9
2002	**Islington**	*3*	Sir M Stoute	K Fallon	2-1	9/11
2003	**Islington**	*4*	Sir M Stoute	K Fallon	8-11f	5/8
2004	**Quiff**	*3*	Sir M Stoute	K Fallon	7-2	3/8

SIR MICHAEL STOUTE has a good grip on what it takes to land this, with five victories from the last ten (three on the bounce), albeit usually at short odds. Super Tassa, the only non-Stoute-trained winner of the last five years, was also remarkable for being the first Italian-trained winner in Britain for 41 years. The Classic generation have the edge, with seven wins in the last decade .

Nunthorpe Stakes (5f) York

1995	**So Factual**	*5*	S bin Suroor	L Dettori	9-2	5/8

1996	**Pivotal**	*3*	Sir M Prescott	G Duffield	100-30	5/8
1997	**Coastal Bluff**	*5*	T D Barron	K Darley	6-1	6/15
	Ya Malak	*6*	D Nicholls	A Greaves	11-1	4/15
1998	**Lochangel**	*4*	I Balding	L Dettori	6-1	2/17
1999	**Stravinsky**	*3*	A O'Brien	M Kinane	Evensf	13/16
2000	**Nuclear Debate**	*5*	J Hammond	G Mosse	5-2f	1/13
2001	**Mozart**	*3*	A O'Brien	M Kinane	4-9f	4/10
2002	**Kyllachy**	*4*	H Candy	J Spencer	3-1f	15/17
2003	**Oasis Dream**	*3*	J Gosden	R Hughes	4-9f	2/8
2004	**Bahamian Pirate**	*9*	D Nicholls	S Sanders	16-1	5/12

A RUN of five consecutive winning favourites (including two at the very skimpy price) suggests that the sprinting division is not so competitive as it has been, despite the healthy field-sizes. Three-year-olds have punched above their weight, claiming their fair share of winners Recent results hint at a draw bias towards low numbers . But the most notable stat last year was the age of the winner (emphasising the lack of top sprinters around).

Stanley Leisure Sprint Cup (6f) Haydock

1995	**Cherokee Rose**	*4*	J Hammond	C Asmussen	5-1	4/6
1996	**Iktamal**	*4*	E Dunlop	W Ryan	10-1	9/11
1997	**Royal Applause**	*4*	B Hills	M Hills	15-8f	9/9
1998	**Tamarisk**	*3*	R Charlton	T Sprake	13-2	5/13
1999	**Diktat**	*4*	S bin Suroor	L Dettori	13-8f	16/16
2000	**Pipalong**	*4*	T Easterby	K Darley	3-1	7/13
2001	**Nuclear Debate**	*6*	J Hammond	G Mosse	11-2	9/12
2002	**Invincible Spirit**	*5*	J Dunlop	J Carroll	25-1	10/14
2003	**Somnus**	*3*	T Easterby	T Durcan	12-1	7/10
2004	**Tante Rose**	*4*	R Charlton	R Hughes	10-1	14/19

CAN OFTEN be run on ground with plenty of give, including two stagings on heavy going in the last five years, which appeared to feature significantly deeper ground than the official good to soft. Older horses appear to have the call over the Classic generation, while a high draw is generally favoured.

St. Leger (1m6f127yds) Doncaster

1995	**Classic Cliche**	S bin Suroor	L Dettori	100-30	7/10
1996	**Shantou**	J Gosden	L Dettori	8-1	10/11
1997	**Silver Patriarch**	J Dunlop	Pat Eddery	5-4f	9/10
1998	**Nedawi**	S bin Suroor	J Reid	5-2	1/9
1999	**Mutafaweq**	S bin Suroor	R Hills	11-2	6/9
2000	**Millenary**	J Dunlop	T Quinn	11-4	5/11
2001	**Milan**	A O'Brien	M Kinane	13-8f	7/10
2002	**Bollin Eric**	T Easterby	K Darley	7-1	3/8
2003	**Brian Boru**	A O'Brien	J Spencer	5-4f	9/12
2004	**Rule Of Law**	S bin Suroor	K McEvoy	3-1f	9/9

THE OLDEST of the five Classics, first run in 1776, and the last to be staged each year. You don't have to have a Classic profile to win and you don't necessarily have to be a stayer. Three of the last nine winners were placed in the Epsom Derby and Mutafaweq was fifth in the Irish version and Rule of Law fourth in their respective years. The key race, aside from the Epsom Classics, has been the Great Voltigeur at York in August won by Rule Of Law and Milan in 2001, when the first three went on to finish 1-2-3 in the Leger in 2002; Brian Boru was second in the Voltigeur).

Queen Elizabeth II Stakes (1m) Ascot

1995	**Bahri**	*3*	J Dunlop	W Carson	5-2	1/6
1996	**Mark Of Esteem**	*3*	S bin Suroor	L Dettori	100-30	5/7
1997	**Air Express**	*3*	C Brittain	O Peslier	9-1	7/9
1998	**Desert Prince**	*3*	D Loder	O Peslier	100-30f	1/7
1999	**Dubai Millennium**	*3*	S bin Suroor	L Dettori	4-9f	3/4
2000	**Observatory**	*3*	J Gosden	K Darley	14-1	6/12
2001	**Summoner**	*4*	S bin Suroor	R Hills	33-1	7/8
2002	**Where Or When**	*3*	T Mills	K Darley	7-1	3/5
2003	**Falbrav**	*5*	L Cumani	D Holland	6-4f	4/8
2004	**Rakti**	*5*	M Jarvis	P Robinson	9-2	13/11

THE TWO stunning results, Maroof and Summoner, were both the result of Richard Hills stealing the race on a supposed pacemaker. Three-year-olds have been firmly in command, with only Falbrav and Rakti) interrupting their hegemony. Some short-priced favourites have also been embarrassed Observatory turned over 11-10 hotpot Giant's Causeway and Where Or When did the same to the 1-2 shot Hawk Wing.

Prix De l'Arc De Triomphe (1m4f) Longchamp

1995	**Lammtarra**	3	S bin Suroor	L Dettori	21-10f	7/16
1996	**Helissio**	3	E Lellouche	O Peslier	18-10f	5/16
1997	**Peintre Celebre**	3	A Fabre	O Peslier	22-10f	2/18
1998	**Sagamix**	3	A Fabre	O Peslier	5-2j	7/14
1999	**Montjeu**	3	J Hammond	M Kinane	6-4c	4/14
2000	**Sinndar**	3	J Oxx	J Murtagh	6-4	7/10
2001	**Sakhee**	4	S bin Suroor	L Dettori	22-10f	15/17
2002	**Marienbard**	5	S bin Suroor	L Dettori	158-10	3/16
2003	**Dalakhani**	3	A de Royer-Dupre	C Soumillon	9-4	14/13
2004	**Bago**	3	J Pease	T Gillet	10-1	5/20

RESULTS HAVE usually been more reliable over the last decade or so, perhaps a reflection of the fact that winners have been trained specifically for the race from the summer. Three-year-olds have dominated recently and, though four-year-old Sakhee succeeded in 2001, he was still lightly-raced. Note that Godolphin have trained both of the only two older winners. Andre Fabre has trained four of the last 13 winners. There are three key trials for the Arc at Longchamp, three weeks prior to the race, which need to be noted. The Derbys all have a major bearing. Marienbard was something of an aberration, being prepared with two races in Germany.

Dubai Champion Stakes (1m2f) Newmarket

1995	**Spectrum**	3	P Chapple-Hyam	J Reid	5-1	1/8
1996	**Bosra Sham**	3	H Cecil	Pat Eddery	9-4	4/6
1997	**Pilsudski**	5	Sir M Stoute	M Kinane	Evensf	1/7
1998	**Alborada**	3	Sir M Prescott	G Duffield	6-1	5/10
1999*	**Alborada**	4	Sir M Prescott	G Duffield	5-1	10/13
						*(*run on July course)*
2000	**Kalanisi**	4	Sir M Stoute	J Murtagh	5-1	3/15
2001	**Nayef**	3	M Tregoning	R Hills	3-1	1/12
2002	**Storming Home**	4	B Hills	M Hills	8-1	4/11
2003	**Rakti**	4	M Jarvis	P Robinson	11-1	3/12
2004	**Haafhd**	3	B Hills	R Hills	12-1	9/11

GUINEAS WINNERS of the same year or the year before have a good record. The overseas races with influence are the Irish Champion Stakes, the Arc de Triomphe and the Coupe de Maisons-Laffitte, which was won by Hatoof and Dernier Empereur. Rakti had only had one run outside Italy before landing this.

Big handicap records

Lincoln Handicap (1m) Doncaster

Year	Winner	Age	Weight	Trainer	Jockey	SP	Draw/ran
1995	**Roving Minstrel**	4	8st3lb	B McMahon	K Darley	33-1	11/23
1996	**Stone Ridge**	4	8st7lb	R Hannon	D O'Neill	33-1	6/24
1997	**Kuala Lipis**	4	8st6lb	P Cole	T Quinn	11-1	21/24
1998	**Hunters Of Brora**	8	9st	J Bethell	J Weaver	16-1	23/23
1999	**Right Wing**	5	9st5lb	J Dunlop	T Quinn	9-2f	8/24
2000	**John Ferneley**	5	8st10lb	P Cole	J Fortune	7-1j	1/24
2001	**Nimello**	5	8st9lb	P Cole	J Fortune	9-2f	1/23
2002	**Zucchero**	6	8st13lb	D Arbuthnot	S Whitworth	33-1	7/23
2003	**Pablo**	4	8st11lb	B Hills	M Hills	5-1	6/24
2004	**Babodana**	4	9st10lb	M.Tompkins	P Robinson	20-1	23/24

BET ANTE-POST or, better still, take a morning price but, whatever you do, don't bet at SP. The perennial question is what effect the draw will have,and athough a high berth prevailed last year, in general low numbers are favoured. The best thing is to watch the Spring Mile, run a day earlier. The 1998 winner, Hunters Of Brora, was the exception; she was the oldest winner since 1963, the first to carry 9st or more to victory since 1985 and was winning for the first time in three years. Carrying the top weight of 9st 10lb was a remarkable feat by Babodana last year and certainly bucked recent trends. The vast majority of both winners and runners were having their first outings of the season. Northern-based trainers no longer dominate and Paul Cole has done particularly well in recent years.

Royal Hunt Cup Handicap (1m) Royal Ascot

Year	Winner	Age	Weight	Trainer	Jockey	SP	Draw/ran
1995	**Realities**	5	9st	G Harwood	M Kinane	11-1	30/32
1996	**Yeast**	4	8st6lb	W Haggas	K Fallon	8-1f	3/31
1997	**Red Robbo**	4	8st6lb	R Akehurst	O Peslier	16-1	17/32
1998	**Refuse To Lose**	4	7st11lb	J Eustace	J Tate	20-1	6/32
1999	**Showboat**	5	8st6lb	B Hills	N Pollard	14-1	30/32
2000	**Caribbean Monarch**	5	8st10lb	Sir M Stoute	K Fallon	11-2	28/32
2001	**Surprise Encounter**	5	8st9lb	E Dunlop	L Dettori	8-1	29/30
2002	**Norton**	5	8st9lb	T Mills	J Fortune	25-1	10/30
2003	**Macadamia**	4	8st13lb	J Fanshawe	D O'Neill	8-1	6/32
2004	**Mine**	6	9st5lb	J Bethell	T Quinn	16-1	8/31

A GREAT betting race in which the draw can play a crucial part, especially if the ground is soft – no less than five of the last ten winners have run from stall 28 or higher. There are few pointers and plots are thick on the ground, so most winners are a working man's price, inlcuding last year's victor Mine, a 16-1 shot. It's recommended that you watch the Victoria Cup at Ascot in May.

Wokingham Handicap (6f) Royal Ascot

Year	Winner	Age	Weight	Trainer	Jockey	SP	Draw/ran
1995	**Astrac**	4	8st7lb	R Akehurst	S Sanders	14-1	16/30

1996	**Emerging Market**	4	8st13lb	J Dunlop	K Darley	33-1	7/29
1997	**Selhurstpark Flyer**	6	8st9lb	J Berry	P Roberts	25-1	5/30
1998	**Selhurstpark Flyer**	7	9st7lb	J Berry	C Lowther	16-1	20/29
1999	**Deep Space**	4	8st7lb	E Dunlop	G Carter	14-1	3/30
2000	**Harmonic Way**	5	9st6lb	R Charlton	R Hughes	12-1	28/29
2001	**Nice One Clare**	5	9st3lb	J Payne	J Murtagh	7-1f	4/30
2002	**Capricho**	5	8st11lb	J Akehurst	T Quinn	20-1	21/28
2003	**Fayr Jag**	4	9st6lb	T Easterby	W Supple	10-1	13/29
	Ratio	5	9st3lb	J Hammond	L Dettori	14-1	22/29
2004	**Lafi**	5	8st13lb	D Nicholls	E Ahern	6-1f	30/29

WAS FIRST run in 1896 and is a tough race in which to find a winner, though the *Outlook* tipped Nice One Clare on the front page ahead of the 2001 race. Winners are often long-priced and low-weighted. A key race is the Victoria Cup (Ascot, May). Winners tend to be aged four to six, with only two winners having been older. Sprint king, Dandy Nicholls also bucked the poor record of favourites when his Lafi won last season.

Northumberland Plate (2m) Newcastle

1995	**Bold Gait**	4	9st10lb	J Fanshawe	D Harrison	12-1	5/17
1996	**Celeric**	4	9st4lb	D Morley	W Carson	2-1f	7/13
1997	**Windsor Castle**	3	8st10lb	P Cole	T Quinn	10-1	20/18
1998	**Cyrian**	4	7st13lb	P Cole	T Sprake	12-1	2/20
1999	**Far Cry**	4	8st10lb	M Pipe	K Darley	9-2j	6/20
2000	**Bay Of Islands**	8	8st4lb	D Morris	K Darley	7-1	4/18
2001	**Archduke Ferdinand**	3	8st4lb	P Cole	F Norton	12-1	17/18
2002	**Bangalore**	6	9st5lb	A Perrett	S Sanders	8-1	9/16
2003	**Unleash**	4	8st11lb	P Hobbs	J Spencer	10-1	1/20
2004	**Mirjan**	8	8st3lb	L Lungo	P Hanagan	25-1	5/19

HAS IN the past been known as a good race for older, experienced stayers but recent winners show a trend towards younger, less exposed types. Paul Cole does well with his three-year-old runners here but other trainers seem happy to stick with older runners. The first bend comes shortly after the start, so those drawn high can be disadvantaged, creating a significant bias towards low numbers that is probably not yet factored into the market.

Bunbury Cup (7f) Newmarket

1995	**Cadeaux Tryst**	3	9st1lb	E Dunlop	W Swinburn	20-1	17/19
1996	**Crumpton Hill**	4	8st12lb	N Graham	M Roberts	7-1	3/16
1997	**Tumbleweed Ridge**	4	9st6lb	B Meehan	M Tebbutt	20-1	19/20
1998	**Ho Leng**	3	9st7lb	L Perratt	M Kinane	14-1	20/20
1999	**Grangeville**	4	9st3lb	I Balding	K Fallon	13-2j	20/19
2000	**Tayseer**	6	8st9lb	D Nicholls	G Mosse	9-1	8/19
2001	**Atavus**	4	8st9lb	G Margarson	J Mackay (3)	10-1	14/19
2002	**Mine**	4	8st12lb	J D Bethell	K Fallon	5-1f	3/17
2003	**Patavellian**	5	9st1lb	R Charlton	S Drowne	4-1f	2/20
2004	**Material Witness**	7	9st3lb	W Muir	M Dwyer	25-1	6/19

A PERSISTENT feature of this race used to be the draw bias towards high numbers, but the current course management appear to have successfully brought an end to that and only one of the last four winners has come from a double-figure draw. With six of the last ten winners carrying 9st or more, weight is clearly no barrier to success, while the bigger yards have failed to make their mark recently – this is a big race in which the smaller stables can put themselves on the map.

John Smith's Cup (1m2f85yds) York

1995	**Naked Welcome**	3	8st4lb	M F'-Godley	D Holland	6-1	9/16
1996	**Wilcuma**	5	9st2lb	P Makin	Pat Eddery	10-1	2/17
1997	**Pasternak**	4	8st3lb	Sir M Prescott	G Duffield	13-2	1/21
1998	**Porto Foricos**	3	8st3lb	H Cecil	J Quinn	6-1	7/20
1999	**Achilles**	4	8st11lb	K Burke	J Weaver	25-1	6/15
2000	**Sobriety**	3	8st8lb	R F J'-Houghton	J Reid	20-1	8/22
2001	**Foreign Affairs**	3	8st6lb	Sir M Prescott	G Duffield	5-2f	8/19
2002	**Vintage Premium**	5	9st9lb	R Fahey	P Hanagan	20-1	9/20
2003	**Far Lane**	4	9st4lb	B Hills	M Hills	7-1	4/20
2004	**Arcalis**	4	9st2lb	J H Johnson	R Winston	20-1	18/21

EVEN THOSE of you who are allergic to draw analysis must take care when playing in this race, which features a notorious bias towards low numbers – for almost the first half of the race, the field are turning left and those on the outside can struggle to get into the contest. Sir Mark Prescott has proved his liking for the race, and the fact that he won one of the most competitive handicaps twice in five years is testament to his skill in this type of race. Runners older than four increasingly struggle. It's almost always worth looking past the market-leader. See also *By The Numbers*, pages 183-187.

Stewards' Cup Handicap (6f) Goodwood

1995	**Shikari's Son**	8	8st13lb	J White	R Hughes	40-1	30/27
1996	**Coastal Bluff**	4	8st5lb	T Barron	J Fortune	10-1j	29/30
1997	**Danetime**	3	8st10lb	N Callaghan	Pat Eddery	5-1	5/30
1998	**Superior Premium**	4	8st12lb	R Fahey	R Winston	14-1	28/29
1999	**Harmonic Way**	4	8st6lb	R Charlton	R Hughes	12-1	8/30
2000	**Tayseer**	6	8st11lb	D Nicholls	R Hughes	13-2	28/30
2001	**Guinea Hunter**	5	9st	T Easterby	J Spencer	33-1	19/30
2002	**Bond Boy**	5	8st2lb	B Smart	C Catlin	14-1	29/28
2003	**Patavellian**	5	8st11lb	R Charlton	S Drowne	4-1	27/29
2004	**Pivotal Point**	4	8st11lb	P Makin	S Sanders	7-1c	1/28

INAUGURATED IN 1840, this is a major betting heat with a strong ante-post market. How-

PIVOTAL POINT (nearside): the cavalry charge that is the Stewards' Cup is within his grasp

ever, the race has been altered in recent seasons by the opening up of a fresh strip of ground on the far rail which has given high numbers a huge advantage, to the detriment of the ante-post market. A high draw is now thought essential and even a casual glance at the results above will tell you why. In 1998, winner Superior Premium was drawn 28 of 29, the second 25 and the third 29 and, though it was more even in 1999, in 2000 Tayseer (28) won from Bon Ami (24). Bond Boy (29) won from horses drawn 9, 22, 16, 7, 25, 30 and 28 in 2002, while Patavellian led home a 1-2-3 for three of the widest four stalls in the penultimate renewal. Do not bet ante-post in this race. The Wokingham Handicap has the most bearing; Knight Of Mercy pulled off the double, Danetime was an unlucky second in the Ascot race. See also *By The Numbers*, pages 183-187.

Ebor Handicap (1m6f) York

1995	**Sanmartino**	3	7st11lb	B Hills	W Carson	8-1	21/21
1996	**Clerkenwell**	3	7st11lb	Sir M Stoute	F Lynch	17-2	2/21
1997	**Far Ahead**	5	8st	J Eyre	T Williams	33-1	10/21
1998	**Tuning**	3	8st7lb	H Cecil	K Fallon	9-2	1/21
1999	**Vicious Circle**	5	8st4lb	L Cumani	K Darley	11-1	7/21
2000	**Give The Slip**	3	8st8lb	Mrs A Perrett	Pat Eddery	8-1	16/22
2001	**Mediterranean**	3	8st4lb	A O'Brien	M Kinane	16-1	20/22
2002	**Hugs Dancer**	5	8st5lb	J Given	D McKeown	25-1	20/22
2003	**Saint Alebe**	4	8st8lb	D Elsworth	T Quinn	20-1	17/22
2004	**Mephisto**	4	9st4lb	L Cumani	D Holland	6-1	3/19

ONE OF the oldest and most famous handicaps, first run in 1847, with a strong ante-post market. Sea Pigeon brought the house down when lumping top-weight home in 1979. Stamina is a premium (as Sea Pigeon showed) and many Ebor winners, such as Further Flight, go on to be top stayers. Unexposed three-year-olds have come to the fore in recent years. Watch the Northumberland Plate (Newcastle, June) and the Duke Of Edinburgh Handicap (Royal Ascot, June).

Ayr Gold Cup Handicap (6f) Ayr

1995	**Royale Figurine**	4	8st9lb	M F'-Godley	D Holland	8-1	27/29
1996	**Coastal Bluff**	4	9st10lb	T Barron	J Fortune	3-1f	28/28
1997	**Wildwood Flower**	4	9st3lb	R Hannon	D O'Neill	14-1	24/29
1998	**Always Alight**	4	8st7lb	K Burke	J Egan	16-1	8/29
1999	**Grangeville**	4	9st	I Balding	K Fallon	11-1	17/28
2000	**Bahamian Pirate**	5	8st	D Nicholls	A Nicholls	33-1	7/28
2001	**Continent**	4	8st10lb	D Nicholls	D Holland	10-1	22/28
2002	**Funfair Wane**	3	9st3lb	D Nicholls	A Nicholls	16-1	16/28
2003	**Quito**	6	8st6lb	D Chapman	A Culhane	20-1	10/26
2004	**Funfair Wane**	5	8st6lb	D Nicholls	P Doe	33-1	8/24

A HISTORIC race first run in 1804, for which there is a lively ante-post book. The effect of the draw can be gleaned from the Ayr Silver Cup, run the day before. A horse with good recent form who can settle in large fields and who can come from off the pace is required. Key races are; the Wokingham Handicap (Royal Ascot, June), the Tote Portland Handicap (Doncaster, September) and the Stewards' Cup (Goodwood, August). Take a second look at Dandy Nicholls' runners - he does run a few - but his record speaks for itself.

Cambridgeshire Handicap (1m1f) Newmarket

1995	**Cap Juluca**	3	9st10lb	R Charlton	R Hughes	11-1	26/39
1996	**Clifton Fox**	4	8st2lb	J Glover	N Day	14-1	17/38
1997	**Pasternak**	4	9st1lb	Sir M Prescott	G Duffield	4-1f	17/36

1998	**Lear Spear**	3	7st13lb	D Elsworth	N Pollard	20-1	33/35
1999*	**She's Our Mare**	6	7st12lb	A Martin	F Norton	11-1	14/33
						*(*run on July course)*	
2000	**Katy Nowaitee**	4	8st8lb	P Harris	J Reid	6-1	34/35
2001	**I Cried For You**	6	8st6lb	J Given	M Fenton	33-1	11/35
2002	**Beauchamp Pilot**	4	9st5lb	G Butler	E Ahern	9-1	26/30
2003	**Chivalry**	4	8st1lb	Sir M Prescott	G Duffield	14-1	17/34
2004	**Spanish Don**	6	8st7lb	D Elsworth	L Keniry	100-1	3/32

THE FIRST leg of the Autumn Double, dating back to 1839. Because of its unusual distance and its straight course, the Cambridgeshire has thrown up a number of specialists. Apart from perennials, look for a late-maturing three-year-old bred to find improvement over longer trips which are not attempted until after the weights are set. Two races at Doncaster on St Leger day, a 0-105 handicap over the straight mile and a 0-95 over an extended 1m2f should provide clues. Longer-priced horses often do well – see last year.

Cesarewitch Handicap (2m2f) Newmarket

1995	**Old Red**	5	7st11lb	Mrs M Reveley	L Charnock	11-1	18/21
1996	**Inchcailloch**	7	7st3lb	J King	R Ffrench	20-1	15/26
1997	**Turnpole**	6	7st10lb	Mrs M Reveley	L Charnock	16-1	6/30
1998	**Spirit Of Love**	3	8st8lb	M Johnston	O Peslier	11-1	19/29
1999*	**Top Cees**	9	8st10lb	I Balding	K Fallon	7-1	17/32
						*(*run on July course)*	
2000	**Heros Fatal**	6	8st1lb	M Pipe	G Carter	11-1	18/33
2001	**Distant Prospect**	4	8st8lb	I Balding	M Dwyer	14-1	32/31
2002	**Miss Fara**	7	8st	M Pipe	R Moore	12-1	36/36
2003	**Landing Light**	8	9st4lb	N Henderson	Pat Eddery	12-1	36/36
2004	**Contact Dancer**	5	8st2lb	M Johnston	R Ffrench	16-1	18/34

THE SECOND leg of the Autumn Double. Normally a race won by five-year-olds and above, Spirit Of Love being a rare three-year-old winner. Fresh horses at the lower end of the weights have a good record. The Tote Ebor and previous runnings of this race itself have the most influence. Go for horses who have shown good autumn form in the past. With such a large field, you can usaually expect the winner to be a good price. A single figure draw is also a disadvantage.

November Handicap (1m4f) Doncaster

1995	**Snow Princess**	3	8st2lb	Lord Huntingdon	R Hills	5-1	10/18
1996	**Clifton Fox**	4	8st10lb	J Glover	N Day	9-1	14/22
1997	**Sabadilla**	3	7st8lb	J Gosden	R Ffrench	10-1	22/24
1998	**Yavana's Pace**	6	9st10lb	M Johnston	D Holland	8-1	12/23
1999	**Flossy**	3	7st7lb	C Thornton	A Beech	5-1	10/16
2000	**Batswing**	5	8st8lb	B Ellison	R Winston	14-1	14/20
2001	**Royal Cavalier**	4	7st10lb	R Hollinshead	P Quinn	50-1	5/14
2002	**Red Wine**	3	8st1lb	J Osborne	M Dwyer	16-1	20/23
2003	**Turbo**	4	9st2lb	G Balding	A Clark	25-1	14/24
2004	**Carte Diamond**	4	9st6lb	B Ellison	K Fallon	12-1	3/24

THE LAST big ante-post race of the season traces back to 1876. Three-year-olds, lightly raced, progressive and with stout pedigrees, are most likely to succeed. The 1m4f Ladbroke Handicap run over course and distance at the previous meeting is worth studying. As far as detailed trends are concerned, there is quite little that stands out. Prices vary (although favourites seem to have a poor record), as does the weight carried to victory. Carte Diamond won last season from the lowest stalls position of the last ten years.

Big Race Dates, By The Numbers and Track Facts

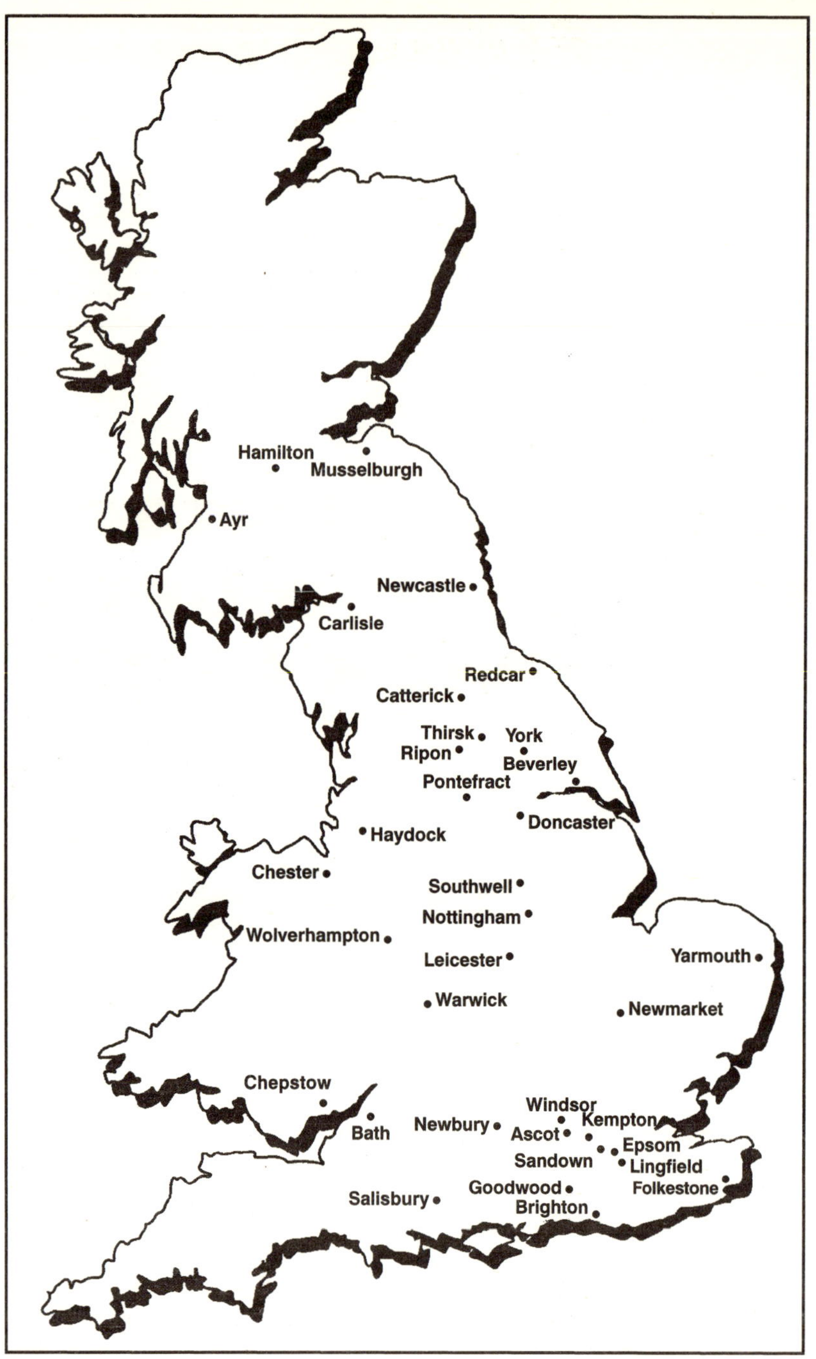
Hamilton
Musselburgh
Ayr
Newcastle
Carlisle
Redcar
Catterick
Thirsk
York
Ripon
Beverley
Pontefract
Doncaster
Haydock
Chester
Southwell
Nottingham
Wolverhampton
Yarmouth
Leicester
Warwick
Newmarket
Chepstow
Windsor
Kempton
Bath
Newbury
Ascot
Epsom
Sandown
Lingfield
Goodwood
Folkestone
Salisbury
Brighton

Fixtures

Key - **Flat**, ***Flat evening***, Jumps, *Jumps evening*

April

1 Friday........**Doncaster, Lingfield**, Newbury
2 Saturday........Bangor, **Doncaster, Kempton**, Newbury, ***Wolverhampton***
3 Sunday........Kelso, Market Rasen, Wincanton
4 Monday........**Southwell, Wolverhampton, Yarmouth**
5 Tuesday........**Folkestone**, Sedgefield, **Southwell**
6 Wednesday........**Catterick, Lingfield, Nottingham**
7 Thursday........**Leicester**, Aintree, Taunton
8 Friday........**Lingfield**, Aintree, **Southwell**
9 Saturday........Hereford, **Lingfield**, Aintree, **Newcastle**
10 Sunday........Hexham, Newton Abbot, Worcester
11 Monday........Kelso, **Lingfield, Southwell**
12 Tuesday........Exeter, **Musselburgh, Newmarket**
13 Wednesday........**Beverley**, Cheltenham, **Newmarket**
14 Thursday........Cheltenham, **Newmarket, Ripon**
15 Friday........Ayr, **Newbury**, *Taunton*, **Thirsk**, ***Wolverhampton***
16 Saturday........Ayr, Bangor, **Newbury**, ***Nottingham***, **Thirsk**, ***Wolverhampton***
17 Sunday........Carlisle, Stratford, Wincanton
18 Monday........Hexham, Plumpton, **Pontefract**, ***Windsor***, ***Wolverhampton***
19 Tuesday........***Brighton***, **Folkestone, Newcastle, Southwell**, *Towcester*
20 Wednesday........**Catterick, Epsom**, ***Lingfield***, Perth, *Worcester*
21 Thursday........***Bath***, **Beverley**, Fontwell, Perth, ***Southwell***
22 Friday........*Chepstow*, *Newton Abbot*, Perth, **Sandown, Wolverhampton**
23 Saturday........***Haydock***, **Leicester**, Market Rasen
........**Ripon, Sandown**, ***Wolverhampton***
24 Sunday........**Brighton**, Ludlow, Wetherby
25 Monday........**Hamilton**, ***Southwell***, Towcester, ***Windsor***, **Wolverhampton**
26 Tuesday........**Bath**, Newton Abbot, **Southwell**, ***Warwick***, ***Yarmouth***
27 Wednesday........*Cheltenham*, Exeter, *Kelso*, **Lingfield, Pontefract**
28 Thursday........Hereford, *Kelso*, ***Lingfield***, **Redcar, Southwell**
29 Friday........*Bangor*, **Musselburgh**, *Fontwell*, **Nottingham**, Southwell
30 Saturday........**Goodwood**, *Hexham*, **Newmarket, Thirsk**, Uttoxeter, *Worcester*

May

1 Sunday........**Hamilton, Newmarket, Salisbury**
2 Monday........**Doncaster, Kempton, Newcastle**, Sedgefield, **Warwick**
3 Tuesday........**Bath**, ***Catterick***, *Exeter*, **Leicester**, Ludlow
4 Wednesday........**Chepstow, Chester**, Fakenham
5 Thursday........***Chepstow***, **Chester, Folkestone**, Newton Abbot, *Wetherby*
6 Friday........**Chester**, ***Hamilton***, **Lingfield, Nottingham**, *Wincanton*
7 Saturday........**Beverley, Haydock**, Hexham, **Lingfield**
........**Newmarket**, ***Thirsk***, *Warwick*
8 Sunday........Plumpton, Uttoxeter, Worcester
9 Monday........**Kempton, Redcar**, *Towcester*, ***Windsor***, **Wolverhampton**
10 Tuesday........**Musselburgh**, Hereford, *Huntingdon*, *Newton Abbot*, **Yarmouth**
11 Wednesday........**Brighton**, Exeter, ***Newcastle***, *Perth*, **York**

12 Thursday........***Carlisle***, *Ludlow*, Perth, **Salisbury, York**
13 Friday........***Hamilton***, *Aintree*, **Newbury, Nottingham, York**
14 Saturday........Bangor, **Newbury, Nottingham, Thirsk**, *Uttoxeter*, *Worcester*
15 Sunday........Fakenham, Market Rasen, **Ripon**
16 Monday........**Bath**, ***Musselburgh***, Newton Abbot, ***Windsor***, **Wolverhampton**
17 Tuesday........**Beverley**, ***Leicester***, **Lingfield, Redcar**, *Towcester*
18 Wednesday........*Folkestone*, **Goodwood**, Kelso, *Sedgefield*, **Southwell**
19 Thursday........***Doncaster***, **Goodwood**, *Kelso*, **Newcastle**, Wetherby
20 Friday........***Bath***, **Goodwood, Haydock, Newmarket**, *Stratford*
21 Saturday........**Catterick, Haydock**, ***Kempton***, **Lingfield, Newmarket**, *Stratford*
22 Sunday........**Brighton**, Hereford, Southwell
23 Monday........**Beverley, Carlisle, Leicester**, ***Thirsk***, ***Windsor***
24 Tuesday........**Lingfield, Nottingham, Ripon**, *Sedgefield*, *Worcester*
25 Wednesday........Cartmel, Fontwell, ***Kempton***, **Lingfield**, ***Ripon***
26 Thursday........**Ayr, Bath**, *Huntingdon*, Newton Abbot, *Wetherby*
27 Friday........**Brighton, Catterick**, ***Pontefract***, *Towcester*, **Wolverhampton**
28 Saturday.*Cartmel*, **Doncaster, Musselburgh, Goodwood**, Hexham, ***Lingfield***
29 Sunday........Fontwell, **Newmarket**, Uttoxeter
30 Monday........Cartmel, **Chepstow, Leicester, Redcar, Sandown**
31 Tuesday........**Carlisle**, *Hexham*, **Leicester, Redcar**, ***Sandown***

June

1 Wednesday........***Beverley***, **Newcastle, Nottingham**, ***Southwell***, **Yarmouth**
2 Thursday........**Brighton, Hamilton, Haydock**, ***Sandown***, *Uttoxeter*
3 Friday........**Epsom**, ***Goodwood***, ***Haydock***, **Thirsk, Wolverhampton**
4 Saturday........***Chepstow***, **Doncaster, Epsom, Haydock**, ***Lingfield***, Worcester
5 Sunday........**Bath**, Perth, Stratford
6 Monday........**Folkestone**, Newton Abbot, ***Pontefract***, ***Windsor***
7 Tuesday........***Chester***, *Huntingdon*, **Redcar, Salisbury**
8 Wednesday........**Beverley**, ***Hamilton***, Hereford, Market Rasen, ***Newbury***
9 Thursday........***Brighton***, **Ripon, Southwell**, *Uttoxeter*, **Yarmouth**
10 Friday........**Catterick**, ***Chepstow***, ***Goodwood***, **Sandown, Wolverhampton**
11 Saturday........**Bath**, Hexham, ***Leicester***, ***Lingfield***, **Ripon, Sandown**
12 Sunday........**Doncaster, Salisbury**, Stratford
13 Monday........**Brighton, Thirsk**, ***Warwick***, ***Windsor***
14 Tuesday........**Carlisle**, *Hereford*, *Newton Abbot*, **York**
15 Wednesday........***Chepstow***, **Hamilton**, ***Kempton***, Worcester, **York**
16 Thursday........***Beverley***, *Aintree*, **Newbury, Southwell, York**
17 Friday........**Ayr**, ***Goodwood***, ***Newmarket***, **Redcar, York**
18 Saturday........**Ayr**, ***Lingfield***, **Newmarket, Redcar**, ***Warwick***, **York**
19 Sunday........Hexham, **Pontefract, Warwick**
20 Monday........**Musselburgh, Nottingham**, ***Ripon***, ***Windsor***
21 Tuesday........**Beverley, Brighton**, ***Newbury***, *Newton Abbot*
22 Wednesday........***Bath***, **Carlisle**, ***Kempton***, **Salisbury**, Worcester
23 Thursday........***Hamilton***, ***Leicester***, **Newcastle, Salisbury, Thirsk**
24 Friday .**Folkestone**, Market Rasen, ***Newcastle***, ***Newmarket***, **Wolverhampton**
25 Saturday...**Chester**, ***Doncaster***, ***Lingfield***, **Newcastle, Newmarket, Windsor**
26 Sunday........Uttoxeter, **Windsor**
27 Monday........***Musselburgh***, **Pontefract**, ***Windsor***, **Wolverhampton**
28 Tuesday........**Brighton, Hamilton**
29 Wednesday........**Catterick**, ***Chepstow***, ***Kempton***, Perth, Worcester
30 Thursday........***Epsom***, **Haydock**, ***Newbury***, Perth, **Yarmouth**

July

1 Friday............................***Beverley***, ***Haydock***, **Sandown**, **Southwell**, **Warwick**
2 Saturday......**Beverley**, ***Carlisle***, **Haydock**, **Leicester**, ***Nottingham***, **Sandown**
3 Sunday...**Brighton**, Market Rasen
4 Monday ....**Bath**, **Musselburgh**, ***Ripon***, ***Windsor***
5 Tuesday...........................**Newmarket**, **Pontefract**, *Uttoxeter*, ***Wolverhampton***
6 Wednesday................**Catterick**, ***Kempton***, **Lingfield**, **Newmarket**, *Worcester*
7 Thursday..................***Doncaster***, ***Epsom***, **Folkestone**, **Newmarket**, **Warwick**
8 Friday..........................***Chepstow***, ***Chester***, **Lingfield**, **Wolverhampton**, **York**
9 Saturday............**Chester**, ***Hamilton***, **Lingfield**, **Nottingham**, ***Salisbury***, **York**
10 Sunday..**Haydock**, Perth, Stratford
11 Monday....................................**Ayr**, Newton Abbot, ***Windsor***, ***Wolverhampton***
12 Tuesday..**Beverley**, **Brighton**
13 Wednesday.....................**Catterick**, ***Kempton***, **Lingfield**, Uttoxeter, *Worcester*
14 Thursday...........................Cartmel, ***Doncaster***, ***Epsom***, **Hamilton**, **Leicester**
15 Friday.........**Carlisle**, ***Hamilton***, ***Newmarket***, ***Pontefract***, Southwell, **Warwick**
16 Saturday....***Haydock***, ***Lingfield***, Market Rasen, **Newbury**, **Newmarket**, **Ripon**
17 Sunday...Newton Abbot, **Redcar**, Stratford
18 Monday...**Ayr**, ***Beverley***, **Brighton**, ***Windsor***
19 Tuesday...**Ayr**, **Yarmouth**
20 Wednesday...................**Catterick**, ***Leicester***, **Lingfield**, ***Sandown***, Worcester
21 Thursday..........................**Bath**, ***Doncaster***, ***Folkestone***, **Sandown**, Uttoxeter
22 Friday..........................**Ascot**, ***Chepstow***, ***Newmarket***, **Wolverhampton**, **York**
23 Saturday.............**Ascot**, ***Lingfield***, **Newcastle**, **Nottingham**, ***Salisbury***, **York**
24 Sunday..**Ascot**, **Newmarket**, **Pontefract**
25 Monday.......................................Sedgefield, **Southwell**, ***Windsor***, ***Yarmouth***
26 Tuesday..**Beverley**, **Goodwood**
27 Wednesday..**Musselburgh**, **Goodwood**, ***Kempton***, ***Leicester***, Newton Abbot
28 Thursday.....................**Carlisle**, ***Musselburgh***, ***Epsom***, **Goodwood**, Stratford
29 Friday.........................Bangor, **Goodwood**, ***Newmarket***, ***Nottingham***, **Thirsk**
30 Saturday....**Doncaster**, **Goodwood**, ***Hamilton***, ***Lingfield***, **Newmarket**, **Thirsk**
31 Sunday...**Chester**, Market Rasen, **Newbury**

August

1 Monday...***Carlisle***, Newton Abbot, **Ripon**, ***Windsor***
2 Tuesday...**Brighton**, **Catterick**
3 Wednesday................**Brighton**, ***Kempton***, **Newcastle**, **Pontefract**, ***Yarmouth***
4 Thursday...................***Brighton***, **Chepstow**, ***Folkestone***, **Haydock**, **Yarmouth**
5 Friday.........................***Haydock***, **Lingfield**, ***Newmarket***, Sedgefield, Worcester
6 Saturday..................***Ayr***, **Haydock**, ***Lingfield***, **Newmarket**, **Redcar**, **Windsor**
7 Sunday...**Leicester**, **Lingfield**, **Redcar**
8 Monday.......................................Southwell, ***Thirsk***, ***Windsor***, **Wolverhampton**
9 Tuesday..**Bath**, Newton Abbot
10 Wednesday..................**Beverley**, ***Hamilton***, **Salisbury**, ***Sandown***, **Yarmouth**
11 Thursday.......................**Beverley**, ***Chepstow***, ***Haydock***, **Salisbury**, **Sandown**
12 Friday....................***Catterick***, **Folkestone**, **Newbury**, **Newcastle**, ***Newmarket***
13 Saturday...Bangor, ***Goodwood***, *Market Rasen*, **Newbury**, **Newmarket**, **Ripon**
14 Sunday...**Bath**, **Pontefract**, Stratford
15 Monday..**Brighton**, **Nottingham**, ***Windsor***, ***Yarmouth***
16 Tuesday..**Hamilton**, **York**
17 Wednesday........................**Carlisle**, ***Kempton***, ***Nottingham***, Worcester, **York**

18 Thursday........................***Chepstow***, **Chester**, *Fontwell*, **Wolverhampton, York**
19 Friday..............................**Ayr, Chester,** ***Salisbury*****, Sandown,** ***Wolverhampton***
20 Saturday......**Beverley, Chester,** ***Lingfield***, Newton Abbot, ***Redcar*****, Sandown**
21 Sunday ....**Folkestone**, Newton Abbot, Southwell
22 Monday ....**Hamilton, Leicester,** ***Windsor*****,** ***Wolverhampton***
23 Tuesday ....**Brighton**, *Perth*, *Worcester*, **Yarmouth**
24 Wednesday ....**Brighton, Catterick**, Perth
25 Thursday ....Bangor, **Musselburgh, Lingfield**
26 Friday ....***Bath*****,** ***Newcastle*****, Newmarket, Salisbury, Thirsk**
27 Saturday......Cartmel, **Goodwood**, *Market Rasen*, **Newmarket,** ***Windsor*****, York**
28 Sunday ....**Beverley, Goodwood, Yarmouth**
29 Monday...................................Cartmel, **Chepstow, Epsom**, Huntingdon
....**Newcastle, Ripon, Warwick**
30 Tuesday..**Leicester, Ripon**, Sedgefield
31 Wednesday...**Lingfield**, Newton Abbot, **York**

September

1 Thursday...**Carlisle, Redcar, Salisbury**
2 Friday...**Chepstow, Haydock, Kempton**
3 Saturday**Folkestone, Haydock, Kempton**, Stratford, **Thirsk,** ***Wolverhampton***
4 Sunday ....Fontwell, Worcester, **York**
5 Monday ....**Bath, Newcastle, Warwick**
6 Tuesday ....**Catterick, Leicester, Lingfield**
7 Wednesday...**Doncaster, Epsom**, Uttoxeter
8 Thursday ....**Chepstow, Doncaster, Epsom**
9 Friday ....Bangor, **Doncaster, Sandown**
10 Saturday ...**Chester, Doncaster, Musselburgh, Goodwood, Wolverhampton**
11 Sunday...**Carlisle, Goodwood**, Stratford
12 Monday...**Musselburgh, Folkestone, Redcar**
13 Tuesday ....**Salisbury, Thirsk, Yarmouth**
14 Wednesday...**Beverley, Sandown, Yarmouth**
15 Thursday..**Ayr, Pontefract, Yarmouth**
16 Friday...**Ayr, Newbury, Nottingham**
17 Saturday ....**Ayr, Catterick, Lingfield, Newbury, Warwick,** ***Wolverhampton***
18 Sunday ....**Hamilton**, Plumpton, Uttoxeter
19 Monday ....**Chepstow, Kempton, Leicester**
20 Tuesday ....**Beverley, Brighton, Newmarket**
21 Wednesday...**Goodwood**, Perth, **Redcar**
22 Thursday..Fontwell, Perth, **Pontefract**
23 Friday ....**Haydock, Lingfield**, Worcester
24 Saturday............................**Ascot, Haydock, Kempton**, Market Rasen, **Ripon**
25 Sunday...**Ascot, Musselburgh**, Huntingdon
26 Monday ....**Bath, Hamilton, Wolverhampton**
27 Tuesday ....**Goodwood, Nottingham**, Sedgefield
28 Wednesday...**Lingfield, Newcastle, Salisbury**
29 Thursday ....**Ayr**, Hereford, **Newmarket**
30 Friday...Hexham, **Lingfield, Newmarket**

October

1 Saturday**Epsom**, Fontwell, **Newmarket, Redcar, Southwell,** ***Wolverhampton***
2 Sunday ....Kelso, Market Rasen, Uttoxeter

3 Monday ....**Brighton, Pontefract, Windsor**
4 Tuesday..**Catterick**, Huntingdon, **Leicester**
5 Wednesday ....Exeter, **Nottingham**, Towcester
6 Thursday..**Southwell**, Wincanton, Worcester
7 Friday..Carlisle, **Newbury, York**
8 Saturday....................Bangor, Chepstow, Hexham, **Salisbury, Warwick, York**
9 Sunday ....**Bath, Goodwood, Newcastle**
10 Monday..**Ayr, Windsor, Wolverhampton**
11 Tuesday..**Ayr, Leicester, Southwell**
12 Wednesday ....**Lingfield**, Uttoxeter, Wetherby
13 Thursday ....Ludlow, **Newmarket, Southwell**
14 Friday..**Brighton, Newmarket, Redcar**
15 Saturday ....**Catterick**, Kempton, **Lingfield, Newmarket**, Stratford
16 Sunday ....**Musselburgh**, Hereford, Market Rasen
17 Monday..Plumpton, **Pontefract, Windsor**
18 Tuesday ....Exeter, **Southwell, Yarmouth**
19 Wednesday..**Bath, Newcastle, Nottingham**
20 Thursday ....**Brighton**, Haydock, Ludlow
21 Friday..**Doncaster**, Fakenham, **Newbury**
22 Saturday....Chepstow, **Doncaster**, Kelso, Aintree, **Newbury, Wolverhampton**
23 Sunday..Aintree, Towcester, Wincanton
24 Monday ....**Leicester, Lingfield, Wolverhampton**
25 Tuesday..**Catterick**, Cheltenham, **Yarmouth**
26 Wednesday..Cheltenham, **Nottingham**, Sedgefield
27 Thursday ....**Lingfield**, Stratford, Taunton
28 Friday ....**Newmarket**, Uttoxeter, Wetherby
29 Saturday...**Ayr**, Lingfield, **Newmarket, Southwell**, Wetherby, ***Wolverhampton***
30 Sunday ....**Ayr**, Carlisle, **Lingfield**
31 Monday ....Plumpton, Warwick, **Wolverhampton**

November

1 Tuesday..**Catterick**, Exeter, Worcester
2 Wednesday..Chepstow, Kempton, **Nottingham**
3 Thursday ....**Musselburgh**, Haydock, Towcester
4 Friday ....Fontwell, Hexham, **Yarmouth**
5 Saturday ....**Doncaster**, Kelso, Sandown
.... **Southwell**, Wincanton, ***Wolverhampton***
6 Sunday ....Ayr, Hereford, Market Rasen
7 Monday..Carlisle, Stratford, **Wolverhampton**
8 Tuesday..Huntingdon, Sedgefield, **Southwell**
9 Wednesday ....Bangor, Lingfield, **Wolverhampton**
10 Thursday..**Lingfield**, Ludlow, Taunton
11 Friday ....Cheltenham, Newcastle, **Wolverhampton**
12 Saturday..Cheltenham, **Lingfield, Southwell**
....Uttoxeter, Wetherby, ***Wolverhampton***
13 Sunday..Carlisle, Cheltenham, Fontwell
14 Monday ....Folkestone, Leicester, **Wolverhampton**
15 Tuesday ....Fakenham, **Lingfield, Southwell**
16 Wednesday ....Hexham, Kempton, **Southwell**
17 Thursday..Hereford, Market Rasen, Wincanton
18 Friday ....Exeter, Kelso, Windsor
19 Saturday ....Haydock, Huntingdon, **Lingfield**

....**Southwell**, Windsor, ***Wolverhampton***
20 Sunday..Aintree, Plumpton, Towcester
21 Monday..**Lingfield**, Ludlow, **Southwell**
22 Tuesday..Sedgefield, **Southwell**, Warwick
23 Wednesday..Chepstow, Lingfield, Wetherby
24 Thursday..Carlisle, Taunton, Uttoxeter
25 Friday..Musselburgh, Newbury, **Wolverhampton**
26 Saturday............**Lingfield**, Newbury, Newcastle, Towcester, ***Wolverhampton***
27 Sunday..Doncaster, Leicester, Newbury
28 Monday..Folkestone, **Southwell**, **Wolverhampton**
29 Tuesday..Hereford, **Lingfield**, **Southwell**
30 Wednesday..Catterick, Plumpton, **Wolverhampton**

December

1 Thursday..Leicester, Market Rasen, Wincanton
2 Friday..Exeter, Sandown, **Wolverhampton**
3 Saturday..............Chepstow, Haydock, Sandown, Wetherby, ***Wolverhampton***
4 Sunday..Kelso, **Southwell**, Warwick
5 Monday..**Lingfield**, Newcastle, **Wolverhampton**
6 Tuesday..Fontwell, Sedgefield, **Southwell**
7 Wednesday..Hexham, Leicester, **Lingfield**
8 Thursday..Huntingdon, Ludlow, Taunton
9 Friday..Cheltenham, Doncaster, **Wolverhampton**
10 Saturday.........Cheltenham, Doncaster, Lingfield, **Southwell**, ***Wolverhampton***
12 Monday..Plumpton, **Southwell**, **Wolverhampton**
13 Tuesday..Folkestone, **Southwell**, Warwick
14 Wednesday..Bangor, **Lingfield**, Newbury
15 Thursday..Catterick, Exeter, **Southwell**
16 Friday..Uttoxeter, Windsor, **Wolverhampton**
17 Saturday..Haydock, **Lingfield**, Newcastle, Windsor
18 Sunday..Musselburgh, **Southwell**
19 Monday..Doncaster, **Lingfield**, **Wolverhampton**
20 Tuesday..Fontwell, **Lingfield**, **Southwell**
21 Wednesday..**Lingfield**, Ludlow, **Wolverhampton**
22 Thursday..Ayr, Fakenham, **Southwell**
26 Monday..Huntingdon, Kempton, Market Rasen
.......................Sedgefield, Towcester, Wetherby, Wincanton, **Wolverhampton**
27 Tuesday.........................Chepstow, Kempton, Leicester, **Southwell**, Wetherby
28 Wednesday..Catterick, Newbury, **Wolverhampton**
29 Thursday..Musselburgh, **Lingfield**, Newbury
30 Friday..Haydock, **Lingfield**, Taunton
31 Saturday..................................Lingfield, Uttoxeter, Warwick, **Wolverhampton**

On their way to Sedgefield on Boxing Day?

Wolver hosts the last flat fixture of the year

Big-race dates

April

2 Sat Doncaster....................................Freephone Stanley Lincoln Handicap (1m)
12 Tue Newmarket ....Shadwell Stud Nell Gwyn Stakes (7f)
13 Wed Newmarket...................................Weatherbys Earl Of Sefton Stakes (1m 1f)
Newmarket...............................Victor Chandler European Free Handicap (7f)
14 Thu Newmarket.......................................Macau Jockey Club Craven Stakes (1m)
16 Sat Newbury ....Dubai Irish Village John Porter Stakes (1m 4f)
Newbury...Lane's End Greenham Stakes (7f)
Newbury..Dubai Duty Free Fred Darling Stakes (7f)
22 Fri Sandown ....Sandown Park Classic Trial Stakes (1m 2f)
23 Sat Sandown ....Betfred Mile Stakes (1m)
24 Sat Sandown ....Betfred Gordon Richards Stakes (1m 2f)
27 Wed Ascot at Lingfield.......................................Bovis Homes Sagaro Stakes (2m)
Ascot at Lingfield ....Sony Victoria Cup (Handicap) (7f)
30 Sat Newmarket................................UltimateBet.com 2000 Guineas Stakes (1m)
Newmarket....................................Victor Chandler Palace House Stakes (5f)

May

1 Sun Newmarket...............................UltimateBet.com 1000 Guineas Stakes (1m)
Newmarket...............................UltimateBet.com Jockey Club Stakes (1m 4f)
Newmarket.......................................R. L. Davison Pretty Polly Stakes (1m 2f)
4 Wed Chester ....Victor Chandler Chester Vase (1m 4f 66yds)
5 Thu Chester.................................UPM-Kyemmene Cheshire Oaks (1m 3f 79yds)
5 Chester ....totesport Chester Cup (Handicap) (2m 2f 117yds)
6 Fri Chester..Betfair.com Ormonde Stakes (1m 5f 89yds)
Chester ....Philip Leverhulme Dee Stakes (1m 2f 75yds)
7 Sat Lingfield ....Derby Trial Stakes (1m 3f 106yds)
Lingfield ....Oaks Trial Stakes (1m 3f 106yds)
11 Wed York...Duke Of York Stakes (6f)
York ....Tattersalls Musidora Stakes (1m 2f)
12 Thu York ....totesport Dante Stakes (1m 2f)
13 Fri York...Yorkshire Cup (1m 5f 194yds)
Newbury...................................Swettenham Stud Fillies' Trial Stakes (1m 2f)
14 Sat Newbury..Juddmonte Lockinge Stakes (1m)
Newbury..Aston Park Stakes (1m 5f 61yds)
18 Wed Goodwood ....Letheby & Christopher Predominate Stakes (1m 2f)
19 Thu Goodwood...Victor Chandler Lupe Stakes (1m 2f)
21 Sat Haydock ....totesport Silver Bowl Handicap Stakes (1m)
Haydock ....Dunwoody Sports Marketing Sandy Lane Rated Stakes (6f)
30 Mon Redcar.......................Totesport Zetland Gold Cup Stakes (Handicap) (1m 2f)
Sandown ....Bonusprint Henry II Stakes (2m)
31 Tue Sandown ....Brigadier Gerard Stakes (1m 2f)

June

3 Fri Epsom ....Temple Stakes (5f)
Epsom...Vodafone Oaks (1m 4f 10yds)
Epsom......................................Vodafone Coronation Cup (1m 4f 10yds)
4 Sat Epsom ....Vodafone Derby (1m 4f 10yds)
Epsom...Vodafone Diomed Stakes (1m 114yds)
Haydock.................................Betfair.com John Of Gaunt Stakes (7f 30yds)
14 Tue Royal Ascot at York ....St James's Palace Stakes (1m)
Royal Ascot at York ....Queen Anne Stakes (1m)
Royal Ascot at York...Coventry Stakes (6f)
15 Wed Royal Ascot at York ....Prince Of Wales's Stakes (1m 2f)
Royal Ascot at York ....Queen Mary Stakes (5f)
Royal Ascot at York ....Jersey Stakes (7f)
Royal Ascot at York..................................Royal Hunt Cup (Handicap) (1m)

16	Thu	Newbury	Ballymacoll Stud Stakes (1m 2f)
		Royal Ascot at York	Gold Cup (2m 4f)
		Royal Ascot at York	Ribblesdale Stakes (1m 4f)
		Royal Ascot at York	Norfolk Stakes (5f)
17	Fri	Royal Ascot at York	Queen's Vase (2m 45yds)
		Royal Ascot at York	Coronation Stakes (1m)
		Royal Ascot at York	King Edward VII Stakes (1m 4f)
18	Sat	Royal Ascot at York	Chesham Stakes (6f)
		Royal Ascot at York	Hardwicke Stakes (1m 4f)
25	Sat	Newcastle	Foster's Lager Northumberland Plate (Handicap) (2m 19yds)
		Newmarket	Criterion Stakes (7f)
		Newmarket	Fred Archer Stakes (1m 4f)

July

2	Sat	Haydock	Lancashire Oaks (1m 4f)
		Haydock	Old Newton Cup (Handicap) (1m 4f)
		Sandown	Coral Eclipse Stakes (1m 2f)
5	Tue	Newmarket	Falmouth Stakes (1m)
		Newmarket	Cherry Hinton Stakes (6f)
		Newmarket	Princess of Wales's UAE Equestrian & Racing Federation Stakes (1m 4f)
6	Wed	Newmarket	TNT July Stakes (6f)
7	Thu	Newmarket	Darley July Cup (6f)
		Newmarket	Ladbrokes Bunbury Cup (Handicap) (7f)
9	Sat	York	John Smith's Cup (Handicap) (1m 2f 85yds)
		York	Webster's Silver Cup Rated Handicap Stakes (1m 5f 194yds)
16	Sat	Newbury	Shadwell Stud Rose Bowl Stakes (6f)
		Newbury	Weatherbys Super Sprint (5f 34yds)
18	Mon	Ayr	Daily Record Scottish Derby (1m 2f)
23	Sat	Ascot at Newbury	King George VI and Queen Elizabeth Diamond Stakes (1m 4f)
		Ascot at Newbury	Princess Margaret Stakes (6f)
26	Tue	Goodwood	Peugeot Gordon Stakes (1m 2f)
27	Wed	Goodwood	Champagne Lanson Sussex Stakes (1m)
		Goodwood	totesport Gold Trophy (Handicap) (1m 4f)
		Goodwood	Veuve Cliquot Vintage Stakes (7f)
28	Thu	Goodwood	Lady O Goodwood Cup (2m)
		Goodwood	Betfair Molecomb Stakes (5f)
29	Fri	Goodwood	Oak Tree Stakes (6f)
		Goodwood	William Hill Mile (Handicap) (1m)
		Goodwood	Glorious Rated Stakes (1m 4f)
30	Sat	Goodwood	Vodafone Nassau Stakes (1m 2f)
		Goodwood	Vodafone Stewards' Cup (Handicap) (6f)

August

6	Sat	Haydock	Petros Rose Of Lancaster Stakes (1m 2f 120yds)
		Newmarket	Sweet Solera Stakes (7f)
12	Fri	Newbury	Newbury Racecourse Washington Singer Stakes (7f)
13	Sat	Newbury	Stan James Geoffrey Freer Stakes (1m 5f 61yds)
		Newbury	Stan James Hungerford Stakes (7f 64yds)
		Newbury	Stan James St Hugh's Stakes (5f)
		Ripon	William Hill Great St Wilfrid Handicap Stakes (6f)
16	Tue	York	Juddmonte International Stakes (1m 2f 85yds)
		York	Great Voltigeur Stakes (1m 4f)
		York	Weatherbys Insurance Lonsdale Cup (2m)
17	Wed	York	Aston Upthorpe Yorkshire Oaks (1m 4f)
		York	Scottish Equitable Gimcrack Stakes (6f)
		York	totesport Ebor Handicap (1m 6f)
18	Thu	York	Victor Chandler Nunthorpe Stakes (5f)
		York	Peugeot Lowther Stakes (6f)
		York	European Breeders Fund Galtres Stakes (1m 4f)
20	Sat	Sandown	Iveco Daily Solario Stakes (7f)
27	Sat	Goodwood	totesport Celebration Mile (1m)
		Goodwood	San Migel March Stakes (1m 6f)

28 Sun Goodwood .... Prestige Stakes (7f)
29 Mon Ripon .... Betfair.com Ripon Champion Two Years Old Trophy (6f)

September

3 Sat Kempton .... Pentax Sirenia Stakes (6f)
Kempton .... Pentax September Stakes (1m 3f)
7 Wed Doncaster .... Park Hill Stakes (1m 6f 132yds)
Doncaster .... £200,000 St Leger Yearling Stakes (6f)
Doncaster .... totesport Portland Handicap Stakes (1m)
8 Thu Doncaster .... Scarbrough Stakes (5f)
Doncaster .... G.N.E.R Park Stakes (1m)
Doncaster .... G.N.E.R Doncaster Cup (2m 2f)
Doncaster .... May Hill Stakes (1m)
9 Fri Doncaster .... Champagne Stakes (7f)
Doncaster .... DBS St Leger Yearling Stakes (1m 6f 132yds)
10 Sat Doncaster .... St Leger Stakes
Doncaster .... Polypipe Flying Childers Stakes (5f)
11 Sun Goodwood .... Select Stakes (1m 2f)
16 Fri Newbury .... Dubai Duty Free Cup (7f)
Newbury .... Dubai Duty Free Mill Reef Stakes (6f)
17 Sat Newbury .... Dubai International Airport World Trophy (5f 34yds)
Newbury .... Dubai Duty Free Arc Trial (1m 3f 5yds)
Ayr .... totesport Ayr Gold Cup (Handicap) (6f)
Ayr .... Doonside Cup (1m 2f 192yds)
Newbury .... John Smith's Handicap Stakes (7f)
24 Sat Ascot at Newmarket .... Queen Elizabeth II Stakes (1m)
Ascot at Newmarket .... Meon Valley Stud Fillies' Mile (1m)
Ascot at Newmarket .... Hackney Empire Royal Lodge Stakes (1m 4f)
Ascot at Newmarket .... Diadem Stakes (6f)
25 Sun Ascot at Newmarket .... Young Vic Theatre Cumberland Lodge Stakes (1m)
Ascot at Newmarket .... Mail On Sunday Mile Final (Handicap) (1m)
27 Tue Goodwood .... Charlton Hunt Supreme Stakes (7f)
30 Fri Newmarket .... Shadwell Stud Middle Park Stakes (6f)
Newmarket .... Cheveley Park Stakes (6f)

October

1 Sat Newmarket .... totesport Cambridgeshire Handicap Stakes (1m 1f)
Newmarket .... Peugot Sun Chariot Stakes (1m 2f)
Redcar .... Two-Year-Old Trophy (7f)
8 Sat Salisbury .... Willmott Dixon Cornwallis Stakes (5f)
Salisbury .... Tom McGee Autumn Stakes (1m 4f)
15 Sat Newmarket .... Emirates Airline Champion Stakes (1m 2f)
Newmarket .... totesport Cesarewitch (Handicap) (2m 2f)
Newmarket .... Victor Chandler Challenge Stakes (1m)
Newmarket .... Darley Dewhurst Stakes (6f)
Newmarket .... Owen Brown Rockfel Stakes (7f)
Newbury .... Jockey Club Cup
21 Fri Doncaster .... Vodafone Horris Hill Stakes (7f)
22 Sat Doncaster .... Racing Post Trophy (1m)
Newbury .... St Simon Stakes (1m 4f)

November

5th Sat Doncaster .... totescoop6 November Handicap (1m 4f)

(All dates may be subject to alteration)

Outlook

By The Numbers

by Chris Cook

See the whole picture

THERE'S A REALLY tremendous amount of nonsense spoken about horseracing, particularly by those who are trying to sell you a tip. *Racing & Football Outlook* aspires to be a nonsense-free zone, which is why we've got *By The Numbers*.

Using trends to analyse races has become very popular, thanks in large measure to Craig Thake of the *Racing Post*. But the level of analysis you hear from most pundits on this subject is shockingly scant.

Many newspaper tipsters content themselves with something like: "Five-year-olds have a good record here, having won three of the last four renewals." Superficially impressive, such stats have absolutely no meaning without more information; as to the number of five-year-old runners, the proportion of all runners which have been aged five, the odds at which you could have backed those five-year-olds.

***By The Numbers* puts you in a position to judge the worth of such glib reasoning. We provide you with all the stats you need to decide what type of animal is really favoured by the conditions of a particular race.**

To give you a flavour of the service, we've set out our approach to two of the Flat season's biggest handicaps, over the next four pages. We start with the John Smith's Cup, to be run at York in early July, and follow with the Stewards' Cup, staged at Goodwood three weeks later.

Each race is spread across two pages. On the left page are stats showing how many of the last ten winners have come from each band of runners within each category, together with full details of those winners.

On the right page, our stats relate to how many placed horses have come from each band, plus there's a commentary offering some insight into the bare numbers.

Let's take some numbers from the John Smith's Cup as an example.

In our 'Win stats' on the left page, the first box shows that 35 runners in the last ten years have been three-year-olds. Four of them have won, at a strike-rate of 11 per cent.

By betting £1 on all of those four-year-olds, you'd have made a net profit of £3.50, which can also be expressed as a profit of 10 per cent of total stakes.

Over on the right page, our 'Place stats' show that, of those 35 four-year-olds, 14 made the frame, a place-rate of 40 per cent.

In the 'Win stats', all bands that have returned a level-stakes profit over the last ten years are shaded.

In the 'Place stats', bands of runners are shaded if their place-rate is above average. So, for the John Smith's, there is shading over the bands for three-year-olds and four-year-olds; both these bands have achieved place rates above the average of 20 per cent.

Take a look and see if you aren't persuaded that you understand these races better after considering our stats and analysis.

If you are, then you'll want to keep an eye on *Racing & Football Outlook* through the summer. Whenever there's a major handicap, we'll analyse it in this feature and give you our idea of the most likely contenders, judging *By The Numbers*.

Win stats

Age

Age	Wins/runs	%	£+-	% of stakes
3	4/35	11	+£3.50	+10
4	4/68	6	-£5.50	-8
5	2/48	4	-£16.00	-33
6	0/20	0	-£20.00	-100
7	0/13	0	-£13.00	-100
8+	0/7	0	-£7.00	-100

Official Ratings

OR	Wins/runs	%	£+-	% of stakes
Under 80	0/20	0	-£20.00	-100
80-84	0/28	0	-£28.00	-100
85-89	2/41	5	-£22.50	-55
90-94	3/34	9	+£6.00	+18
95-99	3/40	8	-£7.50	-19
100+	2/28	7	+£14.00	+50

Draw

Draw	Wins/runs	%	£+-	% of stakes
1-6	4/57	7	-£4.50	-8
7-12	5/58	9	+£1.50	+3
13-18	1/54	2	-£33.00	-61
19+	0/22	0	-£22.00	-100

Wins

Wins	Wins/runs	%	£+-	% of stakes
0	0/3	0	-£3.00	-100
1	2/44	5	-£29.00	-66
2	5/54	9	+£11.00	+20
3	0/36	0	-£36.00	-100
4+	3/54	6	-£1.00	-2

Starting Prices

SP	Wins/runs	%	£+-	% of stakes
Under 5-1	1/10	10	-£6.50	-65
5-1 to 7-1	4/17	24	+£12.50	+74
15-2 to 9-1	0/19	0	-£19.00	-100
10-1 to 12-1	1/22	5	-£11.00	-50
14-1 to 18-1	0/23	0	-£23.00	-100
20-1 to 25-1	4/53	8	+£36.00	+68
28-1 to 33-1	0/14	0	-£14.00	-100
40-1 to 66-1	0/33	0	-£33.00	-100
80-1+	No runners			

Weight

Weight	Wins/runs	%	£+-	% of stakes
Under 8-00	0/27	0	-£27.00	-100
8-00 to 8-06	4/56	7	-£31.00	-55
8-07 to 8-13	2/48	4	-£1.00	-2
9-00 to 9-05	3/33	9	+£7.00	+21
9-06+	1/27	4	-£6.00	-22

Sex

Sex	Wins/runs	%	£+-	% of stakes
Males	4/47	9	-£21.00	-45
Females	0/13	0	-£13.00	-100
Geldings	6/131	5	-£24.00	-18

Handicap wins

Wins	Wins/runs	%	£+-	% of stakes
0	5/58	9	+£11.00	+19
1	2/50	4	-£39.00	-78
2	0/31	0	-£31.00	-100
3	1/23	4	-£2.00	-9
4+	2/29	7	+£3.00	+10

	Winner	Age	Weight	OR	SP	Wins	H'caps	Sex	Draw
2004	*Arcalis*	4	9-02	95	20-1	5	4	gelding	18/21
2003	*Far Lane*	4	9-04	99	7-1	1	0	male	4/20
2002	*Vintage Premium*	5	9-09	101	20-1	5	3	gelding	9/20
2001	*Foreign Affairs*	3	8-06	97	5-2f	2	1	male	8/19
2000	*Sobriety*	3	8-08	100	20-1	2	0	gelding	8/22
1999	*Achilles*	4	8-11	90	25-1	2	0	gelding	6/15
1998	*Porto Foricos*	3	8-03	90	6-1	1	0	male	7/20
1997	*Pasternak*	4	8-03	85	13-2	2	1	male	1/21
1996	*Wilcuma*	5	9-02	89	10-1	4	4	gelding	2/17
1995	*Naked Welcome*	3	8-04	90	6-1	2	0	gelding	9/15

Place stats

THE MOST famous draw bias in British racing was defeated last summer, when Arcalis somehow managed to win from stall 18 of 21.

In the previous decade, nothing had won from wider than stall nine.

Medicean, who subsequently won a Group 1 at this trip, famously trailed in 14th here when asked to race from stall 21 of 22 in the 2000 race.

Even after Arcalis, the draw bias must be respected. After all, there's a perfectly logical reason for it - the course bends sharply left soon after the start.

Those on the outside face a choice between two evils; fly from the gate to get a good position, using up energy early, or settle in behind and hopo to get the gaps when it matters.

It remains the case that six of the last seven winners have come from stalls four to nine (that's 86 per cent of the winners from less than a third of the runners). Those drawn in the bottom six stalls are three times as likely to place as those drawn 13 or higher.

But it's interesting that there's only been one winner from the bottom five stalls in the last seven years. Low-drawn jockeys, familiar with the draw bias, may be trying too hard to take advantage of it by going off too quickly.

Three-year-olds are well treated in relation to their elders at this time of year and would have returned a level-stakes profit here over the last decade. Almost half of all such runners have made the frame. Similarly, you could have made a profit by following all those who'd never previously won a handicap (and are therefore harder for the handicapper to assess).

The market has proved a good guide – blindly backing all those who started at 7-1 or shorter would have been a winning system.

Age	Wins/runs	%
3	14/35	40
4	17/68	25
5	7/48	15
6	0/20	0
7	1/13	8
8+	0/7	0

OR	Wins/runs	%
Under 80	2/20	10
80-84	4/28	14
85-89	6/41	15
90-94	11/34	32
95-99	11/40	28
100+	5/28	18

Draw	Wins/runs	%
1-6	19/57	33
7-12	11/58	19
13-18	7/54	13
19+	2/22	9

Wins	Wins/runs	%
0	0/3	0
1	9/44	20
2	13/54	24
3	6/36	17
4+	11/54	20

SP	Wins/runs	%
Under 5-1	5/10	50
5-1 to 7-1	8/17	47
15-2 to 9-1	8/19	42
10-1 to 12-1	8/22	36
14-1 to 18-1	2/23	9
20-1 to 25-1	7/53	13
28-1 to 33-1	1/14	7
40-1 to 66-1	0/33	0
80-1+	No runners	

Weight	Wins/runs	%
Under 8-00	5/27	19
8-00 to 8-06	13/56	23
8-07 to 8-13	8/48	17
9-00 to 9-05	9/33	27
9-06+	4/27	15

Sex	Wins/runs	%
Males	13/47	28
Females	3/13	23
Geldings	23/131	18

Wins	Wins/runs	%
0	12/58	21
1	7/50	14
2	9/31	29
3	6/23	26
4+	5/29	17

Win stats

Age	Wins/runs	%	£+-	% of stakes
3	1/42	2	-£36.00	-86
4	4/94	4	-£47.00	-50
5	3/64	5	-£10.00	-16
6	1/43	2	-£35.50	-83
7	0/28	0	-£28.00	-100
8+	1/20	5	+£21.00	+105

SP	Wins/runs	%	£+-	% of stakes
Under 5-1	1/4	25	+£1.00	+25
5-1 to 7-1	3/14	21	+£7.50	+54
15-2 to 9-1	0/8	0	-£8.00	-100
10-1 to 12-1	2/27	7	-£3.00	-11
14-1 to 18-1	2/38	5	-£8.00	-21
20-1 to 25-1	0/63	0	-£63.00	-100
28-1 to 33-1	1/46	2	-£12.00	-26
40-1 to 66-1	1/86	1	-£45.00	-52
80-1+	0/5	0	-£5.00	-100

OR	Wins/runs	%	£+-	% of stakes
Under 80	0/14	0	-£14.00	-100
80-84	1/41	2	-£26.00	-63
85-89	0/68	0	-£68.00	-100
90-94	5/62	8	+£18.50	+30
95-99	3/53	6	+£1.00	+2
100+	1/53	2	-£47.00	-89

Weight	Wins/runs	%	£+-	% of stakes
Under 8-00	0/59	0	-£59.00	-100
8-00 to 8-06	3/87	4	-£48.00	-55
8-07 to 8-13	6/76	8	+£6.50	+9
9-00 to 9-05	1/41	2	-£7.00	-17
9-06+	0/28	0	-£28.00	-100

Draw	Wins/runs	%	£+-	% of stakes
1-8	3/79	4	-£52.00	-66
9-16	0/74	0	-£74.00	-100
17-24	1/79	1	-£45.00	-57
25+	6/59	10	+£35.50	+60

Sex	Wins/runs	%	£+-	% of stakes
Males	3/40	8	-£6.00	-15
Females	0/29	0	-£29.00	-100
Geldings	7/222	3	-£100.50	-45

Wins	Wins/runs	%	£+-	% of stakes
0	0/2	0	-£2.00	-100
1	1/21	5	-£8.00	-38
2	2/52	4	-£38.00	-73
3	1/50	2	-£39.00	-78
4+	6/166	4	-£48.50	-29

Handicap wins	Wins/runs	%	£+-	% of stakes
0	1/51	2	-£38.00	-75
1	4/68	6	-£5.00	-7
2	1/51	2	-£40.00	-78
3	2/36	6	-£16.00	-44
4+	2/85	2	-£36.50	-43

	Winner	Age	Weight	OR	SP	Wins	H'caps	Sex	Draw
2004	*Pivotal Point*	4	8-11	91	7-1cf	2	1	gelding	1/28
2003	*Patavellian*	5	8-11	95	4-1	5	3	gelding	27/29
2002	*Bond Boy*	5	8-02	83	14-1	5	3	gelding	29/28
2001	*Guinea Hunter*	5	9-00	98	33-1	4	1	gelding	19/30
2000	*Tayseer*	6	8-11	93	13-2	6	4	gelding	28/30
1999	*Harmonic Way*	4	8-06	92	12-1	1	0	male	8/30
1998	*Superior Premium*	4	8-12	99	14-1	5	1	male	28/29
1997	*Danetime*	3	8-10	100	5-1f	2	1	male	5/30
1996	*Coastal Bluff*	4	8-05	91	10-1j	3	2	gelding	29/30
1995	*Shikari's Son*	8	8-13	92	40-1	11	9	gelding	30/27

Place stats

IT would be a mistake to doubt the bias in favour of high numbers, just because last year's winner came from stall one.

Half of the ten winners prior to 2004 came from one of the top three stalls; in three of the other five years, the runner from stall 30 was beaten less than a length. The other two years were 2003 (when the first three came from stalls 27, 29 and 28) and 1999.

The 1999 result was exceptional, in that low numbers dominated. We know why: the course had employed an 'earthquake' machine to break up compacted ground against the far rail, so that the stands side was left as easily the fastest strip.

No similar explanation has been forthcoming for last summer's result, but perhaps none is needed. The second and third behind Pivotal Point finished hard against the far rail from stalls 24 and 28, while a 40-1 shot from stall 29 was sixth.

Pivotal Point went on to win a Group 2, which means that the only three winners drawn below 19 in the last decade have subsequently either won a Group 2 or been placed in a Group 1. It seems that a horse still has to be very classy to take this from a low berth.

My guess is that some selective watering was used to reduce the far-side bias (a very sneaky thing to do without telling the punters!) but, since the result was a winner from stall one, the course executive may well fight shy of doing something similar. In any case, the far-side bias has proved hard to damp down and will still command respect.

There seems to be a quality threshold for Stewards winners, which would explain why those with less than 8-00 have struggled.

Age

Age	Wins/runs	%
3	4/42	10
4	18/94	19
5	4/64	6
6	7/43	16
7	5/28	18
8+	2/20	10

Official Ratings

OR	Wins/runs	%
Under 80	2/14	14
80-84	5/41	12
85-89	8/68	12
90-94	11/62	18
95-99	7/53	13
100+	7/53	13

Draw

Draw	Wins/runs	%
1-8	10/79	13
9-16	5/74	7
17-24	9/79	11
25+	16/59	27

Wins

Wins	Wins/runs	%
0	0/2	0
1	4/21	19
2	5/52	10
3	6/50	12
4+	25/166	15

Starting Prices

SP	Wins/runs	%
Under 5-1	3/4	75
5-1 to 7-1	7/14	50
15-2 to 9-1	2/8	25
10-1 to 12-1	7/27	26
14-1 to 18-1	7/38	18
20-1 to 25-1	5/63	8
28-1 to 33-1	6/46	13
40-1 to 66-1	3/86	3
80-1+	0/5	0

Weight

Weight	Wins/runs	%
Under 8-00	5/59	8
8-00 to 8-06	16/87	18
8-07 to 8-13	10/76	13
9-00 to 9-05	6/41	15
9-06+	3/28	11

Sex

Sex	Wins/runs	%
Males	11/40	28
Females	3/29	10
Geldings	26/222	12

Handicap wins

Wins	Wins/runs	%
0	6/51	12
1	13/68	19
2	7/51	14
3	4/36	11
4+	10/85	12

Track Facts

WANT TO size up the layout and undulations of the course where your fancy's about to line up? Over the next 30-odd pages, we bring you three-dimensional maps of all Britain's Flat tracks, allowing you to see at a glance task facing your selection. The maps come to you courtesy of the *Racing Post*'s website (www.racingpost.co.uk).

We've listed the top dozen trainers and jockeys at each course, ranked by strike-rate, with a breakdown of their relevant statistics over the last three years. The record of favourites is here as well – Chester (34.8%) has seen the best strike-rate for jollies, while Kempton (25%) has produced the worst. Note that market leaders generated a profit (to level stakes of £1) at only three of the 34 tracks, underlining a basic fact of racing; as a general rule, favourites offer little in the way of value.

We've included addresses, phone numbers, directions and fixture lists for each track, together with Time Test's standard times for all you clock-watchers.

And Graham Wheldon, whose *Sprintline* column is a popular feature of RFO, has chipped in with his views on the draw at every course – see page 226. As his analysis has repeatedly shown, most tracks feature a bias of some kind, so check whether the beast on your betting slip is running on the right side before you hand it over.

Whitletts Road Ayr KA8 0JE.
Tel 01292 264 179

AYR

How to get there – Road: south from Glasgow on A77 or A75, A70, A76. Rail: Ayr, bus service from station on big race days
Features: LH 1m4f oval, easy turns, generally flat, suits galloping types
2005 Flat fixtures: May 26, June 17, 18, July 11, 18, 19, Aug 6, 19, Sep 15, 16, 17, 29, Oct 10, 11, 29, 30
Pointers: For over 20 years Sir Mark Prescott has been selectively picking off small targets here. With only six runners in the last three years, we may not see more than one or two runners this season but they will have a massive chance. Lynda Ramsden has been quiet here recently but Ayr is reputedly her favourite track.

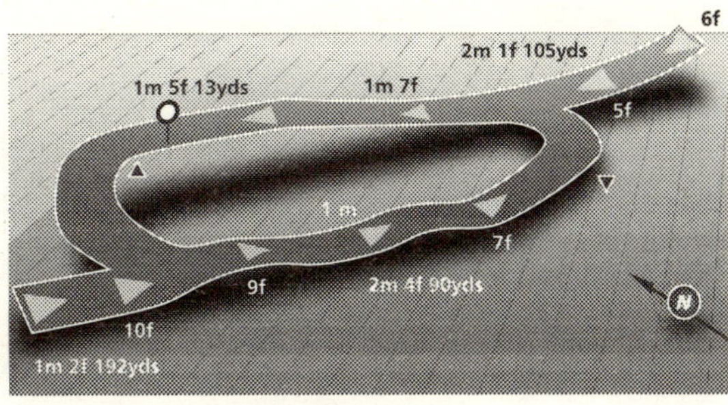

Time Test standard times

5f	57.7	1m2f	2min4.4
6f	1min9.7	1m2f192yds	2min14.3
7f	1min25	1m5f13yds	2min45.4
7f50yds	1min28	1m7f	3min13.2
1m	1min37.7	2m1f105yds	3min46
1m1f20yds	1min50	2m4f90yds	4min25

Favourites

2-y-o	30.0%	-£12.58
3-y-o+	28.4%	-£9.06
Overall	28.8%	-£21.64

Trainers	*Wins-Runs*	*%*	*2yo*	*3yo+*	*£1 level stks*
S bin Suroor	3-6	50.0	1-4	2-2	+0.12
Sir M Prescott	3-6	50.0	1-2	2-4	+7.33
J Howard Johnson	3-7	42.9	1-4	2-3	+8.00
T Easterby	3-16	18.8	1-6	2-10	+35.00
M Johnston	5-31	16.1	4-18	1-13	-11.03
I Semple	8-53	15.1	2-7	6-46	+16.50
M Dods	4-28	14.3	0-5	4-23	+11.00
R Fahey	4-30	13.3	1-3	3-27	-6.33
J Goldie	10-76	13.2	0-9	10-67	-19.75
A Bailey	3-24	12.5	1-6	2-18	+12.50
K R Burke	3-30	10.0	1-8	2-22	-3.50
W Brisbourne	3-46	6.5	0-4	3-42	-8.25

Jockeys	*Wins-Rides*	*%*	*£1 level stks*	*Best Trainer*	*W-R*
D Tudhope	3-11	27.3	+15.50	N Wilson	2-3
K McEvoy	3-12	25.0	-5.89	S bin Suroor	3-6
S Sanders	3-12	25.0	-4.81	Sir M Prescott	2-4
P Mulrennan	6-29	20.7	+31.00	C Fairhurst	1-1
J Egan	3-15	20.0	0.00	J Goldie	2-7
N Mackay	7-35	20.0	+14.75	J Goldie	5-25
P Hanagan	9-53	17.0	+0.30	R Fahey	4-18
K Darley	6-37	16.2	-0.10	M Johnston	2-2
S W Kelly	3-20	15.0	-10.00	D Daly	1-1
J Fanning	6-40	15.0	+16.48	M Johnston	3-16
R Winston	9-69	13.0	-1.09	I Semple	2-15
Darren Williams	5-39	12.8	+11.00	K R Burke	3-23

BATH

Lansdown, Bath,
Gloucestershire BA1 9BU.
Tel 01291 622 260

How to get there – Road: M4, Jctn 18, then A46 south.
Rail: Bath Spa, special bus service to course on race-days

Features: LH oval, uphill straight of 4f.

2005 Flat fixtures: Apr 21, 26, May 3, 16, 20, 26, June 5, 11, 22, July 4, 21, Aug 9, 14, 26, Sep 5, 26, Oct 9, 19

Pointers: Not a great track for meaningful trends. Andrew Balding's runners must be respected and they don't have to travel far. Richard Hannon has a poor strike-rate for such an established trainer.

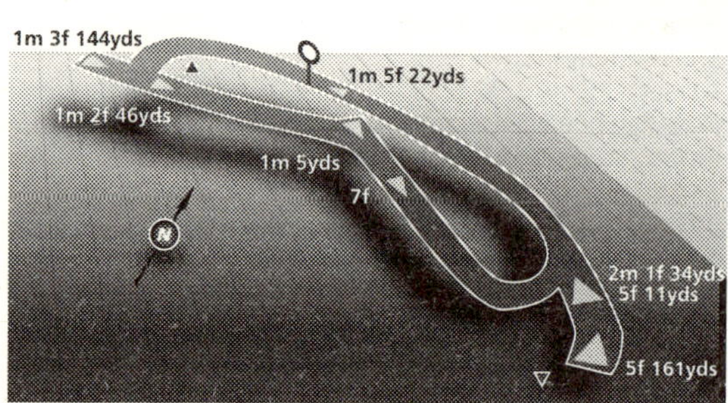

Time Test standard times

5f11yds	1min0.5	1m3f144yds	2min26
5f161yds	1min9	1m5f22yds	2min47.3
1m5yds	1min38	2m1f34yds	3min44
1m2f46yds	2min6.2		

Favourites

2-y-o	31.4%	-£7.42
3-y-o+	24.0%	+£18.89
Overall	25.9%	+£26.32

Trainers	*Wins-Runs*	*%*	*2yo*	*3yo+*	*£1 level stks*
N Callaghan	3-6	50.0	1-1	2-5	+18.83
J Spearing	4-15	26.7	0-0	4-15	+19.75
A Balding	8-34	23.5	2-9	6-25	+41.92
R J Houghton	3-13	23.1	1-6	2-7	+48.50
P Hiatt	3-15	20.0	0-0	3-15	+10.00
B Hills	3-25	12.0	1-6	2-19	-7.00
R Hannon	6-50	12.0	3-25	3-25	+1.50
B Millman	3-26	11.5	3-13	0-13	-0.50
R Hodges	3-27	11.1	0-1	3-26	+14.00
M Channon	5-48	10.4	4-20	1-28	-26.50
P Evans	4-49	8.2	0-9	4-40	-8.50
J Bradley	5-62	8.1	0-13	5-49	+3.25

Jockeys	*Wins-Rides*	*%*	*£1 level stks*	*Best Trainer*	*W-R*
R Hills	4-19	21.1	-7.00	M Tregoning	2-2
D Holland	4-21	19.0	+12.50	V Smith	1-1
K Fallon	3-16	18.8	-5.09	E Vaughan	1-1
F Norton	6-35	17.1	+40.00	M Quinn	2-8
D O'Neill	5-31	16.1	+24.50	R Hannon	2-8
T E Durcan	4-25	16.0	-2.00	M Channon	3-12
S Carson	3-20	15.0	+41.50	R J Houghton	3-10
S Sanders	3-21	14.3	+0.25	R Beckett	2-5
L Dettori	4-31	12.9	-18.83	C Horgan	1-1
T P Queally	3-26	11.5	-13.42	N Littmoden	1-1
D Sweeney	3-28	10.7	+11.50	S Woodman	2-2
J F McDonald	3-30	10.0	+9.88	B Meehan	1-4

York Road, Beverley, E Yorkshire, HU17 8QZ. Tel 01482 867 488

BEVERLEY

How to get there – Road: Course is signposted from the M62.
Rail: Beverley, bus service to course on race-days
Features: RH, uphill finish
2005 Flat fixtures: Apr 13, 21, May 7, 17, 23, June 1, 8, 16, 21, July 1, 2, 12, 18, 26, Aug 10, 11, 20, 28, Sep 14, 20,
Pointers: Tim Easterby has done well here in a short space of time and Newmarket's representatives, though few and far between, must be considered. There's no outstanding jockey though Kevin Darley is a sound booking.

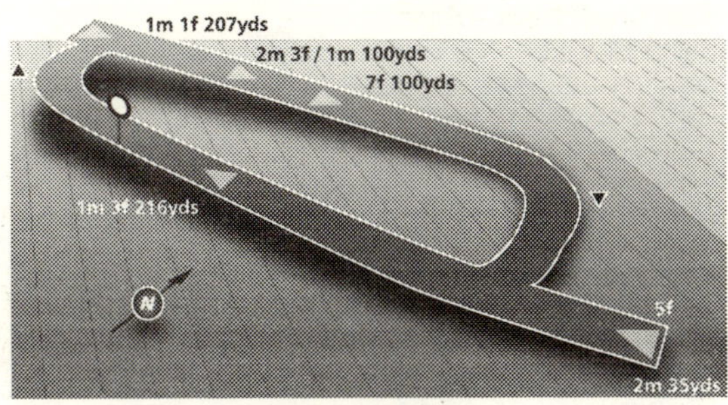

Time Test standard times

5f	1min0.5	1m3f216yds	2min30.6
7f100yds	1min29.5	1m4f16yds	2min32
1m100yds	1min42.4	2m35yds	3min29.5
1m1f207yds	2min0	2m3f100yds	4min16.7

Favourites

2-y-o	40.0%	-£6.74
3-y-o+	23.9%	-£21.02
Overall	27.3%	-£27.75

Trainers	Wins-Runs	%	2yo	3yo+	£1 level stks
W Tinning	3-10	30.0	0-0	3-10	+29.38
M Bell	4-15	26.7	3-8	1-7	+1.49
I McInnes	3-13	23.1	0-0	3-13	+17.50
K Ryan	3-14	21.4	0-4	3-10	+1.50
T Barron	3-14	21.4	1-6	2-8	+7.00
J Given	3-17	17.6	0-3	3-14	+0.25
T Easterby	12-74	16.2	3-25	9-49	+9.67
M Channon	3-20	15.0	2-6	1-14	-4.38
R Fahey	7-47	14.9	1-10	6-37	+35.50
J J Quinn	3-22	13.6	3-9	0-13	+0.37
N Bycroft	3-22	13.6	0-1	3-21	+73.00
D Nicholls	3-24	12.5	0-0	3-24	-6.75

Jockeys	Wins-Rides	%	£1 level stks	Best Trainer	W-R
T Hamilton	5-24	20.8	+40.75	R Fahey	4-14
M Fenton	4-20	20.0	+4.25	J Given	3-11
T Lucas	3-17	17.6	+18.00	M W Easterby	3-16
I Mongan	3-18	16.7	-7.58	G A Butler	1-1
S Sanders	3-19	15.8	-6.50	B Meehan	1-1
G Gibbons	3-19	15.8	-3.00	T Easterby	2-7
K Darley	5-36	13.9	-17.34	N Littmoden	2-4
F Norton	3-22	13.6	+8.50	Mrs J Ramsden	1-1
A Culhane	5-40	12.5	-16.38	M Channon	2-8
R Winston	6-49	12.2	-19.15	W Tinning	2-5
N Callan	4-34	11.8	-7.50	K Ryan	2-7
D Allan	5-45	11.1	+4.00	T Easterby	4-31

BRIGHTON

Freshfield Road, Brighton,
E Sussex BN2 2XZ.
Tel 01273 603 580

How to get there – Road: Signposted from A23 London Road and A27.
Rail: Brighton, bus to course on race-days
Features: LH, sharp and undulating, mainly downhill for last 7f, suitable for handy, speedy types
2005 Flat fixtures: Apr 19, 24, May 11, 22, 27, June 2, 9, 13, 21, 28, July 3, 12, 18, Aug 2, 3, 4, 15, 23, 24, Sep 20, Oct 3, 14, 20
Pointers: Newmarket men Luca Cumani and Sir Mark Prescott have for a long time enjoyed their raids on the seaside track. Ian Wood is coming into the picture with a healthy strike-rate but nearby Gary Moore has a surprisingly lean percentage figure. His son Ryan is a jockey to follow though, along with reliable Seb Sanders.

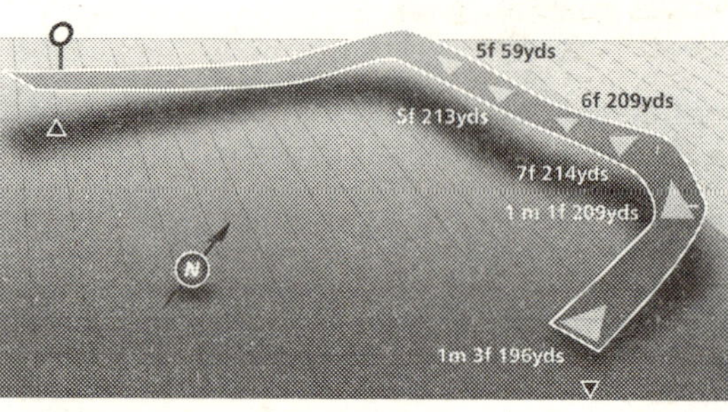

Time Test standard times

5f59yds	59.5	7f214yds	1min32
5f213yds	1min7.5	1m1f209yds	1min57.5
6f209yds	1min19.6	1m3f196yds	2min26

Favourites

2-y-o	31.0%	-£6.54
3-y-o+	28.3%	-£17.77
Overall	28.8%	-£24.31

Trainers	*Wins-Runs*	*%*	*2yo*	*3yo+*	*£1 level stks*
Sir M Stoute	3-4	75.0	0-0	3-4	+9.83
L Cumani	3-6	50.0	0-0	3-6	+14.00
Sir M Prescott	4-10	40.0	0-2	4-8	-0.65
Miss B Sanders	6-15	40.0	0-0	6-15	+40.00
N Callaghan	5-15	33.3	4-11	1-4	+19.07
I A Wood	5-17	29.4	3-6	2-11	+34.75
C Brittain	3-13	23.1	1-2	2-11	+19.50
W G M Turner	3-14	21.4	2-7	1-7	+5.50
D Ivory	3-16	18.8	0-0	3-16	+1.00
M Channon	6-34	17.6	3-9	3-25	+24.25
S Kirk	4-23	17.4	1-6	3-17	+17.00
S Dow	3-22	13.6	0-1	3-21	-2.00

Jockeys	*Wins-Rides*	*%*	*£1 level stks*	*Best Trainer*	*W-R*
B Doyle	3-7	42.9	+6.00	Sir M Stoute	2-3
L Dettori	5-14	35.7	+8.15	M Tompkins	1-1
D Holland	7-25	28.0	+0.05	D Ivory	2-2
S Sanders	14-50	28.0	+19.53	Sir M Prescott	3-4
C Haddon	3-12	25.0	+7.50	W G M Turner	3-6
R L Moore	17-77	22.1	+24.54	S Dow	3-7
K Fallon	3-14	21.4	+1.62	E Vaughan	1-1
S Drowne	6-32	18.8	+29.19	Miss B Sanders	2-2
R Miles	3-19	15.8	+1.00	T Mills	1-2
G Baker	3-20	15.0	+26.50	B Millman	1-1
J Egan	4-33	12.1	+3.83	S Kirk	2-13
C Catlin	4-33	12.1	+1.75	M Channon	2-8

CARLISLE

Durdar Road, Carlisle, Cumbria,
CA2 4TS. Tel 01228 554 700

How to get there – Road: M6 Jctn 42, follow signs on Dalston Road.
Rail: Carlisle, 66 bus to course on race-days
Features: RH, undulating, uphill finish
2004 Flat fixtures: May 12, 23, 31, June 14, 22, July 2, 15, 28, Aug 1, 17, Sep 1, 11
Pointers: Only a handful of trainers and jockeys have managed more than three winners. But Mark Johnston figures still catch the eye, as do Willie Supple's.

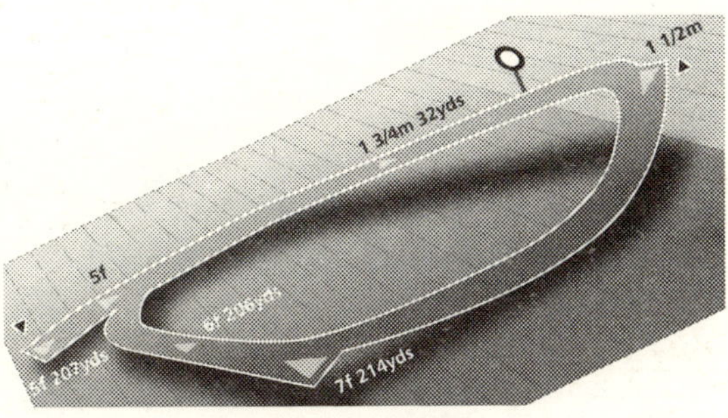

Time Test standard times

5f	59.6	1m1f61yds	1min55
5f193yds	1min11.8	1m3f206yds	2min28.7
6f192yds	1min24.7	1m6f32yds	2min59.2
7f200yds	1min37.6	2m1f52yds	3min42

Favourites

2-y-o	36.6%	-£8.02
3-y-o+	29.2%	-£26.03
Overall	30.4%	-£34.05

Trainers	*Wins-Runs*	*%*	*2yo*	*3yo+*	*£1 level stks*
R Wilman	3-4	75.0	0-0	3-4	+42.00
L Cumani	3-5	60.0	0-0	3-5	+7.62
J R Best	3-6	50.0	1-1	2-5	+25.50
E Dunlop	3-7	42.9	0-0	3-7	+3.50
Sir M Prescott	6-15	40.0	0-2	6-13	-4.37
I Balding	3-8	37.5	1-3	2-5	+16.80
J O'Reilly	3-10	30.0	0-1	3-9	+23.75
Mrs L Stubbs	3-12	25.0	0-3	3-9	+4.63
M Johnston	12-51	23.5	4-13	8-38	+38.25
B Smart	5-25	20.0	2-10	3-15	+37.00
M Channon	4-21	19.0	2-7	2-14	+3.61
I Semple	6-37	16.2	0-1	6-36	+19.42

Jockeys	*Wins-Rides*	*%*	*£1 level stks*	*Best Trainer*	*W-R*
Leanne Kershaw	3-9	33.3	+35.00	J O'Keeffe	2-5
N Mackay	4-14	28.6	+17.50	J S Moore	2-2
E Ahern	3-11	27.3	+15.45	G Chung	1-1
W Supple	8-33	24.2	+24.75	E Alston	4-18
S Sanders	3-14	21.4	-1.80	Sir M Prescott	2-4
K Darley	16-79	20.3	-25.98	L Cumani	2-2
P Robinson	3-16	18.8	-4.92	M Jarvis	2-8
Alex Greaves	4-22	18.2	+3.00	D Nicholls	4-22
D McGaffin	4-23	17.4	+5.67	B Smart	2-5
R Ffrench	5-32	15.6	+8.00	J R Best	1-1
J Egan	3-20	15.0	+5.00	P Harris	1-1
K Dalgleish	5-34	14.7	-4.38	M Johnston	3-16

CATTERICK

Catterick Bridge, Richmond,
N Yorkshire, DL10 7PE.
Tel 01748 811 478

How to get there – Road: A1, exit 5m south of Scotch Corner.
Rail: Darlington or Northallerton and bus.
Features: LH, undulating, tight turns, lends itself to course specialists
2005 Flat fixtures: Apr 6, 20, May 3, 21, 27, June 10, 29, July 6, 13, 20, Aug 2, 12, 24, Sep 6, 17, Oct 4, Oct 15, Oct 25, Nov 1
Pointers: Try a couple of trainer/jockey combinations. Mark Johnston and Joe Fanning; Jimmy Fortune and Paul Cole.

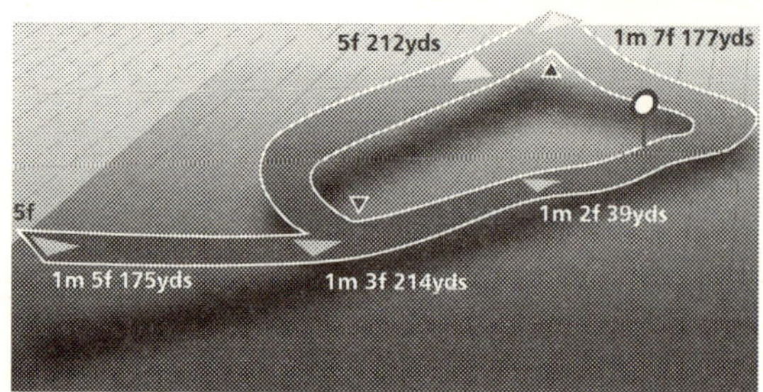

Time Test standard times

5f	57.5	1m3f214yds	2min31
5f212yds	1min10.5	1m5f175yds	2min55.3
7f	1min23.2	1m7f177yds	3min21.2

Favourites

2-y-o	39.5%	+£2.75
3-y-o+	28.7%	-£45.46
Overall	31.4%	-£42.71

Trainers	Wins-Runs	%	2yo	3yo+	£1 level stks
Sir M Stoute	6-15	40.0	3-5	3-10	-0.62
E Dunlop	5-13	38.5	4-7	1-6	+3.19
W Haggas	4-13	30.8	2-5	2-8	+1.48
P Cole	6-21	28.6	5-15	1-6	+5.13
M Bell	5-21	23.8	1-6	4-15	+1.32
M Brittain	3-13	23.1	2-6	1-7	+16.33
M Johnston	25-112	22.3	10-45	15-67	-19.96
Sir M Prescott	6-28	21.4	1-11	5-17	-8.07
R Beckett	3-15	20.0	1-6	2-9	-7.40
A Turnell	4-20	20.0	0-2	4-18	+2.25
J Glover	7-36	19.4	1-10	6-26	+3.88
W Tinning	3-16	18.8	0-0	3-16	+17.50

Jockeys	Wins-Rides	%	£1 level stks	Best Trainer	W-R
G Carter	5-12	41.7	+16.00	A Berry	2-7
J Fortune	3-8	37.5	+4.25	P Cole	3-5
O Urbina	3-8	37.5	+5.67	J Fanshawe	1-2
Paul Scallan	6-20	30.0	+70.44	B Smart	3-11
K Fallon	10-42	23.8	+6.87	D Loder	1-1
J F McDonald	3-14	21.4	+7.75	I A Wood	2-5
I Mongan	3-14	21.4	-3.00	M Jarvis	1-1
N Mackay	3-16	18.8	+9.00	M Tompkins	1-1
L Fletcher	7-42	16.7	+38.50	H Morrison	2-3
K Darley	18-110	16.4	-33.27	M Johnston	5-19
P Hanagan	20-125	16.0	+8.04	R Fahey	6-28
E Ahern	3-20	15.0	-4.67	E Alston	2-4

Chepstow, Monmouthshire,
NP16 6BE. Tel 01291 622 260

CHEPSTOW

How to get there – Road: M4 Jct 22 on west side of Severn Bridge, A48 north, then A446 Monmouth Rd. Rail: Chepstow, bus to course on race-days

Features: LH, undulating

2005 Flat fixtures: May 4, 5, 30, June 4, 10, 15, 29, July 8, 22, Aug 4, 11, 18, 29, Sep 2, 8, 19

Pointers: Roger Charlton and Brian Meehan are the two trainers to follow here, both producing impressive stats Amongst the jockeys, Dane O'Neill has done well, particularly when teaming up with runners from the Henry Candy yard.

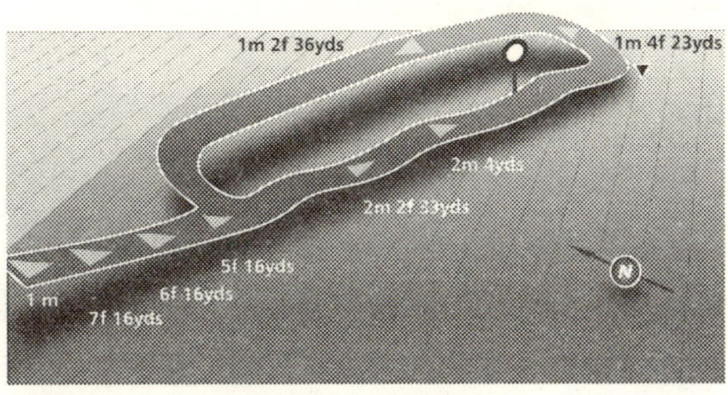

Time Test standard times

5f16yds	57	1m4f23yds	2min31.3
6f16yds	1min8.8	2m49yds	3min28
7f16yds	1min20.5	2m1f40yds	3min41
1m14yds	1min32.6	2m2f	3min52
1m2f36yds	2min4.2		

Favourites

2-y-o	36.5%	-£4.50
3-y-o+	22%	-£97.94
Overall	25.6%	-£102.45

Trainers	Wins-Runs	%	2yo	3yo+	£1 level stks
R Charlton	9-30	30.0	0-5	9-25	+32.38
E Dunlop	11-39	28.2	3-14	8-25	+10.43
H Candy	11-39	28.2	4-9	7-30	+15.40
Sir M Stoute	6-22	27.3	2-3	4-19	-7.91
J Dunlop	11-41	26.8	5-18	6-23	+6.94
B Meehan	12-46	26.1	5-22	7-24	+44.13
M Johnston	5-20	25.0	2-6	3-14	-7.03
Sir M Prescott	5-20	25.0	1-11	4-9	-2.99
G A Butler	6-26	23.1	2-5	4-21	+5.29
J King	5-22	22.7	0-1	5-21	+29.13
M Pipe	5-24	20.8	0-5	5-19	+18.50
C Brittain	3-15	20.0	0-0	3-15	+2.83

Jockeys	Wins-Rides	%	£1 level stks	Best Trainer	W-R
R Ffrench	3-11	27.3	+6.75	A Stewart	2-3
K Fallon	9-34	26.5	-4.75	Sir M Stoute	3-6
R Hughes	9-36	25.0	+0.72	R Charlton	2-2
G Carter	5-21	23.8	+6.80	E Dunlop	3-4
F Norton	10-45	22.2	+13.80	D Haydn Jones	2-3
G Gibbons	5-24	20.8	+50.00	P Evans	3-5
L Newman	7-34	20.6	-4.00	T McGovern	1-1
T Quinn	7-36	19.4	-9.71	H Cecil	2-7
G Duffield	3-16	18.8	-2.00	Sir M Prescott	2-6
D O'Neill	20-109	18.3	+39.08	H Candy	5-10
D Holland	12-66	18.2	-8.82	B Palling	2-3
B Doyle	7-40	17.5	+17.38	B Meehan	3-10

CHESTER

Steam Mill Street,
Chester, CH1 2LY.
Tel 01244 304 600

How to get there – Road: Join Inner Ring Road and A458 Queensferry Road. Rail: Chester General, bus to city centre
Features: LH, flat, almost circular
2005 Flat fixtures:
May 4, 5, 6, June 7, 25, July 8, 9, 31, Aug 18, 19, 20, Sep 10
Pointers: Much as one associates this track with Barry Hills, partly because he has all but made the Dee Stakes his own, the bare facts state that following all his runners only yields a small profit. But Hills has passed on what he knows about the place to his son Michael. As a team they are deadly.

Time Test standard times

5f16yds	59.8	1m3f79yds	2min22.7
6f18yds	1min13	1m4f66yds	2min35
7f2yds	1min24.7	1m5f89yds	2min48.6
7f122yds	1min31.2	1m7f195yds	3min22
1m1f70yds	1min55	2m2f147yds	4min1
1m2f75yds	2min8		

Favourites

2-y-o	52.0%	+£30.12
3-y-o+	28.9%	-£36.83
Overall	34.8%	-£6.71

Trainers	*Wins-Runs*	*%*	*2yo*	*3yo+*	*£1 level stks*
J Noseda	5-11	45.5	3-5	2-6	+6.88
M Tregoning	3-8	37.5	0-0	3-8	+7.62
G Wragg	10-27	37.0	1-1	9-26	+12.27
J Gosden	7-25	28.0	1-3	6-22	+12.82
Sir M Stoute	12-47	25.5	1-6	11-41	+9.52
G A Butler	8-32	25.0	1-5	7-27	+12.63
B Hills	30-126	23.8	12-27	18-99	+4.15
W Jarvis	3-13	23.1	1-4	2-9	+1.50
J Dunlop	7-31	22.6	3-6	4-25	-1.50
M Jarvis	5-24	20.8	1-6	4-18	-3.00
J Eyre	3-15	20.0	1-3	2-12	+17.00
P Cole	11-59	18.6	2-11	9-48	-6.37

Jockeys	*Wins-Rides*	*%*	*£1 level stks*	*Best Trainer*	*W-R*
R Hills	10-38	26.3	+0.41	B Hills	4-11
K Fallon	30-120	25.0	+9.08	Sir M Stoute	9-32
M Hills	19-88	21.6	+2.90	B Hills	15-67
Craig Williams	3-14	21.4	-0.25	M Channon	3-8
P Dobbs	4-20	20.0	-1.00	R Hannon	3-10
R Ffrench	4-21	19.0	-0.50	R Fisher	2-2
D Holland	19-105	18.1	-32.03	G Wragg	5-16
P Hanagan	9-52	17.3	+8.60	R Fahey	4-23
E Ahern	8-47	17.0	-1.38	G A Butler	4-10
J Reid	4-24	16.7	-3.25	A Newcombe	2-4
D Sweeney	5-32	15.6	+6.33	B Palling	2-9
J Quinn	3-20	15.0	+0.40	P Chapple-Hyam	1-1

DONCASTER

Leger Way, Doncaster, DN2 6BB. Tel: 01302 304 200

How to get there – Road: M18, Jncts 3 or 4
Rail: Doncaster, bus to course

Features: LH, flat, easy turns, suits galloping type

2005 Flat fixtures: Apr 1, 2, May 2, 19, 28, June 4, 12, 25, July 7, 14, 21, 30, Sep 7, 8, 9, 10, Oct 21, 22, Nov 5

Pointers: Saeed Bin Suroor's strike-rate is remarkable and he has won the St Leger four times with four different jockeys. Following his horses here is one of the best systems on the Flat. He scored a treble on October 22 last year at odds of 5-1, 6-1 and 4-5. The once mighty Henry Cecil has dropped off the radar.

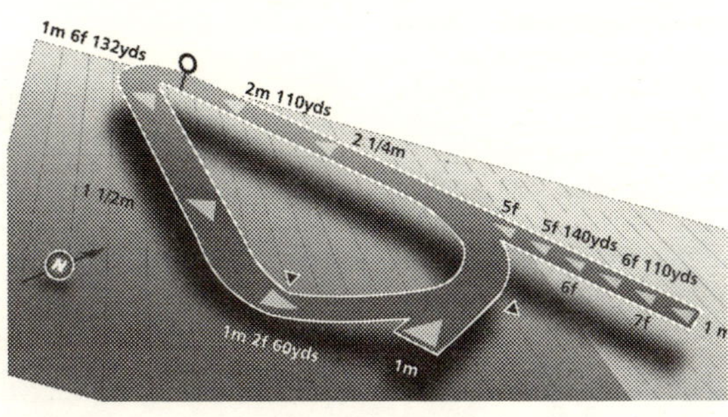

Time Test standard times

5f	58.7	1m(round)	1min37.2
5f140yds	1min7.4	1m2f60yds	2min6
6f	1min11.5	1m4f	2min30
6f110yds	1min18	1m6f132yds	3min3
7f	1min24.3	2m110yds	3min32
1m(str)	1min36.8	2m2f	3min53

Favourites

2-y-o	36.1%	+£6.23
3-y-o+	26.3%	-£76.55
Overall	29.2%	-£70.32

Trainers	*Wins-Runs*	*%*	*2yo*	*3yo+*	*£1 level stks*
S bin Suroor	21-59	35.6	6-15	15-44	+18.15
D Loder	10-39	25.6	8-26	2-13	-12.10
M Ryan	3-14	21.4	1-2	2-12	+38.00
W G M Turner	4-20	20.0	3-17	1-3	+5.00
A P O'Brien	5-28	17.9	3-17	2-11	-9.76
J Dunlop	23-133	17.3	7-54	16-79	-11.41
J Gosden	17-105	16.2	10-48	7-57	+2.41
J Fanshawe	9-56	16.1	0-10	9-46	-29.33
G Wragg	6-38	15.8	3-6	3-32	+3.50
Sir M Stoute	16-102	15.7	6-41	10-61	-28.10
J Noseda	7-45	15.6	5-19	2-26	-8.10
M Bell	10-66	15.2	5-35	5-31	+24.11

Jockeys	*Wins-Rides*	*%*	*£1 level stks*	*Best Trainer*	*W-R*
L Dettori	33-140	23.6	+18.16	S bin Suroor	13-31
J P Murtagh	9-43	20.9	+11.00	Sir M Stoute	4-8
K McEvoy	4-20	20.0	+7.23	S bin Suroor	3-10
K Fallon	26-154	16.9	-31.60	Sir M Stoute	4-27
O Urbina	3-18	16.7	-9.88	J Fanshawe	3-12
Craig Williams	3-20	15.0	+2.50	M Channon	2-13
D Holland	28-187	15.0	-33.44	M Johnston	5-22
R Hills	15-101	14.9	-11.49	B Hills	4-18
M Hills	22-157	14.0	-11.53	B Hills	19-117
F P Ferris	3-22	13.6	+34.00	P Evans	2-11
T McLaughlin	4-30	13.3	0.00	W Brisbourne	2-8
S Hitchcott	6-47	12.8	+23.75	M Channon	3-12

EPSOM

Epsom Downs,
Surrey, KT18 5LQ.
Tel 01372 726 311

How to get there – Road: M25 Jctn 8 (A217) or 9 (A24) 2m south of Epsom on B290
Rail: Epsom & raceday bus, Epsom Downs or Tattenham Corner
Features: LH, undulating, downhill 5f is fastest in the world
2005 Flat fixtures: Apr 20, June 3, 4, 30, July 7, 14, 28, Aug 29, Sep 7, 8, Oct 1
Pointers: A tricky track with no one trainer dominating though Sir Mark Prescott is worth a second look. Considering how inexperienced he is, Tom Queally has done extremely well to rack up six winners from 19 rides. Barney Curley and David Loder have supplied him the ammo.

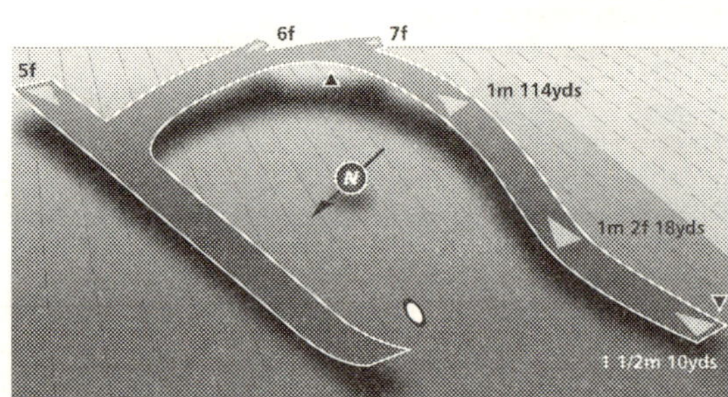

Time Test standard times

5f	53.8	1m114yds	1min41.6
6f	1min8	1m2f18yds	2min3.5
7f	1min20.2	1m4f10yds	2min33.6

Favourites

2-y-o	40.3%	-£2.01
3-y-o+	29.1%	+£25.79
Overall	31.0%	+£23.78

Trainers	*Wins-Runs*	*%*	*2yo*	*3yo+*	*£1 level stks*
H Morrison	6-16	37.5	0-1	6-15	+18.10
Mrs J Ramsden	4-12	33.3	0-0	4-12	+7.00
S C Williams	8-27	29.6	0-1	8-26	+20.37
J Dunlop	12-47	25.5	4-12	8-35	-7.20
Sir M Prescott	5-21	23.8	4-10	1-11	-2.24
D Loder	3-14	21.4	2-4	1-10	-6.69
J Fanshawe	3-14	21.4	0-1	3-13	+12.00
I Balding	10-48	20.8	3-8	7-40	-6.42
Sir M Stoute	9-44	20.5	0-5	9-39	-8.63
S Woods	3-16	18.8	1-3	2-13	+11.50
S bin Suroor	7-40	17.5	1-1	6-39	-13.18
J Noseda	3-18	16.7	2-5	1-13	-9.77

Jockeys	*Wins-Rides*	*%*	*£1 level stks*	*Best Trainer*	*W-R*
R Winston	3-7	42.9	+22.50	B Smart	1-1
T P Queally	6-19	31.6	+16.98	B Curley	2-2
L Dettori	20-75	26.7	+6.10	S bin Suroor	7-25
K Fallon	26-115	22.6	-9.42	Sir M Stoute	5-24
O Urbina	4-18	22.2	+10.75	J Fanshawe	2-4
A Beech	3-14	21.4	+6.50	J Spearing	2-3
J P Murtagh	5-28	17.9	+23.38	J W Payne	1-2
R Hills	7-42	16.7	+4.03	E Vaughan	1-1
K Dalgleish	4-25	16.0	-3.00	M Johnston	4-14
T Quinn	13-84	15.5	-3.09	J Dunlop	3-4
J Fanning	5-33	15.2	+7.25	M Johnston	2-12
R Miles	4-27	14.8	+7.50	T Mills	2-9

Westenhanger, Hythe, Kent,
CT21 4HX. Tel 01303 266 407

FOLKESTONE

How to get there – Road: M20 Jctn 11, A20 south. Rail: Westenhanger from Charing Cross or Victoria
Features: RH, sharp turns
2005 Flat fixtures: Apr 5, 19, May 5, June 6, 24, July 7, 21, Aug 4, 12, 21, Sep 3, 12,
Pointers: Relative newcomer Mick Quinlan has done very well at this venue, both in terms of percentage and level-stakes profit. Alan Berry is a rare visitor to the track, and doesn't often leave empty handed. In the jockeys division, Seb Sanders and Ryan Moore are noteworthy.

Time Test standard times

5f	58.6	1m1f149yds	2min0.2
6f	1min11	1m4f	2min33.6
6f189yds (Rnd)	1min21.8	1m7f92yds	3min19.4
7f(str)	1min24	2m93yds	3min32.7

Favourites

2-y-o	40.5%	-£11.37
3-y-o+	32.8%	-£25.51
Overall	34.6%	-£36.88

Trainers	*Wins-Runs*	*%*	*2yo*	*3yo+*	*£1 level stks*
A Berry	3-5	60.0	0-0	3-5	+15.50
H Cecil	3-6	50.0	0-1	3-5	+19.50
D Nicholls	4-10	40.0	0-1	4-9	+23.25
Sir M Prescott	9-23	39.1	3-8	6-15	+20.96
J W Payne	6-19	31.6	1-4	5-15	+18.46
R Charlton	5-16	31.3	4-6	1-10	-1.96
A Stewart	3-10	30.0	0-2	3-8	+13.60
H Candy	3-10	30.0	1-4	2-6	+1.23
P Hiatt	4-15	26.7	0-0	4-15	+3.00
C Horgan	4-15	26.7	0-0	4-15	+12.25
N Callaghan	5-19	26.3	2-9	3-10	+12.50
M G Quinlan	4-17	23.5	4-7	0-10	+44.00

Jockeys	*Wins-Rides*	*%*	*£1 level stks*	*Best Trainer*	*W-R*
J Fortune	4-9	44.4	+10.88	P Cole	2-2
M Hills	3-8	37.5	+9.55	B Hills	3-6
L Dettori	7-20	35.0	+8.65	D Loder	2-3
G Duffield	4-14	28.6	+9.25	R Guest	1-1
K Fallon	7-28	25.0	-3.70	A Balding	1-1
S Sanders	23-103	22.3	+10.68	Sir M Prescott	6-14
G Carter	9-42	21.4	+4.08	E Dunlop	3-4
T Quinn	12-56	21.4	-2.50	Mrs A Perrett	3-4
S Drowne	16-76	21.1	+7.18	M Channon	5-16
R L Moore	13-63	20.6	+21.71	R Hannon	3-10
M Savage	4-20	20.0	+25.83	J Bradley	2-12
R Hughes	7-38	18.4	-11.38	Mrs A Perrett	2-8

GOODWOOD

Chichester, W Sussex, P018 0PS. Tel 01243 755 022

How to get there – Road: signposted from A27 south and A285 north Rail: Chichester, bus to course on race-days

Features: RH, undulating

2005 Flat fixtures: Apr 30, May 18, 19, 20, 28, June 3, 10, 17, July 26, 27, 28, 29, 30, Aug 13, 27, 28, Sep 10, 11, 21, 27, Oct 9

Pointers: It's extraordinary how revealing statistics can be. Mark Johnston is linked in everybody's mind with Goodwood yet he only has four winners here over the past three years. Having said that do not oppose him in the Goodwood Cup in which last year he had a 1-2-4. Saeed Bin Suroor is the trainer for our money.

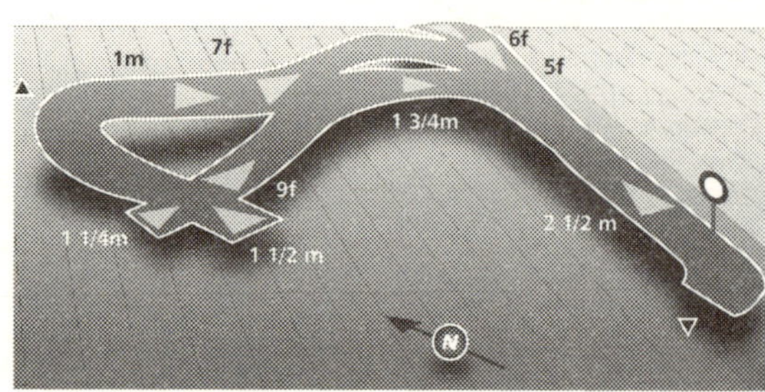

Time Test standard times

5f	56.4	1m3f	2min20
6f	1min10	1m4f	2min32.7
7f	1min24.4	1m6f	2min59
1m	1min36.8	2m	3min22
1m1f	1min52	2m4f	4min13
1m1f192yds	2min2.2	2m5f	4min27.3

Favourites

2-y-o	19.4%	-£20.36
3-y-o+	27.0%	+£2.66
Overall	25.5%	-£17.70

Trainers	*Wins-Runs*	*%*	*2yo*	*3yo+*	*£1 level stks*
P Harris	6-15	40.0	0-0	6-15	+28.50
P Makin	4-13	30.8	0-1	4-12	+24.00
L Cumani	3-10	30.0	0-0	3-10	+8.25
J Boyle	3-10	30.0	0-2	3-8	+10.50
M Tregoning	6-22	27.3	1-7	5-15	+22.33
Sir M Stoute	5-20	25.0	0-1	5-19	+1.65
S bin Suroor	8-33	24.2	1-6	7-27	+20.50
G Wragg	3-13	23.1	1-2	2-11	+0.33
J Gosden	5-27	18.5	2-7	3-20	+1.16
W Muir	4-25	16.0	1-6	3-19	+8.50
J Dunlop	7-45	15.6	0-9	7-36	-6.75
M Johnston	4-37	10.8	2-11	2-26	-17.69

Jockeys	*Wins-Rides*	*%*	*£1 level stks*	*Best Trainer*	*W-R*
S Sanders	6-22	27.3	+76.00	P Makin	3-4
J Murtagh	3-12	25.0	-2.50	J Dunlop	2-2
Lisa Jones	3-14	21.4	+22.00	G A Butler	1-1
L Dettori	10-47	21.3	-0.64	S bin Suroor	4-18
J Fanning	5-24	20.8	+0.31	M Johnston	4-17
K McEvoy	3-16	18.8	+13.25	S bin Suroor	3-7
J Fortune	6-37	16.2	-11.25	L Cumani	1-2
T Quinn	7-45	15.6	+70.25	D Elsworth	2-10
R Hughes	6-40	15.0	-18.13	R Hannon	3-17
R L Moore	10-69	14.5	+96.00	R Hannon	6-24
M Dwyer	8-57	14.0	+8.50	W Muir	2-9
R Hills	4-32	12.5	-18.67	M Tregoning	2-10

HAMILTON

Bothwell Road, Hamilton, Lanarkshire
ML3 0DW. Tel 01698 283 806

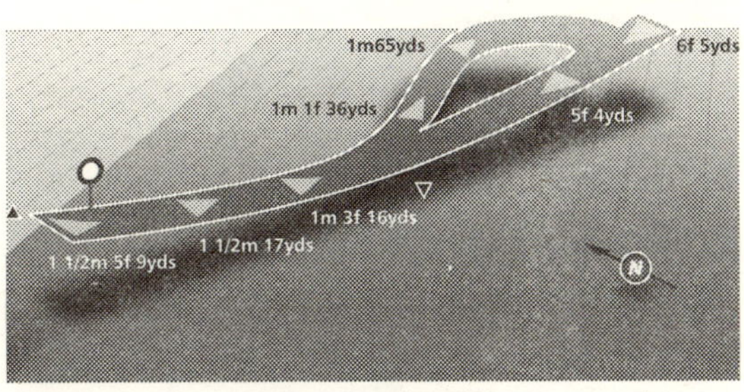

How to get there – Road: M74 Jctn 5, off the A74 Rail: Hamilton West
Features: RH, undulating, dip can become testing in wet weather
2005 Flat fixtures: Apr 25, May 1, 6, 13, June 2, 8, 15, 23, 28, July 9, 14, 15, 30, Aug 10, 16, 22, Sep 18, 26
Pointers: The top five trainers at the Scottish track are from the south. The leading northerner is Karl Burke who struck with a 16-1 shot last year, accounting for most of his profit figure. Watch out for up-and-coming Philip Makin who rode two winners in the space of two days last July, at 6-1 and 8-1.

Time Test standard times

5f4yds	58.2	1m1f36yds	1min54.3
5f200yds	1min9.2	1m3f16yds	2min19.2
6f5yds	1min10	1m4f17yds	2min32.2
1m65yds	1min43.5	1m5f9yds	2min45.4

Favourites

2-y-o	43.5%	+£1.09
3-y-o+	32.7%	-£12.71
Overall	34.7%	-£11.62

Trainers	*Wins-Runs*	*%*	*2yo*	*3yo+*	*£1 level stks*
Sir M Prescott	3-5	60.0	1-2	2-3	-0.43
G A Butler	3-7	42.9	2-4	1-3	-2.15
M Jarvis	3-7	42.9	0-0	3-7	+1.94
M Bell	3-9	33.3	2-3	1-6	+3.63
M Channon	3-10	30.0	2-5	1-5	-2.15
K R Burke	5-19	26.3	3-7	2-12	+16.25
E Alston	3-12	25.0	0-0	3-12	+26.00
B Smart	3-15	20.0	1-7	2-8	+19.50
R Fahey	5-25	20.0	0-0	5-25	-6.71
T Barron	4-27	14.8	0-7	4-20	-2.00
M Johnston	6-46	13.0	2-15	4-31	-32.42
P Monteith	3-24	12.5	0-0	3-24	+13.50

Jockeys	*Wins-Rides*	*%*	*£1 level stks*	*Best Trainer*	*W-R*
T E Durcan	3-6	50.0	+14.17	E Dunlop	1-1
S W Kelly	3-9	33.3	-3.46	G A Butler	1-1
S Sanders	5-15	33.3	-7.37	Sir M Prescott	3-4
G Duffield	3-15	20.0	-5.56	M Tompkins	1-1
J Fanning	5-28	17.9	-15.29	M Johnston	4-18
P Hanagan	8-47	17.0	+18.83	R Fahey	2-6
D Allan	3-18	16.7	+11.33	C J Teague	1-1
A Nicholls	3-18	16.7	+17.50	K R Burke	2-2
P Makin	5-31	16.1	+3.00	T Barron	4-19
T Hamilton	3-19	15.8	-10.71	R Fahey	3-14
T Eaves	3-19	15.8	+6.00	I Semple	2-6
F Lynch	5-32	15.6	+11.60	B Smart	3-11

HAYDOCK

Newton-Le-Willows, Merseyside, WA12 0HQ. Tel 01942 725 963

How to get there – Road: M6 Jctn 23, A49 to Wigan Rail: Wigan & 320 bus or Newton-le-Willows
Features: LH flat track, easy turns, suits the galloping type
2005 Flat fixtures: Apr 23, May 7, 20, 21, June 2, 3, 4, 30, July 1, 2, 10, 16, Aug 4, 5, 6, 11, Sep 2, 3, 23, 24,
Pointers: Veteran Michael Jarvis has lost none of his touch and his horses go off at backable odds. Henry Cecil has always done well here as has Saeed Bin Suroor. Following one of these trainers blind would make a good system. All seven of the Jarvis horses were ridden by Philip Robinson.

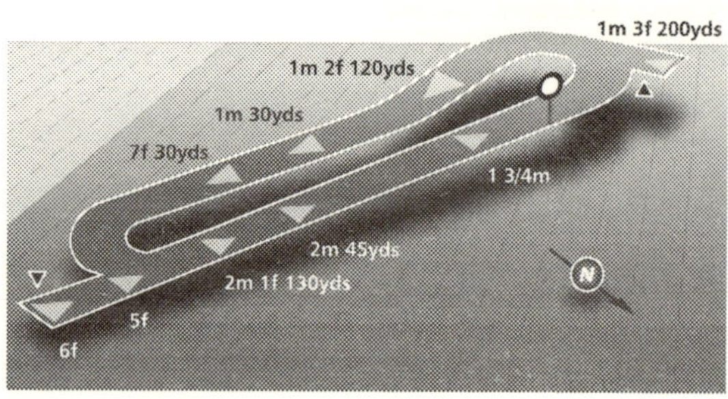

Time Test standard times

5f	59	1m3f200yds	2min28
6f	1min11.3	1m6f	2min54
7f30yds	1min27.4	2m45yds	3min28
1m30yds	1min40.2	2m1f130yds	3min47
1m2f120yds	2min10	2m3f	4min7

Favourites

2-y-o	31.4%	+£4.79
3-y-o+	30.4%	-£1.78
Overall	30.7%	+£3.01

Trainers	Wins-Runs	%	2yo	3yo+	£1 level stks
Sir M Prescott	3-5	60.0	1-1	2-4	+1.52
H Cecil	3-6	50.0	0-0	3-6	+11.63
R Charlton	3-9	33.3	0-1	3-8	+9.75
J Fanshawe	5-15	33.3	0-0	5-15	+23.00
S bin Suroor	4-14	28.6	2-4	2-10	+1.27
M Jarvis	7-25	28.0	2-4	5-21	+11.58
T Barron	5-22	22.7	1-5	4-17	+0.13
R Hannon	3-14	21.4	1-7	2-7	+25.00
L Cumani	3-16	18.8	0-3	3-13	+1.50
B Hills	5-30	16.7	0-4	5-26	+31.15
A Berry	5-32	15.6	4-15	1-17	+3.00
K Ryan	3-22	13.6	1-10	2-12	-3.25

Jockeys	Wins-Rides	%	£1 level stks	Best Trainer	W-R
W Ryan	4-7	57.1	+18.13	H Cecil	3-5
R Hughes	5-17	29.4	+25.25	R Charlton	2-3
F Lynch	4-15	26.7	+17.00	A Berry	2-4
S Sanders	3-13	23.1	-4.19	Sir M Prescott	2-4
P Hanagan	5-22	22.7	+1.67	R Fahey	2-8
F Norton	7-32	21.9	+29.00	A Berry	3-7
R L Moore	3-16	18.8	+2.83	M G Quinlan	2-2
M Hills	3-17	17.6	-7.10	B Hills	2-9
K McEvoy	4-24	16.7	-8.73	S bin Suroor	4-10
P Robinson	7-44	15.9	-7.42	M Jarvis	7-22
S Drowne	3-19	15.8	-3.25	B Ellison	1-1
N Callan	5-40	12.5	-6.75	K Ryan	3-20

Staines Rd East, Sunbury-On-Thames, Middlesex, TW16 5AQ. Tel 01932 782 292

KEMPTON

How to get there – Road: M3 Jctn 1, A308 towards Kingston-on-Thames
Rail: Kempton Park from Waterloo
Features: RH, flat, sharp turn into straight
2005 Flat fixtures: Apr 2, May 2, 9, 21, 25, June 15, 22, 29, July 6, 13, 27, Aug 3, 17, Sep 2, 3, 19, 24,
Pointers: Brian Meehan's horses must be carefully considered as must those of his former teacher Richard Hannon. The Marlborough man invariably gets on the scorecard here at the spring meetings. Brendan Powell's superb profit figure is largely accounted for by the 33-1 shot he had last April.

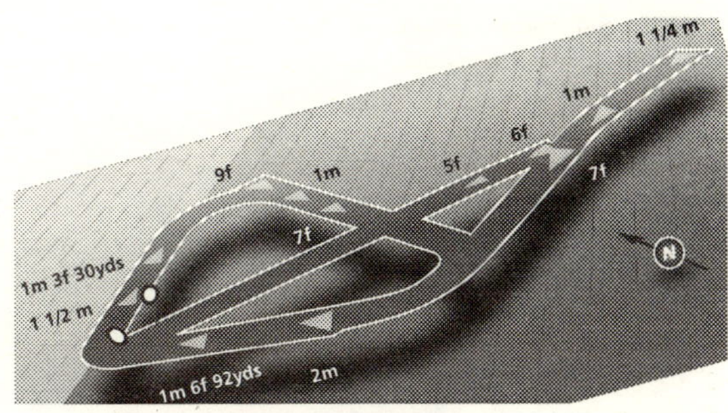

Time Test standard times

5f	58.2	1m1f	1min50
6f	1min10.3	1m2f	2min2
7f(round)	1min24.6	1m3f30yds	2min17.4
7f(Jubilee)	1min24	1m4f	2min30.3
1m(round)	1min37.4	1m6f92yds	3min2
1m(Jubilee)	1min36.6	2m	3min25.5

Favourites

2-y-o	46.4%	+£0.38
3-y-o+	19.2%	-£37.26
Overall	25.0%	-£36.88

Trainers	*Wins-Runs*	*%*	*2yo*	*3yo+*	*£1 level stks*
S bin Suroor	6-19	31.6	4-11	2-8	+1.75
B Powell	4-14	28.6	0-0	4-14	+44.25
B Meehan	6-27	22.2	3-11	3-16	+32.83
J Gosden	4-21	19.0	3-11	1-10	-0.33
R Charlton	3-16	18.8	0-1	3-15	-8.54
J Dunlop	4-22	18.2	0-9	4-13	+16.91
J Hills	3-20	15.0	0-4	3-16	+11.50
D Elsworth	3-22	13.6	0-2	3-20	+20.00
P Evans	3-27	11.1	1-5	2-22	+7.00
M Channon	3-34	8.8	2-13	1-21	-19.00
R Hannon	6-75	8.0	3-25	3-50	-25.77
J Long	3-3	100	0-0	3-3	+26.75

Jockeys	*Wins-Rides*	*%*	*£1 level stks*	*Best Trainer*	*W-R*
Natalia Gemelova	3-6	50.0	+23.75	J Long	3-3
L Dettori	16-60	26.7	+32.92	S bin Suroor	6-18
J Fortune	7-36	19.4	+6.83	B Meehan	3-6
T Quinn	5-31	16.1	+19.00	B Powell	2-3
K Fallon	10-66	15.2	-6.26	G A Swinbank	1-1
P Robinson	3-20	15.0	-4.75	M Jarvis	2-12
R Hughes	6-45	13.3	-27.18	R Charlton	3-5
S Sanders	4-32	12.5	+49.00	Lady Herries	1-1
J Quinn	3-29	10.3	-12.75	P Chapple-Hyam	1-1
E Ahern	4-39	10.3	+6.25	J Hills	2-5
D Holland	4-50	8.0	-26.50	S Kirk	1-2
M Dwyer	3-38	7.9	0.00	M Tregoning	2-6

LEICESTER

London Road, Oadby, Leicester, LE2 4QH. Tel 0116 271 6515

How to get there – Road: M1 Jctn 21, A6, 2m south of city
Rail: Leicester, bus
Features: RH, straight mile is downhill for first 4f, then uphill to finish
2005 Flat fixtures: Apr 7, 23, May 3, 17, 23, 30, 31, June 11, 23, July 2, 14, 20, 27, Aug 7, 22, 30, Sep 6, 19, Oct 4, 11, 24
Pointers: Saeed Bin Suroor likes to use the track as a place to introduce his two-year-olds and 80 per cent of his runners are juveniles. But they tend to go off at short prices. The Godolphin connection explains why Frankie Dettori and Kerrin McEvoy do so well here.

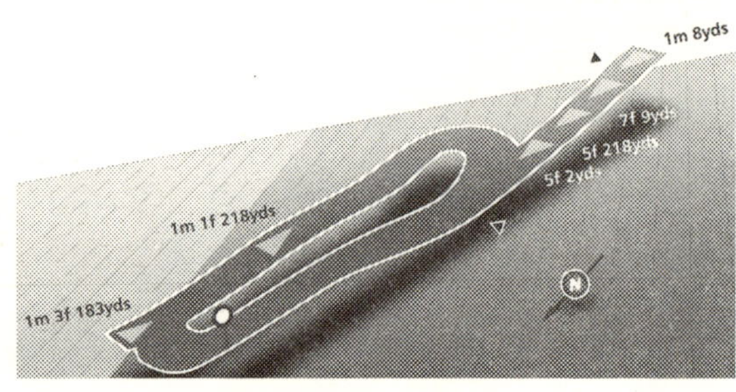

Time Test standard times

5f2yds	58.3	1m (rnd)	1min39.7
5f218yds	1min10.2	1m1f218yds	2min2.7
7f9yds	1min22.3	1m3f183yds	2min28.6
1m8yds	1min38.7		

Favourites

2-y-o	41.6%	+£0.12
3-y-o+	28.2%	-£56.63
Overall	31.6%	-£56.51

Trainers	*Wins-Runs*	*%*	*2yo*	*3yo+*	*£1 level stks*
J Noseda	4-10	40.0	0-2	4-8	+10.80
S bin Suroor	8-20	40.0	5-13	3-7	-4.38
M Saunders	3-9	33.3	0-0	3-9	+30.33
M Tregoning	5-16	31.3	3-6	2-10	+27.91
D Loder	7-24	29.2	5-17	2-7	-10.74
P Cundell	4-15	26.7	0-1	4-14	+6.00
J Fanshawe	15-62	24.2	1-12	14-50	+23.60
J Gosden	11-47	23.4	7-31	4-16	-1.74
J Eustace	5-22	22.7	1-9	4-13	+33.50
J R Best	4-18	22.2	1-5	3-13	+30.00
H Cecil	7-33	21.2	1-8	6-25	-4.39
K Ryan	4-19	21.1	1-5	3-14	+15.50

Jockeys	*Wins-Rides*	*%*	*£1 level stks*	*Best Trainer*	*W-R*
J P Murtagh	4-13	30.8	-1.42	J Fanshawe	2-2
K McEvoy	5-17	29.4	+4.92	S bin Suroor	3-4
L Dettori	18-63	28.6	-5.19	D Loder	4-7
K Fallon	24-105	22.9	+19.13	Sir M Stoute	8-31
R L Moore	7-36	19.4	-5.18	R Hannon	4-9
T Quinn	20-103	19.4	+0.72	H Cecil	5-15
J P Spencer	17-88	19.3	+9.43	D Loder	3-4
R Hills	13-71	18.3	+4.97	J Dunlop	3-16
J Fortune	10-58	17.2	-12.94	J Gosden	4-11
D Holland	20-119	16.8	-2.01	L Cumani	3-5
R Hughes	12-72	16.7	+9.41	Mrs A Perrett	3-7
C Rutter	7-48	14.6	-1.72	H Candy	3-10

LINGFIELD turf

Racecourse Road, Lingfield, Surrey, RH7 6PQ.
Tel 01342 834 800

How to get there – Road: M25 Jctn 6, south on A22, then B2029.
Rail: Lingfield from London Bridge or Victoria

Features: LH, undulating, straight runs downhill

2005 Flat fixtures: Apr 27, May 6, 7, 21, 24, 25, 28, June 4, 11, 18, 25, July 6, 8, 9, 13, 16, 20, 23, 30, Aug 5, 6, 7, 20, 25, 31, Sep 6, 23, 30

Pointers: Sir Michael Stoute and Neville Callaghan have had three winners apiece yet the former has a 60 per cent strike-rate while the latter's percentage is 21. Take your pick. Winningmost jockey Eddie Ahern is far more than an All-Weather rider.

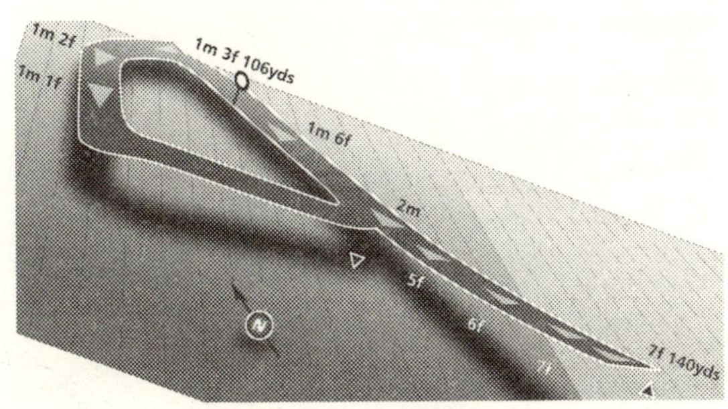

Time Test standard times

5f	56.3	1m2f	2min5.4
6f	1min9	1m3f106yds	2min24.4
7f	1min20.7	1m6f	2min58.6
7f140yds	1min28.2	2m	3min24.6
1m1f	1min52.5		

Favourites

2-y-o	33.3%	-£15.95
3-y-o+	28.4%	-£15.34
Overall	30.0%	-£31.29

Trainers	Wins-Runs	%	2yo	3yo+	£1 level stks
R Guest	3-5	60.0	0-0	3-5	+33.00
Sir M Stoute	3-5	60.0	1-1	2-4	+10.00
M Tregoning	4-12	33.3	2-3	2-9	+4.88
B Millman	5-16	31.3	2-9	3-7	+38.50
C Wall	4-14	28.6	0-2	4-12	+25.00
B Hanbury	3-12	25.0	0-2	3-10	+15.00
J A Osborne	4-16	25.0	2-13	2-3	+17.50
N Callaghan	3-14	21.4	1-10	2-4	+1.25
T Mills	3-14	21.4	0-3	3-11	+9.25
J Dunlop	10-49	20.4	2-21	8-28	-7.26

Jockeys	Wins-Rides	%	£1 level stks	Best Trainer	W-R
K Fallon	5-16	31.3	+18.25	Sir M Stoute	2-3
L Dettori	4-15	26.7	+0.92	J A Osborne	1-1
O Urbina	3-13	23.1	+2.30	Miss D Mountain	1-1
E Ahern	7-32	21.9	+56.00	J Noseda	2-3
S W Kelly	4-23	17.4	+10.00	J A Osborne	2-7
J Egan	3-19	15.8	+0.50	P L Gilligan	2-4
S Sanders	5-33	15.2	+10.37	A Jarvis	1-1
R L Moore	5-36	13.9	+22.75	R Hannon	3-15
D Holland	3-35	8.6	-15.00	J Wainwright	1-1

LINGFIELD sand

Features: LH, polytrack, tight

2005 Flat fixtures: Apr 1, 6, 8, 9, 11, 20, 28, May 17, Sep 17, 28, Oct 12, 15, 24, 27, 30, Nov 10, 12, 15, 19, 21, 26, 29, Dec 5, 7, 14, 17, 19, 20, 21, 29, 30

Pointers: Amanda Perrett has a healthy level stakes profit and a strike-rate above the all-important 25 per cent threshold. She should continue to pay to follow. A rewarding combo is Jamie Spencer when he rides for David Loder.

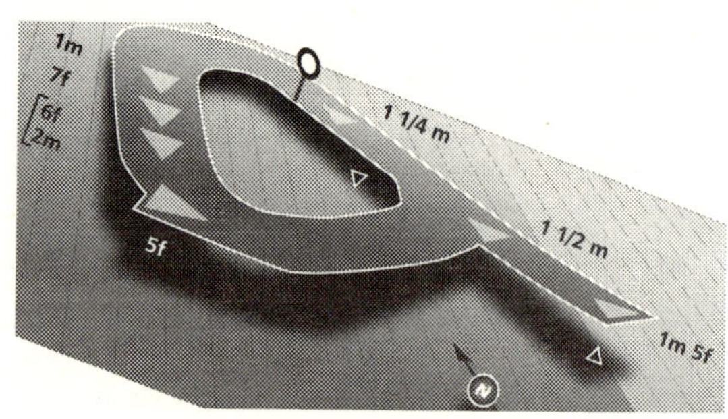

Time Test standard times

5f	58	1m2f	2min3
6f	1min11	1m4f	2min29.6
7f	1min23.2	1m5f	2min43
1m	1min36.6	2m	3min21.5

Favourites

2-y-o	32.6%	-£1.28
3-y-o+	28.2%	-£48.12
Overall	28.8%	-£49.40

Trainers	*Wins-Runs*	*%*	*2yo*	*3yo+*	*£1 level stks*
T J FitzGerald	3-6	50.0	0-0	3-6	+18.50
P Chapple-Hyam	5-11	45.5	0-0	5-11	+4.88
Sir M Stoute	4-13	30.8	2-8	2-5	+1.38
P Hedger	3-10	30.0	0-0	3-10	+14.25
Sir M Prescott	12-43	27.9	5-22	7-21	-15.77
M Dods	3-11	27.3	0-0	3-11	+4.25
S bin Suroor	4-15	26.7	3-13	1-2	-3.47
C Allen	5-19	26.3	2-3	3-16	+6.75
Mrs A Perrett	11-43	25.6	5-18	6-25	+34.12
M Jarvis	6-26	23.1	1-8	5-18	+16.50
G Wragg	5-24	20.8	1-5	4-19	+3.13
D Loder	6-30	20.0	0-9	6-21	-17.74

Jockeys	*Wins-Rides*	*%*	*£1 level stks*	*Best Trainer*	*W-R*
J P Spencer	14-49	28.6	+16.46	D Loder	5-9
L Dettori	15-55	27.3	+10.39	S bin Suroor	3-8
K Fallon	29-111	26.1	-2.36	P Howling	4-5
P Fitzsimons	5-23	21.7	+13.25	D Elsworth	2-3
B Doyle	3-15	20.0	+8.50	R Cowell	2-6
R Hills	4-21	19.0	-3.09	M Tregoning	2-5
D Holland	32-172	18.6	+12.67	N Littmoden	6-24
F Norton	4-22	18.2	+5.00	Bob Jones	1-1
R Hughes	11-61	18.0	+19.67	R Hannon	5-16
R L Moore	17-95	17.9	+61.78	G L Moore	5-31
M Hills	7-43	16.3	-11.68	J Hills	3-20
A Culhane	11-73	15.1	+23.67	P Hiatt	2-8

MUSSELBURGH

Linkfield Road,
Musselburgh,
E Lothian EH21 7RG.
Tel 0131 665 2859

How to get there – Road: M8 Jctn 2, A8 east, follow Ring Road, A1 east. Rail: Musselburgh from Edinburgh Waverley
Features: RH, flat, tight
2005 Flat fixtures: Apr 12, 29, May 10, 16, 28, June 20, 27, July 4, 27, 28, Aug 25, Sep 10, 12, 25, Oct 16, Nov 3
Pointers: Sir Mark Prescott just won't be left out of things on the Scottish circuit but we are more impressed by Gerard Butler's figures. He is the winningmost trainer, has a good strike-rate and shows a profit to level stakes. Neil Callan understands what is required at this tight course and rode a double in mid-September at odds of 16-1 and 2-1.

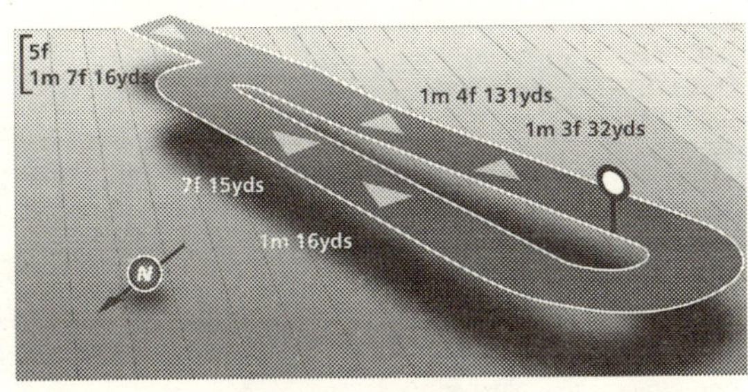

Time Test standard times

5f	57.6	1m4f	2min32.4
7f15yds	1min26.3	1m5f	2min45.3
1m	1min38.3	1m6f	2min58.4
1m1f	1min50.7	1m7f16yds	3min11.3
1m3f32yds	2min20	2m	3min25

Favourites

2-y-o	30.5%	-£40.37
3-y-o+	29.9%	-£19.51
Overall	30.0%	-£59.87

Trainers	*Wins-Runs*	*%*	*2yo*	*3yo+*	*£1 level stks*
Sir M Stoute	3-5	60.0	0-0	3-5	+1.66
M Jarvis	5-10	50.0	1-3	4-7	+0.78
Sir M Prescott	9-20	45.0	2-8	7-12	+22.05
B Meehan	3-8	37.5	3-6	0-2	-1.25
J S Moore	3-9	33.3	3-5	0-4	+3.25
P Harris	5-15	33.3	5-9	0-6	+6.70
W Haggas	7-22	31.8	2-11	5-11	-2.81
G A Butler	11-36	30.6	5-15	6-21	+2.50
S C Williams	5-17	29.4	1-2	4-15	+9.50
M Bell	7-24	29.2	2-6	5-18	+13.25
I A Wood	3-12	25.0	2-3	1-9	-2.52
J J Quinn	5-20	25.0	3-9	2-11	+0.50

Jockeys	*Wins-Rides*	*%*	*£1 level stks*	*Best Trainer*	*W-R*
R Thomas	3-5	60.0	+9.50	C Dore	2-3
J Edmunds	3-8	37.5	+24.00	J Balding	3-8
M Dwyer	3-8	37.5	+0.95	S C Williams	1-1
S Drowne	6-18	33.3	+19.48	M Channon	3-6
E Ahern	6-19	31.6	+5.63	G A Butler	6-9
D Holland	15-63	23.8	-9.05	M Johnston	4-8
T E Durcan	8-37	21.6	-2.24	A Berry	5-15
G Baker	3-14	21.4	+32.25	P Haslam	1-1
J Mackay	8-41	19.5	+17.75	M Bell	2-5
P Robinson	4-21	19.0	-11.48	M Jarvis	3-6
T Lucas	3-16	18.8	+2.63	M W Easterby	3-14
N Callan	5-27	18.5	+4.12	K Ryan	3-8

NEWBURY

Newbury, Berkshire, RG14 7NZ.
Tel: 01635 400 15 or 01635 550 354

How to get there – Road: M4 Jctn 13 and A34 south Rail: Newbury racecourse
Features: LH, wide, flat
2005 Flat fixtures: Apr 15, 16, May 13, 14, June 8, 16, 21, 30, July 16, 31, Aug 12, 13, Sep 16, 17, Oct 7, 21, 22

Pointers: Peter Chapple-Hyam gets his name on the scoreboard after just one season. He always used to have a good record here, especially with his two-year-olds, and we should expect him to resume where he left off. Newbury takes no prisoners and you need a strong jockey. Kieren Fallon fits the bill.

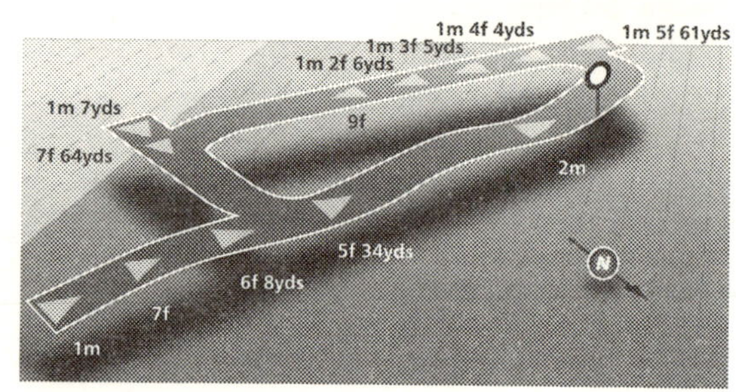

Time Test standard times

5f34yds	1min0	1m1f	1min49.7
6f8yds	1min11.2	1m2f6yds	2min2
7f	1min23	1m3f5yds	2min15.8
7f64yds(round)	1min26.4	1m4f4yds	2min29.3
1m(str)	1min36	1m5f61yds	2min45.8
1m7yds(round)	1min35.3	2m	3min23

Favourites

2-y-o	35.3%	+£1.82
3-y-o+	28.0%	-£2.55
Overall	29.9%	-£0.73

Trainers	*Wins-Runs*	*%*	*2yo*	*3yo+*	*£1 level stks*
G Wragg	3-9	33.3	0-1	3-8	+1.00
E Dunlop	3-12	25.0	0-1	3-11	+32.00
P Chapple-Hyam	3-12	25.0	1-8	2-4	+9.00
Sir M Stoute	5-22	22.7	2-5	3-17	+2.07
H Morrison	4-18	22.2	0-6	4-12	+23.87
M Tregoning	7-34	20.6	0-10	7-24	+8.10
S bin Suroor	4-20	20.0	3-8	1-12	-6.00
S Kirk	4-27	14.8	3-11	1-16	-1.00
J Dunlop	4-36	11.1	0-12	4-24	-14.75
Mrs A Perrett	3-28	10.7	0-11	3-17	-2.30
J Gosden	4-42	9.5	2-8	2-34	-23.50
R Hannon	9-114	7.9	5-52	4-62	-46.00

Jockeys	*Wins-Rides*	*%*	*£1 level stks*	*Best Trainer*	*W-R*
K Fallon	14-60	23.3	-2.85	Sir M Stoute	4-13
L Dettori	12-64	18.8	+10.80	S bin Suroor	4-16
R Hills	8-44	18.2	-13.66	M Tregoning	5-14
J P Murtagh	6-36	16.7	+1.70	Miss K George	1-1
S Sanders	3-19	15.8	+18.00	B McMahon	1-1
R L Moore	7-54	13.0	+14.00	R Hannon	4-26
D Holland	5-47	10.6	-14.50	G Wragg	2-5
E Ahern	3-35	8.6	+6.50	M Magnusson	2-2
M Hills	4-49	8.2	-8.25	J Hills	2-5
S Drowne	4-55	7.3	-2.62	Stef Liddiard	1-1
J Fortune	4-61	6.6	-18.25	S Kirk	1-2
M Dwyer	3-55	5.5	-8.50	J Eustace	1-1

NEWCASTLE

High Gosforth Park,
Newcastle-Upon-Tyne NE3 5HP.
Tel: 0191 236 2020 or 236 5508

How to get there – Road: Signposted from A1 Rail: Newcastle Central, metro to Regent Centre or Four Lane End & bus

Features: LH, 1m6f round, galloping, half-mile straight is all uphill

2005 Flat fixtures: Apr 9, 19, May 2, 11, 19, June 1, 23, 24, 25, July 23, Aug 3, 12, 26, 29, Sep 5, 28, Oct 9, 19

Pointers: Four out of the top five trainers show a profit but there's no guarantee that they will do so again over the next three-year period. Two jockeys to watch are young David Kinsella and experienced Darryll Holland.

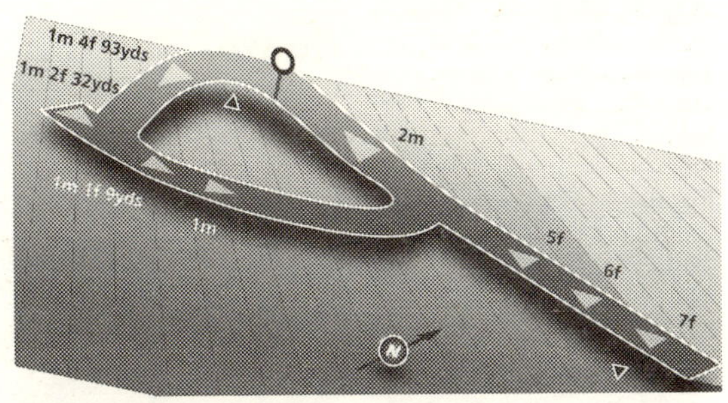

Time Test standard times

5f	59	1m1f9yds	1min52.5
6f	1min11.8	1m2f32yds	2min6.7
7f	1min24.2	1m4f93yds	2min37
1m(round)	1min39.7	1m6f97yds	3min2
1m3yds(str)	1min37.2	2m19yds	3min23.7

Favourites

2-y-o	32.1%	-£20.13
3-y-o+	29.5%	-£44.69
Overall	30.1%	-£64.82

Trainers	*Wins-Runs*	*%*	*2yo*	*3yo+*	*£1 level stks*
H Cecil	5-9	55.6	0-1	5-8	+2.25
D Morris	3-7	42.9	0-0	3-7	+10.00
D Loder	4-10	40.0	1-6	3-4	-1.80
J Noseda	9-26	34.6	2-7	7-19	+2.13
W Haggas	14-41	34.1	3-8	11-33	+6.84
S bin Suroor	3-9	33.3	2-5	1-4	-0.21
R Charlton	4-12	33.3	3-4	1-8	-3.99
M Jarvis	6-18	33.3	1-2	5-16	+2.69
W G M Turner	3-11	27.3	3-10	0-1	+9.00
M Channon	21-81	25.9	6-31	15-50	+16.54
J Dunlop	10-39	25.6	1-5	9-34	-20.73
M Bell	11-47	23.4	5-20	6-27	+27.44

Jockeys	*Wins-Rides*	*%*	*£1 level stks*	*Best Trainer*	*W-R*
K McEvoy	3-8	37.5	+2.50	S bin Suroor	2-3
S Drowne	8-27	29.6	-7.03	M Channon	7-12
L Dettori	4-14	28.6	+1.82	N Graham	1-1
I Mongan	3-11	27.3	+29.80	N Littmoden	3-4
D Kinsella	4-15	26.7	+30.00	M Polglase	1-1
M Hills	3-14	21.4	+5.08	B Hills	3-8
P Robinson	6-30	20.0	-9.31	M Jarvis	6-12
D Holland	15-76	19.7	+12.91	Mrs M Reveley	2-2
S Sanders	10-51	19.6	-12.25	R Charlton	2-2
K Fallon	13-67	19.4	-24.89	T Easterby	2-2
C Poste	3-18	16.7	-1.00	R Fahey	3-14
A Beech	4-24	16.7	+27.87	P Haslam	1-1

NEWMARKET

How to get there – Road: from south M11 Jctn 9, then A11, from east or west A45, from north A1 or A45
Rail: Newmarket

Features: RH, wide, galloping, uphill finish

2005 Flat fixtures: Apr 12, 13, 14, 30, May 1, 7, 20, 21, 29, June 17, 18, 24, 25, July 5, 6, 7, 15, 16, 22, 24, 29, 30, Aug 5, 6, 12, 13, 26, 27, Sep 20, 29, 30, Oct 1, 13, 14, 15, 28, 29

Pointers: With the racing so competitive here, even the best trainers struggle to establish strike-rates above the key 25 per cent threshold. David Elsworth managed it but whether he can maintain such a percentage is doubtful. Brian Meehan has terrific two-year-old figures and won the Cheveley Park Stakes with Magical Romance at 40-1.

Rowley Mile Course

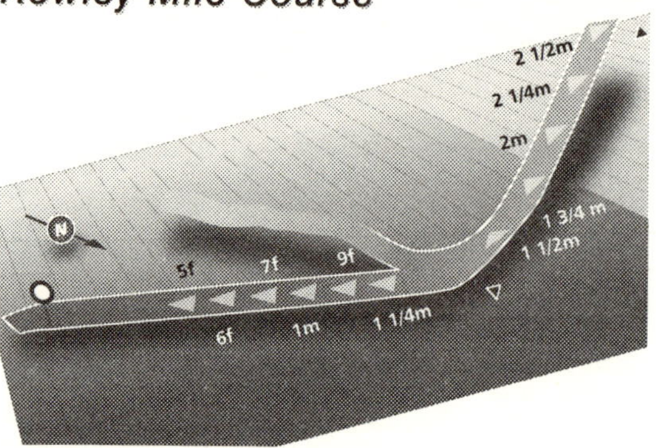

Time Test standard times

5f	57.5	1m2f	2min1.4
6f	1min10.5	1m4f	2min27.7
7f	1min22.7	1m6f	2min54.4
1m	1min35.7	2m	3min20.3
1m1f	1min48.6	2m2f	3min48

Trainer stats below apply for both Newmarket courses.

Trainers	*Wins-Runs*	*%*	*2yo*	*3yo+*	*£1 level stks*
D Flood	3-5	60.0	0-0	3-5	+21.63
D Elsworth	8-26	30.8	4-11	4-15	+131.50
B Meehan	12-55	21.8	9-33	3-22	+62.58
Sir M Stoute	16-75	21.3	4-23	12-52	+29.10
M Johnston	12-66	18.2	1-20	11-46	+24.01
R Charlton	5-28	17.9	0-3	5-25	+0.75
J Gosden	8-46	17.4	4-20	4-26	+33.13
S bin Suroor	15-93	16.1	10-43	5-50	-32.42
P Evans	3-19	15.8	0-4	3-15	+1.00
B Hills	13-97	13.4	2-32	11-65	+9.83
J Noseda	6-45	13.3	2-15	4-30	+7.66
D Loder	7-53	13.2	4-29	3-24	-9.50
W Haggas	3-24	12.5	1-5	2-19	+16.00
L Cumani	4-33	12.1	0-5	4-28	-8.50
C Wall	3-26	11.5	0-4	3-22	+1.50
P Chapple-Hyam	3-27	11.1	2-17	1-10	-10.34
Mrs A Perrett	5-49	10.2	2-18	3-31	+12.00
J Dunlop	9-89	10.1	2-40	7-49	-29.25
J Fanshawe	6-60	10.0	0-3	6-57	-10.50

Westfield House, The Links,
Newmarket, Suffolk, CB8 0TG.
Tel 01638 663 482 or 01638 662 762

How to get there: see facing page
Features: RH, wide, galloping, uphill finish
2004 Flat fixtures: June 18-19, 25-26, July 6-8, 16-17, 23, 25, 30-31, Aug 6-7, 13-14, 27-28
Pointers: See facing page.

July Course

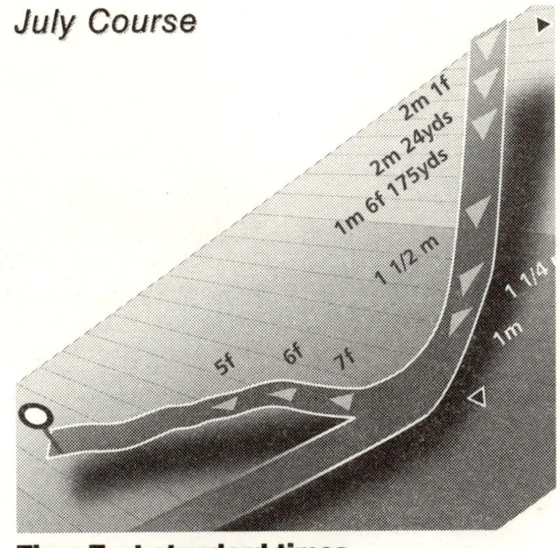

Time Test standard times

5f	57.7	1m2f	2min1
6f	1min10	1m4f	2min26.7
7f	1min22.8	1m6f175yds	3min3
1m	1min35.7	2m24yds	3min21.2
1m110yds	1min42	2m1f65yds	3min36

Favourites
(apply for both Newm't courses)

2-y-o	35.9%	-£17.31
3-y-o+	27.1%	-£71.64
Overall	29.7%	-£88.95

Jockey stats apply for both Newmarket courses.

Jockeys	*Wins-Rides*	*%*	*£1 level stks*	*Best Trainer*	*W-R*
L Keniry	3-12	25.0	+102.00	D Elsworth	3-3
J Murtagh	6-31	19.4	+29.50	Mrs A Perrett	2-3
L Dettori	21-110	19.1	-18.88	S bin Suroor	12-56
P Hanagan	5-28	17.9	+35.00	R Beckett	1-1
J Fortune	9-51	17.6	-12.06	J Gosden	3-9
M Kinane	3-20	15.0	+13.00	Mrs A Perrett	2-4
J P Murtagh	9-66	13.6	-17.83	J Fanshawe	3-16
R Hills	10-74	13.5	+18.68	B Hills	3-9
K Fallon	19-144	13.2	-69.77	Sir M Stoute	8-48
S Drowne	8-62	12.9	+4.00	R Charlton	3-15
T Quinn	8-65	12.3	-13.27	D Elsworth	3-8
M Dwyer	8-66	12.1	+32.00	L Cumani	1-1
T P Queally	6-51	11.8	-10.50	D Loder	5-23
J Fanning	4-35	11.4	-16.07	M Johnston	4-25
M Hills	9-87	10.3	-5.00	B Hills	7-55
E Ahern	9-87	10.3	+9.16	J Noseda	6-38
D Holland	11-111	9.9	-11.75	L Cumani	2-11
S Sanders	8-84	9.5	-30.13	J Dunlop	3-6

NOTTINGHAM

Colwick Park, Colwick Road,
Nottingham, NG2 4BE.
Tel 0115 958 0620

How to get there – Road: M1 Jctn 25, A52 east to B686, signs for Trent Bridge, then Colwick Park
Rail: Nottingham
Features: LH, flat, easy turns
2005 Flat fixtures: Apr 6, 16, 29, May 6, 13, 14, 24, June 1, 20, July 2, 9, 23, 29, Aug 15, 17, Sep 16, 27, Oct 5, 19, 26, Nov 2

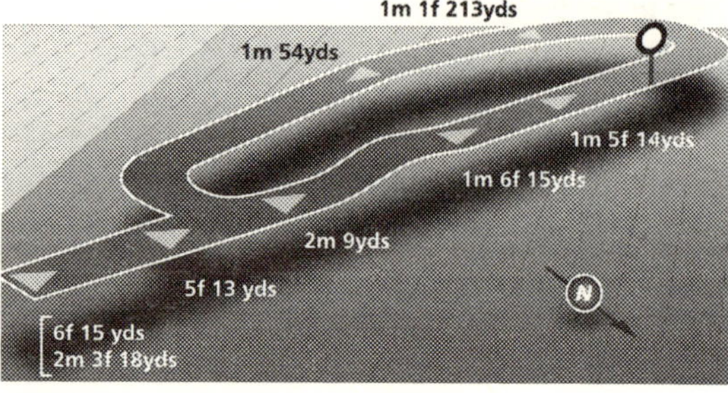

Pointers: Once again that wily old fox Sir Mark Prescott feasts at the top table at one of Britain's smaller venues. All his winners were booted home by Seb Sanders. Johnny Murtagh is well up in the jockeys' numbers chart while Darryll Holland's tactical prowess has proved an asset.

Time Test standard times

5f13yds	58.7	1m6f15yds	2min58.5
6f15yds	1min11.3	2m9yds	3min24.3
1m54yds	1min40.3	2m2f18yds	3min52.3
1m1f213yds	2min2.4		

Favourites

2-y-o	27.8%	-£7.26
3-y-o+	27.9%	-£12.49
Overall	27.9%	-£19.75

Trainers	*Wins-Runs*	*%*	*2yo*	*3yo+*	*£1 level stks*
N Callaghan	3-5	60.0	3-4	0-1	+12.60
Mrs A Perrett	3-6	50.0	0-1	3-5	+15.50
Sir M Prescott	4-9	44.4	1-2	3-7	+4.55
J Spearing	3-8	37.5	1-2	2-6	+18.83
M Jarvis	3-10	30.0	1-5	2-5	+11.41
P Hiatt	3-11	27.3	0-0	3-11	+18.33
J Fanshawe	4-16	25.0	0-0	4-16	+3.05
M Johnston	4-16	25.0	3-8	1-8	+4.47
P Harris	4-17	23.5	1-2	3-15	-4.87
D Ivory	3-13	23.1	0-1	3-12	+38.00
H Candy	3-14	21.4	1-3	2-11	+12.63
B McMahon	4-23	17.4	0-10	4-13	+11.25

Jockeys	*Wins-Rides*	*%*	*£1 level stks*	*Best Trainer*	*W-R*
M Howard	3-8	37.5	+43.00	D Ivory	3-7
J P Murtagh	6-22	27.3	+5.37	J Fanshawe	2-6
R Miles	3-13	23.1	+6.20	R J Price	1-1
D Allan	3-13	23.1	+8.00	S C Williams	1-1
T Quinn	4-18	22.2	+4.25	H Cecil	1-1
B Swarbrick	3-16	18.8	+22.00	W Brisbourne	2-9
S Sanders	11-61	18.0	+24.43	Sir M Prescott	4-8
D Holland	4-23	17.4	+18.00	G A Butler	1-1
L Dettori	4-25	16.0	-11.76	S bin Suroor	2-8
I Mongan	4-29	13.8	-8.50	P Harris	2-3
K Fallon	4-32	12.5	+0.38	Sir M Stoute	2-5
S Drowne	4-35	11.4	+22.33	J Spearing	1-1

33 Ropergate, Pontefract,
WF8 1LE. Tel 01977 703 224

PONTEFRACT

How to get there – Road: M62 Jctn 32, then A539 Rail: Pontefract Monkhill or Pontefract Baghill from Leeds

Features: LH, undulating, sharp home turn, last half-mile is all uphill

2005 Flat fixtures: Apr 18, 27, May 27, June 6, 19, 27, July 5, 15, 24, Aug 3, 14, Sep 15, 22, Oct 3, 17

Pointers: A good strike-rate from Sir Michael Stoute from a meaningful quota of runners. Kieren Fallon's figures look tasty particularly when riding for his boss.

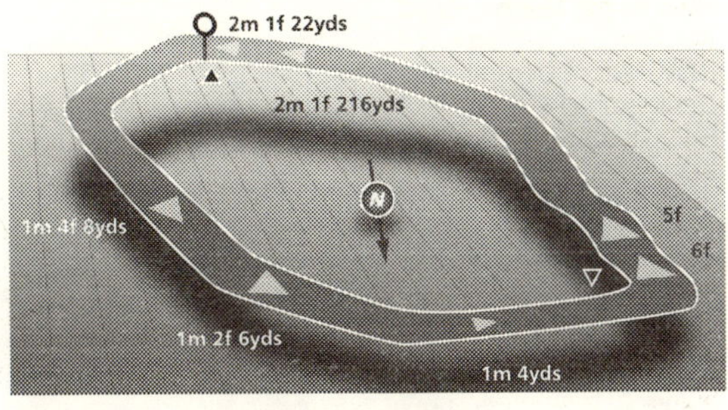

Time Test standard times

5f	1min1.3	1m4f8yds	2min34.5
6f	1min14.2	2m1f22yds	3min42.2
1m4yds	1min41.8	2m1f216yds	3min52
1m2f6yds	2min7.2	2m5f122yds	4min48

Favourites

2-y-o	41.4%	-£0.50
3-y-o+	26.7%	-£50.52
Overall	29.8%	-£51.02

Trainers	Wins-Runs	%	2yo	3yo+	£1 level stks
T Mills	3-6	50.0	0-0	3-6	+15.00
P Cole	10-24	41.7	5-8	5-16	+3.35
H Cecil	8-23	34.8	0-1	8-22	+9.87
Sir M Stoute	18-58	31.0	4-9	14-49	+14.59
M Jarvis	9-30	30.0	3-9	6-21	+12.13
W Haggas	11-42	26.2	5-14	6-28	+5.35
R Charlton	3-12	25.0	1-2	2-10	+2.29
Mrs A Perrett	3-12	25.0	0-1	3-11	-4.00
J Noseda	3-12	25.0	1-4	2-8	+6.36
L Cumani	6-25	24.0	0-3	6-22	+2.26
J Toller	3-13	23.1	0-0	3-13	+22.50
J Dunlop	11-51	21.6	4-9	7-42	-10.44

Jockeys	Wins-Rides	%	£1 level stks	Best Trainer	W-R
L Dettori	9-26	34.6	+9.12	J Gosden	2-3
K Fallon	37-122	30.3	+26.51	Sir M Stoute	9-23
T Quinn	16-55	29.1	+54.42	H Cecil	3-7
P Robinson	16-67	23.9	+29.63	M Jarvis	8-19
M Hills	9-38	23.7	-6.83	B Hills	6-28
J P Spencer	12-55	21.8	+11.86	Mrs J Ramsden	3-4
A Clark	5-23	21.7	+32.00	M Dods	3-9
R Hughes	4-19	21.1	-7.17	B Hills	2-6
G Faulkner	3-16	18.8	+62.50	K R Burke	1-1
R Hills	6-35	17.1	-18.48	Sir M Stoute	2-3
D O'Neill	4-24	16.7	-3.00	R Hannon	2-8
J Fortune	7-43	16.3	-1.79	I Balding	2-2

REDCAR

Redcar, Teesside,
TS10 2BY. Tel 01642 484 068

How to get there – Road: A1, A168, A19, then A174 Rail: Redcar Central from Darlington
Features: LH, flat, galloping
2005 Flat fixtures: Apr 28, May 9, 17, 30, 31, June 7, 17, 18, July 17, Aug 6, 7, 20, Sep 1, 12, 21, Oct 1, 14,
Pointers: There's only one trainer to recommend here and that is Jeremy Noseda, who scores with exactly half of the runners he brings. Be wary of Tim Easterby's horses. Very few of them score and they often start short in the betting. Frankie Dettori doesn't come up here very often, but when he does he makes it pay 50% of the time.

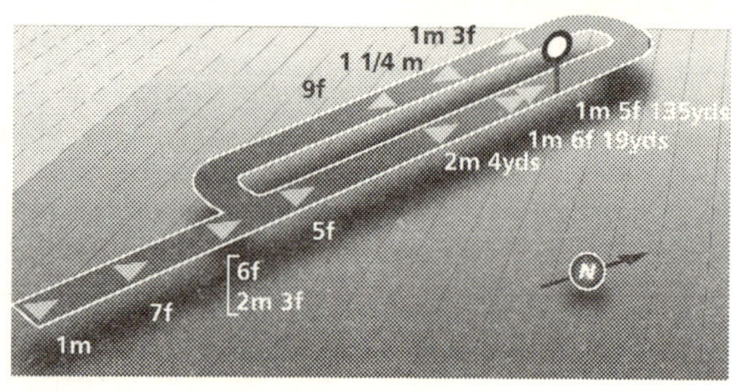

Time Test standard times

5f	56.7	1m3f	2min17
6f	1min9.4	1m4f	2min30
7f	1min22	1m5f135yds	2min54.7
1m	1min34.7	1m6f19yds	3min0
1m1f	1min49.3	2m4yds	3min25
1m2f	2min2.6	2m3f	4min5.3

Favourites

2-y-o	40.3%	-£18.89
3-y-o+	24.9%	-£92.12
Overall	28.7%	-£111.01

Trainers	*Wins-Runs*	*%*	*2yo*	*3yo+*	*£1 level stks*
D Loder	6-12	50.0	5-9	1-3	+0.02
J Noseda	12-24	50.0	3-6	9-18	+20.74
M Ryan	3-8	37.5	1-1	2-7	+6.07
J Gosden	10-33	30.3	2-13	8-20	-4.48
R Charlton	3-10	30.0	1-5	2-5	-0.49
Sir M Stoute	5-18	27.8	2-6	3-12	+15.23
P L Gilligan	3-11	27.3	1-1	2-10	+15.38
L Cumani	7-26	26.9	1-5	6-21	+21.38
M Bell	8-33	24.2	5-14	3-19	-3.55
N Callaghan	3-13	23.1	1-7	2-6	+2.25
H Cecil	3-13	23.1	1-3	2-10	-5.03
J Hills	3-13	23.1	0-2	3-11	+0.63

Jockeys	*Wins-Rides*	*%*	*£1 level stks*	*Best Trainer*	*W-R*
L Dettori	3-6	50.0	+7.08	P D'Arcy	1-1
T Quinn	4-12	33.3	+9.97	H Cecil	2-3
D Corby	3-11	27.3	+9.25	M Channon	2-2
J Weaver	7-27	25.9	-3.18	J Noseda	4-7
K McEvoy	3-13	23.1	-0.27	S bin Suroor	2-5
M Henry	3-13	23.1	-1.05	M Jarvis	2-2
J Mackay	5-22	22.7	-0.87	M Bell	4-5
S Drowne	4-19	21.1	+7.12	R Charlton	2-6
J Egan	5-24	20.8	-1.88	Mrs H Dalton	1-1
N Callan	11-55	20.0	+6.83	K Ryan	3-14
K Darley	29-148	19.6	-20.59	G A Butler	4-6
I Mongan	6-31	19.4	+59.50	N Littmoden	3-10

77 North Street, Ripon, N Yorkshire
HG4 1DS. Tel 01765 602 156 or 01765 603 696

RIPON

How to get there – Road: A1, then B6265
Rail: Harrogate, bus to Ripon centre, 1m walk
Features: RH, sharp
2005 Flat fixtures: Apr 14, 23, May 15, 24, 25, June 9, 11, 20, July 4, 16, Aug 1, 13, 29, 30, Sep 24
Pointers: Mark Brisbourne has a terrific record when sending runners here, with a £66 level stakes profit. Barry Hills and Paul Cole are also worthy of note, when making the long trip up. Female star Lisa Jones has done well amongst the 'jocks' particularly when teaming up with David Chapman.

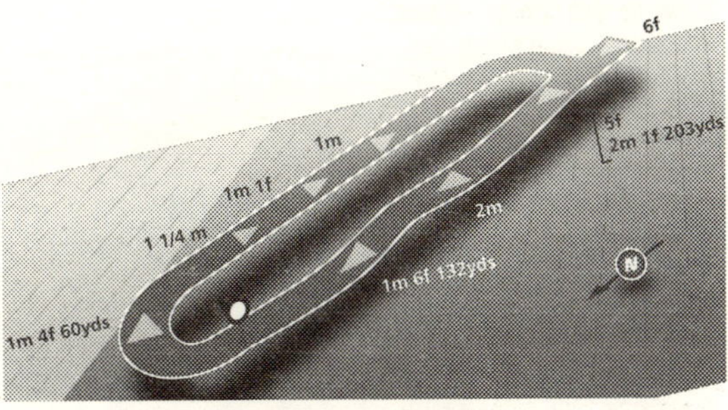

Time Test standard times

5f	57.8	1m2f	2min3.3
6f	1min10.6	1m4f60yds	2min34
1m	1min37.8	2m	3min27
1m1f	1min50.8	2m1f203yds	3min52

Favourites

2-y-o	40.4%	-£2.95
3-y-o+	32.9%	-£17.83
Overall	34.6%	-£20.79

Trainers	*Wins-Runs*	*%*	*2yo*	*3yo+*	*£1 level stks*
Sir M Prescott	4-7	57.1	2-3	2-4	+9.75
H Cecil	9-21	42.9	0-0	9-21	+7.75
M Jarvis	6-17	35.3	2-2	4-15	-2.03
M Tregoning	5-15	33.3	1-2	4-13	+3.76
B Hills	22-74	29.7	5-9	17-65	+12.71
P Cole	5-17	29.4	0-2	5-15	+15.81
J Dunlop	17-64	26.6	3-6	14-58	-15.19
Sir M Stoute	9-37	24.3	1-1	8-36	-18.88
J Gosden	6-26	23.1	0-2	6-24	-6.06
C Brittain	4-18	22.2	0-4	4-14	+16.50
G Wragg	3-14	21.4	0-0	3-14	+5.00
W Brisbourne	6-34	17.6	0-0	6-34	+66.00

Jockeys	*Wins-Rides*	*%*	*£1 level stks*	*Best Trainer*	*W-R*
P Robinson	13-34	38.2	+39.01	M Jarvis	5-11
T Quinn	9-33	27.3	+0.08	H Cecil	6-8
M Hills	5-20	25.0	+4.80	B Hills	2-15
R Hills	6-24	25.0	-4.30	J Dunlop	2-7
W Ryan	5-23	21.7	+5.50	H Cecil	3-10
Lisa Jones	3-15	20.0	+61.00	D Chapman	2-4
J Fortune	6-30	20.0	+1.55	J Gosden	3-6
J P Spencer	8-42	19.0	+0.63	L Cumani	2-5
S Sanders	10-55	18.2	-12.01	J Fanshawe	2-2
Alex Greaves	5-28	17.9	+2.50	D Nicholls	5-27
D Holland	10-56	17.9	-7.04	B Hills	2-2
R Havlin	3-17	17.6	-2.06	J Gosden	2-10

SALISBURY

Netherhampton, Salisbury, Wilts, SP2 8PN. Tel 01722 326 461

How to get there – Road: 2m west of Salisbury on A3094
Rail: Salisbury, bus
Features: RH, uphill finish
2005 Flat fixtures: May 1, 12, June 7, 12, 22, 23, July 9, 23, Aug 10, 11, 19, 26, Sep 1, 13, 28, Oct 8
Pointers: Respectable figures indeed from Michael Jarvis and even better ones from his stable jockey Philip Robinson who wins on 35.3% of his rides here. The combination of Johnny Murtagh and Amanda Perrett is a potent one.

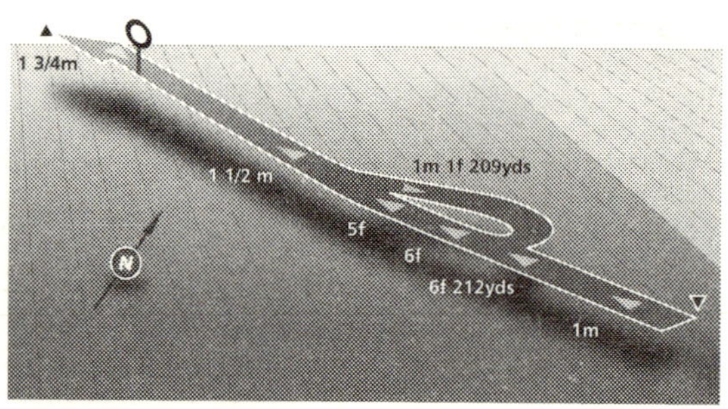

Time Test standard times

5f	59.6	1m1f209yds	2min5
6f	1min12	1m4f	2min32
6f212yds	1min25.2	1m6f15yds	2min58.3
1m	1min39.2		

Favourites

2-y-o	35.6%	-£6.37
3-y-o+	28.0%	-£52.89
Overall	30.1%	-£59.25

Trainers	Wins-Runs	%	2yo	3yo+	£1 level stks
M Jarvis	6-14	42.9	4-5	2-9	+4.23
P L Gilligan	3-8	37.5	0-0	3-8	+28.50
W Haggas	6-17	35.3	2-2	4-15	+20.88
S bin Suroor	7-22	31.8	3-8	4-14	+1.90
G Wragg	6-19	31.6	0-2	6-17	+10.00
J Fanshawe	8-28	28.6	1-6	7-22	+11.75
J Gosden	25-105	23.8	9-42	16-63	-2.58
K Ivory	3-13	23.1	0-2	3-11	+3.50
A Reid	4-18	22.2	0-4	4-14	+16.75
R Charlton	18-84	21.4	2-21	16-63	-0.83
R Guest	3-17	17.6	0-2	3-15	+1.50
C Brittain	3-18	16.7	1-6	2-12	-7.25

Jockeys	Wins-Rides	%	£1 level stks	Best Trainer	W-R
P Robinson	6-17	35.3	+2.23	M Jarvis	5-7
J Murtagh	3-9	33.3	+7.12	Mrs A Perrett	2-5
L Dettori	14-56	25.0	-12.95	S bin Suroor	7-16
K Fallon	20-96	20.8	-0.45	Sir M Stoute	4-20
R Hughes	37-188	19.7	+0.97	R Hannon	12-69
R Hills	13-67	19.4	+3.28	M Tregoning	4-15
Hayley Turner	3-18	16.7	+26.00	J King	3-7
D Holland	12-72	16.7	-4.50	G Wragg	5-7
M Hills	9-58	15.5	-15.49	B Hills	6-35
Craig Williams	4-26	15.4	-1.00	M Channon	4-20
J Fortune	22-143	15.4	-18.87	J Gosden	11-31
J Egan	8-53	15.1	+19.50	S Kirk	3-9

SANDOWN

Esher, Surrey, KT10 9AJ.
Tel 01372 463 072 or 01372 464 348

How to get there – Road: M25 Jctn 10 then A3
Rail: Esher from Waterloo
Features: RH, last 7f uphill
2004 Flat fixtures: Apr 22, 23 (mixed), May 30, 31, June 2, 10, 11, July 1, 2, 20, 21, Aug 10, 11, 19, 20, Sep 9, 14
Pointers: A real Grade 1 track where only the best win races so it's no surprise to see names like John Gosden, David Loder and Geoff Wragg on the leaderboard. Saeed Bin Suroor, who has won the Eclipse four times (last year with Refuse To Bend) is notable for his absence. Britain's two top riders, Frankie Dettori and Richard Hills, score heaviest.

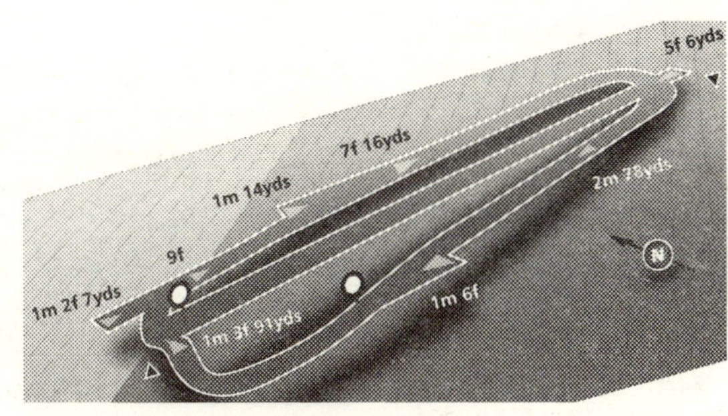

Time Test standard times

5f6yds	59.2	1m2f7yds	2min5
7f16yds	1min27	1m3f91yds	2min21.7
1m14yds	1min40	1m6f	2min57
1m1f	1min52	2m78yds	3min30.4

Favourites

2-y-o	37.0%	-£4.64
3-y-o+	29.7%	-£14.67
Overall	31.3%	-£19.31

Trainers	Wins-Runs	%	2yo	3yo+	£1 level stks
J J Quinn	4-8	50.0	1-1	3-7	+13.88
Sir M Prescott	6-19	31.6	3-6	3-13	+7.50
N Callaghan	7-24	29.2	3-7	4-17	+14.00
S C Williams	6-21	28.6	0-0	6-21	+37.25
R J Price	3-11	27.3	0-0	3-11	+15.00
D Loder	7-27	25.9	6-17	1-10	+0.78
J Given	3-12	25.0	0-1	3-11	+16.50
R Fahey	3-12	25.0	0-1	3-11	0.00
J Gosden	21-87	24.1	7-28	14-59	-7.53
G Wragg	7-30	23.3	0-1	7-29	+2.08
H Cecil	8-36	22.2	0-5	8-31	-13.26
E Vaughan	11-51	21.6	0-1	11-50	+13.79

Jockeys	Wins-Rides	%	£1 level stks	Best Trainer	W-R
R Hills	25-107	23.4	+21.61	J Gosden	6-11
L Dettori	28-123	22.8	+37.40	D Loder	4-14
K Dalgleish	5-22	22.7	-0.77	M Johnston	4-17
W Supple	11-49	22.4	+42.25	J Gosden	2-3
G Carter	6-33	18.2	+62.00	Miss D Mountain	2-3
K Fallon	36-209	17.2	-33.68	Sir M Stoute	13-57
B Doyle	4-24	16.7	+9.44	L Cottrell	1-1
M Roberts	8-48	16.7	-2.63	A Stewart	4-9
D Holland	21-130	16.2	-15.25	G Wragg	5-17
J Fanning	4-26	15.4	-5.59	M Johnston	3-18
P Robinson	16-105	15.2	+50.98	M Jarvis	9-43
J P Spencer	9-60	15.0	+1.25	L Cumani	2-5

SOUTHWELL

Rolleston, Newark,
Notts, NG25 0TS.
Tel 01636 814 481

How to get there – Road: A1 to Newark, then A617 or M1 to Nottingham then A612; Rail: Rolleston

Features: LH fibresand, sharp

2005 Flat fixtures: Apr 4, 5, 8, 11, 19, 21, 25, 26, 28, May 18, June 1, 9, 16, July 1, 25, Oct 1, 6, 11, 13, 18, 29, 5, 8, 12, Nov 15, 16, 19, 21, 22, 28, 29, Dec 4, 6, 10, 12, 13, 15, 18, 20, 22, 27

Pointers: Of the bigger trainers to come here, Sir Mark Prescott and James Fanshawe have respectable statistics. Karl Burke is of a similar mould. Neil Callan has ridden twice as many winners here as his nearest pursuer while Jamie Spencer is top-notch on the sand.

NB: Due to the shortage of meetings on the turf course, our trainer, jockey and favourite stats relate to AW racing only.

Time Test standard times

5f	57.7	1m4f	2min34
6f	1min13.5	1m5f	2min47.4
7f	1min27	1m6f	3min1.7
1m	1min40	2m	3min30
1m3f	2min21.6	2m2f	3min58

Favourites

2-y-o	46.2%	+£9.32
3-y-o+	30.2%	-£44.63
Overall	32.0%	-£35.31

Trainers	Wins-Runs	%	2yo	3yo+	£1 level stks
M Ryan	3-5	60.0	0-0	3-5	+42.50
J Fanshawe	3-6	50.0	0-1	3-5	+2.51
Sir M Prescott	7-15	46.7	2-4	5-11	+1.32
M Bell	4-11	36.4	0-1	4-10	+5.75
S C Williams	6-17	35.3	0-2	6-15	+30.02
B Pearce	4-13	30.8	0-0	4-13	+8.25
W Jarvis	3-12	25.0	2-2	1-10	+0.23
Miss J Feilden	5-21	23.8	0-1	5-20	-4.95
T Barron	19-81	23.5	3-9	16-72	+1.70
K R Burke	16-69	23.2	6-14	10-55	+15.65
A Reid	4-18	22.2	0-0	4-18	-2.22
W G M Turner	4-19	21.1	1-8	3-11	-4.93

Jockeys	Wins-Rides	%	£1 level stks	Best Trainer	W-R
J P Spencer	6-13	46.2	+0.20	T Barron	2-2
M Dwyer	3-9	33.3	-0.90	C Egerton	1-1
R Price	4-14	28.6	+49.00	M Ryan	2-2
S Sanders	9-33	27.3	-9.44	Sir M Prescott	4-5
C Haddon	5-19	26.3	+13.57	W G M Turner	2-8
D Mernagh	10-38	26.3	+40.63	T Barron	9-28
B Reilly	12-53	22.6	+29.67	Miss J Feilden	5-12
N Callan	25-128	19.5	+7.30	K Ryan	11-44
Rory Moore	7-37	18.9	-4.41	P Haslam	6-19
O Urbina	3-16	18.8	-1.88	J Fanshawe	2-4
J D O'Reilly	3-16	18.8	+4.00	J O'Reilly	3-15
G Faulkner	6-33	18.2	+16.00	P Haslam	3-17

Station Road, Thirsk, N Yorkshire, YO7 1QL. Tel 01845 522 276

THIRSK

How to get there – Road: A61 from A1 in the west or A19 in the east
Rail: Thirsk, 10 min walk
Features: LH, sharp, tight turns, drains well
2005 Flat fixtures: Apr 15, 16, 30, May 7, 14, 23, June 3, 13, 23, July 29, 30, Aug 8, 26, Sep 3, 13,
Pointers: You won't go far wrong backing Saeed bin Suroor's horses though the profits may be on the thin side of slim. Kerrin McEvoy did well on his first year riding the track while Kevin Darley, although riding plenty of winners here, does so at a loss.

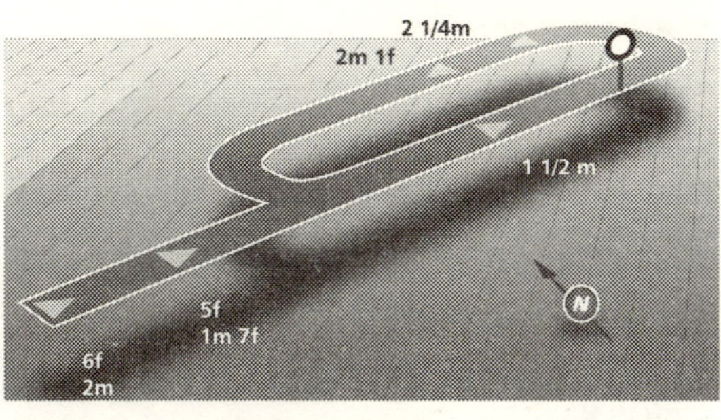

Time Test standard times

5f	57.4	1m	1min35.8
6f	1min9.5	1m4f	2min30
7f	1min23	2m	3min22.6

Favourites

2-y-o	39.3%	-£5.62
3-y-o+	32.4%	+£2.76
Overall	34.1%	-£2.87

Trainers	*Wins-Runs*	*%*	*2yo*	*3yo+*	*£1 level stks*
S bin Suroor	4-6	66.7	1-2	3-4	+3.28
M Tregoning	7-13	53.8	0-0	7-13	+1.31
E Dunlop	8-18	44.4	1-3	7-15	+20.15
J Dunlop	11-25	44.0	0-4	11-21	+8.29
G Wragg	3-7	42.9	0-0	3-7	+1.88
J Toller	4-10	40.0	0-0	4-10	+12.00
B Meehan	4-11	36.4	2-5	2-6	+9.23
H Cecil	5-15	33.3	0-1	5-14	+1.91
J Fanshawe	6-21	28.6	0-2	6-19	-0.82
B Hills	7-25	28.0	1-2	6-23	-1.26
Sir M Stoute	8-29	27.6	0-2	8-27	+5.70
A Balding	3-11	27.3	3-5	0-6	-1.25

Jockeys	*Wins-Rides*	*%*	*£1 level stks*	*Best Trainer*	*W-R*
O Urbina	4-10	40.0	+0.39	J Fanshawe	4-6
K McEvoy	3-8	37.5	+3.50	S bin Suroor	1-2
S Whitworth	3-8	37.5	+1.75	J Toller	2-4
D Sweeney	4-11	36.4	+13.37	K R Burke	2-3
M Hills	3-9	33.3	-2.34	B Hills	3-3
R Hills	4-12	33.3	+8.03	S bin Suroor	1-1
D Corby	3-10	30.0	+12.67	J A Osborne	1-1
T Quinn	4-14	28.6	-2.80	H Cecil	2-3
M Henry	3-11	27.3	-3.70	J Dunlop	2-2
P Robinson	3-11	27.3	+3.75	M Jarvis	2-5
B Doyle	4-15	26.7	+0.26	B Meehan	1-1
K Darley	25-112	22.3	-15.03	T Easterby	5-21

WARWICK

6 Hampton Street, Warwick
CV34 6HN. Tel 01926 491 553

How to get there – Road: M40 Jctn 14, A429
Rail: Warwick

Features: LH, sharp turns

2005 Flat fixtures: Apr 26, May 2, June 13, 18, 19, July 1, 7, 15, Aug 29, Sep 5, 17, Oct 8

Pointers: Peter Chapple-Hyam, being a keen Warwickshire supporter, passes through here to saddle a few winners. He has lost none of his gift and should be kept firmly on the right side. Ryan Moore has a good record for Ian Wood.

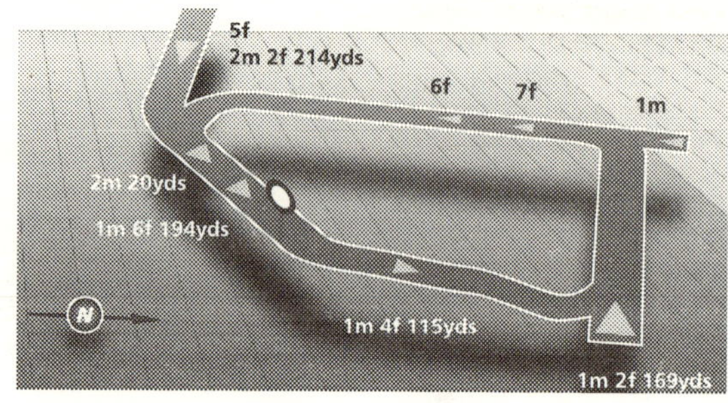

Time Test standard times

5f	58	1m4f115yds	2min34.6
5f110yds	1min4	1m6f194yds	3min6
6f	1min10.6	2m20yds	3min24
7f	1min22.2	2m2f214yds	3min58
1m	1min35.3	2m3f13yds	4min0
1m2f169yds	2min12		

Favourites

2-y-o	43.1%	+£5.68
3-y-o+	27.7%	-£55.06
Overall	31.1%	-£49.38

Trainers	*Wins-Runs*	*%*	*2yo*	*3yo+*	*£1 level stks*
N Callaghan	3-6	50.0	3-6	0-0	+10.50
T Watson	3-8	37.5	0-1	3-7	+11.50
D Loder	4-11	36.4	3-6	1-5	+12.38
Sir M Stoute	11-31	35.5	2-12	9-19	+22.22
P Chapple-Hyam	3-9	33.3	2-6	1-3	-2.35
M Johnston	10-37	27.0	3-10	7-27	+14.92
A Reid	4-16	25.0	0-0	4-16	+19.00
H Cecil	3-13	23.1	0-1	3-12	-1.72
M Pipe	5-22	22.7	0-2	5-20	-1.02
L Cottrell	4-18	22.2	0-2	4-16	+16.00
N Graham	3-14	21.4	0-2	3-12	+11.00
J Dunlop	8-38	21.1	3-16	5-22	-14.65

Jockeys	*Wins-Rides*	*%*	*£1 level stks*	*Best Trainer*	*W-R*
N Mackay	4-10	40.0	+5.88	M Pipe	2-2
K Fallon	8-27	29.6	-0.46	D Cantillon	1-1
L Dettori	3-11	27.3	+7.00	C Brittain	2-2
R L Moore	9-33	27.3	+43.88	I A Wood	2-3
R Miles	4-16	25.0	+20.50	A Reid	1-1
Pat Eddery	9-40	22.5	+14.86	B Meehan	2-8
J F McDonald	5-23	21.7	+18.75	B Meehan	2-3
J Fanning	7-33	21.2	+31.00	M Johnston	3-12
T Quinn	7-33	21.2	+0.91	N Littmoden	1-1
Craig Williams	4-19	21.1	+12.00	A Berry	1-1
M Hills	15-73	20.5	+32.76	B Hills	8-39
F Lynch	3-15	20.0	+2.50	Sir M Stoute	2-6

WINDSOR

Maidenhead Road, Windsor,
Berkshire SL4 5JJ.
Tel 01753 498 400

How to get there – Road: M4 Jctn 6, A355, A308 Rail: Windsor Central from Paddington or Windsor Riverside from Waterloo
Features: Figure of eight, flat, easy turns, straight almost 5f long
2005 Flat fixtures: Apr 18, 25, 9, 16, 23, June 6, 13, 20, 25, 26, 27, July 4, 11, 18, 25, Aug 1, 6, 8, 15, 22, 27, Oct 3, 10, 17
Pointers: A competitive track with lots of large fields so well done to Middleham man Karl Burke for his four winners from 15 contenders. 'Bad' Manners had a particularly good time of it here last season which explains his prominence in the list.

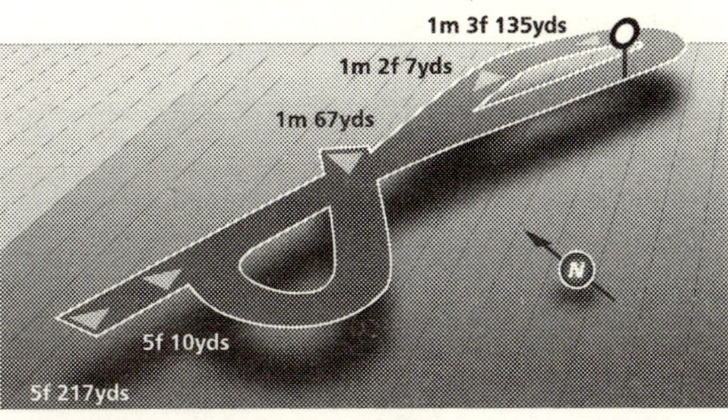

Time Test standard times

5f10yds	59	1m2f7yds	2min3.6
5f217yds	1min10.2	1m3f135yds	2min22.6
1m67yds	1min41.6		

Favourites

2-y-o	36.4%	+£1.04
3-y-o+	26.7%	-£39.06
Overall	29.1%	-£38.03

Trainers	*Wins-Runs*	*%*	*2yo*	*3yo+*	*£1 level stks*
H Manners	3-6	50.0	0-0	3-6	+26.00
R Charlton	4-13	30.8	2-2	2-11	+17.25
K R Burke	4-15	26.7	1-2	3-13	+18.00
J Noseda	4-19	21.1	2-6	2-13	-11.11
D Elsworth	3-17	17.6	2-4	1-13	-2.75
M Bell	5-30	16.7	1-12	4-18	+16.00
Mrs A Perrett	3-19	15.8	0-2	3-17	-3.92
P Cole	3-20	15.0	1-6	2-14	-1.75
Sir M Stoute	4-28	14.3	0-5	4-23	-18.73
P Evans	6-44	13.6	1-10	5-34	+6.00
H Candy	3-23	13.0	1-5	2-18	-10.65
S Kirk	3-24	12.5	1-9	2-15	+9.37

Jockeys	*Wins-Rides*	*%*	*£1 level stks*	*Best Trainer*	*W-R*
F Norton	3-13	23.1	+17.00	B Gubby	2-2
L Dettori	10-56	17.9	-9.79	J Jenkins	2-4
K Fallon	9-52	17.3	-13.67	Sir M Stoute	3-14
Hayley Turner	3-19	15.8	+33.50	M Bell	2-3
R L Moore	13-92	14.1	-22.13	R Hannon	6-29
T Quinn	8-57	14.0	+52.75	P Cole	2-7
F P Ferris	3-22	13.6	+10.00	H Manners	3-4
S Drowne	11-82	13.4	+23.08	R Charlton	4-8
R Hughes	5-44	11.4	-1.37	R Hannon	3-22
J Quinn	4-37	10.8	+40.25	J Dunlop	1-1
P Robinson	3-29	10.3	-9.42	M Jarvis	2-11
J Fortune	5-50	10.0	-35.06	J Gosden	2-11

WOLVES

Dunstall Park, Gorsebrook Road, Wolverhampton, West Midlands, WV6 0PE. Tel 08702 202 442

How to get there – Road: of A449, close to M6, M42 and M54
Rail: Wolverhampton, bus
Features: LH, fibresand, very sharp
2005 Flat fixtures: Apr 2, 4, 15, 16, 18, 22, 23, 25, May 9, 16, 27, 3, 10, 24, 27, July 5, 8, 11, 22, Aug 8, 18, 19, 22, Sep 3, 10, 17, 26, Oct 1, 10, 22, 24, 29, 31, Nov 5, 7, 9, 11, 12, 14, 19, 25, 26, 28, 30, Dec 2, 3, 5, 9, 10, 12, 16, 19, 21, 26, 28, 31
Pointers: Mick Channon runners warrant close attention according to the stats, as do Ralph Beckett's. Michael Fenton rides the course well, and often teams up successfully with Gay Kelleway.

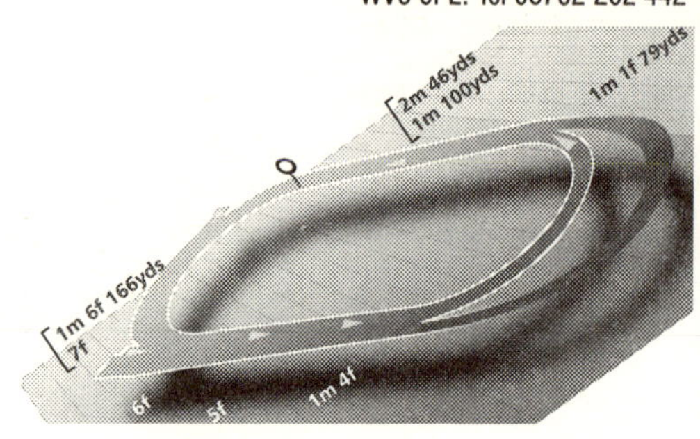

Time Test standard times

5f	1min0.3	1m1f79yds	1min57.6
6f	1min13.2	1m4f	2min35.3
7f	1min27	1m6f166yds	3min11.7
1m100yds	1min46.8	2m46yds	3min36.7

Favourites

2-y-o	36.7%	+£8.31
3-y-o+	27.2%	-£65.22
Overall	28.3%	-£56.91

Trainers	*Wins-Runs*	*%*	*2yo*	*3yo+*	*£1 level stks*
B Pearce	3-6	50.0	0-0	3-6	+18.50
R Beckett	3-8	37.5	2-4	1-4	+24.10
W Jarvis	3-9	33.3	0-1	3-8	+6.00
E Dunlop	4-13	30.8	2-5	2-8	+5.42
B Hills	8-26	30.8	1-1	7-25	+15.66
R J Price	3-10	30.0	0-0	3-10	+13.50
P Harris	4-14	28.6	1-4	3-10	+27.75
M Usher	4-14	28.6	1-2	3-12	+13.25
R Fisher	3-11	27.3	1-2	2-9	+14.00
D Bridgwater	5-20	25.0	0-0	5-20	-1.77
M Channon	6-24	25.0	1-12	5-12	+27.00
J Jay	4-17	23.5	1-2	3-15	-1.50

Jockeys	*Wins-Rides*	*%*	*£1 level stks*	*Best Trainer*	*W-R*
L Newnes	5-9	55.6	+12.25	M Usher	3-3
W Supple	4-9	44.4	+9.63	D Loder	1-1
G Faulkner	8-18	44.4	+25.00	P Haslam	4-9
K Fallon	10-35	28.6	+8.13	N Littmoden	2-3
L Dettori	4-15	26.7	-0.25	J A Osborne	2-2
D Fox	4-16	25.0	+11.25	C Dwyer	3-7
B Reilly	8-33	24.2	+22.82	Miss J Feilden	2-5
E Ahern	18-80	22.5	-0.23	G A Butler	3-7
D Holland	12-59	20.3	-13.96	R Brotherton	2-4
D Mernagh	3-16	18.8	+2.50	T Barron	2-11
M Dwyer	4-22	18.2	-2.06	B Hills	2-4
M Fenton	20-110	18.2	+46.79	Miss G Kelleway	8-39

Jellicoe Road, North Denes, Great Yarmouth, Norfolk, NR30 4AU. Tel 01493 842 527

How to get there – Road: A47 to end, A1064
Rail: Great Yarmouth, bus
Features: LH, flat, drains well
2005 Flat fixtures: Apr 4, 26, May 10, June 1, 9, 30, July 19, 25, Aug 3, 4, 10, 15, 23, 28, Sep 13, 14, 15, Oct 18, 25, Nov 4
Pointers: Very few non-Newmarket trainers get a look in here. The likes of Loder, Callaghan, Stoute and Bin Suroor bring plenty of two-year-old debutants to the party. The top jockey, both in terms of numbers and strike-rate, is the peerless Kieren Fallon.

YARMOUTH

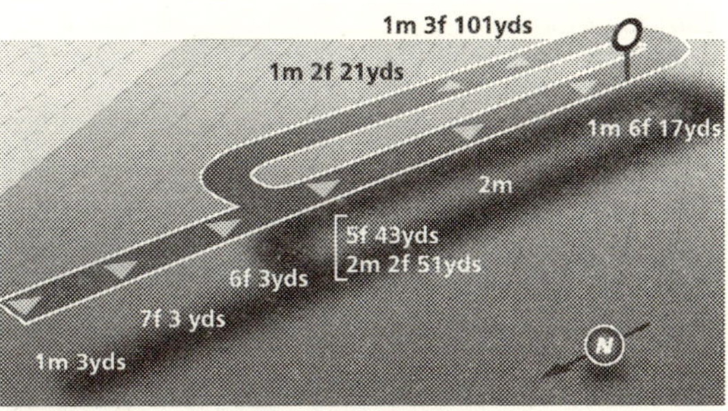

Time Test standard times

5f43yds	1min0.4	1m3f101yds	2min23
6f3yds	1min10.7	1m6f17yds	2min58
7f3yds	1min23	2m	3min25
1m3yds	1min35.5	2m1f170yds	3min48
1m2f21yds	2min3.3	2m2f51yds	3min54

Favourites

2-y-o	35.9%	-£7.71
3-y-o+	26.6%	+£5.40
Overall	29.1%	-£2.31

Trainers	*Wins-Runs*	*%*	*2yo*	*3yo+*	*£1 level stks*
Sir M Prescott	4-10	40.0	1-3	3-7	+5.75
H Cecil	3-8	37.5	0-2	3-6	+11.50
J Eustace	3-9	33.3	1-5	2-4	+16.33
M Jarvis	3-11	27.3	1-6	2-5	+3.33
J Noseda	3-12	25.0	2-9	1-3	+0.17
V Smith	3-12	25.0	1-1	2-11	-0.46
N Callaghan	4-16	25.0	3-10	1-6	-3.13
Sir M Stoute	4-17	23.5	3-12	1-5	+9.21
S bin Suroor	4-19	21.1	4-14	0-5	+4.75
S C Williams	4-19	21.1	0-3	4-16	+6.50
J R Best	3-15	20.0	0-2	3-13	+18.00
W Brisbourne	3-17	17.6	0-3	3-14	+9.00

Jockeys	*Wins-Rides*	*%*	*£1 level stks*	*Best Trainer*	*W-R*
K Fallon	9-33	27.3	-5.40	Sir M Stoute	3-6
L Dettori	8-30	26.7	+5.88	N Callaghan	2-2
N Callan	6-24	25.0	+46.50	J C Poulton	2-7
E Ahern	5-23	21.7	+12.17	J Noseda	3-9
F P Ferris	3-14	21.4	+20.50	Mrs S Lamyman	1-2
K Darley	3-18	16.7	+13.50	C Wall	1-1
S Sanders	7-43	16.3	-13.25	Sir M Prescott	3-8
O Urbina	4-25	16.0	+19.75	J Jay	2-2
T E Durcan	3-22	13.6	+15.00	M Channon	2-12
T P Queally	7-54	13.0	-2.67	M G Quinlan	2-5
Lisa Jones	4-32	12.5	+31.00	P Felgate	1-3
Hayley Turner	3-25	12.0	+87.50	Mrs C Dunnett	3-11

YORK

York, YO23 1EX.
Tel 01904 620 911

How to get there – Road: Course south of city on Knavesmire Road. From north, A1, A59 to York, northern bypass from A19 to A64. Otherwise, A64
Rail: York, bus
Features: LH, flat
2005 Flat fixtures:
May 11, 12, 13, June 14, 15, 16, 17, 18, July 8, 9, 22, 23, Aug 16, 17, 18, 27, 31, Aug 4, Sep 7, 8,
Pointers: You want a top trainer at this top track especially with the Royal meeting coming up in June. Who better to side with than Sir Michael Stoute and Saeed Bin Suroor. And don't forget Richard Fahey, who had a 33-1 winner with Sualda last season at the Ebor meeting, and is a man to be respected in handicaps.

Time Test standard times

5f	56.6	1m2f85yds	2min7
6f	1min9.2	1m3f195yds	2min26.4
6f214yds	1min21.7	1m5f194yds	2min53
7f202yds	1min35.4	1m7f195yds	3min20
1m205yds	1min48		

Favourites

2-y-o	35.5%	+£2.55
3-y-o+	25.0%	-£8.08
Overall	27.7%	-£5.53

Trainers	*Wins-Runs*	*%*	*2yo*	*3yo+*	*£1 level stks*
Sir M Stoute	5-16	31.3	0-1	5-15	+10.00
M Bell	3-11	27.3	3-5	0-6	+7.00
S bin Suroor	7-27	25.9	2-13	5-14	-11.60
B McMahon	4-17	23.5	3-9	1-8	+23.50
J Noseda	3-13	23.1	1-3	2-10	+29.44
P Evans	3-18	16.7	0-3	3-15	+18.00
L Cumani	3-18	16.7	0-0	3-18	-2.00
M Tompkins	3-22	13.6	1-7	2-15	+5.50
M Johnston	5-46	10.9	3-20	2-26	-13.00
R Fahey	4-44	9.1	0-10	4-34	+19.50
T Easterby	5-60	8.3	2-22	3-38	-19.50
D Nicholls	4-57	7.0	0-0	4-57	-21.25

Jockeys	*Wins-Rides*	*%*	*£1 level stks*	*Best Trainer*	*W-R*
A McCarthy	3-9	33.3	+3.30	M Bell	1-1
L Dettori	8-42	19.0	-15.10	S bin Suroor	6-19
D Holland	5-28	17.9	+15.00	J A Osborne	2-2
R L Moore	3-17	17.6	+39.50	M Magnusson	1-1
K Fallon	10-58	17.2	+17.58	Sir M Stoute	4-13
S Sanders	5-30	16.7	+56.75	J Spearing	1-1
R Hills	3-20	15.0	+11.00	M Johnston	2-7
D Allan	3-24	12.5	+25.00	T Easterby	2-17
K Darley	7-59	11.9	-22.63	W Jarvis	1-1
M Hills	3-26	11.5	-13.00	B Hills	2-20
J Fanning	4-35	11.4	+8.00	M Johnston	3-20
E Ahern	3-28	10.7	+2.94	J Noseda	2-8

ASCOT: No stands, and no course stats in this section as racing is off the agenda for now

IT'S AMAZING to me how many otherwise-savvy punters and journalists still don't take the draw into account when sizing up a Flat race.

However sure you may be that you've found the best horse in a race, the simple truth is that, until you've considered the possibility of a draw bias, you won't be able to assess the chances of any runner with any accuracy.

It's fundamental. On some courses, a particular draw is almost impossible to overcome, while on others there are draws that confer a tremendous advantage – if you don't know which is which, you'd be as well finding your winners with a pin.

What follows is my outline of the factors you need to consider when betting at Britain's many Flat tracks. During the turf season, I'll be updating these thoughts every week in *Racing & Football Outlook*. I'll also be pointing out horses that have run well from poor draws, so you can back them next time out and turn these biases into profit.

Course by course: your guide to Britain's draw biases

AYR (left-handed)

The draw only usually becomes a major issue in sprints at the Western Meeting, with fields rarely big enough the rest of the season for groups to form (high is almost always best in fields of 25 or fewer, whatever the ground).

Throughout the 90's high numbers were massively favoured in the Gold and Silver Cups, but this changed in 2003, with the far side (low) dominating both races. This was down to a fresh (hardly watered) strip of ground being unveiled down that side, but it was back to normality last season, with the stands' side best again.

The centre of the course looked much slower than the remainder last year, meaning low numbers were favoured in big fields over 7f50y and 1m.

Stalls: Usually go up the stands' side (high) in sprints, but occasionally go on the other side (normally in the run-up to the Western Meeting to preserve the ground).

Biases: High numbers are usually best in sprints whatever the ground, apart from the odd occasion when the stalls are placed up the far side (low).

Splits: Fields only usually split in the Silver and Gold Cups.

BATH (left)

The draw is basically of far less importance than the pace at which races are run.

In big fields, runners drawn low are often inclined to go off too fast to hold a rail position (the course turns left most of the way, including one major kink) and this can see hold-up horses drawn wide coming through late.

Conversely, in smaller fields containing little pace, up front and on the inside is often the place to be.

Stalls: Always go on the inside (low).

Splits: Fields always stick together, but soft ground (very rare) can see a split, with the outside rail (high) favoured.

BEVERLEY (right)

A high draw is essential on good to soft or faster ground over 5f and also on the round course, particularly in races of 7f100y and 1m100y.

In sprints, runners have to negotiate a right-handed jink not long after the start and it seems harder here than at probably any course for runners drawn low to get over to the favoured rail (there's also a camber).

The course management experimented with moving stalls to the stands' side over 5f in 2002 (unsuccessfully, as it led to a huge low bias) and are planning to do so again this summer, following major work over the winter.

Stalls: Go on the inside (high) at all distances, but will be tried stands' side again over 5f at some point this season.

Biases: High numbers are massively favoured at 5f on good to soft or faster ground and are also best on the round course.

Splits: Splits are very rare, and only likely over 5f on soft ground.

BRIGHTON (left)

Much depends on the going and time of year; on good to soft or slower ground runners often head for the outside rail (high), while in late season it's often just a case of whichever jockey finds the least cut-up strip of ground. Otherwise, low-drawn prominent-racers tend to hold sway in fast-ground sprints, with double figures always facing an uphill task over 5f 59y.

Stalls: Always go on the inside (low) in sprints.

Splits: These occur frequently in the second half of the season, as jockeys look for a fresh strip on ground that seems to churn up easily.

CARLISLE (right)

For the past few seasons, runners racing with the pace and hardest against the inside rail (high) have done well in big fields on decent ground early in the campaign.

This is entirely down to the fact that the Flat course and NH course are one and the same, and that those racing nearest the fence are running where the hurdle wings were positioned, while those wider out are on the raced-on surface.

Things have tended to level out as the year has progressed, though. On soft ground, the bias swings completely, with runners racing widest (low) and grabbing the stands' rail in the straight, favoured at all distances.

Stalls: Normally go on the inside (high) but can go down the middle in sprints (usually on slow ground).

Biases: High numbers are best in early-season sprints as long as the ground is no slower than good. Look to back low numbers on soft/heavy ground.

Splits: Rarely will two groups form, but on easy ground, runners often spread out.

CATTERICK (left)

When the ground is testing, the stands' rail is definitely the place to be, which suits high numbers in 5f races, and high-drawn prominent-racers at all other distances.

However, when the ground is good to firm or faster, horses drawn on the inside (low) often hold the edge, and there have been several meetings over the last two seasons in which those racing prominently hardest against the inside rail have dominated (over all distances, presumably as a result of watering).

Stalls: Go on the inside (low) at all distances these days (they often used to go on the outer over 5f212y).

Biases: Low numbers are best in sprints on fast ground (particularly watered firm going) but the stands' rail (high) rides faster under slower conditions.

Splits: Are common over 5f.

CHEPSTOW (left)

High numbers enjoyed a massive advantage in straight-course races in 2000, and the course management duly took steps to eradicate the faster strip, using the same 'earthquake' machine as had been employed at Goodwood in the late 90s.

This led to little in the way of a draw bias for the next two years, but it's been back in the last two campaigns, although not so much in the second half of last season.

Expect a major high bias in the first half of this year.

Stalls: Always go on the stands' side (high) on the straight course.

Biases: High numbers are favoured on the straight course (up to 1m14y) whatever the ground.

Splits: Splits are common, as jockeys drawn low often head far side in the realisation that it's hard to win down the middle.

CHESTER (left)

It's well known that low numbers are favoured at all distances here, even in the 2m2f Chester Cup, and the bias is factored into the prices these days.

That said, sprints (and in particular handicaps) are still playable, as it almost always pays to stick to a runner drawn 1-4.

Stalls: Go on the inside (low) at all distances bar 1m2f75y and 2m2f117y (same starting point) when they go on the outside. Certain starters ask for the stalls to come off the inside rail slightly in sprints.

Biases: Low numbers are favoured at all distances. Soft

CHESTER: get trapped on the outside and you've got no chance - even in the Chester Cup

ground seems to accentuate the bias until a few races have been staged. Although a higher draw becomes less of a disadvantage when the ground on the inside becomes chewed up.

DONCASTER (left)

Draw biases here are usually as reliable as they come, with high numbers dominating in sprints, low numbers taking over on the straight 1m (as long as there are enough runners for a split) and with either rail having the advantage at 7f.

Stall 1 has a tremendous record over the straight 1m.

Stalls: Always go on the stands' side (high) on the straight course.

Biases: High numbers are best in sprints, very high and very low numbers are favoured over 7f, while very low draws are best over the straight 1m (as long as they're taken to the far side).

The softer the ground becomes, the greater the biases.

Splits: Fields tend to stick together in sprints, apart from in fields of 20+, but it's not uncommon for a few to go far side at 7f and 1m.

EPSOM (left)

When the going is on the soft side, jockeys tack over to the stands' side for the better ground (this strip rides quicker in such conditions as the course cambers away from the stands' rail towards the far side).

In 5f races, the stalls are invariably placed on the stands' side, so when the going is soft the majority of the runners are on the best ground from the outset. Prominent racers drawn low in round-course races are able to take the shortest route around Tattenham Corner, and on faster ground have a decisive edge over 6f, 7f and 1m114y.

Over 5f, high numbers used to hold quite an advantage, but the bias is not so great these days.

Stalls: Always go on the outside (high) over 5f and 6f (races over the latter trip start on a chute) and inside (low) at other distances, bar 1m4f10y (centre).

Biases: Low-drawn prominent racers are favoured at between 6f and 1m114y.

Splits: Good to soft ground often leads to a few trying the stands'-side route.

FOLKESTONE (right)

Prior to '98, Folkestone was never thought to have much in the way of a bias, but nowadays the draw is often crucial on the straight course (up to 7f).

Whatever the ground, the far rail (high) rides faster than the stands' rail, which in turn rides quicker than the middle of the track.

Runners now invariably go across to the far side over 6f and 7f (jockeyship often playing a part, with several races going to whichever horse had secured the front up the rail). However, over 5f, when the stalls are up the stands' rail, fields often split, with low numbers just about holding sway (it seems the ground lost by switching across over the minimum trip can't be regained from racing on the faster surface). Slow ground swings things even more in favour of high numbers.

Stalls Usually go up the stands' side (low) on the straight track, but occasionally down the centre (they can't go up the far side as the ambulance needs access).

Biases: High numbers are favoured over 6f and 7f, and also over the minimum trip when 14 or more line up.

However, very low numbers have a good record in smaller fields over 5f.

Front-runners are well worth considering at all distances.

Splits: Fields only tend to divide over 5f these days.

GOODWOOD (right and left)

The course management took steps to end the major high bias seen in the Stewards' Cup throughout the late 90s by breaking up the ground by machine in '98.

This led to the stands' side (low) dominating the race in '99 before the far side gradually took over again.

However, last year, things turned full circle again, with the stands' rail dominating both the Stewards' Cup and the consolation race, but nobody is letting on as to whether the machine has been back in action.

A watching brief is advised through the early part of this season.

Stalls: Invariably go on the stands' side (low).

Biases: High numbers are best at between 7f-1m1f, and the faster the ground, the more pronounced the bias (keep an eye out for the rail on the home turn being moved during Glorious week).

Splits: Although fields tend not to break into groups in most sprints, runners often spread out to about two-thirds of the way across in fields of around 20.

HAMILTON (right)

Extensive drainage work was carried out in winter 2002 in a bid to level up the two sides of the track, but after encouraging early results, the natural bias in favour of high numbers (far side) kicked in again.

Basically the course is stuck with this bias, which can only be altered by watering on faster going (be careful after a dry spell, as things can often swing in favour of low numbers).

High numbers are also best over 1m65y, thanks to runners encountering a tight right-handed loop soon after the start.

Stalls: It's not uncommon for the ground to become too soft for the use of stalls, but otherwise they go either side.

Biases: High draws are best in soft/heavy-ground sprints, but the bias becomes middle to high otherwise (often switching to low on watered fast ground).

Despite the stiffness of the course, front-runners do particularly well at all distances.

Splits: Look for high numbers to peel off in fields of 8+ when the stalls are stands' side, unless the ground is very fast.

HAYDOCK (left)

High numbers used to enjoy a major advantage in soft-ground sprints, but that seems to have been turned full circle by drainage work carried out in the late 90s, with the far side (low) now best on very bad ground.

Otherwise, runners usually head for the centre these days, the draw rarely making much of a difference (although very high numbers can be worst off in big fields on faster going).

Stalls: Usually go down the centre in the straight.

KEMPTON (right)

This has become one of the most complicated bias courses in the country during the past couple of seasons. Ground, watering, field size and stall positioning are factors to consider in every sprint.

In mid-summer, when fast ground and small fields usually prevail, the stalls are generally put down the centre, and jockeys tend to stay there in one group.

However, more than once last year, one or more jockeys tried going to the far side, a move that paid off.

Runners usually stick to either rail if the stalls are stands' side (low) or far side (high), when very low numbers or very high numbers respectively, enjoy the advantage respectively.

In big fields (16-20 (the course can take 24 but no more than 20 are allowed to run under new BHB rules)) it's not uncommon for fields to split wherever the stalls are positioned, and much then comes down to watering.

The judgement call continues to be low (definitely on soft ground) but the far side (high) has been known to dominate, particularly in early season.

High-drawn prominent racers are best over 7f and 1m (Jubilee and Round courses).

Stalls: Can go anywhere, and often down the centre in midsummer.

Splits: Splits are common in sprints when 16-20 line up

.

LEICESTER (right)

There was a four-year spell between '98 and '01 when the centre-to-far-side strip (middle to high) enjoyed a decisive advantage over the stands' rail, jockeys eventually choosing to avoid the near side.

However, that's changed recently, with very low numbers more than holding their own.

Stalls: Invariably go up the stands' side (low).

Splits: Still occur occasionally.

LINGFIELD (left)

Turf

The draw advantage is nothing like as defined as in years past, but the stands' rail (high) went through a good spell in the second half of last season.

The one factor that can have a massive effect on the draw is heavy rainfall on firm ground.

Presumably because of the undulating nature of the track and the fact that the far rail on the straight course is towards the bottom of a slope where it joins the round course, rainfall seems to make the middle and far side ride a deal slower.

In these conditions, the top three or four stalls have a massive edge.

Stalls: Go up the stands' side (high) at between 5f and 7f, and down the middle over 7f140y.

Biases: High numbers are massively favoured on fast ground after recent rain, but otherwise the most recent meeting is often the best guide.

Splits: It's unusual to see two distinct groups, but runners often fan out centre to stands' side in big fields.

All-Weather

There's not much in the draw at longer distances, but there certainly is over 5f, with stalls 1 to 5 enjoying a major advantage over boxes 6 to 10.

It's also best to be low-to-middle in 6f races and over 1m2f, where those drawn wider than 7 tend to struggle.

That said. being drawn next to the inside railcan also be a disadvantage, with stalls 1 and 2 not performing well (boxes 3 to7 are favoured)

MUSSELBURGH (right)

The bias in favour of low numbers over 5f didn't look as pronounced last season. It could be that a few more try going to the far side (inside) this year on genuinely fast ground.

The bias in favour of high numbers at 7f and 1m isn't as major as many believe.

Stalls: Usually go up the stands' side (low) over 5f nowadays, but they can be rotated.

Splits: Look out for runners drawn very high in big-field 5f races on fast ground, as they occasionally go right to the far rail.

NEWBURY (left)

There's basically little between the two sides these days, apart from on soft ground, in which case the stands' rail (high) is definitely the place to be.

When the ground is testing it's not uncommon to see runners race wide down the back straight and down the side at between 1m3f56y and 2m (particularly over 1m5f61y). In such circumstances, a high draw becomes a huge advantage.

Stalls: Can go anywhere for straight-course races.

NEWCASTLE (left)

It's always been a case of high numbers best at up to an including 7f on good or firmer, and low numbers having the advantage when the ground is good to soft or softer.

Over the straight 1m, the stands' rail (high) is the place to be apart from on bad ground.

Stalls: Invariably go on the stands' side (high), only being switched to the inside under exceptional circumstances.

Splits: Two groups are usually formed when 14+ go to post, and often when 8-13 line up. The majority tend to go far side in sprints, but most stick stands' side over the straight 1m.

NEWMARKET (right)

July Course

The major draw biases seen under the former Clerk of the Course have become a thing of the past since Michael Prosser took over, and now only the occasional meeting will be affected.

The course is permanently divided into two halves by a rail (the Racing Post now carry information regarding which side is to be used) and, as a rule of thumb, the two outside rails (stands' rail when they're on the stands'-side half, far rail when they're on the far-side half) ride faster than the dividing rail.

Stands'-side half - On fast ground (particularly watered) very high numbers are often favoured at up to 1m, when there's a narrow strip hard against the fence that rides quicker.

However, on good to soft or slower ground, runners racing down the centre are favoured.

Far-side half – There's rarely much in the draw, apart from on slow ground, when the far side (low) rides much faster.

Stalls: Can go either side on either half of the track.

Splits: Runners just about tend to form two groups in capacity fields, but are more likely to run to their draw here than at tracks such as Newcastle.

Rowley Mile

Similarly to the July Course, the draw seems to have been evened out since the Clerk of the Course change. Occasionally a bias will appear, but they're hard to predict these days.

Stalls: Can go anywhere and are rotated.

Biases: High numbers have dominated the 2m2f Cesarewitch in recent years, the logic here being that those on the inside can be switched off early, while low numbers have to work to get into position before the sole right-handed turn.

Splits: It's not unusual for jockeys to come stands' side on slow ground in round-course races.

NOTTINGHAM (left)

On the straight course, it used to be a case of low numbers being favoured when the stalls were on the far rail, and high numbers when they were stands' side. With low being best when the stalls spanned the entire course. These days, though, it's less clear-cut and the going makes biggest difference.

On soft ground low numbers are best but high tend to be favoured on good to firm or faster.

Stalls: Tend to go on the stands' side (high) unless the ground is very soft.

Splits: Fields usually split in sprints when 14+ line up.

PONTEFRACT (left)

Low numbers have always been considered best here for the same reason as at Chester, in that the course has several distinct left-hand turns with a short home straight, but this is not always true.

High numbers at least hold their own over 6f now, whatever the ground, but massively so on soft/heavy.

Drainage work was carried out in the late 90s to try and eradicate the outside-rail bias on slow ground, and this worked immediately afterwards, but during the last two seasons there have been definite signs that it's now riding much faster.

Stalls: Go on the inside (low) unless the ground is very soft, when they're switched to the outside rail.

Splits: Although it's uncommon to see distinct groups, high numbers usually race wide these days on good to soft or slower ground.

REDCAR (left)

It's not unusual to see big fields throughout the season here, but the draw rarely plays a part, with runners inclined to converge towards the centre.

Stalls: Go towards the stands' side (high).

Splits: Splits are unusual and usually of little consequence when they are seen.

RIPON (right)

The draw is often the sole deciding factor in big-field sprints and watering plays a major part.

As a general rule, low numbers are best when the ground is good to firm or faster, while the far side is always best on softer going but, ultimately, the best guide here these days is the most recent meeting.

Stalls: Go on the stands' side (low) apart from under exceptional circumstances.

Biases: Front-runners (particularly from high draws over 1m) have an excellent record, and any horse trying to make ground from behind and out wide is always facing a tough task.

Splits: Fields tend to stay together in races of 12 or fewer, but a split is near guaranteed when 15 or more line up. Look for 'draw' jockeys who might chance going far side in fields of 13-14.

SALISBURY (right)

It's difficult to win from a single-figure draw in big-field fast-ground sprints, and also over 7f, but proven stamina and race suitability become the most important factors over the testing straight 1m.

This far-side bias is at its greatest early and late season, before and after the erection of a temporary rail (which usually goes up in July).

The draw swings full circle on slower ground, as jockeys then invariably head towards the stands' rail (good to soft seems to be the cut-off point).

Stalls: Go on the far side (high) unless the ground is soft, when they're often moved to the near side.

Biases: High numbers are best on the straight course on fast ground, there's not much in it on good to soft, while low take over on soft/heavy.

Splits: Fields only tend to divide on good to soft ground; otherwise they all converge towards either rail, dependant upon going.

SANDOWN (right)

On the 5f chute, when the going is on the soft side and the stalls are on the far side (high), high numbers enjoy a decisive advantage.

On the rare occasions that the stalls are placed on the stands' side, low numbers enjoy a slight advantage when all the runners stay towards the stands' rail, but when a few break off and go to the far side high numbers comfortably hold the upper hand again.

High numbers enjoy a decent advantage in double-figure fields over 7f and 1m on good going or faster, but jockeys invariably head for the stands' side on slow ground.

Stalls: Usually go far side (high) over 5f, as the course is more level that side.

Splits: It's unusual for runners to split over 5f, with capacity fields rare and jockeys all inclined to head for the far rail.

SOUTHWELL (right, All-Weather)

During last year, the bias over 5f seemed to swing back towards the stands' side (high) following a couple of years of far-side domination.

It's best to be drawn low over 6f, due to the start's proximity to the first bend, but over 7f and beyond it's generally preferable to be drawn middle-to-high, especially over those distances with a long run to the first bend.

THIRSK (left)

This used to be the biggest draw course in the country, back in the days of the old watering system (which was badly affected by the wind) but, while biases still often show up, they're not as predictable as used to be the case. Field sizes, watering and going always have to be taken into account in fields of 12 or more (11 or fewer runners and it's rare to see anything bar one group up the stands' rail, with high numbers best).

Otherwise, low numbers are almost always favoured on good or softer ground, while either rail can enjoy the edge on watered fast ground (the one place not to be under any circumstances is down the middle).

Low-drawn prominent-racers are well worth considering whatever the distance.

Stalls: Always go up the stands' side (high).

Biases High numbers are best in sprints when 11 or fewer line up, but it's hard to know which side is likely to do best in bigger fields on fast ground.

The far (inside) rail is always best on slow going (the softer the ground, the greater the advantage).

Splits: Runners invariably stay towards the stands' side in sprints containing 12 or fewer runners (unless the ground is soft) and frequently when 13-14 line up. Any more and it becomes long odds-on two groups.

WARWICK (left)

Low numbers are favoured in fast-ground sprints, but not by as much as many believe, and the prices often overcompensate.

However, when the ground is genuinely soft, high numbers can enjoy an advantage, although not so much last year.

Stalls: Always go on the inside (low).

WINDSOR (figure of eight)

It's typical to see large fields all season, and the draw almost always plays a part.

In sprints, things are set in stone, with high numbers best on good or faster going (particularly watered fast ground),

with not much between the two sides on good to soft, and with the far side (low) taking over on soft or heavy ground. It can be difficult for runners who switch off the stands' rail to make up the leeway (because the course turns sharply left soon after the finish, those pulled wide must think they're being asked to quicken up into a dead-end).

On slower ground, jockeys head centre to far side, and right over to the far rail on genuine soft/heavy (again it's difficult to make ground from behind under such conditions).

Stalls: Can be positioned anywhere for sprints.

Biases: High-drawn prominent-racers are favoured in fast-ground sprints, and also over 1m67y. On good to soft going, there's rarely much between the two sides, but it's a case of nearer to the far rail (low) the better on bad ground.

Splits: Splits only tend to occur on good to soft ground, and even then it's rare to see two defined groups.

WOLVERHAMPTON (left, All-Weather)

At most meetings, the ground against the inside rail rides much deeper than the rest of the track, the exception being after very wet or very cold weather, when the track is usually deep-harrowed.

The bias is at its strongest over 5f, with stalls 1 and 2 having a poor record, although over 7f100y and 1m100y it's also a disadvantage to be drawn on the extreme outside, as both starts are very close to the first bend.

YARMOUTH (left)

High numbers enjoyed a major advantage for much of the 90s, but this was put to an end by the course switching from pop-up sprinklers (which were affected by the offshore breeze) to a Briggs Boom in '99. These days a bias will appear occasionally but it's hard to predict, and runners often head for the centre whatever the going.

Stalls: Go one side or the other.

Splits: It's common to see groups form, often including one down the centre, in big fields.

YORK (left)

The draw is nothing like as unpredictable in sprints as many believe, although things are never quite as clear-cut in September/October as earlier in the season.

Essentially, on good or faster ground, the faster

strip is to be found centre to far side, which means in capacity fields, the place to be is stall 6-12, while in fields of 12-14 runners drawn low are favoured (the course is only wide enough to house 20 runners).

On soft/heavy ground, the stands' side (high) becomes the place to be, and high numbers often get the rail to themselves, as this is not a bias well known among jockeys. Low numbers are best on fast ground on the round course, although watering can reduce the bias.

Stalls: Can go anywhere.

Biases: Prominent-racers drawn down the centre are favoured in fast-ground

sprints, but high numbers take over on genuine soft/heavy ground. Low

numbers are best in big fields on the round course, apart from on slower

going, when runners leave the inside in the home straight.

Splits: Defined groups are rare.

WINDSOR: Is a "figure-of-eight" shape

Win – free form!

THIS YEAR'S QUIZ could hardly be more simple, and the prize should prove invaluable to our lucky winner. We're offering a free subscription to Raceform, the BHB's official form book – every week from May to November, you could be getting the previous week's results in full, together with note-book comments highlighting future winners, adjusted Official Ratings and Raceform's *Performance* ratings. The winner will also get a copy of last year's complete form book.

All you have to do is this: have a look at the following pictures of three leading ladies in the Flat game today. All three had reasons to be cheerful after last season. One landed a job with Godolphin for the winter, one successfully rode out her claim, while the other caused a stir in the Emerald Isle. If you think you know the answer – write their names in the box below in the order in which they appear.

Send your answers along with your details on the entry form below, to:

2005 Flat Annual Competition, Racing & Football Outlook, Floor 23, 1 Canada Square, London, E14 5AP.

Entries must reach us no later than first post on Monday April 25. The winner's name and the right answers will be printed in the RFO's May 2 edition.

Six runners-up will each receive a copy of last year's form book.

1

2

3

Name

Address

Town

Postcode

In the event of more than one correct entry, the winner will be drawn at random from the correct entries. The Editor's decision is final and no correspondence will be entered into.

BETTING CHART

ON	ODDS	AGAINST
50	Evens	50
52.4	11-10	47.6
54.5	6-5	45.5
55.6	5-4	44.4
58	11-8	42
60	6-4	40
62	13-8	38
63.6	7-4	36.4
65.3	15-8	34.7
66.7	2-1	33.3
68	85-40	32
69.2	9-4	30.8
71.4	5-2	28.6
73.4	11-4	26.6
75	3-1	25
76.9	100-30	23.1
77.8	7-2	22.2
80	4-1	20
82	9-2	18
83.3	5-1	16.7
84.6	11-2	15.4
85.7	6-1	14.3
86.7	13-2	13.3
87.5	7-1	12.5
88.2	15-2	11.8
89	8-1	11
89.35	100-12	10.65
89.4	17-2	10.6
90	9-1	10
91	10-1	9
91.8	11-1	8.2
92.6	12-1	7.4
93.5	14-1	6.5
94.4	16-1	5.6
94.7	18-1	5.3
95.2	20-1	4.8
95.7	22-1	4.3
96.2	25-1	3.8
97.2	33-1	2.8
97.6	40-1	2.4
98.1	50-1	1.9
98.5	66-1	1.3
99.0	100-1	0.99

The table above (often known as the 'Field Money Table') shows both bookmakers' margins and how much a backer needs to invest to win £100. To calculate a bookmaker's margin, simply add up the percentages of all the odds on offer. The sum by which the total exceeds 100% gives the 'over-round' on the book. To determine what stake is required to win £100 (includes returned stake) at a particular price, just look at the relevant row, either odds-against or odds-on.

RULE 4 DEDUCTIONS

When a horse is withdrawn before coming under starter's orders, but after a market has been formed, bookmakers are entitled to make the following deductions from win and place returns (excluding stakes) in accordance with Tattersalls' Rule 4(c).

	Odds of withdrawn horse	*Deduction from winnings*
(1)	3-10 or shorter	75p in the £
(2)	2-5 to 1-3	70p in the £
(3)	8-15 to 4-9	65p in the £
(4)	8-13 to 4-7	60p in the £
(5)	4-5 to 4-6	55p in the £
(6)	20-21 to 5-6	50p in the £
(7)	Evens to 6-5	45p in the £
(8)	5-4 to 6-4	40p in the £
(9)	13-8 to 7-4	35p in the £
(10)	15-8 to 9-4	30p in the £
(11)	5-2 to 3-1	25p in the £
(12)	100-30 to 4-1	20p in the £
(13)	9-2 to 11-2	15p in the £
(14)	6-1 to 9-1	10p in the £
(15)	10-1 to 14-1	5p in the £
(16)	longer than 14-1	no deductions

(17) ....When more than one horse is withdrawn without coming under starter's orders, total deductions shall not exceed 75p in the £.

**Starting-price bets are affected only when there was insufficient time to form a new market.*

Feedback!

If you have any comments or criticism about this book, or suggestions for future editions, please tell us.

Write Nick Watts,
2005 Flat Annual
Racing & Football Outlook
Floor 23,
1 Canada Square,
London E14 5AP

email rfo@mgn.co.uk

Fax FAO Nick Watts, 0207 510 6457

Horse index

All horses discussed, with page numbers, except for references in the Group 1 and two-year-old form sections (pages 83-107), which have their own indeces.